INTERREGIONAL MIGRATION AND PUBLIC POLICY ͗N CANADA

CARLETON LIBRARY SERIES

The Carleton Library Series publishes books about Canadian economics, geography, history, politics, public policy, society and culture, and related topics, in the form of leading new scholarship and reprints of classics in these fields. The series is funded by Carleton University, published by McGill-Queen's University Press, and is under the guidance of the Carleton Library Series Editorial Board, which consists of faculty members of Carleton University. Suggestions and proposals for manuscripts and new editions of classic works are welcome and may be directed to the Carleton Library Series Editorial Board c/o the Library, Carleton University, Ottawa K1S 5B6, at cls@carleton.ca, or on the web at www.carleton.ca/cls.

Interregional Migration and Public Policy in Canada

An Empirical Study

KATHLEEN M. DAY AND STANLEY L. WINER

Carleton Library Series 223

McGill-Queen's University Press
Montreal & Kingston • London • Ithaca

© McGill-Queen's University Press 2012

ISBN 978-0-7735-3744-6 (cloth)
ISBN 978-0-7735-3745-3 (paper)

Legal deposit first quarter 2012
Bibliothèque nationale du Québec

Printed in Canada on acid-free paper that is 100% ancient forest free
(100% post-consumer recycled), processed chlorine free

This book has been published with the help of a grant from the Canadian
Federation for the Humanities and Social Sciences, through the Aid
to Scholarly Publications Program, using funds provided by the Social
Sciences and Humanities Research Council of Canada.

McGill-Queen's University Press acknowledges the support of the Canada
Council for the Arts for our publishing program. We also acknowledge the
financial support of the Government of Canada through the Canada Book
Fund for our publishing activities.

Library and Archives Canada Cataloguing in Publication

Day, Kathleen Mary, 1958–
   Interregional migration and public policy in Canada : an empirical
study / Kathleen M. Day and Stanley L. Winer.

(Carleton library series ; 223)
Includes bibliographical references and index.
ISBN 978-0-7735-3744-6 (bound). – ISBN 978-0-7735-3745-3 (pbk.)

   1. Migration, Internal – Canada. 2. Migration, Internal – Economic
aspects – Canada. 3. Canada – Economic conditions – Regional disparities.
4. Canada – Economic policy – 1991– . I. Winer, Stanley L., 1947–
II. Title. III. Series: Carleton library ; 223

HB1989.D39 2011   304.80971   C2011-905591-0

Typeset by Jay Tee Graphics Ltd. in 10/13 Sabon

To Elie and Rima
K.D.

To my parents, Albert and Shirley
S.W.

Contents

Tables

Figures

Preface

In this book we investigate the empirical relationship between internal migration and public policy in Canada. Each of us has pursued this challenging issue, on and off, for more than two decades, and for one of us, it has been more than three since the study of policy-induced migration began. Our collaboration goes back to 1994 when we undertook a review of the literature for the Ontario Fair Tax Commission. The basic work for the present study was undertaken at Statistics Canada over about a four-year period beginning with our initial proposals for research and ending in 2001 after our results were cleared for publication by Statistics Canada. We completed a long technical report on our work in 2002, and then published a short journal article, which for various reasons appeared in print only in 2006. We sought support for publication of the full study, undergoing the associated reviewing, and once that lengthy process had been successfully completed, we undertook the substantial revisions that are required to turn the technical report into a book. All of this has taken time, and so we are pleased to finally be able to present our work here along with our assessment of the state of the Canadian literature on policy-induced migration.

Our original research was financed by a grant from the federal department of Human Resources, and by many services-in-kind from Statistics Canada under their Visiting Research Fellowship program. Winer's research was also partly supported by the Canada Research Chairs program. The publication of the book itself is supported by the Aid to Scholarly Publications Program of the Canadian Federation for the Humanities and Social Sciences. We are grateful for all of this financial help, without which our research and this book would not have been possible.

Programming was provided by Manohar Surkund. Our debt to him is substantial. He has worked on migration almost as long as we have. Long before he retired, he was the programmer for the study on internal migration

that Stanley Winer and Denis Gauthier completed in 1983 for the Economic
Council of Canada, the first study in Canada to use migration data derived
from tax files. It was our good fortune that he retired from the Public Service just before we began the present work and that our paths crossed at
the right time. Processing the tax tapes to derive the migration data we use
for our empirical work is a huge, difficult, and time-consuming enterprise,
one that for obvious reasons of confidentiality must be done only at Statistics Canada under its careful oversight. We could not have completed the
task without Manohar's expertise. The task was actually enormous for all
concerned, and when we reflect on this project now, we are at times amazed
that we decided to undertake it.

The book before you is a substantially revised version of Human Resources Development Canada Technical Report W-01-3E, which was made available by them on the web in 2002, and on Stanley Winer's website at www.
carleton.ca/~winers. Selected results from the full study appeared in *International Tax and Public Finance* 13 (2006), 535–64, under the title "Policy-
Induced Internal Migration: An Empirical Investigation of the Canadian
Case." We are grateful to editors Michael Devereux and John Wilson for
their helpful comments and editorial assistance.

Some of the material in the book is taken from our journal article and
some from the review (Day and Winer 1994) that we did for the Ontario
Fairtax Commission. We extend our appreciation to Springer and to the
University of Toronto Press for permission to use this published work here.

We are also grateful to a great number of people who assisted us in vari-
ous ways in the course of our research. To Louis Grignon, Marcel Bédard,
Patrick Hayes, and Anne Tweddle at HRDC, and to Garnett Picot, Richard
Dupuy, Len Landry, Shawna Brown, Lise Champagne, Dan Finnerty, Michel
Girard, Pat Grainger, Mark Levesque, Brian Murphy, Ronald Rioux, Abe
Tarasovsky, and Karen Wilson at Statistics Canada. (The long gestation per-
iod of the manuscript is such that Abe, Garnett, and Len are now retired.)
We also want to thank several anonymous referees as well as John Cragg,
Ross Finnie, Pierre Lefebvre, Tim Sargent, François Vaillancourt, and Jean-
Pierre Voyer for assistance with various aspects of the project. Michael
Francis, Jafar Khondaker, Richard Levesque, and Déla Hoyi provided able
research assistance in the conduct of the research and in the preparation of
the manuscript.

Finally, we would like to express our appreciation to Philip Cercone,
Ron Curtis, and Susanne McAdam and the production team at McGill-
Queen's University Press for their patience and their help in the preparation
of the book.

INTERREGIONAL MIGRATION AND PUBLIC POLICY IN CANADA

Public Policy and Interregional Migration: An Introduction to the Issues

Choosing where to live and when to move are important decisions for the individuals who make them. In this book we investigate the impact of public policy on the internal migration decisions of Canadians during the period from 1968 to 1996. We consider the influence of two types of policies: incremental changes in long-established programs of the sort that often occur over the decades, with special attention to the role of unemployment insurance reforms; and large, dramatic "policy shocks," including the election of the Parti Québécois government in Quebec in 1976 and the closing of the East Coast cod fishery in 1992. The period we investigate is among the longest studied in any empirical investigation of Canadian interprovincial migration. It is arguably an excellent period for a study of the sort we undertake because it encompasses considerable "action" in the data that is relevant to an investigation of the connection between internal migration and public policy.

Our search for policy-induced migration, like that of the researchers who have come before us, is generally motivated by an understanding that in the aggregate, the internal migration decisions of individual Canadians may have important consequences for the level and distribution of economic well-being in the country as a whole. The seminal academic impetus for these endeavours in Canada is Thomas Courchene's (1970) empirical work that was reported in the *Canadian Journal of Economics* four decades ago. Courchene argued, and provided some empirical evidence for the view, that direct and indirect public support of various kinds for people who live in more disadvantaged regions retards economic development and regional convergence by reducing migration out of the less prosperous provinces of the country.

The central problem Courchene addressed, which we will briefly state here and return to at greater length later on, begins with the observation that economic migration between regions depends on interregional differences in the *comprehensive* incomes that people expect to receive in the origin and destination locations, and not just on regional differences in their actual earned incomes or labour productivities. It follows that if comprehensive incomes in disadvantaged regions, where real wages are lower and unemployment rates higher, are supplemented by various government programs to a greater extent than they are in more prosperous parts of the country, too few people – from a national point of view – may migrate out of places where real wages are relatively low and unemployment is relatively high. If this does happen, earned income in the country as a whole will be lower, the national unemployment rate will be higher, and regional disparities in earned incomes will be increased compared to a situation where the public policy-related components of comprehensive incomes do not vary across the provinces.

Economists, at least, find this argument straightforward. And as a result, over the last four decades, it has become commonplace for many of them, as well as for some policy analysts and journalists, to point an accusing finger at regional subsidies, and especially towards the regionalized nature of the unemployment insurance system in Canada.[1] It is easy to see why the insurance system is often singled out. Consider, for example, the stylized facts presented in table 1.1, which covers the 1978–2008 period. Panel A of the table, for the years 1978 to 1996, corresponding to a period we shall use later to assess the importance of the policy-induced migration revealed by our own work, shows how the generosity of the Unemployment Insurance program, or UI as it was then called, varies regionally as measured by the minimum number of weeks required to qualify for insurance payments (shown by the column labelled "*MIN*" in the table) and by the weeks of benefits to which a person with this minimum number of weeks of employment would be entitled (shown as *MINWKS*). We can see from the table that the weeks for qualification are lower and the weeks of benefit entitlement are higher in the less-developed provinces of the lower-wage Atlantic region compared to, say, the higher-wage provinces of Ontario, Alberta, and British Columbia. Qualifying weeks vary from 10 to 15, and associated weeks of benefits from 22 to 39, indicating that at least for individuals who are weakly attached to the labour market, regional differentials in the generosity of the UI system can be quite large.

We have also included data on social assistance in the table, in part to alert the reader to the fact that we shall consider other aspects of public policy besides unemployment insurance, including social assistance as well

Table 1.1

Some Stylized Facts concerning Earnings, Unemployment Insurance and Social Assistance in the Canadian Federation, 1978–2008

	Panel A: 1978–96, by Province			
Province	Average Weekly Earnings (1) (Current dollars)	MIN[1] (weeks)	MINWKS[2] (weeks)	Annual Social Assistance Benefits[3] (Current dollars)
NFLD	418	10	39	9,030
PEI	363	10	38	9,614
NS	391	11	35	9,632
NB	397	11	36	7,445
QUE	429	11	34	8,641
ONT	453	13	26	11,289
MAN	401	14	25	8,770
SASK	396	15	22	10,059
ALTA	446	14	25	9,805
BC	458	13	31	10,555
Average	415	12.2	31.1	9,484
CV[4]	0.07	0.15	0.20	0.12
Corr. with (1)[5]		0.36	−0.35	

	Panel B: 1997–2008, by Province				
Province	Average Weekly Earnings (1) (Current dollars)	MINH[6] (hours)	MIN[1] (weeks)	MINWKS[2] (weeks)	Annual Social Assistance Benefits[8] (Current dollars)
NFLD	640	420	11	32	14,353
PEI	570	426	12	29	12,697
NS	613	475	13	24	12,384
NB	620	461	12	24	11,886
QUE	659	496	13	23	13,219
ONT	735	610	16	18	14,629
MAN	631	621	17	17	12,000
SASK	642	650	18	16	12,545
ALTA	733	624	17	17	11,617
BC	695	560	15	20	13,501
Average	654	534	14.4	21.8	12,883
CV[4]	0.08	0.17	0.17	0.25	0.08
Corr. with (1)[5]			0.53	−0.58	

Source: See first section of appendix A.

[1] Minimum weeks required to qualify for insurance payments.

[2] Weeks of insurance benefit entitlement of a person with MIN weeks of employment.

[3] Annual social assistance benefits for a single parent with 2 children.

[4] Coefficient of variation (standard deviation divided by mean).

[5] Correlation coefficient.

[6] Hours of insurance benefit entitlement of a person with MIN weeks of employment. (After 1996, MIN depends on hours of work instead of weeks of work.)

[7] MINH converted to weeks of work assuming 1 week = 37 hours.

[8] Social assistance for a single parent with 1 child.

as taxation and public expenditures of various kinds. In addition, we want to suggest that since social assistance appears in the table to be a substitute for unemployment insurance, tending to be more generous where insurance is less generous, it seems wise to model unemployment insurance and social assistance together, and we will do so.

The unemployment insurance system was adjusted in 1996, as well as at various points between 1971 and 1996, in ways that we shall discuss at some length as we proceed. In 1996, its official name was also changed, perhaps unwisely, to Employment Insurance (EI). As indicated in panel B of the table, qualification for insurance benefits subsequently depended on hours of work, a more stringent requirement than the previous weeks of work, especially for some part-time workers. However, the pattern of regional variation observed in the period since 1996 remains similar to that of the earlier period: qualifying requirements still tend to be less stringent and weeks of benefits longer in the less-developed regions. While our empirical work does not include the later period, we have included the second panel of table 1.1 here to suggest that since the pattern of regional differentiation in insurance benefits is similar to that of the earlier period, our empirical work based on the 1968 to 1996 period is relevant to contemporary policy debates. We will come back to this matter at the end of the book.

A second type of policy often pointed to by Courchene and by others concerned with the adverse consequences of regional bias in public policies is the Canadian system of intergovernmental grants. These grants, including equalization and federal contributions for provincial social programs, in various ways subsidize the governments and the citizens of poorer provinces to a greater extent than those of richer provinces, thereby indirectly sustaining differences across regions in the portion of an individual's total or comprehensive income that originates in the public sector. Just as with regionalized unemployment insurance benefits, regional differences in the public component of comprehensive incomes supported by the grant system may also lead to a misallocation of labour (Graham 1964; Boadway and Flatters 1982a,b).

The argument raised by Courchene and others both before and since does not rest here, however, even in principle. Mobility of labour is not perfect and is much less than that of capital because of the need for people to change their place of residence as well as their place of work. A personal decision to move carries with it substantial transactions and psychological costs that do not burden investors in capital markets. The high personal cost of migration means that migration flows may not be affected by existing regional differentials in the public component of comprehensive incomes if these differentials are not "too big." It is possible that not even the unemployment insurance program has a large enough impact on comprehensive incomes in different regions to alter migration decisions substantially.

The challenge of actually uncovering empirically the extent to which policies like unemployment insurance and federal grants-in-aid actually alter internal migration patterns is substantial. While certain extraordinary events such as the election of a separatist government in Quebec in 1976 and the closing of the cod fishery on the East Coast in 1992 may precipitate substantial migration responses – ones that we will investigate – in ordinary times the relationship between migration and government policies is quite hard to study. In ordinary circumstances, people move to take a better job, to get married, for adventure, to retire, and for other reasons that have little to do with the public sector. Migration decisions may also be influenced in ordinary times by public policies that affect the quality of schools, the regional generosity of unemployment insurance and social assistance, and the size of tax burdens. Common sense tells us that all of these factors together, to a greater or lesser extent, weigh in the decision to migrate. Anyone who wishes to study the connection between public policy and migration faces the challenging task of untangling the multiple causes of migration decisions in an environment where there is a substantial risk of confusing the influence of small changes in public policies with the influence of many private factors, including changes in the nature of employment opportunities over the course of business cycles.

In the following sections of this introductory chapter, we proceed as follows. We first show that internal migration is a substantial phenomenon in Canada. If that were not so, the rest of our work would not make much sense. Then we return to consider more carefully the issues and arguments concerning policy-induced internal migration that we have introduced only briefly so far. The chapter concludes with a brief outline of what is to come in the rest of the book.

INTERNAL VERSUS INTERNATIONAL MIGRATION IN CANADA

Migration continues to play an important role in the demographic history of Canada. International migration, of economic migrants and of refugees, is mostly what one reads about in the newspapers and on the Web. However, internal migration – the focus of this book – which in normal times is more or less ignored by the press also has been, and continues to be, an important determinant of the regional allocation of labour in Canada.

Table 1.2 illustrates the roles of both international and internal migration over the periods from 1976 to 1986 and from 1986 to 1996, respectively, covering much of the sample period addressed by the empirical work we will present. An alternative, useful discussion that covers about the same period is found in Beaujot and Kerr (2004).

In the ten-year period between 1976 and 1986 covered in panel A of the table, we see that net immigration from other parts of the world added almost nine hundred thousand people to the country, a number roughly equal to 45 percent of the natural increase of about two million. Approximately 47 percent of the (net) immigrants went to the province of Ontario, the economic heartland of the country. We can also see from column 6 that internal migration redistributed the population westward to Alberta and British Columbia and, at the same time, to Ontario. Underlying these observations is the continuing migration from the East Coast to Ontario and from Ontario and (to some extent) from the Prairie Provinces to the West Coast, a pattern that has continued for years.

Internal migration over the decade covered after 1976 was substantial relative to international migration. Between 1976 and 1986, out-migration from the relatively less prosperous provinces of Newfoundland and New Brunswick was more important than immigration from abroad in determining overall population changes in these provinces, as indicated by the ratios of interprovincial to international migration in column 8 of the table. Net in-migration from other parts of Canada to Alberta and British Columbia, especially from Ontario, and out-migration from Quebec to the rest of Canada have also been substantial relative to international flows. Over the ten-year period after 1976, net internal migration to Alberta and from Quebec was in each case about one and a half times as large as the corresponding international inflow.[2] In total, according to the ratios in column 8, net internal migration was at least as important as net international migration in six of the ten provinces as well as in the northern territories.[3]

Panel B of table 1.2 shows that the overall pattern of net migration flows changed to some extent in the decade from 1986 to 1996, but not by very much. Ontario continues to be a magnet for both internal and international migrants, and people continue to move westward. This pattern is most likely the result of the continuing economic dominance of central Canada, fluctuations in economic activity associated with the export price of natural resources, and the continuing attraction of life on the West Coast.

A comparison of columns 8 in the two panels of the table indicates that internal migration continues to be an important determinant of the distribution of the Canadian population. Over the decade after 1986, internal

Table 1.2
International and Internal Migration, Canada and the Provinces (Numbers are in thousands, unless otherwise specified)

Panel A: 1976–86[1]

	Population 1986 (1)	Population Distribution (percent) (2)	Natural Increase (3)	Net International Migration[2] (4)	Distribution of (4) by Province (percent) (5)	Net Inter-Provincial Migration[3] (6)	Net Inter-provincial Migration Rates (6)/(1)[3] (percent) (7)	Inter-provincial vs. International Migration[4] (6)/(4) (8)
Newfoundland	576.5	2.2	63.4	2.6	0.3	−34.8	−6.03	−13.4
PEI	128.4	0.5	9.1	1.2	0.1	−0.2	−0.16	−0.2
Nova Scotia	889.3	3.4	53.9	11.2	1.3	−0.2	−0.02	0.0
New Brunswick	725.2	2.8	54.4	4.4	0.5	−10.4	−1.38	−2.4
Quebec	6,708.5	25.7	483.0	161.8	18.1	−236.5	−3.52	−1.5
Ontario	9,438.1	36.2	620.7	416.0	46.6	69.7	0.74	0.20
Manitoba	1,091.7	4.2	80.3	40.3	4.5	−45.3	−0.42	−1.1
Saskatchewan	1,029.3	3.9	95.5	18.7	2.1	−13.1	−1.27	−0.7
Alberta	2,430.9	9.3	281.4	99.2	11.1	147.9	−6.08	1.5
British Columbia	3,004.1	11.5	207.2	136.8	15.3	133.6	4.44	1.0
Yukon	24.5	0.1	3.8	0.3	0.0	−5.4	22.04	−18.0
NWT and Nunavut	54.7	0.2	11.2	0.8	0.1	−5.0	−9.14	−6.3
Canada	26,101.2	100.0	1,963.7	893.3	100.0	0.0	−2.025	n/a

Table 1.2 (continued)

Panel B: 1986–96

	Population 1986 (1)	Population Distribution (percent) (2)	Natural Increase (3)	Net International Migration[2] (4)	Distribution of (4) by Province (percent) (5)	Net Inter-Provincial Migration[3] (6)	Net Inter-provincial Migration Rates (6)/(1)[3] (percent) (7)	Inter-provincial vs. International Migration[4] (6)/(4) (8)
Newfoundland	559.8	1.9	32.3	3.0	0.2	-36.7	-6.56	-12.2
PEI	135.8	0.5	7.3	1.4	0.1	1.9	1.40	1.4
Nova Scotia	931.4	3.1	43.7	16.2	0.9	-6.8	-0.73	-0.4
New Brunswick	752.3	2.5	36.9	1.4	0.1	-7.0	-0.93	-5.0
Quebec	7,246.9	24.5	414.9	301.6	17.4	-92.7	-1.23	-0.3
Ontario	11,083.1	37.4	718.9	938.4	54.2	23.6	0.21	0.0
Manitoba	1,134.2	3.8	77.5	34.5	2.0	-60.4	-5.32	-1.8
Saskatchewan	1,019.1	3.4	73.1	14.5	0.8	-93.0	-9.12	-6.4
Alberta	2,775.2	9.4	269.1	105.9	6.1	-27.4	-0.99	-0.3
British Columbia	3,874.3	13.1	208.0	313.1	18.1	301.9	7.79	1.0
Yukon	31.4	0.1	3.8	0.6	0.0	1.3	4.14	2.2
NWT and Nunavut	67.4	0.2	13.3	0.7	0.0	-4.6	-6.82	-6.6
Canada	29,610.8	100.0	1,898.8	1,731.3	100.0	0.0	-1.555	n/a

Source: Statistics Canada CANSIM tables 051-0001 and 051-0004, accessed 27 June 2009 and Beaujot (1991), table 3, 165.

[1] The numbers in this table differ somewhat from those in the Day and Winer (1994), table 2, and from Beaujot's (1991) table 3, because of data revisions and modifications to estimation methods, especially for net international migration.

[2] Net international migration in column (4) is the difference between the number of immigrants and emigrants.

[3] A minus sign in columns (6) and (7) indicates a net out-flow.

[4] A minus sign in column 8 indicates interprovincial and international net flows are opposite in directions.

[5] Average excludes the north.

migration was once again more important than international net migration in determining the regional distribution of people in five of the ten provinces. The role of internal in- and out-migration has become somewhat more important compared to the earlier decade for Prince Edward Island, New Brunswick, Manitoba, and Saskatchewan, and somewhat less important relative to net international flows for Newfoundland, Quebec, and Alberta. But the changes are not dramatic.

All in all, we can conclude that for the period up to 1996 that we study in this book and, in fact, for more recent years too, internal migration is quantitatively at least as important as international migration in determining the regional distribution of the Canadian population. Further evidence on the matter is provided by Finnie (1998a), Vachon and Vaillancourt (1999), Beaujot and Kerr (2004), and Kapsalis (2008). Kapsalis, for example, concludes that for most provinces, labour force changes resulting from internal migration flows are comparable to, or exceed, labour force changes owing to natural population growth and external migration in the 2002 to 2006 period, and we should expect that a similar characterization applies to the earlier periods we are studying here.

Two remarks will be useful before we turn to the connection between internal migration and public policy. First, we note that in the case of Newfoundland and Quebec, one study finds that over half of all Canadian native-born in-migrants aged five and over were return migrants in the 1991–96 period (Bélanger 2002, 55). Newbold and Cicchino (2007), using census data disaggregated by census metropolitan area (CMA), find that substantial return migration is a general phenomenon, characteristic of many CMAs across Canada. Return migration may play a role in the interpretation of the stylized facts we will generate later concerning the effects of large shocks on interprovincial migration patterns.

Second, it is important to take note of the variability of the migration flows for each province. This is hinted at by a comparison of columns 7 in the two panels of table 1.2. For example, in panel A, the net internal migration rate for Ontario over the 1976–86 period as a percentage of the 1986 population is 0.74, while for the following decade, in panel B, the comparable figure is just 0.21. For other provinces this comparison is even more dramatic, and for some there is little change. The variability of migration flows is even more apparent when one looks at the graphs of the province-specific gross outflow we present in chapter 5. Modelling migration flows in this environment of variable flows is not an easy task.

One should note that it is hard to know how well most empirical models do in predicting internal migration history, since their forecasting abilities are almost never revealed in published work. We will try to be open about this matter.

THEORETICAL ARGUMENTS CONCERNING "FREE" INTERNAL MIGRATION

It is useful to begin a more extensive discussion of the arguments about why policy-induced migration may be important for economic well-being with a discussion of the consequences of migration decisions that are entirely free of the influence of public policy. Before we do so, however, it is important to note that the phrase "free of the influence of public policy" in an economic context refers to a situation in which individuals face no impediments or inducements to move other than those that result from the operation of private market forces. The word "free" as it is used here is not intended to imply that the private transportation or psychological costs of moving are negligible.

In this hypothetical world, labour resources will be allocated across regions or provinces according to the productivity of labour services in different locations, adjusted for the cost of moving. As a result, total national output and earned income in the country as a whole will be as high as possible, given stocks of capital and other economic conditions, including the real costs of relocating. Moreover, as we will see, "free" mobility will also lead to the equalization of earned incomes across regions, thereby reducing regional disparity.

Free Migration and National Economic Efficiency

An intuitive demonstration that free internal migration results in a nationally desirable allocation of resources may be usefully decomposed into three parts. We must first establish a standard of reference – an ideal regional allocation of labour that may be used to judge the consequences of internal migration. We will use economic efficiency in the national economy as our standard. This requires that labour services be allocated across regions so that the marginal physical product of labour, or addition to total output of the last person placed in each region, is equalized.

To see why national efficiency in the allocation of human resources requires the equalization of marginal productivities across regions, consider the case in which a person has a marginal contribution to output of MP_S in a sending or origin region s and a marginal product of MP_D ($> MP_S$) if he or she is employed in a destination region D, such as at point B illustrated in figure 1.1.[4]

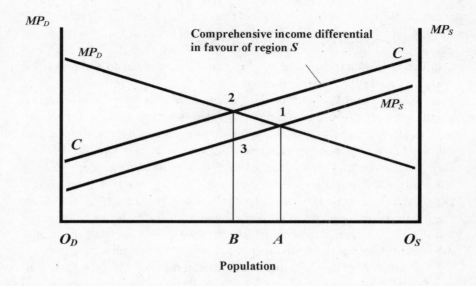

The comprehensive income differential line CC lies above the marginal product (MP) curve for region S because of the additional net fiscal benefits a person in region S enjoys relative to a person living in region D.

Figure 1.1. Interregional migration, public policy, and the allocation of labour services in the national economy

In such a case, *national* output can be increased if that person moves from S to D. Output falls by MP$_S$ in the sending region when the worker leaves, but it is increased by an even greater amount when the individual is re-employed in the destination. (There is no unemployment in our smoothly functioning hypothetical economy.) Only when people are allocated across regions so that marginal productivities are equalized, as at point A in the figure, where there is O$_D$A labour in region D and AO$_S$ labour remaining in region S, will the potential contribution of available human resources in the country as a whole be realized.

Choosing a standard of reference does not inform us about how the allocation of labour is actually determined. The second part of the argument begins to fill that gap by establishing a connection between wages paid to workers and their marginal products. To maximize their profits, private firms must balance the cost of an additional worker, which in our fully competitive world is just his or her real wage, with the benefit to the firm of hiring this person as indicated by that person's marginal contribution to the firm's output. As long as the prevailing real wage paid to workers is less than the marginal product of the next person hired, the total profit of the firm will increase when its labour force is expanded. For this reason, profit maximization leads firms in each region to hire workers until the marginal product of labour for the last worker hired is just equal to the prevailing real wage in the local labour market.

In the third and last part of the story, we connect wages and marginal products to migration, and conclude. Without loss of generality we can consider an initial situation in which real wages are higher in some regions than others. Those regions with relatively high wages attract workers because their welfare is higher there, and the resulting increase in the supply of labour leads to the bidding down of real wages in these locations of net in-migration. Similarly, in regions of net out-migration where wages are initially low, the diminished supply of labour leads to wage increases. If migration is not influenced by government policies, this process continues until real wages are effectively equalized across regions, at which point migration ceases.

One should note that regional differences in the cost of living or in non-market amenities such as a warm climate may be reflected in interregional nominal wage differentials in the migration equilibrium. But this does not alter the basic nature of the equilibrium if we think of real wages as having been suitably adjusted to incorporate such factors.

Then, to conclude, since profit maximizing firms hire additional units of labour until the marginal product of labour is equal to the prevailing real wage, free migration across regions that equalizes real wages also results in the equalization of marginal productivities. The result, from the first part of the argument, is an efficient national allocation of human resources in a migration equilibrium.[5]

It is important to reiterate that this chain of reasoning does not depend on an assumption that the costs of migration are negligible. Migration costs and transactions costs generally may lead to regional wage differentials opening up, but this does not invalidate the conclusion reached if an efficient allocation is understood to encompass the costs of market exchange.

The preceding argument does require that non-labour income, such as from investments, may be received by workers regardless of where they choose to sell their labour services. If the generation of income has no geographical location attached to it at all – the stereotypical day trader in financial markets or the computer specialist who works at home may be examples of such a situation – the economic importance of interregional migration is reduced. But this sort of employment is not a dominant feature of our economy at this time, and location continues to be an important factor determining earned income for most people.

Together the three parts of the argument suggest that there is an "invisible hand" process at work here, to use Adam Smith's apt label. No individual migrant or business firm cares about the social allocation of labour services. However, in seeking the highest wage or the greatest profit, each person and firm contributes to an outcome in which labour services are allocated according to marginal productivities in alternative destinations, thereby maximizing aggregate income in the country as a whole.

Free mobility is a right that is codified in section 6 of the Canadian Charter of Rights, with qualifications allowing for certain kinds of public policy actions. This part of the Charter is bolstered by the demonstration that, under certain conditions, migration that is free of government interference leads to a socially desirable allocation of human resources.

Regional Disparities in Earned Income, and a Word of Caution

Earned income is the product of the real wage per hour and hours of work. Since hours of work for similar types of labour are more or less the same in different locations, the equalization of real wages and of marginal productivities that tends to occur in response to interregional migration also leads to the equalization of earned incomes. Thus, as an important by-product of its consequences for economic efficiency, "free" migration reduces regional disparity in earned incomes.

We are now ready to return to the role of public policy. But before we do so, a word of caution about the role of internal migration is in order. In assessing the arguments we have presented, it should be kept in mind that there are many factors besides labour mobility that play a role in establishing both the level and the distribution of earned incomes. To take just one example, the regional allocation of physical capital is an essential determinant of the total level and distribution of economic well-being. Arguments for and about the free movement of people do not imply that labour mobility is the only, or even the most important, factor involved in the complicated processes that lie behind regional development in a market economy. However, they do suggest that the mobility of labour can contribute in a substantial manner to the well-being of Canadians.

PUBLIC POLICY, INTERREGIONAL MIGRATION, AND ECONOMIC WELFARE

We turn from our hypothetical world to the world as it is, one where public policies exist and play an important role in peoples' lives. There are at least two reasons why the relationship between public policy and individual migration decisions is important for the level and distribution of earned income in the country as a whole. In the first, perhaps older, but still important (and still controversial) view, the more responsive are individual migration decisions to interregional differences in economic circumstances, the worse are the real consequences of public policy actions for national efficiency. This argument is often referred to as the transfer dependency hypothesis for reasons that will become clear in a moment. In a second, more recent view, the willingness of individuals to move in response to interregional differences in public benefits attenuates and, in the limit, eliminates the adverse consequences of internal migration, at least under certain conditions.

We will consider each point of view at some length, beginning with the older argument first. In between, the role of federal grants will arise. Before starting this discussion, however, it should be noted that regardless of which view one favours, the degree of responsiveness of migration to public policy is crucial.

A First Argument: Fiscally Induced Migration Reduces Economic Efficiency

In the first view, public policy is assumed to be determined independently of migration patterns. The problem then pointed to is that because the net effects of the public sector are not uniform across the country, migration induced by responses to regional policy differences leads to a misallocation of labour services in the country as a whole (Courchene 1970, 1978; Gordon 1983). This argument is illustrated in figure 1.1, which shows a comprehensive income line CC (that we previously ignored) lying above the marginal product of labour curve in region S because of the receipt of public sector benefits by a citizen if he or she resides in region S rather than in D.[6] As we saw before, efficiency from a national standpoint occurs when there is $O_D A$ labour in region D and AO_S labour remaining in region S, because with that allocation of labour, marginal products of labour are equalized across provinces and so national income is maximized.

But now, because the federal and provincial governments subsidize citizens in region S, comprehensive incomes in S are greater than earned incomes there. Since people care only about their comprehensive incomes, the process of migration strictly according to earned incomes is then short-circuited, with fewer people leaving S than in the original scenario we discussed earlier. The resulting equilibrium allocation of labour now is at point B, where earned income for the marginal migrant in region D is equal to the total comprehensive (private plus public) full income he or she receives in *s*. Marginal labour productivity and earned income in this new equilibrium is higher in region *D* than in *S* and, consequently, total earned income in the country as a whole is reduced relative to the situation in which public policy (of all governments combined) does not discriminate in favour of one region or another. The total loss in real income is represented by triangle "123" in figure 1.1.[7]

The actual size of the welfare loss resulting from policy-induced migration is an empirical question. But when thinking about its potential importance, one should recall our demonstration earlier that internal migration each year is substantial, often outweighing international immigration as a source of labour market developments. This is especially so for some poorer provinces. Moreover, as we shall document carefully in the next chapter, regional differences in the generosity of public programs continue to be an important feature of the public sector in Canada.

In his seminal work on policy-induced migration, Courchene pointed to the regionalized structure of the unemployment insurance system illustrated in table 1.1, which provides greater support to people in more depressed regions and to federal grants like equalization payments that go only to poorer provinces. Such policies create incentives to remain in poorer regions even though earned incomes would be higher if people moved to a more prosperous province like Ontario.[8] For this reason, he referred to the relationship between the public sector, migration, and national economic welfare as the *transfer dependency hypothesis*.

To this list of policies we can add the public use of natural resource rents. The same kind of problem may occur if individuals move between provinces to capture a share of natural resource rents, or returns above total costs of production (Wilson, Percy, and Norrie 1980; Boadway and Flatters 1982a; Helliwell 1994). Migration to Alberta in the years following the OPEC price increase in 1973, for example, may have been partly motivated by attempts to take advantage of employment opportunities or lower taxes that were supported directly or indirectly by government resource revenues. To the extent that such rent-seeking occurs, migration decisions are not based only on marginal productivities of labour in alternative locations, and a reduction in earned income in the country as a whole must result.

The incorporation of other ideas has led to an even fuller understanding of the consequences of policy-induced migration. It turns out that, in principle at least, the same sort of reasoning that underlies the transfer dependency thesis could lead to *higher* rather than lower earned incomes in the poorer provinces as a result of public policy, an argument made quite early on in the debates over policy-induced migration by Graham (1964) and developed later by Boadway and Flatters (1982a,b). Consider, for example, the case of people from the Atlantic provinces who are attracted to Ontario because of the fiscal benefits they can enjoy there in the form of better schools accompanied by lower taxes, a situation made possible by the larger and richer Ontario population coupled with economies of scale in the production of public services. The resulting migration adds to the Ontario labour force and depresses the real wage and the marginal productivity of labour in Ontario. Workers will continue to migrate to Ontario even if the wage they earn is less than in the Atlantic region as long as they receive compensatory benefits in the form of better or cheaper public services. They will continue to migrate until the resulting decline in the real wage in Ontario just compensates for the advantages that in-migrants receive from the relatively richer Ontario public sector.

In the Atlantic provinces, to continue this example, the outflow of people leads to a reduced supply of labour and thus to an increase in the real wage and in the marginal product of labour. This increase in the real wage compensates those who stay for the disadvantages of the less generous fiscal treatment that they receive from Atlantic governments. The overall result of migration in this case is a situation in which the real wage and marginal productivity are *higher* in the Atlantic region than in Ontario. In this example, national output and average earned income in the country as a whole could be increased by moving workers out of Ontario and *back* into the Atlantic region.

It is important to keep in mind that regardless of which of the cases we have discussed are of interest or appear to be relevant, they all hinge on the strength of the relationship between the public component of expected comprehensive income and internal migration flows. Many other factors will also be important, not the least of which are the probabilities attached by prospective migrants to various components of expected comprehensive income, some of which will vary with labour market status. Migration costs are also important, and if substantial, such costs may make small or even large differentials in expected comprehensive incomes irrelevant. In the end, the matter *is* an empirical one.

An Efficiency Argument for Equalization Grants

The recognition that the public sector in richer provinces may induce too much migration from poorer regions leads to an interesting argument about the role of federal grants. It is worth pursuing this matter a little, despite the fact that grants will not appear in our empirical model, since doing so helps in understanding the general economic logic of policy-induced migration.

The Canadian system of equalization, now enshrined in the 1982 Constitution, can (perhaps somewhat generously) be viewed as a clever policy response to the inefficiency created by fiscally induced migration or to migration that has as its purpose the harvesting of resource rents. This efficiency argument for grants is based on the idea that when properly computed, equalization payments allow all provinces to deliver the same level of fiscal benefits to its citizens with comparable tax burdens. By so doing, the equalization system eliminates regional differences in the fiscal component of comprehensive incomes that are the source of inappropriate migration signals, thereby allowing interregional differences in marginal productivities to remain as the primary determinants of internal migration flows (Graham 1964, Boadway and Flatters 1982a,b).[9]

In the context of figure 1.1, the well-functioning equalization system can be represented by creating a comprehensive income line for region D that is above its marginal product curve by exactly the same amount that CC is above the marginal product curve in region S. The fiscal differential in favour of region S that we introduced initially is then exactly offset, and an efficient allocation of labour across the country once again emerges as a result of private economic decisions. Since equalization results in efficiency as well as equality of net fiscal benefits across the provinces, such a system represents a policy – one of few perhaps – for which underlying social efficiency and equity concerns do not *necessarily* conflict.[10]

A major problem with this efficiency argument for equalization payments is that such grants have to be properly computed and then actually used on behalf of the people for whom they are intended.[11] In the example of migration from the Atlantic region to Ontario, grants must be just large enough to allow fiscal benefits in the Atlantic provinces to be brought up to the level in Ontario, but not larger.[12] If, for example, the equalization paid to the poorer provinces is "too high," some workers will not leave them even when their marginal productivity and real wage is lower than in other, more prosperous parts of the country. In that case, the national allocation of labour will not be efficient, since fiscal differentials continue to influence migration decisions (Winer and Gauthier 1982a; Usher 1995).[13]

A Second View: When Public Policy Choices Are Tightly Constrained by Migration

In the analysis so far we have assumed that public policy is formulated independently of any migration that it may induce. But what if migration or its threat is a constraint on the policy choices made by provincial governments? For example, suppose that provincial governments maximize the welfare of a representative citizen and that all citizens everywhere are essentially alike. Moreover, suppose that migration is cheap relative to average income. Then migration plays quite a different role. Instead of leading to a misallocation of resources across regions, in the manner indicated in figure 1.1, it leads to the loss triangle 123 being fully internalized when each government decides on its own policy actions (Myers 1990; Wellisch 2000).[14] This happens because cheap mobility imposes a tight constraint on each government. Whatever it does, it must maintain the welfare of its residents at the same level as anywhere else in the country, for that is the only outcome possible when citizens can move cheaply between jurisdictions.

In such a situation, each government will behave more or less as if it is maximizing the welfare of the representative citizen in the country as a whole. It will take into account the possibility that the benefits it provides to its residents may spill across provincial borders and so affect the utility of its own residents through the consequences of migration, that tax competition to attract economic activity may led to inefficient tax cuts and the under-provision of public services in the country as a whole, and that the exporting of taxes to non-residents will reduce welfare elsewhere and hence in this province too via the migration responses such actions precipitate.[15]

This is of course a polar case, and many things can go wrong. In particular, if migration is subject to high fixed costs rather than being costless, a government maximizing its own residents' welfare will be tempted to take advantage of people elsewhere by exporting taxes, because this action will not then precipitate substantial offsetting migration that effectively forces the home government to face the national consequences of its actions.[16] This effect of fixed costs stands in stark contrast to the role of such costs in the first view we analyzed. There, migration costs reduce the inefficiency of the equilibrium by reducing the magnitude of fiscally induced migration flows (as well as migration for any other reason). Note though that in either case, the costs of migration matter.

So far we have been dealing with competition between provincial governments. The obvious question arises as to whether the federal government's influence on regional comprehensive income differentials is similarly constrained. Indeed, it is reasonable to expect that the federal government is more able to differentiate its policies across regions because it can optimize over several regions at the same time. This means that it can trade off economic and political benefits in one part of the country against losses from interregional migration in another, while a province will generally tend to enjoy or suffer only one of these.

At this point we are on the edge of an analysis of how the costs of migration and government behaviour are related. We will resist going further in that direction in this book, because our focus is on the empirical consequences of government policies for individual migrations decisions, however these policies come about. We will only point out here that the connection between migration costs and the nature of political behaviour has long been recognized. For example, as Scott and Bloss (1988) pointed out over two decades ago, "To the extent that political action to obtain preferred policies at home is a substitute for moving to another province where more attractive policies are already in force, increases in travel costs will make political investment in the home province a more attractive course of action" (185).

What If the Generosity of Fiscal Policy Is Uniform across the Country?

To complete our discussion of the theory of fiscally induced migration, we must ask ourselves if policy-induced migration would in principle cease if fiscal policies (of all governments) were uniformly applied across the country. In considering that question, which is more difficult to answer than might seem to be the case, it is interesting to focus on the role of unemployment insurance, an aspect of public policy in Canada that will be given special, though not exclusive attention in the following chapters. Suppose then that all aspects of the current unemployment insurance system that differentiate its benefit structure by region were eliminated. Would there then be any systematic connection between the insurance system and internal migration?

One answer is that there may still be a relationship between UI and migration because of the implicit subsidization of job search activities that insurance payments provide.[17] The reporting requirements of the insurance system do not prevent claimants from temporarily travelling to look for work in other cities or provinces. This activity is costly and time-consuming, and by offering financial support while recipients hunt for a job, the system may make them more mobile than if they had received no benefits while unemployed. On the other hand, and again because migration is costly, they may use their insurance payments to support themselves while searching for a job at home rather than moving somewhere else where job prospects may be better. (Exiting the labour force is not permitted under the unemployment insurance rules.) Which of these effects dominates will depend in part on the value of "location" in individual preferences, just as will the actual effect on migration of differences in comprehensive incomes that arise for reasons unrelated to unemployment insurance. Some people may stay put no matter what, while others may be footloose, and in the end, it is an empirical matter.

We should also point out that the job search effects of unemployment insurance on an individual's location choices and the effects of regional differences in comprehensive incomes, to the extent that either exist, will both be present at the same time in the same data. To the best of our knowledge, no one has succeeded in separating out the job search effects of UI on migration from the migration response to regional variation in the generosity of the insurance system, nor will we be able to do so.

A second answer to the question revolves around the general equilibrium effects of unemployment insurance on the macroeconomy. Unemployment insurance has a vital role to play in maintaining aggregate demand in times of recession, and there is no reason why the consequences of insurance for aggregate demand will be felt uniformly across regions or provinces even if the benefit structure of the insurance system is the same everywhere. Thus insurance payments, even when uniformly available, may precipitate internal migration by boosting demand and regional employment prospects in some regions more than in others. As with job search migration, this effect will also be embedded in observed migration patterns, and we will not be able to separate out the aggregate demand part of migration either.

GOVERNMENT REGULATIONS AND THE FLEXIBILITY OF LABOUR MARKETS

So far we have been concerned with the adverse consequences of regional differences in comprehensive incomes created by the fiscal policies of one or another government in the federal system. The effects of federal and provincial government regulations on mobility and on the flexibility of labour markets is also a matter of concern. Regulations that have the effect of making it harder for people in some occupations to move across provincial boundaries are not prohibited by the mobility provisions of section 6 of the Canadian Charter of Rights. For this reason, regulatory barriers to mobility were the focus of chapter 7 of the Agreement on Internal Trade signed by the provinces and the federal government in 1994.[18]

Provincial residency requirements, restrictive labour market regulations, and professional licensing requirements do not show up in measures of comprehensive income. But they may, nonetheless, adversely affect the regional allocation of labour (Lazar 1992; Gunderson 1994; Green and Harrison 2006; Grady and Macmillan 2007). For completeness we discuss these regulatory barriers to migration briefly here, even though it is not possible to quantify these regulations in a way that allows them to be included in our own empirical model.

Labour market regulations generally increase the cost of interregional mobility independently of the real resource costs that must be incurred by individuals who are changing their location of work. For example, restrictive regulations in the construction industry may make it expensive in terms of time and money for construction workers to find employment in other provinces. Social-welfare residency requirements make it more risky, and hence more expensive in a general sense, for lower-income Canadians to search for work in other provinces.

In principle, these sorts of policies reduce average earned income in the country by slowing down the interregional adjustment of workers in response to changing labour market conditions. In the limit, they fracture the common market and force individuals to search for work within a smaller, and therefore less rewarding, labour market. By reducing the ability of unemployed individuals in economically distressed regions to search for work in other places, they also contribute to an increase in the disparity of earned income in the country as a whole.

This is another aspect of public policy that may affect migration even if it is uniform across the country. It is easy to see why this is so. Imagine a country in which restrictive provincial regulations and laws are identical across provinces, so that, for example, someone in a particular profession must register, and in the same manner, in each province separately in order to work there. The uniformity of such regulations will not be of much comfort to potential migrants on whom their cost directly falls.[19]

THEORY, OUR EMPIRICAL RESEARCH, AND THE PLAN OF THIS BOOK

Theory tells us that in principle, internal migration matters economically because the regional allocation of labour services is a factor in the determination of both the average size of and regional disparity in earned incomes. Internal migration can also serve as an important constraint on the behaviour and performance of governments at different levels in our federal system and as an adjustment mechanism in times of economic stress.

In the course of our discussion we have seen that governments at various levels conduct polices that may interfere with or, if properly structured, may enhance the role the market plays in allocating labour services in the country. What matters most in the fiscal realm are public policies that are different in various parts of the country. Aspects of public choices, like the regionally differentiated benefit schedules that are built into the unemployment insurance system, create differentials in expected comprehensive incomes that are of concern to individual Canadians when they are planning when to move and where to live.

The relevance to economic well-being of the arguments about the relationships between internal migration decisions and public policy that we have introduced in this chapter depends crucially on the actual strength of the relationship between individual migration decisions and the economic impact on individuals of the actions of various governments in our federal system. If the relationship is generally weak, the force of the arguments we have summarized is blunted. On the other hand, if there is a substantial amount of policy-induced migration, these arguments are more relevant for policy-making. The purpose of the empirical work we present in the rest of this book is to assess the nature and quantitative strength of the relationship between fiscal policies of federal and provincial governments and internal migration in Canada.

We pointed out that in conducting our empirical work, we will pay special attention to the role of the unemployment insurance system in determining expected comprehensive income differentials across the country and the subsequent effects of such differences in full income on internal migration. This makes good empirical sense. Because insurance payments are an important source of income for recipients and the program explicitly differentiates among recipients depending on their location, we are as likely to see policy-induced migration result from regional differences in the generosity of unemployment insurance as from any other aspect of public sector activity.

The Rest of the Book

Before describing our own empirical model of fiscally induced migration, we will look more carefully at the nature of regional variation in public policies in Canada. We show in the next chapter that there is substantial regional variation in a variety of fiscal policies, including the provision of goods and services as well as unemployment insurance, that could be relevant to prospective migrants and that if we fail to find substantial policy-induced migration it will not be because there is insufficient "action" in the data we use. Following this exploration of the regional dimension in public policy, chapter 3 provides a comprehensive survey of the last four decades of research on policy-induced migration in Canada.

The stage is then properly set for the presentation of our own approach to the empirical study of internal migration, which follows in chapter 4. In chapter 5 we discuss the construction of the migration and other data that we use to implement our empirical framework, and the estimates of various versions of our basic migration model are presented in chapter 6.

The remainder of the book then explores the implications of the models we have estimated. In chapter 7, we consider the effects of small or marginal changes in selected policies represented in the estimating equations. To put the effects of the marginal policy reforms we consider in perspective, we compare their effects to those of small changes in market wages. In chapter 8, we use simulation to assess the quantitative importance of the policy-induced migration that is revealed by our new empirical work. Here we construct and simulate several interesting counterfactuals designed to explore the consequences of eliminating regional variation in the operation of the unemployment insurance system and in the tax system. Again to provide perspective, we construct analogous counterfactuals for market conditions, including probabilities of employment.

We also simulate the hypothetical consequences for internal migration flows of three extraordinary events: the October crisis of 1970, the election of the Parti Québécois in 1976, and the closing of the East Coast cod fishery in 1992. These large policy shocks are especially interesting because they are likely to have created incentives to move that are substantial relative to the kinds of policy reforms or changes that we experience in normal times and relative to the full direct and indirect costs of moving.

In the last chapter, we summarize what we think we have learned in this study and also offer an assessment of the current state of knowledge concerning fiscally induced migration in Canada, with some emphasis on the consequences of regional variation in the generosity of the unemployment insurance system. Sources of data and further details about data construction, marginal effects and simulations that may be of use in further research on internal migration in Canada are provided in an extensive set of appendixes.

2

Regional Dimensions of Public Policy
in Canada

In chapter 1 we described mechanisms through which public policy can affect economic well-being because of its effects on internal migration patterns. One possibility among others is that fiscal policies may short-circuit the tendency for migration to contribute to regional economic convergence. But for this result or for almost all the other consequences of policy-induced migration we discussed to become a reality, two conditions must be satisfied. The first is that substantial regional differences in fiscal policy must exist or be created, while the second is that migration has to be sensitive to such policy differences. In this chapter we focus on the first of these preconditions.

The fiscal policies that people are likely to take into account when they consider where to live are the taxes they pay and the personal transfers and the goods and services that they or their families receive from governments when residing in a particular location.[1] In what follows, we take a careful look at how such fiscal policies vary across regions in Canada.

In practice it is not always easy to measure the relevant fiscal policy variables on a regional basis in a manner that is relevant to the study of internal migration. Taxes and transfer payments can differ greatly across individuals, leading to incentive effects that differ as well. The consumption of publicly provided goods also varies across individuals and households. For example, families with young children care a great deal about publicly provided education, but such education may be of less value to the childless or to those whose children have grown up. Measuring the contribution of publicly provided goods and services to regional differences in net fiscal benefits (the benefits from goods and services, plus transfer payments less tax liabilities) is further complicated by the fact that in principle such measurement requires the valuation of public services. While time-series data on fiscal aggregates do exist on a regional or a provincial basis, these data measure total government spending on broadly defined government functions rather than the value of the benefits that are relevant to particular types of individuals in alternative locations.

No one has yet been able to provide valuations of net benefits on a provincial basis even for a representative person. What we can do here is to examine provincial differences over the 1966–96 period in a variety of fiscal aggregates reflecting different aspects of government policy that might affect individuals. These variables, all of which will later be incorporated in our empirical models as prospective, underlying determinants of the net benefits relevant to migration decisions, include real per capita provincial government spending on health, education, and all other functions (excluding debt relief and social assistance); real social assistance benefits (for a single mother with two children); the basic real income tax burden for an individual with average income and no deductions other than the personal deduction or tax credit; the minimum weeks of insurable employment required to qualify for unemployment insurance benefits; the maximum weeks of benefits available to someone with the minimum weeks of insurable employment; and real per capita current plus net capital spending by the federal government.[2]

The first three variables reflect provincial differences in publicly provided services, with health and education being singled out because they are among the services that most directly affect individuals and thus are the most likely to influence migration decisions. The level of social assistance benefits measures the generosity of the provincial social safety net, which is likely to be important not just to the unemployed but also to any individual who faces a great deal of uncertainty about future employment prospects. Income taxes are clearly of importance to migration decisions, since they directly influence individuals' after-tax income.

In contrast to the first five variables, the remaining three are controlled by the federal government.[3] The federally designed and administered unemployment insurance (UI) system is of particular interest to our study because since 1971 it has explicitly linked benefits received to local labour market conditions. Moreover, the amounts of money involved can be substantial.

While the provisions of the unemployment insurance system have changed greatly over the years – table 2.1 outlines the principal changes between 1955 and 1996, the end of the period we study – when considering policy influences on interregional migration, certain changes in the insurance system stand out. The first of these is the introduction in 1971 of regional extended benefits, which tied weeks of benefits received to the unemployment rate in each designated insurance region. The second is the additional regional variation in benefits introduced in late 1977 in the form of the variable entrance requirement, under which the minimum weeks of work required to qualify for insurance were also tied to the unemployment rate in each official UI region. The fact that these two major changes to the insurance system occurred in the 1970s suggests that it is desirable to include these years in the sample period under investigation, as we do in this book. Including this history makes it more likely that we will be able to detect any migration effects of unemployment insurance that might exist. These two important provisions of the unemployment insurance system underlie the two UI indicators we examine in this chapter.

Federal government policy decisions also lie behind variation across the regions in government spending on goods and services. Because regional development is of interest to voters living in each part of the country and because some places may be more politically influential at one time or another for various reasons, federal spending is unlikely to be evenly distributed and will vary over time as well. These regional differences in federal spending may affect individuals' evaluations of job prospects in different places, and to the extent that they do, such differences in federal spending may influence migration decisions.

To help us assess whether the observed provincial differences in any of these public policy variables are "big" in a migration context, we also examine the regional dispersion of two private sector factors – real average weekly earnings and unemployment rates. These are the two labour market variables that are most commonly associated with migration decisions in the empirical literature on interregional migration, and they are widely believed to provide individuals with a strong incentive to move. If regional differences in the public policy variables we look at are at least as great as those in average weekly earnings or unemployment rates, then they may well be large enough to influence individual migration decisions. Of course, even large regional differences in public policies may not influence migration decisions if individuals do not care much about those particular policies, just as small regional differences in public policies may have big effects if individuals care about them a great deal. Nonetheless, it is useful to have a point of reference, and the two private labour market variables are logical choices for this role.

The remainder of this chapter is divided into three parts. In the next section, we examine regional dispersion in each of the private market and public policy variables over the 1966–96 period. Then in the following section we look more closely at the nature of regional differences. Does one

Table 2.1
Changes In Relevant Unemployment Insurance Parameters, 1955–96 (regular benefits only)

UI Act of 1955
- waiting period of six days
- minimum of 30 weeks of insurable employment required to qualify for regular benefits
- one week of regular benefits awarded for every two weeks of insurable employment, up to a maximum of 36 weeks
- maximum weekly insurable earnings equal to $57
- schedule showing weekly benefit payments as a function of previous weekly earnings, up to a maximum of $23 for those without dependents and $30 for those with dependents
- seasonal benefits introduced, payable from 1 January to 15 April
- minimum of 15 weeks of insurable employment since 31 March prior to claim required to qualify for seasonal benefits
- one week of seasonal benefits payable for every 3 qualifying weeks, for minimum of 10 weeks to maximum of 15 weeks of benefits

Amendments effective 1 December 1957
- seasonal benefit period extended to include 1 December to 15 May
- weeks of seasonal benefits increased to minimum of 13 weeks and maximum of 16–24 weeks

Amendments effective 27 September 1959
- maximum benefit duration increased to 56 weeks
- maximum weekly insurable earnings increased to $69
- schedule of weekly benefits altered such that maximum weekly benefit increased to $27 for those without dependents and $36 for those with dependents

Amendments effective 30 June 1968
- maximum weekly insurable earnings increased to $100
- schedule of weekly benefits altered such that maximum weekly benefit increased to $42 for those without dependents and $53 for those with dependents

UI Act of 1971 (effective 27 June 1971)
- two-week waiting period introduced
- minimum weeks of insurable employment required to qualify for benefits reduce to 8 weeks
- maximum insurable earnings to be adjusted annually with the help of an earnings index; set at $150 for 1972
- wage replacement rate fixed at 66²/₃% for all claimants without dependents and at 75% for all claimants with dependents, regardless of previous earnings, up to a maximum weekly benefit of ²/₃ of the annual MIE
- five-phase benefit schedule introduced: phase 1 consisted of from 8 to 15 weeks of benefits, depending on previous weeks of insurable employment (initial benefit period); phase 2 consisted of up to 10 additional weeks (re-established initial benefit period); phase 3 consisted of additional weeks of benefits for those with 20 or more qualifying weeks (labour force extended benefit period); phase 4 consisted of additional benefits in the event the national unemployment rate exceeded 4% (national extended benefit period); and phase 5 consisted of regional extended benefits of up to 18 weeks, depending on the relationship between the national and regional unemployment rates

Amendments effective January 1976 (Bill C-69, given Royal Assent 20 December 1975)
- difference between wage replacement rates for those with and without dependents eliminated; wage replacement rate set equal to 66²/₃% for all claimants

Table 2.1 (continued)

Amendments effective 1977 (Bill c-27, given Royal Assent 5 August 1977)
· variable entrance requirement (VER), which permitted the minimum weeks of insurable work required to qualify for benefits to vary from 10 to 14 weeks depending on the regional unemployment rate, came into force on 4 December 1977
· five-phase benefit structure replaced by a three-phase benefit structure that came into effect on 11 September 1977: phase 1 consisted of 1 week of benefits for each week of insurable employment, up to a maximum of 25 weeks; phase 2 (labour force extended benefits) consisted of 1 week of benefits for every 2 weeks of insurable employment over 26 weeks, up to a maximum of 13 weeks; phase 3 (regional extended benefits) consisted of from 2 to 32 additional weeks of benefits, depending on the regional unemployment rate

Amendment effective 7 January 1979 (Bill c-14, given Royal Assent 22 December 1978)
· replacement rate reduced to 60% of average weekly insurable earnings

11 February 1990
· minimum number of qualifying weeks reverts to 14 weeks nationwide, because legislation to amend VER failed to pass Senate;

Amendments effective 18 November 1990 (Bill c-21, given Royal Assent 23 October 1990)
· VER restored and increased from 10 to 20 weeks of insurable employment, depending on the regional unemployment rate
· three-phase benefit structure replaced by a single table showing weeks of benefits given number of qualifying weeks and the regional unemployment rate

Amendment effective 4 April 1993 (Bill c-113, given Royal Assent 2 April 1993)
· replacement rate reduced to 57%

Amendments effective 1994 (Bill c-17, given Royal Assent 15 June 1994)
· single benefit table revised, effective 3 April 1994
· VER raised from 12 to 20 weeks, effective 3 July 1994
· replacement rate reduced to 55% for most claimants; raised to 60% for low-income claimants with dependents, effective 3 July 1994

EI Act of 1996, provisions effective 30 June 1996
· maximum weekly insurable earnings for benefit purposes is reduced to $750
· maximum weekly benefits reduced to $413
· maximum number of weeks of benefits reduced to 45; otherwise benefit structure remains the same until January of 1997

Note: For a more complete summary of the many changes to Canada's unemployment insurance system over the years, see Lin (1998) or Dingledine et al. (1995).

province always stand out from the others, or have the relative positions of the provinces remained relatively constant over time? Does the pattern of dispersion of one migration determinant suggest that it will have the same or a different effect on migration flows than other migration determinants? The answers to these questions will allow us to draw some tentative

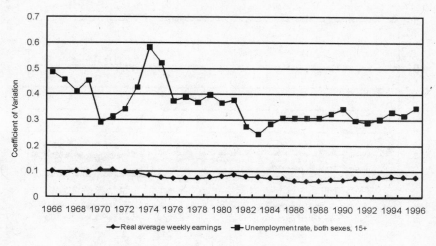

Figure 2.1   Regional variation in labour market variables

conclusions regarding how likely it is that regional differences in public policies in Canada will create substantial incentives relevant for migration decisions. A final section summarizes our findings regarding the nature of regional differences in public policy in Canada.

REGIONAL DISPERSION OF MARKET CONDITIONS AND PUBLIC POLICIES IN CANADA

To measure regional dispersion, we will rely primarily on the coefficient of variation (cv), a standard statistical measure of relative dispersion. Defined as the standard deviation of a variable divided by its mean, the coefficient of variation is unit-free and so allows comparisons to be drawn across variables that differ widely in terms of their units of measurement (e.g., dollars versus weeks).[4] In all calculations we use data for the ten Canadian provinces only.

It is convenient to begin with the coefficients of variation of our two reference variables, real average weekly earnings and the unemployment rate, which are presented in figure 2.1. We see there that the regional dispersion of average weekly earnings across provinces hovered at or just below the 0.1 level throughout the 1966 to 1996 period. In contrast, dispersion of provincial unemployment rates across Canada is both much higher and more variable, with a cv ranging from a high of 0.58 in 1974 to a low of 0.24 in 1983.

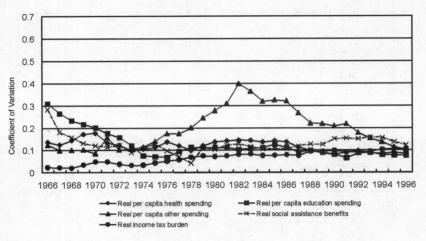

Figure 2.2   Regional variation in provincial/local government policies

Figure 2.1 reveals the important regional differences in unemployment rates that existed during the 1966–96 period, but do any of our public policy variables display as much dispersion across regions? Figure 2.2 presents the coefficients of variation of the five policy variables that are determined at the provincial/local level: real per capita spending on health, real per capita spending on education, real per capita spending on "other" functions (excluding debt charges), real social assistance benefits (for a single mother with two children), and the real combined federal-provincial income tax burden.[5] This income tax burden is computed for illustrative purposes as the total income tax owed in each province by a non-mover who is employed all year, earns the average weekly wage, receives average nonwage income, and claims only the personal deduction or tax credit.

The figure shows that with the exception of the "other" category of provincial non-interest spending, which includes a broad mix of items, the coefficients of variation are quite similar to each other and to those of real average weekly earnings in figure 2.1. Moreover, it appears that the regional dispersion of the per capita health and education spending of the provinces was quite stable over the entire period, although before 1974, spending on education and social assistance benefits seems to have varied more across provinces than in later years. Of the five public sector variables, the real income tax burden displayed the lowest level of variation across provinces between 1966 and 1996, and the "other spending" category exhibits the highest level of provincial variation throughout most of the period. Although it is not

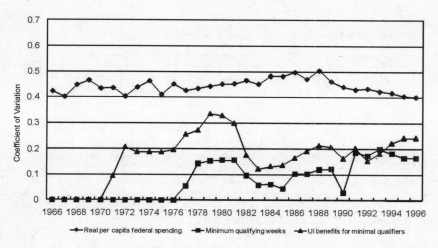

Figure 2.3   Regional variation in federal government policies

apparent from the graph, the high level of regional dispersion in the "other" spending category appears to have been due in large measure to big changes in spending in Alberta and Saskatchewan following the oil shocks of 1973 and 1979.

The fact that social assistance benefits and per capita spending on health and education display less dispersion across regions than "other spending" is perhaps not surprising, in view of the fact that these provincial programs are supported by conditional grants from the federal government. One of the justifications for these grant programs is to ensure that Canadians have similar access to health care, education, and welfare regardless of where they live, and to the extent that per capita spending is a good measure of such access, this comparison of the variability of the grant-supported and "other spending" categories suggests that the federal grant system has achieved some success in this regard.

Next, figure 2.3 displays the coefficients of variation of the three variables that are determined by federal government policy: two parameters of the unemployment insurance system, the minimum number of weeks required to qualify for UI and the maximum weeks of benefits that a person with minimum qualifying weeks can receive, and real per capita federal government spending. The first two variables are constructed by applying the relationship between the regional unemployment rate, on the one hand, and qualifying weeks and weeks of benefits, on the other hand, to the provincial average unemployment rate.[6] As we should expect, there is no regional

Table 2.2
Changes to Regional Extended Benefit Provision

Date of Legislation	Regional Extended Benefit Provision
UI Act of 1971	Introduction of regional extended benefit as fifth phase of benefits. Individuals eligible to receive regional extended benefits if the regional unemployment rate was at least 4% and the regional unemployment rate was at least 1 percentage point higher than the national rate. Eligibility for these benefits was determined after all other benefits had been exhausted and was continually re-evaluated from week to week. The maximum number of weeks of regional extended benefit was 18.
1977 amendments	Number of benefit phases reduced to three. Two weeks of regional extended benefit for every half percentage point by which the regional unemployment rate exceeds 4.0%, up to a maximum of 32 weeks.
1990 amendments	Single benefit schedule. Table 2 of schedule relates weeks of benefits to regional unemployment rate.
1994 amendments	Two weeks of regional extended benefit for every percentage point by which regional unemployment rate exceeds 4%. Weeks of benefits range from 14 to 50 weeks.

variation in maximum weeks of benefits for minimal qualifiers prior to the introduction of regional extended benefits in 1971. Similarly, there is no regional variation in minimum qualifying weeks until after the variable entrance requirement came into effect in 1978. Not surprisingly, after the introduction of these two insurance provisions the behaviour of the coefficients of variation of the two unemployment insurance variables bears some similarity to that of the unemployment rate. However, regional variation in these indicators is somewhat less than that of the unemployment rate.

Changes over time in the degree of regional variation of provincial unemployment rates constitute only one of the factors underlying the observed fluctuations in the coefficients of variation of our two unemployment insurance parameters. The numerous policy changes that occurred during the 1966–90 period also play a role. The changes to regional extended benefits that occurred during our sample period are summarized in table 2.2. When first introduced in 1971, the regional extended benefit provision entitled individuals to up to eighteen weeks of additional benefits if the regional unemployment rate was at least 4 percent *and* exceeded the national rate by at least one percentage point. This somewhat cumbersome formula, which also involved constant re-evaluation of the conditions for receipt of benefits, was replaced in 1977 by a simpler formula in which weeks of regional extended benefits depended on the extent to which the regional unemployment rate exceeded 4 percent. This change may be responsible for the increase in the coefficient of variation of UI benefits for minimal qualifiers (*MINWKS*) that occurs in the late 1970s despite the fact that regional dispersion of unemployment rates remained relatively stable. Then, in 1990, the three-phase benefit formula was replaced by a single schedule for regular benefits that did, however, continue to link benefits received to the regional unemployment rate. Regional extended benefits were reintroduced as a separate category of benefits in 1994, but the new formula was less generous than the 1977 one, two weeks of benefits were awarded for each percentage point (not each half percentage point) by which the regional unemployment rate exceeded 4 percent. Perhaps as a result of this change, regional dispersion of unemployment insurance benefits for minimal qualifiers drops in 1990, despite an increase in the regional dispersion of unemployment rates in the same year.

The other important source of regional variation in the unemployment insurance system is the variable entrance requirement, changes in which are summarized in table 2.3. Before the 1977 revisions to the UI Act, the minimum weeks of insurable employment required to qualify for benefits was the same across Canada, although it decreased from 30 weeks in 1966 to 8 weeks in the early seventies. Under the 1977 revisions, which did not come into effect until December of that year, minimum qualifying weeks varied from 10 to 14 weeks as the regional unemployment rate increased from 6 percent to 9 percent and over. In 1990, the variable entrance requirement, or VER, was temporarily eliminated when the Senate failed to pass the necessary enabling legislation, resulting in a sudden drop in the coefficient of variation of minimum qualifying weeks in that year. The new legislation that eventually came into effect in November of that year made the VER more stringent, with weeks of insurable employment required to qualify for UI rising from 14 to 20 in regions with unemployment rates of 6 percent or less. The final change in the VER during our sample period raised qualifying weeks in high unemployment regions – that is, regions with unemployment rates of at least 14 per cent – from 10 or 11 weeks to 12 weeks. These changes underlie the fluctuations in the coefficient of variation of minimum qualifying weeks observed in figure 2.3.

A particularly interesting fact that emerges from figure 2.3 is the relatively high degree of regional variation in per capita federal spending. While the coefficient of variation of this variable has been relatively stable from 1966 to 1996 (although it does decline somewhat after 1986), it is much higher than that of the provincial per capita spending variables, and also that of the unemployment rate since 1976. The suggestion here is that the federal government used its spending powers to differentiate between the

Table 2.3
Variable Entrance Requirement, 1977–96

Regional Unemployment Rate	Weeks of Insurable Employment Required to Qualify for Benefits
As of 4 December 1977[1]	
6% and under	14
over 6.0% to 7%	13
over 7.0% to 8.0%	12
over 8.0% to 9.0%	11
over 9.0%	10
As of 11 February 1990	
0% to 100%	14
As of 18 November 1990[2]	
6% and under	20
over 6.0% to 7%	19
over 7.0% to 8.0%	18
over 8.0% to 9.0%	17
over 9.0% to 10%	16
over 10% to 11%	15
over 11% to 12%	14
over 12% to 13%	13
over 13% to 14%	12
over 14% to 15%	11
over 15%	10
3 July 1994 to 31 December 1996[3]	
6% and under	20
over 6.0% to 7%	19
over 7.0% to 8.0%	18
over 8.0% to 9.0%	17
over 9.0% to 10%	16
over 10% to 11%	15
over 11% to 12%	14
over 12% to 13%	13
over 13%	.12

[1] *Source*: Dingledine (1981), 92.

[2] *Source*: Table 1 of Schedule, Unemployment Insurance Act 1971, revised 1990; McFarlane et al. (1992).

[3] *Source*: Table 1 of Schedule, Unemployment Insurance Act, 1971, revised 1993–94; Rudner (1995).

provinces to a substantial extent, even when compared to the differentiation that results from provincial government policies.

A CLOSER LOOK AT PROVINCIAL POLICY DIFFERENTIALS

In examining migration incentives, it is important to look not just at the overall extent of regional dispersion but also at the nature of that dispersion.

Looking at the position of each province relative to the unweighted ten-province average in each year during the 1966–96 period can tell us more about the nature of the migration incentives arising from regional differences. In the graphs that follow, the Canadian average is assigned the value 100 in each year. A value of 120 for a particular province thus implies that its value lies 20 percent above the Canadian average, while a value of 80 would imply that the province lies 20 percent below the Canadian average. To minimize clutter in the graphs, for each variable we have divided the provinces into two groups: Quebec and provinces to the east, and Ontario and those to the west.

As figures 2.4a,b and 2.5a,b illustrate, there are some regularities in the pattern of regional dispersion of the two market variables that we use as a point of comparison, real average weekly earnings and the unemployment rate. Throughout the 1966–96 period the three Maritime provinces and Saskatchewan had below average values of average weekly earnings, while average weekly earnings were always above the ten-province average in Quebec, Ontario, Alberta, and British Columbia. Holding all else equal, then, we would expect to see positive net migration flows from the provinces with below-average earnings to those with above average earnings. This was in fact more or less the case over this period (recall table 1.2), though Quebec is a notable exception. As we see from figure 2.5a, the unemployment rate in Quebec was usually above the ten-province average, which might explain the unattractiveness of that province as an internal migration destination, although similarly high unemployment rates in British Columbia do not seem to have prevented that province from enjoying positive net inflows of people.

This phenomenon of positive net in-migration to high unemployment regions has been observed elsewhere as well, leading Harris and Todaro (1970) to hypothesize that what migrants really care about is expected income, which they defined as the product of the probability of employment and income if employed. The fact that British Columbia was on balance an attractor of migrants suggests that people thought their expected incomes would be higher there *despite* the high rate of unemployment. In contrast, in our sample period the four Atlantic provinces suffer the dubious distinction of offering potential migrants an unattractive combination of both relatively low average wages and above-average unemployment rates, which would tend to lower expected incomes.

Turning now to provincial/local government per capita spending, figures 2.6a to 2.8b show that per capita spending on health and other functions exhibit similar patterns, in that the "have-not" provinces generally provided relatively low levels of per capita spending and the "have" provinces

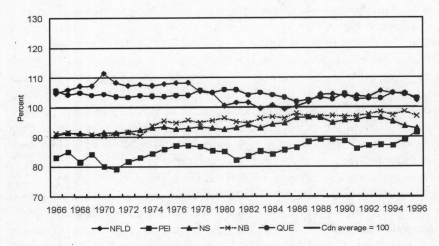

Figure 2.4a　Average weekly earnings relative to 10-province average

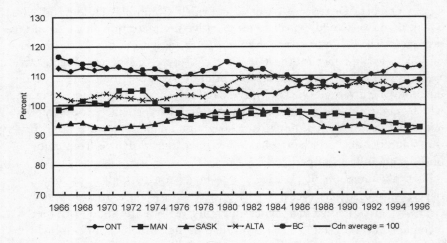

Figure 2.4b　Average weekly earnings relative to 10-province average

generally provided higher levels. The detailed patterns, however, are a bit more complicated. For instance, in 1995 per capita spending in the health and "other" categories in the "have" province of Alberta dropped below the average in 1995. In addition, per capita "other" spending in Ontario remained below the ten-province average between 1971 and 1996, while in Saskatchewan it remained above the average from 1974 to 1996. The relatively high levels of per capita spending in areas other than health and

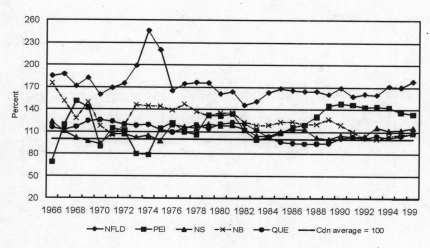

Figure 2.5a   Unemployment rate, both sexes, 15+ relative to 10-province average

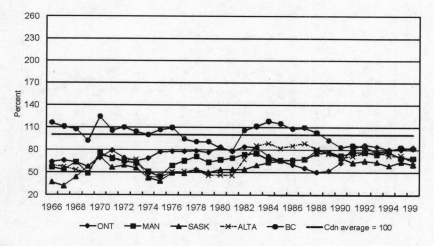

Figure 2.5b   Unemployment rate, both sexes, 15+ relative to 10-province average

education in Alberta and Saskatchewan that began in the mid-seventies were no doubt driven by commodity booms.

The pattern with respect to education spending is also not quite what one expects. Although figure 2.7b shows that Alberta led the other provinces until 1991, by 1995 it had fallen below the national average here too. Per capita spending on education in Quebec (figure 2.7a) remained above average levels between 1974 and 1996, and during that period often

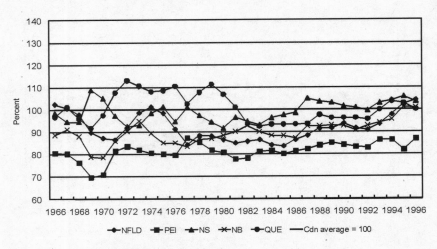

Figure 2.6a Per capita spending on health relative to 10-province average

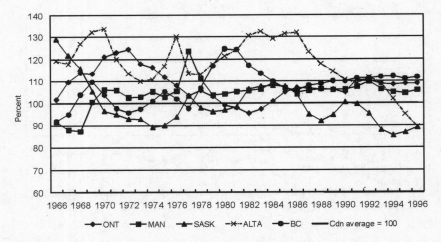

Figure 2.6b Per capita spending on health relative to 10-province average

exceeded that in Ontario. Among the Atlantic provinces per capita spending on education was generally highest in Newfoundland (which even exceeded the ten-province average for a number of years), while in relatively wealthy British Columbia per capita spending on education generally lay below the national average.

A striking feature of figures 2.6a to 2.8b is the number of changes in the relative positions of the provinces. While certain provinces display a

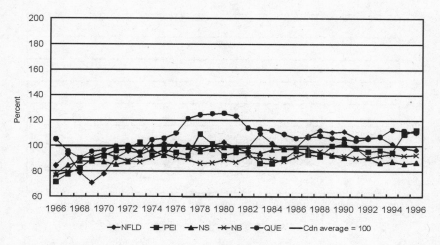

Figure 2.7a   Per capita spending on education relative to 10-province average

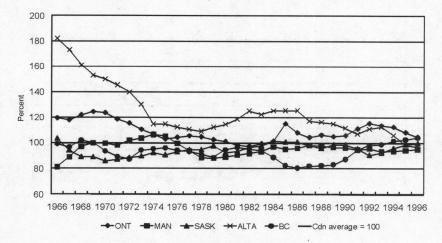

Figure 2.7b   Per capita spending on education relative to 10-province average

tendency to remain either above or below the average, the ranking of most with respect to other neighbouring provinces changes often over the years. The same can be said of real social assistance benefits, which are shown in figures 2.9a,b. In fact, the most consistent finding there is that New Brunswick was the least generous of the ten provinces throughout the 1979–95 period. Alberta moved from providing below-average benefits to single mothers with two children until 1979, to above-average benefits from 1980

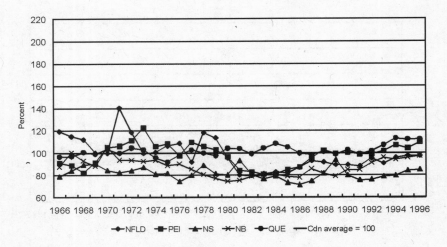

Figure 2.8a   Per capita other spending relative to 10-province average

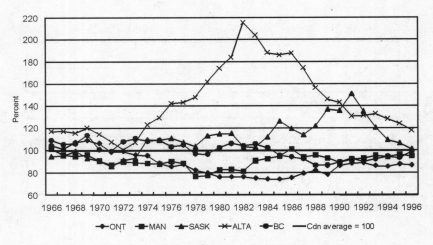

Figure 2.8b   Per capita other spending relative to 10-province average

to 1988, to a level of benefits in 1996 that was at or just below the ten-province average.

As far as the provincial policy indicators go, the one that perhaps displays the most stable pattern is the income tax burden, displayed in figures 2.10a,b. The most interesting feature here is the large gap between Quebec and the rest of the provinces, which began to open up in 1976 and remained fairly constant from 1988 to 1996. Not surprisingly, basic income taxes fell

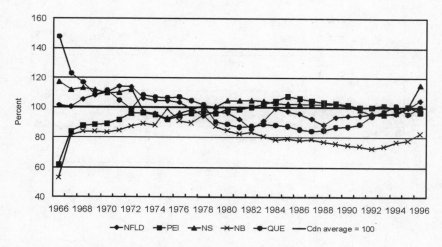

Figure 2.9a   Social assistance benefits relative to 10-province average

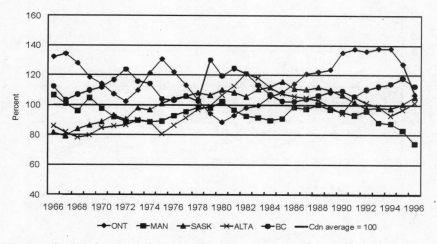

Figure 2.9b   Social assistance benefits relative to 10-province average

more in oil-rich Alberta than in any other province beginning in 1975. From 1978 to1996 Newfoundland imposed the second-highest basic income tax in the country, although throughout this period it remained within five percentage points of the ten-province average. We will pay careful attention to tax incentives in our empirical work.

Turning now to the federal policy variables, the behaviour of the two unemployment insurance variables in figures 2.11a,b and 2.12a,b (minimum

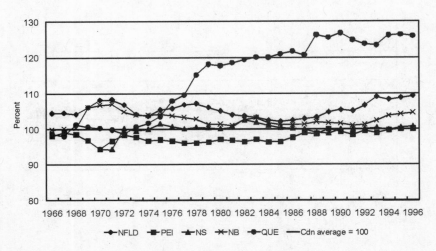

Figure 2.10a   Real income tax burden relative to 10-province average

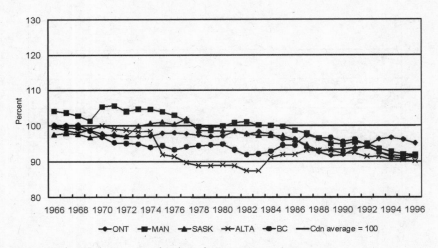

Figure 2.10b   Real income tax burden relative to 10-province average

qualifying weeks and maximum benefits with minimum qualifying weeks) is very similar to that of the unemployment rate, a correspondence that follows from the dependence of these two indicators on the unemployment rate. Provinces with relatively high unemployment rates tend to have relatively low minimum qualifying weeks and relatively high maximum benefits with minimum qualifying weeks. For a closer look at what this means for individuals, figures 2.13 and 2.14 compare just two provinces, Ontario

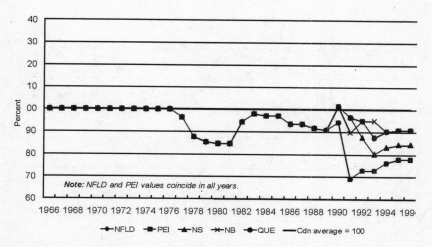

Figure 2.11a   Minimum qualifying weeks for UI relative to 10-province average

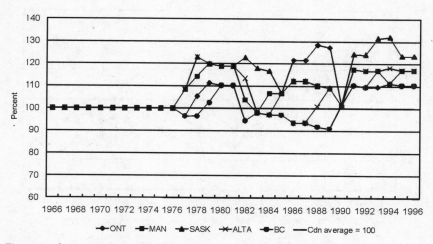

Figure 2.11b   Minimum qualifying weeks for UI relative to 10-province average

and Newfoundland. These figures suggest that during our sample period the migration incentives embodied in the unemployment insurance system have indeed fluctuated over time, with the gap between the two provinces in minimum weeks required to qualify for benefits ranging from zero weeks between 1982 and 1984 (and of course prior to the introduction of regional extended benefits) to six weeks in 1991. Similarly, the difference in maximum weeks of benefits for minimal qualifiers ranged from just four weeks

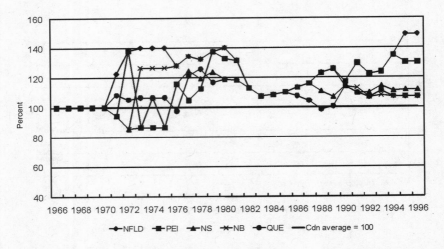

Figure 2.12a   Maximum UI benefit weeks at *MIN* relative to 10-province average

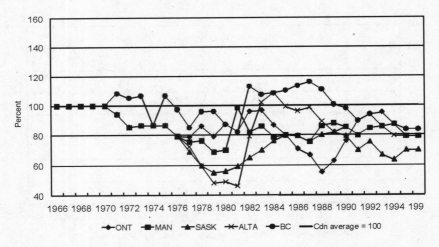

Figure 2.12b   Maximum UI benefit weeks at *MIN* relative to 10-province average

in 1983 to twenty-two weeks in 1988. The two figures also show that the switch from Unemployment Insurance to Employment Insurance in 1997 did not result in any important changes in these differentials.

The pattern of regional differences in the last of the three federal policy variables we examine is displayed in figure 2.15a,b. What is most interesting about these figures is the stability of the pattern of dispersion across provinces. Note that there is far less switching of relative positions than in the graphs of the provincial spending variables.

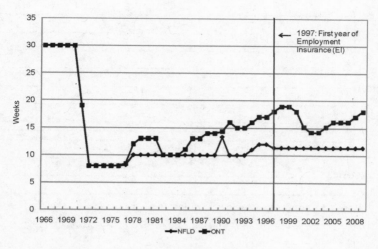

Figure 2.13   Minimal qualifying requirement for UI/EI, 1966–2009

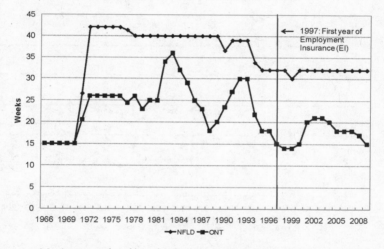

Figure 2.14   Maximum weeks of benefits for a minimal UI/EI qualifier, 1966–2009

The two provinces that benefited most on a per capita basis from federal spending during the 1966–1996 period were Nova Scotia and Prince Edward Island. In fact, per capita federal spending in these two provinces was so high that between 1978 and 1996, the only other province in which per capita federal spending lay consistently above the ten-province average was New Brunswick. The provinces that benefited least in per capita terms from federal current and capital spending were the three westernmost provinces and Quebec.

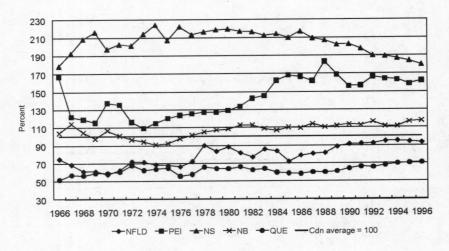

Figure 2.15a   Per capita federal spending relative to 10-province average

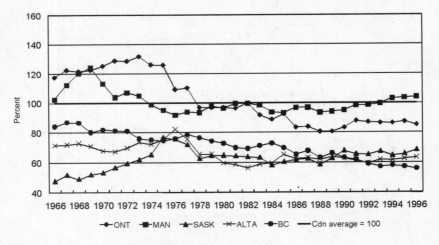

Figure 2.15b   Per capita federal spending relative to 10-province average

CONCLUSION

After examining the pattern of regional disparities in all these potential migration determinants, what general conclusions can we draw about regional differences in public policy in Canada and their implications for interregional migration? First, if the standard for measuring the potential importance to migration of policy differentials is the level of regional variation in average weekly earnings and the unemployment rate, then all the policy variables examined here are potentially important, since they exhibit as much or more variation across provinces, as measured by the coefficient of variation, as these essential private market indicators. The same can be said of the federal policy variables, since they display at least as much variation, or more, than the provincial policy variables. It is clear that regional differences in the various public sector determinants of migration considered do exist.

Second, the figures indicate that provinces where wages are above the Canadian average and unemployment rates are below the average, such as Ontario and Alberta, also tend to offer residents relatively high levels of publicly provided goods and services (at least at the provincial level) accompanied by relatively low tax rates. This observation suggests that the migration incentives resulting from provincial differences in publicly provided goods and services tend to reinforce those resulting from provincial differences in private market variables, rather than offset them. On the other hand, the pattern of regional differences in the three federal policy variables examined does raise the spectre of the transfer dependency thesis, with greater government spending and more generous unemployment insurance benefits in provinces with higher unemployment rates and lower wages.

However, we would be getting ahead of ourselves if we were to draw any further conclusions about the nature or strength of policy-induced migration at this point, since the effect of any policy on migration depends not only on the extent of regional differences but also on how people respond to the additions to comprehensive income in any location that result from the actions of governments at various levels in the federal system. The literature review in the next chapter and the parameter estimates to be presented in later chapters will shed more light on the importance to individuals of the various incentives to migrate created by private markets and by the public sector. The one thing we can say at this point is that if regional differentials in fiscal policies turn out to have weak effects on migration compared to variation in labour market conditions, we cannot attribute such a result to a lack of regional variation in the public sector variables we use in our empirical work.

3

A Review of Four Decades of Empirical Research

The evidence we examined in chapter 2 indicates that various aspects of public policy in Canada alter the public components of individual comprehensive incomes to a greater extent in some regions and provinces of the country than in others. Often the regional differentiation is deliberate, as in the case of unemployment insurance, and at times it may simply result from the combined and uncoordinated actions of different levels of government. The result of such regional discrimination may be either good or bad from the perspective of the country as a whole, depending on which of the various theoretical perspectives on policy-induced migration introduced in chapter 1 we choose to follow. In all cases, though, the seriousness of the situation depends on the strength of the relationship between public policy and the volume and pattern of internal migration. Only if the relationship is substantial will any of the theoretical arguments we introduced be of practical concern.

The fact that internal migration is an important determinant of the regional allocation of labour in Canada, coupled with the potential importance of policy-induced migration, led to an extensive empirical search over the past four decades, beginning with Courchene's seminal paper in 1970. Before turning to our own empirical models and results, in this chapter we review the past forty years of research on the nature and strength of fiscally induced migration in Canada. The review will help to place our own work in perspective so that what is new can more easily be sorted out. It also serves as a background to the state-of-the-art assessment about policy-induced migration, encompassing the research presented in this book as well as the literature considered here, that we offer in our concluding chapter.

Courchene's work, as well as much of the research that followed it, was motivated by a suspicion that public support of various kinds for people living in poorer provinces is partly responsible for the persistence of regional disparities in Canada. Courchene identified two types of policies that he thought should be indicted: unemployment insurance and inter-governmental grants from the federal to the provincial governments that are biased towards relatively poor regions. With respect to unemployment insurance, his concern was that recipients of benefits might be unwilling to risk losing those benefits by moving to look for work in regions with lower unemployment. Similarly, he argued that intergovernmental transfer payments, by allowing governments in low-income provinces to offer more services at a given level of taxation, would reduce migration from low-income to high-income provinces. The empirical relevance of these argu-ments – which collectively have become known as *the transfer dependency thesis* – remains controversial.

Courchene tested his hypotheses using aggregate cross-section data from the 1961 Census, and aggregate time-series data for the period 1952–67. He estimated a number of simple linear models explaining the rate of migration from province i to province j of the form

$$M_{ij} = \beta_0 + \beta_1 X_{1ij} + \beta_2 X_{2ij} + \ldots + \beta_K X_{Kij} + \varepsilon_{ij}, \tag{3.1}$$

where M_{ij} is either the rate of migration from i to j or its natural log; X_{1ij} to X_{Kij} are the explanatory variables he believed influenced the flow of migrants between i and j; $\beta_0, \ldots, \beta_K$ are the parameters to be estimated; and ε_{ij} is a random error term.

Using the ratio of total unemployment insurance benefits to earned income and intergovernmental transfers per worker in the origin province i (or, in an alternative equation, the ratio of total federal transfers to earned income in the origin) to measure unemployment insurance and intergovernmental transfer payments respectively, Courchene estimated these linear equations and found that his hypotheses were verified. Subsequent research, however, has not always led to the same conclusion.

Although all the studies that build on Courchene's work begin with the premise that provincial differences in fiscal structure may influence migra-tion decisions, they differ in many respects, including the type of econo-metric model estimated, the type of data used, and their representation of fiscal structure, as well as in their conclusions. These differences are not completely independent. To a large extent, the type of data selected deter-mines both the types of econometric model that can be estimated and the manner in which the variables reflecting public sector influences may be measured and represented. For example, linear models cannot be estimated using individual microdata, since such models require a continuous measure of migration as the dependent variable, something that is not available in a microdata set. Similarly, dummy variable indicators of receipt of unemployment insurance benefits are found only in studies that use microdata, a fact that we will return to later on. Moreover, studies that use aggregated, time-series data are able to, and do, include a wider range of policy variables, including indexes of the generosity of unemployment insurance, than do studies relying on microdata. In addition, in some cases these studies are able to take a structural approach to the representation of public policy, embedding various policy parameters in the model used to represent decision making by a prospective migrant.

We could arrange our review of prior research either (i) by type of migration equation used – and in particular, whether it models a simple move-stay decision or takes all possible destinations into account; (ii) by the way in which fiscal policies are represented in the model; (iii) by the type of data utilized; or (iv) according to some combination of these characteristics. Since it is such an important determinant of the empirical model that can be used, it is convenient to divide this chapter into sections according to the type of data analyzed, while paying careful attention in each case to the other two dimensions of modelling choices.

We first review studies that attempt to model aggregate internal migration flows in the section, "Studies that Use Aggregate Data." By "aggregate data," we mean migration data that do not consist of observations on individuals but that may be disaggregated in various ways, such as by gender or income. (Of course such data have been built up from observations of individual moves.) Then in the next section we turn to studies that use individual microdata, most of which have been published since 1990, because little in the way of microdata suitable for the study of fiscally induced migration was available beforehand. The final section of the chapter summarizes our conclusions. Here our concern is primarily methodological, before the presentation of our own migration model in chapter 4. As we noted, we will offer an overall assessment of what we think the literature as well as our own work tells us about fiscally induced migration in our final chapter.

For the convenience of the reader table 3.1 at the end of this chapter summarizes the most important characteristics of all the studies examined, including the type of data used, the sample period, the type of model estimated, the fiscal variables included, and each study's principal results concerning policy-induced migration.

To help keep things in perspective, it should be noted at the outset that although we focus on the role of public policy, virtually all studies of internal migration find that private market factors – such as regional wage differentials, unemployment rates, moving costs, and the age of migrants – consistently perform well as predictors of individual migration decisions and of general migration patterns. The issue we are concerned with in our survey of previous work is whether or not, and to what extent, public polices of various kinds are also important. In addition, in order to keep the length of our review manageable, we do not include in our survey the vast literature on the topic from other countries, though we are aware of this literature and make use of it in a general way in formulating our own work on Canada.[1]

STUDIES THAT USE AGGREGATE DATA

One great advantage of using aggregate data to study migration is that such data cover relatively long time periods that encompass many important policy changes relevant to a study of policy-induced migration. These policy changes are important because they contribute much of the variation needed to identify the effects on migration of particular government policies. Moreover, when using such data, it turns out to be easier to include explanatory variables that explicitly measure regionally specific variation in fiscal policies of various types.

Collectively the studies we review in this section cover the period 1952–2004, during which there were several major revisions to Canada's intergovernmental transfer system as well as to the unemployment insurance system. Although no one study covers the entire time period, at least one (Basher and Fachin 2008) uses a sample period of over thirty years, about the same length as our own, while several others examine periods of twenty years or more.

Although studies of aggregate migration flows vary considerably in terms of the number of fiscal variables they include and the manner in which the fiscal variables are incorporated in their estimating equations, one thing they have in common is that they all use fiscal aggregates of some sort. By "fiscal aggregates" we mean a value that pertains to the entire provincial economy, usually a per capita measure. Fiscal aggregates have the advantage of being readily available, but they may not always be accurate measures of the theoretical quantities they are intended to represent. For example, provincial differences in per capita government spending on health may not accurately reflect provincial differences in publicly provided health services, since both the mix and the quality of services may differ from province to province as well. Furthermore, different individuals may value a particular bundle of publicly provided goods and services differently. Among the

studies we review here, only Winer and Gauthier (1982a) are able to par-
tially compensate for the latter problem by estimating different migration
functions for different income classes. We will pay particular attention to
differences between studies in their choice of fiscal variables in the discussion that follows.

Of the first three studies to follow Courchene, all estimate simple linear
models of migration, but they do not all include the same fiscal variables as
Courchene. Boadway and Green (1981) come closest to Courchene's specification, including both the ratio of average weekly unemployment insurance
benefits to average weekly earnings in Newfoundland and per capita federal
transfers to Newfoundland in their equation explaining net migration *to*
Newfoundland from the rest of Canada. They find that only the insurance
benefit variable has a significant (positive) impact on migration to the province during the 1951–78 period.

Like Boadway and Green, Schweitzer (1982) focuses on a single province, in this case Alberta. The only fiscal variable he includes in his equations explaining in- and out-migration to Alberta between 1961 and 1979
is per capita provincial government natural resource revenues. He finds that
resource revenues have a significant (positive) effect only on in-migration to
Alberta. Our guess is that here we are seeing the consequences of attempts
by individuals to effectively take part in resource booms associated with the
oil and gas sectors of the Alberta economy.

Dean (1982) also restricts his attention to one component of provincial
government revenues, in this case taxes. However, he examines all ten provinces over the 1972–79 period, rather than just one. He includes both origin
and destination values of two tax variables in an equation describing the
rate of migration from province i to province j: the personal income tax
rate (which during his sample period is a percentage of basic federal tax)
and direct taxes as a percentage of personal income. When the equation is
estimated using pooled data for all ten provinces, all the tax variables have
significant coefficients. Surprisingly, the coefficients of the origin as well as
the destination variables have negative signs, suggesting that high taxes in
the province of origin will tend to reduce out-migration rather than increase
it. Dean reports that the negative sign of the coefficient on the province of
origin tax variable disappears in most cases when separate equations are
estimated for each province of origin.

Winer and Gauthier (1982a,b) provide the first study of fiscally induced
migration in Canada to estimate a discrete choice model of migration rather
than a linear model.[2] One problem with the linear models of migration discussed so far is that it is impossible to include the characteristics of more

than just the actual origin and destination regions in the estimating equations without making some extremely restrictive assumptions. In principal, other destinations are relevant to any individual who is deciding where to go (if anywhere). Discrete choice models, in which choices result from individual optimization across all possible alternatives, including the staying option, provide a nice way of representing such decision making.

The conditional logit model, first proposed by McFadden (1974a), has since proved to be particularly popular among migration researchers everywhere.[3] In this model the probability of migrating from i to j, P_{ij}, is given by

$$P_{ij} = \frac{e^{V_{ij}}}{\sum_{k=1}^{K} e^{V_{ik}}},$$ (3.2)

where e is the exponential function, K is the number of possible destinations, and V_{ij} is in practice defined as a linear function of the variables believed to influence migration:

$$V_{ij} = \beta_1 X_{1ij} + \ldots + \beta_K X_{Kij}.$$ (3.3)

Although all the variables on the right-hand side of (3.3) have both i and j as subscripts, in some aggregate studies many of them vary only with the destination j, so that the characteristics of only one destination appear in the numerator of expression (3.2). However, the characteristics of all the other destinations appear in the denominator of (3.2), guaranteeing that all of them influence the rate of migration from i to j. Another desirable property of this model that is not shared by linear models is that the sum over all destinations j of the migration probabilities P_{ij} is guaranteed to equal one.

The conditional logit model has the convenient feature that the log of the odds of choosing destination j over destination i is a linear equation. Although for individuals the choice probabilities are not directly observable, the log-odds version of the model can be estimated using aggregate data by substituting the observed migration rate M_{ij} for the choice probability P_{ij}, resulting in the following linear estimating equation:[4]

$$\ln\left[\frac{M_{ij}}{M_{ii}}\right] = \beta_1 + \beta_2(X_{1ij} - X_{1ii}) + \ldots + \beta_K(X_{Kij} - X_{Kii}) + \varepsilon_{ij}.$$ (3.4)

The relative simplicity of equation (3.4), coupled with the other advantages of the conditional logit model, has led many migration researchers using aggregate data to choose it over simple linear specifications like (3.1).

In addition to being the first to estimate a conditional logit model, Winer and Gauthier (1982a) also include a much fuller representation of the public sector in their model than did previous authors, using migration flows based on income tax data for the 1967–77 period. Their fiscal variables include the difference in per capita federal expenditures between origin and destination, the difference between origin and destination in per capita unconditional grants received from the federal government, the difference between origin and destination in per capita natural resource revenues, per capita federal transfers excluding unemployment insurance benefits in the province of origin, and origin and destination values of an index of the generosity of unemployment insurance benefits. The index of insurance generosity they use is

$$UIDEX_k = \frac{MAX_k}{MIN_k} \cdot \frac{CA_k}{CF_k}, \tag{3.5}$$

where k represents the province, MAX_k is the maximum number of weeks of benefits to which a person with minimum qualifying weeks is entitled, MIN_k is the minimum number of weeks required to qualify for benefits, CA_k is the number of claims accepted, and CF_k is the number of initial claims filed. Increases in the generosity of the system will lead to increases in the value of the index.

In addition, their data set allows them to estimate separate models of migration for each of seven different income classes. This is possible because their migration data were constructed from a 10 percent sample of income tax files. Since the impact of fiscal structure may vary systematically with the level of income, this disaggregation is obviously useful in a study of policy-induced migration when individualized measures of fiscal surplus, as opposed to province-wide fiscal aggregates, are not available.

Apart from their results with respect to unemployment insurance, Winer and Gauthier's results concerning most of the fiscal variables they utilized are somewhat inconclusive. They do find that migration to Alberta and the West is significantly positively correlated with natural resource revenues, as does Schweitzer. The possibility remains, however, that this result is tainted by the general collinearity between public and private sector variables in the West following the dramatic rise in the price of oil after 1973, a problem that affects all studies that attempt to look at the role of such tax revenues. Natural resource revenues may simply be a proxy for job opportunities or other private sector determinants of migration decisions not included in the estimating equations.

On the other hand, federal grants to the provinces do have the expected effect, discouraging out-migration and encouraging in-migration, but only when the Atlantic provinces are included as possible destinations and then only for the poorer income group. Simulations Winer and Gauthier conduct concerning the quantitative effects of changes in equalization grants between 1971 and 1977 confirm the nature of these results. The finding that there is a significant, negative impact of grants on out-migration for lower-income people who live in the poorer Atlantic region where these grants are most important does suggest that grants do retard out-migration, as Courchene hypothesized.

Winer and Gauthier's results with respect to unemployment insurance benefits are stronger than those for other fiscal variables, in the sense that the signs and statistical significance of coefficients are more consistent across various samples. They find that out-migration of poorer people from the Atlantic provinces is significantly and negatively related to increases in the generosity of unemployment insurance benefits in that region, and positively related to increases in the generosity of insurance benefits elsewhere. The fact that unemployment insurance payments are a relatively important source of income for poorer people and for people in relatively depressed regions of the country enhances the intuitive plausibility of these results.

Like Winer and Gauthier, Shaw (1985, 1986) estimates a conditional logit model of migration and includes multiple variables representing fiscal structure: a measure of UI generosity (average weekly UI benefits relative to average weekly wages), a measure of the probability of receiving UI (the ratio of total weeks of benefits paid to total weeks of unemployment in the province), real per capita unconditional federal grants to the province, and real provincial natural resource revenues. Both origin and destination values of each variable are included. However, his work differs from that of previous studies that use aggregate data in that he uses census data for the period 1965–81 and examines migration between census metropolitan areas (CMAs), not provinces, although his fiscal variables are defined on a provincial basis.

He finds that real per capita unconditional intergovernmental grants to the destination province increase migration to that province, while grants to the province of origin either have no effect or an unexpected positive effect on out-migration. The natural resource revenues of a provincial government have no discernible effect on migration flows, nor does the probability of receiving UI benefits, but increases in the generosity of unemployment insurance payments in the census CMA of origin significantly reduce out-migration. Furthermore, when Shaw restricts his sample to the post-1971 period, when the regional generosity of the unemployment insurance system was substantially increased, he finds that the negative effect of an increase in insurance generosity in the province of origin on outflows from that province is larger in magnitude and that increases in the generosity of benefits in the potential destinations also tend to increase out-migration. Thus his results with respect to unemployment insurance benefits support those of Winer and Gauthier.

While adding more variables to represent provincial differences in fiscal structure would seem to be desirable, not all studies pursued this avenue of research. Mills, Percy, and Wilson (1983), Foot and Milne (1984), and Vanderkamp (1988) chose instead to rely on a single indicator of fiscal structure, a measure of net fiscal surplus essentially equal to the dollar amount of expenditures minus all taxes collected in each region. As a representation of fiscal structure, this measure is not a good one because it does not allow for the subjective evaluation of the benefits individuals receive from government services. All three of these studies also estimate linear migration models rather than conditional logit models.[5]

Otherwise, the models estimated in these three studies are quite different. Mills, Percy, and Wilson look at annual gross migration flows, Foot and Milne at net in-migration, and Vanderkamp at net out-migration. In addition, the first two studies use annual data for the periods 1961–78 and 1961–81 respectively, while Vanderkamp uses Census data covering the period 1931–40 to 1971–80.

Both Mills, Percy, and Wilson and Foot and Milne find that their fiscal surplus variables have the expected effect only in some provinces. It is particularly noteworthy that Ontario is one of the provinces for which both studies find that fiscal surpluses seem to have either no impact on migration or an effect opposite to what was anticipated. Vanderkamp, whose data were pooled across provinces, finds that an increase in fiscal surplus reduces out-migration from a province.

The relatively weaker performance of fiscal variables other than unemployment insurance in most of the studies discussed thus far seems to suggest that federal grants and provincial fiscal policies have little effect on interprovincial migration flows. However, MacNevin (1984) and Day (1992) dispute this conclusion, arguing that the explanation for the inconclusive results obtained by other studies may lie in their choice of variables representing fiscal structure. Individuals making migration decisions are unlikely to pay direct attention to the levels of interprovincial grants or natural resource revenues received by different provincial governments. Similarly, few individuals are likely to make a detailed calculation of their fiscal surplus in the manner implied by Mills et. al., Foot and Milne, and Vanderkamp. Instead, the aspects of fiscal structure that individuals are most likely to be aware of are the public services that they consume, the taxes they pay, and the transfer payments, including unemployment insurance, that they directly receive. MacNevin and Day further suggest that finding that the level of public services has a significant impact on interprovincial migration provides indirect evidence that intergovernmental grants and natural resource revenues influence migration, since changes in provincial government revenues will clearly have an impact on the supply of public services. Of course, the strength of this indirect route cannot be uncovered by such an approach; the migration model would have to be supplemented by a model of provincial government decision making in order to determine the precise impact of grants on migration.

Note that this argument does not imply that including grants and natural resource revenues in a migration equation is wrong. Because expenditures, taxes, federal grants, and natural resource revenues are linked through the provincial government budget constraint, including the latter three variables in an estimating equation instead of a measure of provincial government services constitutes a reduced-form approach to the modelling of fiscal structure in which grants appear instead of the level of public services because grants are a (possibly endogenous) determinant of the level of those services. The empirical models of Winer and Gauthier (1982a), Shaw (1985, 1986), and others can be viewed in this light. Indeed, absent an explicit structural model of how grants alter provincial decision making and how provincial fiscal policy in turn affects migration decisions, this reduced-form approach is the only way that the role of grants can be directly investigated in a migration study. On the other hand, in a model of the individual migration decision, one can argue that it is desirable to include factors that are as closely related to individual decision making as possible. Our work in this book is grounded in the latter view about how to represent public policy.

MacNevin and Day, both of whom estimate conditional logit models of migration, choose real per capita provincial government expenditures as their measure of the level of public services. Although MacNevin's results with respect to this variable are not consistent across different specifications of his estimating equations, Day's results are stronger. She finds that higher per capita levels of provincial government spending attract in-migrants to a province, holding all other determinants of migration constant. In addition, she finds that the mix of services provided matters. Migrants are attracted to provinces with higher per capita levels of spending on health and education but repelled by higher levels of spending on social services. Precisely why spending on social services is a deterrent is not clear. It is possible that its effect is related to the income or employment status of migrants, or that per capita expenditures on social services are acting as a proxy for types of unemployment that are not adequately captured by the usual Labour Force Survey measure of unemployment that she used.[6] The aggregate data used by Day do not permit the exploration of such possibilities.

MacNevin and Day also include taxes and transfer payments to individuals in their models of interprovincial migration, although they do so in a somewhat different manner than do other studies discussed so far. Income taxes and transfer payments affect individuals primarily through their effect on disposable income, and thus MacNevin and Day argue that they should be included in migration equations through measures of disposable income, rather than as separate explanatory variables. Day also incorporates unemployment insurance benefits and the probability of receiving them in the measure of disposable income in some versions of her model. Since the measures of disposable income included by MacNevin and Day do have a significant impact on in-migration to a region – the higher is disposable income in province i, the greater will be in-migration to that province, holding all else equal – income taxes and provincial government transfer payments also have a significant influence on migration through this channel. This approach to the measurement and role of income is one that we employ in the empirical work to be presented in later chapters.

Authors such as Winer and Gauthier (1982a) argue that empirical models of migration should ideally go a step further in constructing an appropriate income variable by including the expected present value of the gain in disposable income resulting from a move rather than current disposable income, which is the income variable utilized by Day and MacNevin. This is because the gains from migration are realized not solely in the period immediately after the individual moves but over an extended period after the move is made. Moreover, they argue that individuals may have different expectations about how the different components of disposable income – before-tax income, income taxes, and transfer payments – are likely to evolve through time. If so, and given that it is possible only to approximate the process through which individuals form expectations of these quantities, it may be more appropriate to treat expected before-tax income, expected income taxes, and expected transfer payments as separate explanatory variables rather than using one comprehensive measure of income.

Winer and Gauthier (1982a) follow this latter strategy by including measures of expected gross or before-tax income and per capita transfer payments to individuals as separate explanatory variables in their estimating equations.[7] They deliberately exclude income taxes because including them would introduce a serious econometric complication: the high correlation between income taxes and before-tax income would make it difficult to identify the separate effect of the two explanatory variables.[8] Note that this problem does not arise when disposable income is used, because income, income taxes, and transfers are combined into a single variable. As was noted earlier, their results with respect to their transfer payments variable were mixed.

Of the remaining aggregate studies, that of Liaw and Ledent (1987) can be viewed as following an approach similar to that of MacNevin and Day in that they include only fiscal variables that directly affect individuals. Their sample period of 1961–83 is also similar to those of MacNevin and Day. However, their primary focus is on the estimation of an extension of the conditional logit model, namely the nested logit model, rather than on fiscally induced migration. They include only two fiscal variables – the ratio of unemployment insurance benefits per person in the destination to unemployment insurance benefits per person in the origin, and per capita government transfers to persons in the province of origin.[9] They find that per capita transfers have only a weak effect on migration. Their results with respect to unemployment benefits, however, contrast sharply with those of other researchers: they find that higher relative unemployment insurance benefits in the destination province will actually reduce in-migration, not increase it. They argue that this result is to be expected because they have included this variable as a proxy for the unemployment rate rather than as a measure of the insurance system.

Liaw and Ledent's (1987) results with respect to their relative unemployment insurance benefits variable illustrate the difficulties inherent in interpreting econometric results. Average benefits, of which their variable is a measure, do rise with unemployment rates because of the variable entrance requirement and regional differences in the maximum benefit period. Thus in principal, unless the ratio of unemployment rates is also included as an explanatory variable in the model, one cannot distinguish between the deterrent effect of relatively high unemployment rates in a province and the attraction of relatively higher unemployment insurance benefits. Consequently, Liaw and Ledent's results do not necessarily contradict the findings of Winer and Gauthier and Shaw; instead, they may simply indicate that the deterrent effect is the stronger of the two.[10]

Rosenbluth (1996) and Benarroch and Grant (2004) also follow the lead of MacNevin and Day in including measures of per capita government spending rather than intergovernmental grants in their migration models. Using data for all ten Canadian provinces for the period 1966–91, Rosenbluth tested three potential fiscal variables in his linear migration equations, but obtained consistent results with respect to only one of them – real per capita transfer payments to persons. His results indicate that increases in real per capita transfers to persons in a province significantly increase the rate of in-migration to that province.

Benarroch and Grant's (2004) study is more specialized in that they study the interprovincial movements of doctors between 1976 and 1992, not of the general population or the labour force as do other studies. So their fiscal variables relate specifically to doctors: the effective rate of income tax on physicians, health care spending (net of expenditures on physicians) per capita, and the number of hospital beds per capita. The last two of these variables are included to reflect working conditions for physicians, rather than government services consumed. They also include two variables related to the fee structures governing physician compensation in their conditional logit models. Their results show that in-migration of doctors is significantly higher where fee schedules are more generous and where provinces spend more on health care. This too is evidence of policy-induced migration.

The two most recent aggregate studies of fiscally induced migration in Canada abandon the conditional logit model used by so many previous researchers in favour of linear models. In the case of Basher and Fachin (2008), this choice is motivated by their desire to use time-series techniques not previously applied in the migration literature in investigating the causes of the downward trend in interprovincial migration rates over the 1980s and 1990s. Like Boadway and Green (1981) and Schweitzer (1982) before them, Basher and Fachin focus on a single province of origin – Ontario – but model gross rather than net in-migration to that province, using aggregate time-series data for the period 1974–2004. In contrast to previous studies that employ time-series data, they emphasize the potential problem of obtaining spurious results due to nonstationarity of the data, leading them to test first for unit roots and then for cointegration of the variables in their otherwise fairly simple linear model of migration.[11] Only one fiscal variable is included – the difference between the origin province and Ontario in per capita federal transfers to persons.[12] After finding that the variables of their model are indeed cointegrated, which implies that their estimation results will not be spurious, they conclude that provincial differentials in per capita federal transfers to persons do not play an important role. Instead, they find that regional unemployment differentials and income in the sending provinces appear to drive the decline in migration rates observed over the sample period they study. They interpret these results as evidence that convergence among provincial economies is at least partly responsible for the downward trend in interprovincial migration rates.[13]

Finally, Bakhshi, Shakeri, Olfert, Partridge, and Weseen (2009) follow Winer and Gauthier (1982a) in adopting the reduced-form approach to modelling fiscal structure. Like Basher and Fachin, they employ a linear specification for their migration equations but do not test for stationarity or cointegration. As fiscal variables, they include the origin values of three separate components of provincial government revenues – per capita equalization payments, per capita transfers from the federal and local governments (less equalization payments), and per capita provincial other revenue (i.e., own-source revenues) – and experiment with different lag lengths for these variables. They find that neither federal equalization payments nor other federal grants have any quantitatively important impact on (the log of) interprovincial migration flows in the 1982 to 2004 period, though their coefficients are statistically significant.[14] In an interesting simulation, they also show that if all federal equalization grants were somehow magically transformed into an equivalent, individualized wage increase, the effect, like that of a change in the wage differentials also included in their migration equation, would be substantial. This appears to demonstrate that federal grants to the provinces and personal transfers received directly by individuals are not close substitutes.

Before we move on to microdata studies, a comment on the implications of the literature on regional convergence may be useful. There is some work, including Helliwell (1994), Coulombe and Lee (1995), Cousineau and Vaillancourt (2000), DeJuan and Tomljanovich (2005), and Coulombe (2006), that indicates that provincial per capita incomes have converged to some extent since 1945. This suggests that whatever the impact of the public sector has been, it has not posed a complete barrier to the reallocation of labour and other resources across regions in the country as a whole (but see Afxentiou and Serletis 1998, who find no convergence over the 1961 to 1991 period). However, the question remains as to why convergence has not been more complete after five or six decades and why it is not occurring more rapidly.[15]

Could the public sector have something to do with the slow pace of regional convergence? Coulombe and Day (1999) compare northern US states and Canada to try to get at this question. They find that Canadians are more likely to remain in regions where they do not have jobs than are Americans in northern states. This result is consistent with a migration-retarding effect of public policy in Canada that is more substantial than in the United States, though it is not a direct test of that hypothesis. It could also be that migration costs for interregional adjustment are greater in Canada.

What conclusions can be drawn from these aggregate studies regarding the existence of fiscally induced migration? First, it seems to us that the evidence that provincial differences in the generosity of unemployment insurance benefits influences migration is fairly strong, at least as far as statistical significance is concerned. The empirical strength of this relationship has not, however, been established. Furthermore, most of the existing aggregate studies can be criticized on the grounds that a single insurance-related explanatory variable cannot capture all the relevant aspects of the system. For example, although the ratio of unemployment insurance benefits to earnings is likely to increase with both the ease of qualifying for benefits and the generosity of benefits, it does not allow these two aspects of the system to influence migration decisions independently. Shaw (1985, 1986) is the only author who includes separate measures of the generosity of benefits and the probability of receiving them in his equations, although the latter did not seem to have a statistically significant effect.

In addition, only Winer and Gauthier (1982a) define their index of unemployment insurance generosity so as to ensure that it is unaffected by the existence of various types of special benefits (e.g., maternity benefits). In contrast, other authors' measures can change simply because of regional differences in the utilization of special benefits whose provisions do not vary across regions. Consequently, their measures of the effects of regional variation in the unemployment insurance system may be less accurate than one would like.

Second, there is some evidence that provincial government spending, as well as provincial taxes and transfer payments, have an impact on inter-provincial migration. Much of the evidence regarding interprovincial differences in taxes and transfer payments is indirect, though, as it relies on the use of comprehensive after-tax income variables. There is also some evidence that intergovernmental grants from the federal government influence migration decisions, especially for lower-income people moving to or from the Atlantic region.

In terms of the modelling of fiscally induced migration, despite the fact that conditional logit models have a number of advantages over linear ones, the latter still have their uses, particularly in multi-equation models such as those of Boadway and Green (1981), Schweitzer (1982), Vanderkamp (1988), and Rosenbluth (1996). When one is interested in the consequences as well as the causes of migration, as these authors are, a linear specification is a sensible choice, since it would be difficult to incorporate a highly non-linear migration function in a multi-equation model of migration and the labour market.[16] Much work remains to be done on the consequences of fiscally induced migration in Canada, and these studies constitute important contributions in this respect.

Finally, it is worth noting that the work of Winer and Gauthier (1982a) suggests that the degree of fiscally induced migration may differ across population subgroups. That this would be the case makes sense, especially in the case of transfers to persons such as unemployment insurance. The probability of needing such transfers may vary considerably from one person to the next, and those with low probabilities of requiring transfers probably do not pay them much attention when making migration decisions. However, aggregate migration data for population subgroups, particularly income classes or groups defined by labour force status, is difficult to obtain. Only in rare instances (as in the case of our own study) can the money be found to subsidize the creation of such data. Microdata may provide the best avenue for future exploration of the differences in migration responses to fiscal variables across population subgroups.

STUDIES THAT USE MICRODATA

For many years, the only Canadian microdata set that contained information about migration was the decennial census. Even these data were limited by the fact that until 1991, the census asked people only whether their current location was the same as their location five years earlier. This definition of mobility is not ideal because the same individual could have moved more than once during that five-year period. Further complicating the estimation of migration functions using these data was the fact that income and employment information were available only for the location at the time of the census, not for the individual's location five years earlier. The unavailability of this key information meant migration researchers had to deal with the problem of estimating the missing incomes as well as a migration function.

Since the late 1980s, a number of microdata sets with a panel dimension that provide information about mobility, such as the Labour Market Activity Survey (LMAS), the Longitudinal Administrative Database (LAD), and the Survey of Labour and Income Dynamics (SLID), have become available and have been put to use by migration researchers.[17] These data sets provide information about year-to-year mobility, about income and, except for the LAD, about employment both before and after the move. Although information about what incomes would have been if a different alternative had been chosen is still lacking, this additional information constitutes an important advantage over census microdata.

Because the nature of the migration information provided in a microdata set is quite different from that in an aggregate data set, the models estimated with microdata differ from those estimated using aggregate data. In an aggregate data set, the dependent variable is a flow or rate that can be regarded as a continuous variable. But in a microdata set, the outcome of a migration decision takes the form of one or more dummy variables that indicate whether the individual has moved or not, and/or which destination has been chosen. Nonlinear discrete choice models are typically used with data of this type. In the Canadian literature, most microdata studies of migration examine only the move-stay decision, because the associated econometric models are simpler and easier to estimate than models of multiple choices. Binomial probit and logit models have both been used. Only three of the microdata studies we examine – Liaw and Ledent (1988); Ostrovsky, Hou, and Picot (2008); and Bolduc, Fortin, and Fournier (1996) – estimate multinomial choice models.

When it comes to defining variables that represent fiscal structure, users of microdata face different challenges than users of aggregate data. The use of fiscal aggregates such as per capita intergovernmental transfer payments or per capita government expenditures is much more problematic because these measures do not vary across individuals. Even if there existed enough variation across regions in these variables to identify their coefficients, it is by now well known that the standard errors of these coefficients will tend to be underestimated in studies using microdata, resulting in the coefficients appearing to be more statistically significant than they actually are.[18] In the case of fiscal variables such as unemployment insurance and social assistance benefits that affect individuals directly, the relevant values are not observable for all possible destinations, a problem that has already been alluded to above.

Because of these problems, most studies of fiscally induced migration that use microdata include a very limited range of fiscal variables. All but two of the studies we discuss in this section restrict their attention to transfers to persons in the form of social assistance and unemployment insurance benefits. Most studies simply use dummy variable indicators of receipt of benefits in the previous year to represent unemployment insurance and social assistance, rather than indices of program generosity or the amount of benefits received. The use of dummy variable indicators sidesteps the problem of trying to estimate benefits received in different locations by concentrating on the sending region and ignoring all others. However, this approach has serious limitations, the most important of which is that because a dummy variable is independent of the amount of benefit received, it cannot capture the effect of greater generosity of benefits in a particular location *once one has qualified for benefits*. Only regional differences in the ease of qualifying for benefits will be reflected to some extent in the estimated coefficients of the dummy variables. A further problem in the case of unemployment insurance benefits is that the data underlying the dummy variable indicator do not distinguish between regular benefits, which are tied to regional unemployment rates, and other types of benefits that are not.

Keeping these limitations of microdata studies in mind, we now turn to the studies themselves. The first study of fiscally induced migration in Canada that uses microdata is that of Liaw and Ledent (1988). This study uses microdata from the 1981 Census, and focuses on migration of the elderly, rather than of all Canadians. Only one fiscal variable is included in their nested logit model, namely per capita government transfers (net of UI benefits) to persons. They find that per capita government transfers do not have a significant impact on migration of the elderly.

Islam (1989) also uses data from the 1981 Census. Like Shaw (1985, 1986), Islam examines intermunicipal (between census metropolitan areas, or CMAs) rather than interprovincial migration and considers differences in two aspects of fiscal structure, namely transfers to persons and property taxes.[19] Islam is also one of the few researchers who have corrected for selectivity bias in the estimation of the income gains attributable to migration, using the procedure of Heckman (1979). To estimate the income gain due to migration, which is an important explanatory variable in any migration equation, one has to compare a migrant's observed post-migration income with an estimate of what they would have earned had they not moved. A bias in estimating what income would have been had the individual not moved may occur if migrants are systematically different from stayers, and this difference is not explicitly allowed for through the use of an appropriate estimation technique that recognizes the correlation between the error terms in the equations used to describe migration choices and to model income. Ordinary least squares is not an appropriate estimation technique in these circumstances.

Although Islam uses after-tax income as his income variable, like Winer and Gauthier (1982a) he chooses to include transfer payments and property taxes in his estimating equation independently of income. Both these variables (and disposable income) enter the model in the form of a gain (or loss) due to moving, with the gain in transfer payments being estimated using a selectivity correction as well. Islam's results suggest that individuals will tend to move to municipalities with higher transfer payments than the place of origin and that intermunicipal differences in property taxes do not have a significant effect on migration.

A difficulty in interpreting Islam's results concerning property taxation stems from the manner in which he constructed his data. Since Islam's 1981 Census data set does not contain direct observations on property tax payments, he estimates them by regressing monthly rental payments on average household income and various characteristics of the housing unit. Because this method assumes that variations in individual rental payments from municipality to municipality are due entirely to property taxes, problems may arise. Differences in the frequency with which assessed values are changed, among other things, may result in differences across municipalities in the relationship between rental payments and property taxes. In addition, since Islam includes renters as well as owners in his data set, differences in the degree of rent control and in the proportion of rental properties that are subject to rent control will also distort the relationship between rental payments and property taxes. Thus it is likely that Islam's estimates of property taxes are subject to measurement error, which will tend to bias the coefficient estimates.

The next four studies we review consider only transfers to persons and use a dummy variable approach to incorporate social assistance and unemployment insurance benefits in their models. Osberg, Gordon, and Lin (1994) study a sample of men residing in the Atlantic and Prairie provinces drawn from the Labour Market Activity Survey for the short period 1986 to 1987. Using a bivariate probit model of interregional and inter-industry migration, they find that the receipt of unemployment insurance, social assistance, and training services does not significantly affect interprovincial migration decisions. Lin (1995) also uses data from the LMAS, but for the 1988–90 period, which he divides into two subperiods. He estimates logit models of the move-stay decision and finds that interprovincial migration does not depend on the receipt of either unemployment insurance or social assistance, except in the case of adult women in 1990. In this case, receipt of unemployment insurance benefits in the previous year increases the probability of migrating. For men, Lin's results are identical to those of Osberg et al. (1994). However, both studies look at migration from only one year to another and thus reflect only the effects of provincial differences in the generosity of social programs, rather than important policy changes across time.

Bolduc, Fortin, and Fournier (1996), like Benarroch and Grant (2004) in their aggregate study, examine the mobility of doctors. This narrow focus renders their results less general, but they do provide evidence to the effect that government policies can influence migration flows. They look at newly trained doctors in Quebec during the 1976 to 1988 period, using multinomial probit models to model the choice between eighteen different regions. They show that government measures to induce doctors to move, such as settlement grants, relocation expenses, training leaves, and income subsidies, have had an impact on the location choices of newly trained doctors.

Returning now to the general population, Finnie (2004) estimates a panel logit model of the move-stay decision using data that cover a much longer period, 1982–95. These data are from the Longitudinal Administrative Data set, which is derived from individual tax files. He finds that the receipt of unemployment insurance is associated with a significant *increase* in out-migration of prime-aged men and women. More specifically, his estimates imply increases in the probability of migrating that vary with age and sex, ranging from 0.18 (for women aged 45–64) to about 0.06 (for women aged 20–24).[20] Men aged 20–24 constitute the only group for which receipt of unemployment insurance benefits has no significant effect on the probability of moving.[21]

Audas and McDonald (2003) also employ dummy variables for the receipt of unemployment insurance and social assistance benefits and examine the move-stay decision but in their estimation allow for differences in responsiveness related to the nature of an individual's labour market attachment. The categories of labour market attachment they define resemble closely those defined in the technical report upon which this book is based (Day and Winer 2001).[22] Their data come from the Survey of Labour and Income Dynamics for 1993–99, a data set that permits them to study intraprovincial moves between unemployment insurance regions. They use the SLID's detailed information about labour force status to identify the degree of labour market attachment of individual migrants. In some estimations, and with mixed success, these authors also attempt to allow for the possibility that migration choices and receipt of unemployment insurance benefits may be simultaneously affected by unobservable individual characteristics such as personal motivation. Finally, because their data set spans the period both before and after the switch from Unemployment Insurance (UI) to Employment Insurance (EI) in 1996, Audas and McDonald exploit the change in the insurance regime over the course of their sample period in an attempt to gain further insight into the impact of unemployment insurance benefits on migration decisions. This change lies outside the sample period we will employ in our work, although our sample period includes earlier and in our view more fundamental changes in the unemployment insurance system that Audas and McDonald cannot consider.

In modelling the unemployment insurance system, Audas and McDonald do not rely solely on a dummy variable for receipt of benefits as do other microdata studies. In some models they also include *the sum* of minimum weeks and maximum weeks of insurance benefits available to a qualified individual in each unemployment insurance region of residence as a proxy for the generosity of the system. In addition, they test for changes in the coefficient of the Employment Insurance region unemployment rate after 1996. Such a change would suggest that the changes to the program had indeed had some effect on mobility.

The Audas-McDonald results show that the relationship between unemployment insurance and migration depends on the degree of attachment to the labour market, a result echoed in the work we describe in subsequent chapters, as well as in our earlier technical report.[23] They find some evidence that receipt of insurance payments inhibits migration of people who are moderately attached to the labour market, although the magnitude of the effect is sensitive to the estimation method used. Standard probit estimates of two different specifications imply that a moderately attached individual will be almost one percentage point less likely to move to another EI region if he/she has received insurance benefits in the previous year, but the magnitude of the effect jumps to four percentage points when instrumental variables estimation is used to correct for the potential endogeneity of the receipt of benefits.[24] In addition, they find that the tightening of the eligibility rules after 1996 likely gave marginally attached workers a stronger incentive to leave high unemployment regions. This last effect appears to be small in magnitude (an increase of less than 0.1 percentage points in the probability of moving). Receipt of social assistance benefits in the previous year appears to affect only those who are unattached to the labour market, reducing the probability of moving from one EI region to another by about 0.7 percentage points.

Most recently, Ostrovsky, Hou, and Picot (2008) use the LAD, combined with Citizenship and Immigration records, to compare the migration behaviour of immigrants and long-term Canadians aged 20 to 54 during 1996–2000 and 2001–5, two boom periods when economic activity and provincial population surged in Alberta. Although the authors are primarily concerned with migration *to* Alberta, this study is of particular interest because it is one of only two (Audas-McDonald is the other) that deal with the period after the implementation of changes associated with the retitling of the insurance program as Employment Insurance in 1996. The overall conclusion of the study is that immigrants are more likely than comparable non-immigrants to move to Alberta in response to Alberta's labour demand boom post-2000, especially if they have been living in Canada for less than five years.

For both groups they find that receipt of government benefits significantly affects migration behaviour. Their initial results indicated that receipt of unemployment insurance in the origin province reduced out-migration of immigrants to provinces other than Alberta and had no effect on migration to Alberta. However, the results change after additional information about immigration class and region of origin are added to the model. In the expanded model, migration to Alberta of both immigrants and long-time residents is significantly positively affected by receipt of EI benefits. For immigrants, receipt of social assistance has positive effects on migration that are generally bigger in absolute value than for EI. For example, receipt of employment insurance benefits is associated with an increase in the probability of moving to Alberta of 0.011, while receipt of social assistance is associated with an increase of 0.028.

All in all, these results indicate that the effect of the welfare system on the behaviour of recent immigrants is different from that for long-time residents. Because of attachments to one's place of residence that are built up over the years – which we can think of as a type of migration cost – this difference in behaviour is not surprising and adds credibility to their results.

What conclusions can be drawn from these microdata studies regarding the existence of fiscally-induced migration? In general, as we have already noted, microdata studies are more limited than aggregate studies in terms of the fiscal variables they include because measures of fiscal benefits are not available on an individual basis. Hence, most have restricted their attention to the relationship between the receipt of unemployment and social assistance benefits and migration. In so doing most authors have relied on simple zero-one dummy variables indicating the receipt of benefits during the year prior to moving. While these studies have certainly provided new insights into the determinants of migration, the dummy variable approach to investigating the effects of unemployment insurance and social assistance has serious limitations. As has already been noted, most of these studies restrict their attention to the move-stay decision, rather than investigating destination choice.[25] By way of contrast, most aggregate studies include both origin and destination characteristics among their explanatory variables. But in the case of both unemployment insurance benefits and social assistance, the nature of the relationship between receipt of benefits and the migration decision is likely to be affected by the identity of the provinces of origin and destination. When all destinations are pooled, only the average effect of destination characteristics will be captured.

Dummy variable indicators of receipt of benefits also share some of the limitations of the benefits indices used in aggregate studies. As has already been noted, in the case of unemployment insurance they do not capture regional differences in weeks of benefits, an important aspect of regional variation in the Canadian insurance system. In addition, microdata sets do not provide information regarding the type of benefits received, so that the dummy variable cannot distinguish between recipients of regular and special benefits.

A last criticism of the microdata studies is that if some of the explanatory variables included in the model are correlated with unobservable factors that also influence migration, the parameter estimates will be biased and cannot be interpreted as causal. As Audas and McDonald (2003) and several others have pointed out, it is quite possible that such a correlation exists. In fact, it is possible that the conflicting results of these studies with respect to unemployment insurance – Finnie (2004) and Ostrovsky, Hou, and Picot (2008) find a positive relationship, while studies based on the LMAS and SLID find little or no relationship – can be blamed on the shared dependence of both mobility and receipt of benefits on the same unobservable personal characteristics. In support of this argument, we note that studies that include more personal characteristics (e.g., level of education) are less likely to find a significant positive relationship between these variables, while the one study that does try to control for this problem using instrumental variables estimation – Audas and McDonald (2003) – finds that the change in estimation method does affect the results.

Of course, endogeneity problems that lead to correlations between the explanatory variables and the error terms of a migration model may also exist in studies that use time-series data. In fact, economic theory suggests that wages, unemployment rates, and migration flows are all jointly determined. Flows of migrants between labour markets in response to wage and unemployment rate differentials should in principle lead to changes in those wage and unemployment rate differentials, leading to further changes in migration flows. But because annual rates of net in-migration to the Canadian provinces tend to be small, aggregate studies may face a less serious endogeneity problem than do microdata studies.[26]

As for other insights gained from microdata studies, the work of Bolduc et al. (1996), who look at measures that target a specific group, and Audas and McDonald (2003), who estimate separate migration functions for individuals with different degrees of labour market attachment, provides further support for the view that the effects of various fiscal policies on migration vary across population subgroups. However, the microdata studies as a whole provide little evidence regarding the effects of government spending, taxes, and intergovernmental grants on migration decisions, because so few studies have tried to incorporate these variables in their models. It is also disappointing, although understandable in light of the associated technical problems, that so few microdata studies have considered alternative destination choices in their basic frameworks of analysis.

It should be noted, as we have before, that few of the microdata studies consider situations in which the generosity of the unemployment insurance system varies substantially. Two of them, however – Audas and McDonald (2003) and Ostrovsky, Hou, and Picot (2008) – do cover the period after the introduction of Employment Insurance, when the basis for qualification was changed from weeks to hours of work, likely making qualification for insurance more difficult for some part-time workers.[27] The fact that their results do not seem to differ in an important way from those of previous studies using similar data for earlier periods implies that the changes in the system have not greatly altered the relationship between unemployment insurance benefits and mobility. This observation strengthens our argument that the results of studies of the effect of unemployment insurance on migration prior to 1997 have important implications for those interested in the relationship between Employment Insurance and migration in Canada today.

CONCLUDING REMARKS

Although a search for fiscally induced migration has been conducted by numerous authors using different types of data, in our view the questions posed by Courchene (1970) have yet to be definitively answered. The empirical evidence on the effects of grants and government expenditures on migration remains inconclusive. The role of unemployment insurance in influencing migration decisions also remains somewhat unclear, since the microdata studies that have been published to date do not capture all aspects of regional variation in benefits, while the indices of unemployment insurance generosity used in aggregate studies are also somewhat limited in their representation of the insurance system. More attention to the way in which the important parameters of the insurance system are represented in an empirical study is warranted.

The results of Winer and Gauthier (1982a) and Audas and McDonald (2003), together with those of Bolduc et al. and Benaroch and Grant (2004) for physicians, further suggest that in studying interregional migration, it is worthwhile to disaggregate the data as much as possible while still retaining a relatively long sample period. A long sample period is desirable because it allows the researcher to include more important policy changes. And disaggregation along the lines of income class and labour force status allows one to identify the specific groups most affected by government policies.

In the empirical work in this book, we follow Winer and Gauthier in disaggregating our data by income class, and also disaggregate by age and sex. Our sample period also ranges from the late 1960s until 1996, years during which there were important changes to public programs such as unemployment insurance, including the introduction of regionally differentiated benefits in 1971 and the variable entrance requirement in 1977.

At this point it is appropriate to point out that in any study of public policy, it is possible to consider only how year-to-year variation or variation between provinces affects migration patterns. It is not possible to study how the *existence* of the policies themselves influences migration patterns, because the effect of the complete elimination of a program such as equalization grants or unemployment insurance is not a shock that is represented in the data. The fact that marginal changes in insurance or social assistance or in other programs have a small effect on migration does not rule out the possibility that the program as a whole – its inception, or its complete elimination – is important, especially since migration costs may blunt or eliminate the force of normal year-to-year changes in public policy.

None of the studies we have reviewed distinguish between the effects of marginal or normal, year-to-year, changes in policy variables, on the one hand, and large discrete changes in public policies, on the other. Fortunately for us (though perhaps not for everyone who was affected) there are some policy-related shocks of a very large magnitude that effectively provide the opportunity to study situations akin to large, discreet changes in public policy. These include the events in Quebec associated with the October crisis of 1970, the election of the Parti Québécois in 1976, and the closing of the cod fishery in 1992. We consider the consequences of these extraordinary events in our own empirical work, along with the normal policy changes that occur frequently over the years.

After we have presented our work in the following chapters, we will be in a better position to look back at the four decades of research reviewed in this chapter in combination with our own in order to assess the nature and strength of policy-induced migration in Canada.

Table 3.1
A Summary of Empirical Studies of Fiscally Induced Migration in Canada

Study	Migration Data and Model Type	Fiscal Variables	Results
Courchene (1970)	Gross interprovincial migration rates, 1961 Census; linear model	Intergovernmental transfers per worker in the sending province	Transfers have significant negative effect on out-migration.
	Gross interprovincial migration rates of family allowance recipients, 1952–67; log-linear model	Ratio of total federal transfers to earned income in the sending province, ratio of total UI benefits to earned income in the sending province	Both federal transfers and UI benefits have significant negative effect on out-migration.
Boadway and Green (1981)	Net migration to Newfoundland, 1951–78 (net migration estimated by annual change in population less natural increase); linear model	Average weekly UI benefits per claim divided by average weekly earnings, per capita federal transfers to Newfoundland	Increases in ratio of average weekly UI benefits to average weekly earnings significantly increase net migration to Newfoundland. However, per capita federal transfers do not seem to have significant effect.
Schweitzer (1982)	Gross in- and out-migration to Alberta, 1961–79; linear model	Per capita provincial government natural resource revenues in Alberta relative to those in the rest of Canada	Increases in per capita natural resource revenues in Alberta relative to rest of Canada significantly increase in-migration to Alberta, but do not have significant effect upon out-migration.
Dean (1982)	Gross interprovincial migration rates of family allowance recipients, 1972–79; linear model	Personal income tax rate (origin and destination), direct taxes paid as a percentage of personal income (origin and destination)	Origin and destination values of both variables have negative and usually significant impact on out-migration when provinces are pooled.
Winer and Gauthier (1982a)	Gross interprovincial migration rates of family allowance recipients, 1951–78; log-linear model (attempt to replicate Courchene's results)	Ratio of average weekly UI payments to average weekly wages, ratio of total federal transfers to persons (excluding UI) to labour income in sending province, ratio of unconditional intergovernmental grants divided by labour force in sending province	Coefficients are significant and imply that more generous UI impedes out-migration and encourages in-migration in 10 of 18 equations. Federal transfers and unconditional grants have significant negative impact on out-migration.

Table 3.1 (continued)

Study	Migration Data and Model Type	Fiscal Variables	Results
	Gross interprovincial migration rates of individuals in a 10% sample drawn from income tax records, 1967–77; CL model	Index of UI generosity in both origin and destination, difference between origin and destination in per capita federal purchases, difference between origin and destination in per capita unconditional intergovernmental grants, per capita transfer payments to persons excluding UI benefits, difference between origin and destination in per capita natural resource revenues	In general, fiscal structure seems to have larger impact on poor and middle-income class. Also, out-migration from Atlantic provinces is negatively related to increases in generosity of UI in the Atlantic region, and positively related to increases in generosity of UI benefits elsewhere. Results somewhat mixed with respect to other policy variables.
Mills, Percy, and Wilson (1983)	Gross interprovincial migration rates of family allowance recipients, 1961–78; linear model	Difference in fiscal surplus between destination and origin provinces, where fiscal surplus is defined as per capita provincial government expenditures less per capita revenues from direct and indirect taxes	Positive fiscal difference seems to increase out-migration from Atlantic and Western provinces, but not Ontario and Quebec.
Foot and Milne (1984)	Net interprovincial flows, 1961–81; linear model	Real per capital fiscal surplus in region under consideration, defined as difference between federal transfers to persons plus provincial government expenditures less provincial and local direct and indirect taxes and other transfers to provincial government from persons; weighted average of fiscal surpluses in other regions	Increase in fiscal surplus in province i will increase net in-migration to six provinces, but has no effect or negative effect in Ontario, Manitoba, Saskatchewan, and BC. Increases in fiscal benefits in other provinces have expected significantly negative effect only in case of Ontario.
MacNevin (1984)	Gross interprovincial migration rates, 1962–78; CL model	Real per capita provincial government expenditures, total provincial and local taxes as a percentage	Results with respect to government expenditures not robust. Both tax specifications perform well.

Table 3.1 (continued)

Study	Migration Data and Model Type	Fiscal Variables	Results
MacNevin (1984)	Gross interprovincial migration rates, 1962–78; CL model	of provincial personal income, provincial and local taxes disaggregated by type (personal taxes deducted from income, and commodity taxes expressed as a percentage of gross provincial expenditures)	Higher taxes in origin province will increase out-migration, while higher taxes elsewhere will reduce out-migration.
Shaw (1985, 1986)	Gross migration rates between 17 census metropolitan areas, 1961, 1971, 1976, and 1981 censuses; CL model	Average weekly payment of UI benefits in the province divided by the average weekly wage in the CMA (generosity of UI), ratio of total weeks of UI benefits paid to total number of weeks of unemployment in province (probability of receiving UI), real per capita unconditional federal grants to province, real provincial government natural resource revenues	Increased generosity of UI benefits in origin CMA will significantly reduce out-migration. Increased grants to government of destination province will increase out-migration. When sample is restricted to post-1971, generosity of UI benefits in destination CMA and grants to province of origin will also have significant effect on out-migration –positive in first case, negative in second. Changes in natural resource revenues do not have significant effect on migration.
Liaw and Ledent (1987)	Gross interprovincial migration rates, 1961–83; nested logit model	Unemployment benefit per unemployed person in destination relative to that in origin, level of per capita government transfers to persons in province of origin	Unemployment benefits per employed person have no significant effect on out-migration from region, and increases in per capita government transfers provide no more than a weak disincentive to out-migration. Higher relative unemployment benefits in destination province seem to provide significant deterrent to in-migration.

Table 3.1 (continued)

Study	Migration Data and Model Type	Fiscal Variables	Results
Liaw and Ledent (1988)	Micro data from the 1981 census, interprovincial moves of elderly only; nested logit model	Per capita government transfers per person, net of UI benefits	Per capita government transfers do not have significant impact on migration of the elderly.
Vanderkamp (1988)	Rate of net out-migration between census years, pooled across provinces, for the period 1931–40 to 1971–80; linear model	Fiscal surplus (defined as provincial government expenditures less residence-based taxes) as proportion of earned income	Fiscal surplus appears to act as deterrent to net out-migration.
Islam (1989)	Micro data from the 1981 census; probit model of move/stay choice	Estimated difference between origin and destination in transfers to persons, estimated difference between origin and destination in property taxes	Property tax differentials do not have a significant effect on intermunicipal migration, but differences in transfer payments do. Individuals will tend to move to municipalities where transfer payments are higher.
Day (1992)	Gross interprovincial migration rates, 1962–81; CL model	Real per capita expenditures on health, social services, education, and all other goods by provincial and local governments and hospitals; income and wage variables corrected for income taxes, provincial transfers, and UI benefits	In general, increases in government spending on health and education in a province increase in-migration to that province. But increased spending on social services has significantly negative impact on in-migration. Tax, transfer, and UI variables have a significant impact through income and wage variables.
Osberg, Gordon, and Lin (1994)	Longitudinal sample of men residing in the Atlantic and Prairie provinces from the LMAS, 1986–87; bivariate probit model	Receipt of SA payments, UI benefits and training services in year before moving	Receipt of SA, UI, or training services does not significantly affect interregional migration.
Lin (1995)	Longitudinal data from the LMAS, 1988–90; logit model of move-stay decision	Receipt of UI benefits, SA benefits and/or participation in federal government funded training programs in the year before moving	UI benefits have significant positive impact on mobility of adult women in 1990, but not in 1989. None of the other variables have statistically significant coefficients.

Table 3.1 (continued)

Study	Migration Data and Model Type	Fiscal Variables	Results
Bolduc, Fortin, and Fournier (1996)	Annual surveys of newly trained general practitioners and their location in Quebec, 1976–88; multinomial probit, nested logit models	Provincial government incentives (bursaries, settlement grants net of taxes, allowances, training leaves, relocation expenses reimbursement), income subsidies	All government measures have significant impact on initial location choices of newly trained GPs in Quebec. Combined subsidies and incentives increase migration numbers the most. Individually, income subsidies have a smaller impact on location choice of physicians than incentive measures.
Rosenbluth (1996)	Rate of net in-migration, estimates based on migration of family allowance recipients, pooled across provinces for the period 1966–91; linear model	Real per capital transfer payments to persons, real per capita government expenditures, real per capita taxes on persons	Increases in real per capita transfer payments to persons significantly increase rate of net in-migration to province. Results with respect to other two variables are not robust.
Audas and McDonald (2003)	SLID data, 1993–99; probit model of move/stay decision	Receipt of UI benefits and SA in previous year, region-specific UI benefit generosity (minimum weeks plus maximum weeks of UI benefit available), interaction between regional unemployment rate and an indicator for the post-1996 UI reform. (The 1996 reforms changed the eligibility definition from required *weeks* to required *hours* of work.)	Receipt of UI/EI benefits inhibits migration of people who are moderately attached to labour market. 1996 reforms increase mobility of those with low or no labour market attachment.
Finnie (2004)	LAD, 1982–95; panel logit model	Receipt of UI and SA in previous year	Receipt of UI is associated with an increase in out-migration for prime-aged men and women, and to a lesser extent for younger men and women and new-

Table 3.1 (continued)

Study	Migration Data and Model Type	Fiscal Variables	Results
			entrant women. Out-migration is also positively related to the receipt of social assistance, especially for men.
Benarroch and Grant (2004)	Annual interprovincial migration rates of physicians from the CIHI's physician database, 1976–92; CL model	Effective (average) tax rate on physicians; health care expenditures on physicians per physician in the province; health care expenditures (net of expenditures on physicians) per capita; measures of fee-for-service rates; and, number of hospital beds per capita	After-tax income, expenditure per physician, fee-per-service rates, the number of hospital beds and non-physician expenditures per capita have a significant positive impact on in-migration. Income tax rate differentials do not seem to have a significant impact on a physician's decision to move.
Basher and Fachin (2008)	Annual in-migration rates to Ontario by province of origin, 1971–2004; log-linear model	Difference in per capita federal transfers to persons between the origin province and Ontario	Federal transfer differentials have a minor effect on out-migration from BC, Alberta, and Nova Scotia to Ontario.
Ostrovsky, Hou, and Picot (2008)	Interprovincial migration to Alberta, or to other provinces, for recent immigrants and for long-time residents; LAD combined with immigration records, 1996–2005; MNL model	Receipt of EI, receipt of SA in previous year	In expanded model, receipt of EI has significant positive effect on migration to Alberta of immigrants and long-term residents. Receipt of SA has significant positive impact on migration of both population groups. For immigrants impact of SA is more important than that of EI.

Table 3.1 (continued)

Study	Migration Data and Model Type	Fiscal Variables	Results
Bakhshi, Shakeri, Olfert, Partridge, and Weseen (2009)	Gross annual inter-provincial migration flows, 1982–2004; log-linear model	Per capita federal equalization grants, sum of all other federal-provincial transfers (such as for health care and universities), provincial-local transfers per capita, provincial per capita own source revenues	Equalization has statistically significant but very small impact on migration flows. Hypothetical per worker wage increase equivalent in total to equalization has much greater negative impact on migration flows. Other federal transfers have slightly negative impact on in-migration with a three- to four-year lag. Own-source provincial revenues generally have significantly positive impact on out-migration.

Note: In this table we use the following mnemonics: UI = Unemployment Insurance, EI = Employment Insurance; SA = social assistance; LMAS = Labour Market Activity Survey; LAD = Longitudinal Administrative Data (LMAS); SLID = Survey of Labour and Income Dynamics; CMA = Census Metropolitan Area; CIHI = Canadian Institute for Health Information; CL = conditional logit model; MNL = multinomial logit model.

4

An Empirical Model of Interprovincial Migration

Our review of the existing literature shows that a variety of approaches have been used over the past four decades to search for policy-induced migration. Some authors allow all fiscal variables to enter the estimating equation separately, while others use composite measures of fiscal benefits. Some use grants and natural resource revenues as explanatory variables, while others use measures of government spending, and yet others rely on dummy variables indicating whether or not individuals received unemployment insurance or social assistance benefits. To some extent differences among the approaches can be explained by the features and limitations of the data employed, while in other cases there are differences in deliberate modelling choices on the part of the researchers.

Our approach to the search for policy-induced migration is motivated by the following educated guess: if we are to observe such migration in the data, it is as likely to be associated with the effects of the unemployment insurance system as with any other part of the fiscal system. There are three sensible reasons for our view about the centrality of unemployment insurance. First, as we have seen, the generosity of this income support program varies across regions in Canada by design, being more generous where unemployment rates tend on average over time to be higher. Second, the amounts of income involved for insurance recipients and the regional differentials in comprehensive income that are created are substantial. And third, we can measure the resulting income differentials created by the program at least as well as, if not better than we can estimate the effects on comprehensive incomes of other aspects of the fiscal system. Some of the stylized facts concerning regional variation in the generosity of the unemployment insurance system have already been presented in chapters 1 and 2.

While the model we outline in this chapter focuses in the first instance on the role of unemployment insurance, it will become clear in the course of our analysis that the structure of the model allows us to investigate the role of other public programs that have a direct effect on individual after-tax and transfer incomes, including social assistance and personal income taxation. Additional aspects of public policy that affect individuals directly can also be represented in the framework, including federal and provincial public services, as well as certain extraordinary events such as the election of a separatist government in Quebec and the closing of the cod fishery. These unusual events will also be investigated.

The basic model of migration behaviour we will employ is straightforward in principle. Every individual participant or potential participant in the labour force is assumed to maximize expected utility defined over all potential destinations, including his or her current place of residence. The uncertainty the individual faces concerns their employment status in alternative locations. We discuss the nature of this uncertainty and its relationship to unemployment insurance informally in the next section. Then we address the problem of how best to model other aspects of fiscal structure that vary across regions. These informal discussions set the stage for our formal model of policy-induced migration.

THE RELATIONSHIP BETWEEN UNEMPLOYMENT INSURANCE AND LABOUR MARKET UNCERTAINTY

As table 2.1 illustrated, the Canadian unemployment insurance program has undergone many complicated and substantial changes over the last three decades. This insurance system has many parameters, some of which are more likely than others to influence interregional migration. In particular, because they vary with regional unemployment rates, the regionally extended benefits introduced in 1972 and the variable entrance requirement that was introduced in 1977 are the most likely aspects of the unemployment insurance system to affect the decisions of potential migrants who are unsure about their job prospects in alternative destinations. Our use of data for the 1970s stems from a desire to capitalize on this history of the unemployment insurance system.

The issue that then arises in the present context is how to incorporate the important parameters of the insurance system in a model of interregional migration. Our solution to this problem takes advantage of the fact that labour market uncertainty and unemployment insurance are inextricably linked since, in principle, only unemployed individuals are eligible to receive unemployment insurance payments.[1] As we explain in more detail later, we assume that with respect to weeks of work a discrete number of states of the world are possible, with some of these states involving the receipt of unemployment insurance and social assistance. Of course individuals do not have perfect information about which state will occur in any particular location, and we assume that each person chooses their location so as to maximize expected utility defined over all possible locations and states of the labour market.

Harris and Todaro (1970) were probably the first to highlight the role of labour market uncertainty in determining migration, arguing that it is the origin-destination differential in *expected* income, rather than in actual income, that underlies migration decisions. Authors such as Stark (1991) and Daveri and Faini (1996) subsequently pointed out that the original Harris-Todaro model does not allow for risk-averse behaviour. In other words, faced with the prospect of unemployment if she moves, an agent may prefer to stay at home even though her expected income would be higher in a new location. The role of risk aversion as well as the original argument of Harris and Todaro is dealt with here, as it usually now is in the migration context, by treating the migrant as an expected utility maximizer who chooses the location where expected utility is highest.

The model bears a technical resemblance to those used in the literature on risk sharing and full insurance, such as Mace (1991), Cochrane (1991) and Townsend (1994), where the consequences of optimization of expected utilities over exogenously given states of the world are also considered. However, in that literature there is usually a social planner who shares risk among individuals in a given location by maximizing a weighted sum across individuals of expected utilities defined over possible states of the world. In our model of individual choice, in contrast, there is no social planner. Risk sharing across individuals might be said to occur in our context through the provision and operation of the unemployment insurance and social assistance systems, although of necessity we consider these systems to be exogenous with respect to individual decision making.

It should be noted that we do not consider individual migration that might result from diversification within a family. While families may be able to reduce the overall variance of family income for a given mean family income by strategically locating family members, the individual tax filers in the data we construct and use are not linked to other family members. And even if we had the data, taking such family behaviour into account is very difficult.

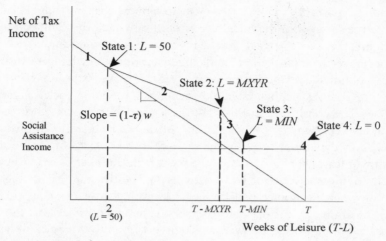

Figure 4.1 The four labour market states

Note: The following parameters will generally vary with location: the average weekly wage w; the marginal tax rate on labour income π; the minimum weeks of work required to qualify for unemployment insurance MIN; the weeks of work such that additional weeks beyond this reduce the maximum possible weeks of unemployment insurance available for the current year $MXYR$; and the level of social assistance income SA available to those not in the labour force.

As a further simplification, we assume that the probability that each state of the world will occur is exogenously fixed as far as the individual is concerned. Thus, in our approach, there is no labour-leisure choice problem for the individual to solve within any potential location. Individuals can choose only their place (or province) of residence, not the number of weeks they will work once they get there.[2] Then, since the number of weeks of labour supplied is in principle a continuous variable, with a range from zero to fifty-two, empirical implementation of our model requires that we define the discrete states of the world carefully. Our choice of states is motivated by a consideration of the budget constraints facing a representative individual who, in different states of the world, might receive wage income, unemployment insurance, social assistance, or some combination of these types of income.

Figure 4.1, adapted from Phipps (1990), illustrates the set of annual budget constraints that a representative individual in a given location would face in each of four states of the world defined by the level of labour supply if the only restriction on access to unemployment insurance was a minimal number of weeks of work.[3] Although Phipps uses the figure to illustrate a person's labour-leisure choice in the presence of unemployment insurance, for our purposes it is more convenient to assume that individuals cannot choose the segment of the budget constraint on which they will end up. In the figure, the after-tax wage $(1-\tau)w$ is assumed to be constant.

The line segment labelled "1" in the figure represents the budget constraint facing an individual who is employed at least fifty weeks per year and who therefore receives neither unemployment insurance nor social assistance income.[4] The constraint labelled "2" is relevant to a person who receives unemployment benefits over the course of the year and who is "strongly" attached to the labour force, in the sense that their weeks of work for the year are at least equal to MXYR, where MXYR is the number of weeks beyond which additional weeks of work actually reduce the number of weeks of unemployment insurance benefits possible during a one-year period. The third constraint, "3", is relevant to the individual who has at least the minimum weeks of work (MIN weeks) required to qualify for unemployment insurance, but whose weeks of work are less than MXYR. In this case, under the Canadian unemployment insurance system, additional weeks of work make the individual eligible for additional weeks of insurance over the year, and in this sense, the worker may be said to be weakly attached to the labour market. Finally, there is the constraint, or more exactly, the point labelled "4", which represents the situation relevant to the person who is on social assistance. The figure here reflects the assumption that anyone receiving social assistance must not work as a condition of the receipt of this assistance.[5]

Between MIN and MXYR weeks of work, the slope of the budget constraint is greater than the after-tax weekly wage rate because for each week of work, the individual receives the after-tax wage plus a week's worth of unemployment insurance benefits. The slope decreases between MXYR and full-time employment because in this interval, additional weeks of work reduce the individual's total weeks of entitlement to benefits. In comparison to the interval from MIN to MXYR weeks, where the unemployment insurance system acts as a wage subsidy, between MXYR and fifty weeks of work benefits are effectively subject to a tax that reduces the value to the individual of additional weeks of work.

The nature of the constraints in figure 4.1 suggests the following simplified definitions of the four states of the world: in state 1, weeks of work are equal to fifty; in state 2, weeks of work are equal to MXYR; in state 3, weeks of work are equal to MIN; and in state 4, weeks of work are equal to zero.[6] Even with this simplification, as will become clear later in this chapter, many important parameters of the unemployment insurance system, including the replacement rate (ρ), the variable entrance requirement (VER), and regionally extended benefits (*EXT*), as well as *MXYR* and *MIN*, can be incorporated in the model through the definition of an individual's income in the four states of the world.

Concerning the interpretation of state 4, since it is likely that many social assistance recipients do not file tax returns and are therefore not represented in our data, especially in the years before the introduction of refundable child tax benefits in 1994, this state is probably best regarded as one that might, but does not currently, apply to individuals in the data, and that may affect a migration decision by providing a floor, of varying height across provinces, beneath which income does not fall.

The decision to simplify the model by treating weeks of work as a discrete random variable is similar in spirit to the approach of Zabalza et al. (1980) in their study of the impact of social security on retirement decisions. While their model does not involve uncertainty, they argue that in the real world individuals do not have full control over their hours of work, and it is appropriate to model the choice of hours of work as a discrete choice between full-time jobs, part-time jobs, and retirement. We assume here that an analogous argument holds for weeks of work. From this perspective, states 1, 2, and 3 can be viewed as corresponding to long-term, medium-term, and short-term jobs respectively.

Is this approximation to the distribution of job durations a realistic one? Unfortunately there is very little evidence available on job durations in Canada. Christofides and McKenna (1995) provide some evidence on job durations, obtained from the 1986–87 and 1988–90 Labour Market Activity Surveys (LMAS). They find, among other things, that the observed probability density functions for weeks of work for completed job spells are heavily skewed towards the low end of the distribution, with the mode in each year ranging from ten to fourteen weeks. These values are similar to the range of *MIN* across provinces under the Canadian unemployment insurance system. Thus the distribution of actual job durations in Canada is definitely not uniform and does appear to reach a peak in the vicinity of *MIN* (although the extent to which the location of this peak is influenced by the unemployment insurance system is not clear). Christofides and McKenna also report that the mean length of all spells of employment in their two LMAS samples were 243 weeks and 332 weeks respectively, implying that a high proportion of jobs last 50 weeks or more. These findings provide some empirical support for our choice of labour market states.

In any event, the approach depicted in figure 4.1 to defining the nature of possible work-leisure outcomes facing a prospective migrant in any location has the considerable advantage of highlighting the role that migration plays in individual adjustments to labour market conditions. In the model, migration is the *only* means through which individuals can alter their labour market outcomes. At the same time, the model does not preclude the possibility that individuals might move to a region with a lower probability of employment than the region in which they originated. They might well do so if unemployment insurance benefits, social assistance benefits, and/or other fiscal benefits in that region were sufficiently high. Moreover, as will be seen when the model is described more formally, this approach leads "naturally" to the specification of unemployment insurance-related explanatory variables, as well as of the role of taxation, that are appropriate for a study of migration behaviour. This is a distinct advantage relative to almost all of the work we reviewed in chapter 3, where a more ad hoc approach to the treatment of unemployment insurance generosity and other policy variables such as taxation is frequently adopted.

REPRESENTING THE EFFECTS OF OTHER POLICY INSTRUMENTS: SCALE, MIX, AND INCIDENCE EFFECTS

Unemployment insurance may be the public policy we think most likely to have a measurable impact on interprovincial migration. But as we have seen in earlier discussion, it is not the only public policy with the potential to influence migration flows. Other aspects of fiscal policy – government spending, taxes, and intergovernmental grants – all differ from province to province as well. As we saw in chapter 3, previous studies of migration have taken different approaches to dealing with these variables: some have taken a structural approach that involves including government spending and income taxes in the model but not grants (MacNevin 1984, Day 1992), while others have taken a reduced-form approach in which spending is replaced by grants and other components of provincial government income (Winer and Gauthier 1982a; Bakhshi et al. 2009). Studies also vary in terms of how they allow the chosen public policy variables to enter into the estimating equation. Here we will stick as closely as possible to an approach in which the variables that appear in the migration equation reflect the public policies that have immediate consequences for prospective migrants.

In the tradition of the Tiebout (1956) class of models of "voting with the feet," in our model every individual is assumed to take into account the consequences of expected differences in net fiscal surpluses between his or her current location and all potential destinations, as well as differences in expected labour incomes. But while in principle it is straightforward to incorporate such fiscal surpluses into a migration model, in practice the matter is difficult to deal with because suitable measures of expected net fiscal surpluses by origin and destination are not available. As noted earlier, perhaps the most important reason for the lack of data is that a measure of fiscal surplus requires the valuation of public services. An additional problem is that public accounts on a province-wide basis measure fiscal aggregates rather than the fiscal quantities that are immediately relevant to individuals. Whether measured on a per capita basis or not, these fiscal aggregates may not be good measures of the public services received and taxes paid by an individual. For example, equalization affects federal and provincial government budget restraints, federal and provincial fiscal decisions and, then, individual taxes, transfers and public services in amounts that depend on the collective choice process and, in turn, the nature of fiscal incidence within each province.

Similar problems arise with respect to the use of aggregate federal and provincial expenditures or taxes from own sources as explanatory variables. When fiscal aggregates like the total public expenditures on health or education in a province appear in a migration equation, it must be assumed that the estimated coefficients on these variables effectively translate each fiscal aggregate into a variable that is relevant to individual migration choices. This is a strong assumption. This is why it is desirable to use determinants of net fiscal surpluses that are as closely related as possible to individual decision making. In this study, we employ parameters of the unemployment insurance system and the tax system, as well as standardized levels of social welfare assistance, because they are likely to be highly correlated with the individual migration incentives these programs create. The use of variables that measure the incentive effects for individuals of important aspects of the fiscal system places less of a burden on the coefficients in estimating equations.

However, to represent the effects of federal, provincial, and local government spending on current and capital goods and services, it is necessary to continue to rely on fiscal aggregates. Time series by province on the quantity and quality of various kinds of public services actually consumed by individuals are simply not available. The impact on migration of regional differences in these fiscal aggregates can be considered to consist of three effects: the effect of differences in the *scale* of public spending and taxing, in the *mix* of goods and services provided for a given scale, and in the *incidence* of the impact of the public sector across individuals for a given scale and mix (Winer and Gauthier 1982a). Scale is captured in the model by the per capita size of the fiscal aggregate, and the mix effect is allowed for by using as explanatory variables per capita current and capital spending by provinces on health, education, and all other (non-interest) categories of expenditure; and federal per capita spending on goods, services, and capital goods in each province.

Since the incidence of public spending and taxing is likely to vary systematically with the level of income, we use disaggregation of migration flows by income class (and sometimes age and sex also) as a means of capturing the incidence effect. This disaggregation also helps to distinguish between types of individuals who may be affected by unemployment insurance and social assistance. Disaggregation of spending by major category and disaggregation of migration flows by income class thus places less of a burden on the coefficients of variables representing the migration incentives embodied in fiscal aggregates. In what follows we rely heavily on migration data disaggregated into three income classes.

Further issues in the representation of the role of the public sector that must be addressed include the possibility of correlation between public and private sector variables, structural relationships between public sector variables, and the potential role of non-fiscal policy instruments such as regulations. Correlations between fiscal variables and those used to represent the effects of employment opportunities and wage rates may arise because of the impact of the public sector on private activity and because of the effect of changing market conditions on government decisions. To the extent that this is so, fiscal and employment-related variables will be correlated. Estimated coefficients will still be consistent in the face of such correlation. But when such correlations exist it is no longer a simple matter to distinguish clearly between private and public sector influences on interprovincial migration. We will use variations on our basic model to guard against making over-optimistic conclusions.

Structural relationships between public sector explanatory variables may occur if federal and provincial intergovernmental grants of various kinds, as well as provincial and local public spending and taxing, are all included in the same migration equation (Winer and Gauthier 1982a). The reason is that provincial fiscal policies, especially those of the poorer provinces, are influenced by federal grants. Such a relationship creates a high degree of correlation between intergovernmental grants and other fiscal variables, making reliable estimation of the effects of the public sector on migration behaviour difficult. Moreover, when both grants and provincial fiscal variables are included in an estimating equation, the effects of provincial fiscal policies that are partly funded by these grants are accounted for twice. This is why previous empirical studies reviewed in chapter 3 that have included variables such as intergovernmental grants and natural resource revenues in their estimating equations do not also include all other government tax and expenditure variables; as pointed out, something has to be omitted to avoid the double counting.

Since individuals making location decisions care directly about the services they will receive and the taxes they will pay in any potential destination, and only indirectly if at all about which level of government finances those services, we omit federal grants from the estimating equations to avoid structural dependency of the sort described above. This is not to say that the reduced form approach is not useful, provided one can avoid double counting the effect of grants and the effect of the additional public services or lowered taxation that these grants make possible. However, in our own work we think it more worthwhile to take an approach that focuses on what is actually paid to or received from the public sector by individuals. The effects on interregional migration of intergovernmental grants such as equalization or the Canada Health and Social Transfer may be calculated by combining the results of the migration model presented here with a model of the effects of such grants on provincial policy choices. This is a task that we must leave for the future.

Another task that we leave to the future is modelling the impact of non-fiscal policies, such as the regulation that we discussed in chapter 1. In principle, the effects on migration of labour market regulations should be considered along with the effects of fiscal policies. Provincial licensing restrictions, labour and education regulations, and restrictive language laws vary across jurisdictions and may be important determinants of migration behaviour. However, it is difficult to construct time series that can be used as proxies for the effects of these programs in a migration equation. While it may be possible to develop such data in the future, we focus here on the influence of fiscal policies, except for the extraordinary events in Quebec in the 1970s and the closing of the cod fishery, to which we shall return later on.

AN EXPECTED UTILITY MODEL OF LABOUR MIGRATION WITH CONSTRAINED LABOUR SUPPLY

We begin a more formal presentation of the framework we employ with a simplified annual decision-making model. For the benefit of the reader, all the variables of the model are listed and defined in table 4.1. An individual initially living in province i is assumed to choose province j over all other provincial destinations in any year if and only if his or her utility is higher there. Everyone is similarly considered to be a potential interprovincial

Table 4.1
Variable Definitions: Theoretical Model

Variable	Definition
τ_{ijs}	Top marginal income tax rate applying to taxable income in state s, facing an individual from i who moves to j
w_j	Wage rate in province j
$MXYR_j$	Number of weeks of work in j such that additional weeks of work beyond this point do not permit the individual to receive additional weeks of unemployment insurance benefits during the year
$MXYRWKS_j$	Weeks of insurance benefits that a person with $MXYR$ qualifying weeks can receive (= 50−$MXYR$)
MIN_j	Minimum weeks of work required to qualify for unemployment insurance benefits in j
$MINWKS_j$	Maximum weeks of benefits that an individual with MIN weeks of insurable employment in region j is entitled to receive
T	Total time available for work or leisure, equal to 52 weeks
L_{js}	Labour supply in region j in state s, with $L_{j1} = 50$, $L_{j2} = MXYR_j$, $L_{j3} = MIN_j$, and $L_{j4} = 0$
π_{js}	*ex ante* probability, as seen by the individual, that state s will occur in region j
EU_{ij}	Expected utility of a person moving from i to j
U_{ijs}	Utility in state s of an individual who moves from i to j
J	Total number of possible destinations (equal to 10 in the empirical model)
V_{ij}	Random utility associated with move from i to j
ε_{ij}	Random error term associated with move from i to j
P_{ij}	Probability of moving from i to j
X_{ijs}	Consumption of a person moving from i into state s in j
$T\text{-}L_{js}$	Leisure time of a person in province j in state s
F_j	Vector of real fiscal benefits in j
A_j	Vector of amenities in j that affect individual utility
α_1	Coefficient of $\ln X_{ijs}$ in the direct utility function (4.5)
α_2	Coefficient of $\ln (T - L_{js})$ in the direct utility function (4.5)
α_3	Vector of coefficients of $\ln F_j$ in the direct utility function (4.5)
α_4	Vector of coefficients of $\ln A_j$ in the direct utility function (4.5)
q_j	Price of consumption goods X in region j
UI_{js}	Unemployment insurance benefits in state s in j
SA_{js}	Social assistance benefits in region j in state s
B_{is}	Non-wage income (interest, dividend and other investment income) in state s of individual originating in i (B_{i4} is assumed to be zero)
TR_i	Transfers from the federal government, excluding unemployment insurance, to individual originating in i
C_{ij}	Monetary cost of moving from i to j
$TOTALTAX_{ijk}$	Total income tax owed to all governments by a person who moves from i to j and is in state s.
INC_{ijs}	After-tax income in state s of individual who moves from i to j
$INCOME_{ij}$	Probability-weighted sum of logs of real income for individual moving from i to j, defined in (4.8)
$LEISURE_{ij}$	Probability-weighted sum of logs of leisure time for individual moving from i to j, defined in (4.9)
ρ	Benefit replacement rate for unemployment insurance
w^R_j	Replaceable wage in j, defined as $w^R_j = wj$ if $w_j < MIE$; otherwise $w^R_j = MIE$, where MIE is the maximum insurable earnings

Table 4.1 (continued)

Variable	Definition
WUI_j	Weekly rate of unemployment insurance benefit $= \rho \ w^R_j$
$\overline{SA}_1$	Maximum full-time, yearly social assistance benefit in location j
P_{ijh}	Aggregated probability of moving from i to j for individuals in group h
β	Discount factor, defined as $[1/(1+\eta)]$
η	Individual's subjective real rate of discount

Note: Subscripts i, j, and s refer, respectively, to province of origin i, province of destination j, and state of the world s ($=1,2,3,4$). Time subscripts apply to all variables but have been omitted for convenience.

migrant in every year, and the move/stay decision is treated as just another (important) margin on which people continually optimize.

This simple framework may be applied in a manner that allows us to focus on how uncertainty about employment prospects in different regions interacts with the unemployment insurance system to affect migration decisions. As explained in section 4.1, we assume that for each individual, the number of weeks of work in each possible destination is a discrete random variable that can have the four possible values illustrated in figure 4.1. These four states correspond, in a stylized manner, to important kinks in an individual's annual budget constraint induced by the unemployment insurance and social assistance systems in Canada over the sample period.

We recall that in state 1, individuals work a total of fifty weeks, leaving them two weeks of leisure time.[7] In state 2, individuals work a total of MXYR weeks, where MXYR is the number of weeks of work such that the individual would be able to spend the remainder of the year collecting insurance benefits. In state 3, individuals work only MIN weeks, the minimum number of weeks required to qualify for benefits, and they spend the remainder of the year collecting a combination of insurance and social assistance benefits. The unemployment insurance system and the social assistance systems of the provinces thus jointly determine income in state 3. Finally, in state 4, it is assumed that individuals spend the entire year on social assistance and do not work. Given this characterization of labour supply opportunities, the utility maximizing migration decision can be formalized in the following manner.

Let π_{js} be the ex ante probability, as seen by the individual, that state s ($s = 1, ..., 4$) will occur in province j. Assume further that these province-specific aggregate probabilities are independent of any *individual's* migration decisions and independent of the region of origin. Then, from the perspective of a person currently resident in province i, expected utility in potential destination j is

$$EU_{ij} = \sum_{s=1}^{4} \pi_{js} U_{ijs} \, , \tag{4.1}$$

where U_{ijs} is the *maximum* utility that an individual originating in i would enjoy in province j in state s. Since the individual chooses the province that yields the highest expected utility, he or she moves to j if

$$EU_{ij} > EU_{ik} \, , \quad \forall \, k \neq j, \quad k = 1,...,J \, , \tag{4.2}$$

where J is the total number of provinces (equal to ten in the Canadian case). If j happens to be the individual's province of origin i, the individual will not move.

As McFadden (1974a) has shown, this model of choice can be converted into an econometric model by assuming that the expected utility of an individual chosen at random from the population is given by

$$V_{ij} = EU_{ij} + \varepsilon_{ij} \, , \tag{4.3}$$

where ε_{ij} is a random error representing attributes of alternative j that are pertinent to the individual but that the researcher cannot systematically observe. Since Pudney (1989, 112) points out that it is implausible to assume that the form of the function EU_{ij} is the same for all alternatives, we will include an additive alternative-specific constant to this function in our empirical work.

Then, if the ε_{ij} are independently and identically distributed with a Type I extreme value distribution, the probability that an individual in region i will choose to move to j is given by

$$P_{ij} = \frac{e^{EU_{ij}}}{\sum_{k=1}^{J} e^{EU_{ik}}} \, . \tag{4.4}$$

The probability of staying in i rather than moving is P_{ii}.

Result (4.4) is the conditional logit model of migration, so called because the log of the ratio of P_{ij} to P_{ii}, the log of the odds of moving from i to j rather than staying put, depends on the difference between expected utilities in the two locations. This log of the ratio of the probabilities does not depend on the characteristics of any other potential destination besides i and j, a property of the model referred to as independence of irrelevant alternatives. It is a limitation of the model that we accept.

As we noted earlier, the framework we are developing emphasizes the role of migration in utility optimization because labour supply is assumed to be fixed in each state of the world over which expected utility in (4.4) is defined, so that location is the *only* margin on which individuals base their decisions.[8] It is also important to note that (4.4) embodies condition (4.2) – that migration decisions depend on differences in *total* expected utility across alternatives. Thus, for example, while some aspects of the unemployment insurance system may affect the relative price of leisure, as interesting studies of this effect (such as Sargent 1995) have shown, what matters in the present context is how the insurance system alters total expected utility in different locations. For this reason, the representation of the unemployment insurance system in this paper must be different than in studies designed to measure the effects of this system on the relative price of leisure. We will return to this important point later on.

One limitation of equations (4.3) and (4.4) is that they refer to an individual. Since we will estimate our model using grouped data (which is, nonetheless, highly disaggregated by various characteristics of migrants), the following argument is of some importance. If one assumes that V_{ij} in equation (4.3) is the utility function of a representative individual with average income, average wages, etc. in some group, ε_{ij} in equation (4.3) is the mean over individuals in the group of the random terms in their utility functions, and all individuals have independent, identical random utility terms with a Type I extreme value distribution, then one can show that the distribution of the mean random utility term in (4.3) can be approximated to the first order by a Type I extreme value distribution (Day 1989, chapter 2 and appendix 1). In this sense the model estimated with grouped rather than individual data can be viewed as a first-order approximation to the model of migration probabilities derived by explicit aggregation over individual probabilities of moving.

Before turning to the detailed specification of utility and income in each of the four states, some further remarks concerning the nature of the data to be used to estimate the model defined by (4.4) may be helpful. First, we note that in the context of using grouped data, P_{ij} in (4.4) refers to a gross flow, from i to j, rather than to a net migration flow between two locations. Moreover, P_{ij} is a probability, and therefore its value must lie between zero and one. Accordingly, we use gross migration rate data in our estimation, a choice that is also appropriate on more practical grounds. A migration equation estimated using net flow data may mask differences between the behaviour of those moving out of, and into, a region, such as between first-time job seekers and those returning because of disappointments in the labour market (Sjaastad 1962). Furthermore, while changes in net flows can always be inferred from equations for gross flows, the reverse is not true.

Second, since the gross flow migration data we have constructed are from tax files that record the characteristics of individuals, it is obvious that the empirical work we carry out must be designed to deal with the behaviour of individuals rather than of families. But which sorts of individuals? Since we want to focus on the consequences of unemployment insurance, we need to choose a sample of people who are, or who want to be, labour market participants, even if they have received some unemployment insurance or social assistance payments over the year. Accordingly, the migration data we employ in estimation – which include those who do not migrate as well – omit tax filers younger than twenty years of age, many of whom are students or are supported in part by parents; students older than twenty (insofar as they can be identified by tuition fee deductions); and those over sixty-four years of age, since they are likely to be retired. For these groups, unemployment insurance generosity is basically irrelevant. For the same reason, the migration data we use also exclude tax filers who have not reported any labour income or income from unemployment insurance or social assistance, as well as tax filers whose only source of income is from investments or rentals.[9]

Detailed Specification of Expected Utility and Incomes in the Four States of the World

As with most applications of the conditional logit model, we choose a functional form for EU_{ij} that is linear in parameters. In particular, assume individuals maximize a Cobb-Douglas utility function:

$$U_{ijs} = \alpha_1 \ln X_{ijs} + \alpha_2 \ln(T - L_{js}) + \alpha_3{}' \ln(F_j) + \alpha_4{}' \ln(A_j), \qquad (4.5)$$

where α_1 and $\alpha2$ are individual coefficients, and α_3 and α_4 are vectors of coefficients. As before, the subscript i indicates the province of origin, j the province of destination, and s the state of the world. X is real consumption; T is the total time (in weeks) available for work or leisure; L is weeks of work; F is a vector of real fiscal benefits, such as those associated with the provision of education and health care; and A is a vector of locational amenities, including cultural and linguistic factors, that may affect the individual's utility. (Several elements of A will be used in unlogged form.)

In each province and each state of the world, the individual also faces a budget constraint and a labour supply constraint that defines the number of weeks of work available:

$$q_j X_{ijs} + w_i(T - L_{js}) = w_j T + UI_{js} + SA_{js} + B_{is} + TR_i - C_{ij} \tag{4.6a}$$
$$- TOTALTAX_{ijs}$$

$$L_{js} = \begin{cases} 50 & \text{if } s = 1 \\ MXYR_j & \text{if } s = 2 \\ MIN_j & \text{if } s = 3 \\ 0 & \text{if } s = 4. \end{cases} \tag{4.6b}$$

In the budget constraint, q is the price of consumption goods; w is the individual's wage, which is assumed to be identical in all states of the world; UI is income from unemployment insurance benefits; SA is social assistance income; B is interest and investment income; TR is personal transfers from the public sector other than UI and SA; C is the sum of the before-tax direct and indirect (foregone wage) monetary costs of moving; and $TOTALTAX$ is total federal and provincial income tax. Turning to the labour supply constraint, we recall that $MXYR$ is the number of weeks of work required to ensure that the individual will receive unemployment insurance benefits for the remainder of the year, while MIN is the minimum number of weeks of work required to qualify for regular insurance benefits.

Note that by replacing $TOTALTAX$ with a formula for computing total tax paid, it is possible to rewrite the budget constraint in terms of the marginal tax rate. While its form has no bearing on estimation, it is convenient to reformulate the budget constraint as a function of the marginal tax rate in order to derive the derivatives of the migration rates P_{ij} with respect to the various components of income in order to study the comparative statics of the model, especially the marginal effects of changes in policy variables. We discuss such derivatives in chapter 7. Appendix F contains the reformulated versions of after-tax income net of moving costs.

Based on specific institutional features of the Canadian case, some components in (4.6a) and (4.6b) depend on i and j, while others are assumed to depend on either i or j but not both. Three components of income – UI, SA, and B – depend on the state of the world. In the case of UI and SA, this is because receipt of these forms of income are contingent on the individual being unemployed. Interest and investment income are assumed to be zero in state 4 because unemployed individuals with a substantial amount of interest and investment income would not be eligible to receive social assistance benefits. Otherwise, B is assumed to depend only on the province of origin.

Maximum utility for each *ijs* combination is derived by maximizing (4.5) subject to the constraints (4.6). The results are substituted into equation (4.1) to obtain the following expression for expected utility:

$$EU_{ij} = \alpha_1[\pi_{j1}\ln INC_{ij1} + \pi_{j2}\ln INC_{ij2} + \pi_{j3}\ln INC_{ij3} + \qquad (4.7)$$
$$\pi_{j4}\ln INC_{ij4} - \ln q_j]$$
$$+ \alpha_2[\pi_{j1}\ln(T-50) + \pi_{j2}\ln(T-MXYR_j) +$$
$$\pi_{j3}\ln(T-MIN_j) + \pi_{j4}\ln T]$$
$$+ \alpha_3'\ln(F_j) + \alpha_4'\ln(A_j).$$

where INC_{ijs} is the income received in province j in state s by an individual originating in province i, as specified below. Note that the consumption good's price, q_j, appears separately from the income terms in (4.7) because it is assumed to be the same in all states of the world.[10]

For the purposes of simplifying the discussion in later chapters, it is convenient to re-write equation (4.7) as follows:

$$EU_{ij} = \alpha_1 INCOME_{ij} + \alpha_2 LEISURE_{ij} + \alpha_3'\ln(F_j) + \alpha_4'\ln(A_j), \qquad (4.7')$$

where

$$INCOME_{ij} = \pi_{j1}\ln INC_{ij1} + \pi_{j2}\ln INC_{ij2} + \pi_{j3}\ln INC_{ij3} \qquad (4.8)$$
$$+ \pi_{j4}\ln INC_{ij4} - \ln q_j,$$

and

$$LEISURE_{ij} = \pi_{j1}\ln(T-50) + \pi_{j2}\ln(T-MXYR_j) + \qquad (4.9)$$
$$\pi_{j3}\ln(T-MIN_j) + \pi_{j4}\ln(T).$$

The composite variables INCOME and LEISURE are the probability-weighted sums of the logs of real income (net of moving costs) and leisure time respectively, or in statistical terms, the expected values of the log of real income and the log of leisure time.

In equations (4.7) and (4.8), after-tax incomes net of moving costs in the four states of the world are defined precisely as follows:

$$INC_{ij1} = 50w_j + B_i + TR_i - C_{ij} - TOTALTAX_{ij1} \qquad (4.10)$$
$$INC_{ij2} = w_j MXYR_j + \rho w_j^R(50 - MXYR_j) + B_i + TR_i - C_{ij} - TOTALTAX_{ij2}$$

$$INC_{ij3} = w_j MIN_j + \rho w_j^R MINWKS_j + (\overline{SA_j}/52) \bullet (50 - MIN_j - MINWKS_j)$$
$$+ B_i + TR_i - C_{ij} - TOTALTAX_{ij3}$$
$$INC_{ij4} = \overline{SA_j} + TR_i - C_{ij}$$

where, in addition to previous definitions, w_j^R is the replaceable wage in j, defined as $w_j^R = w_j$ if $w_j < MIE$; otherwise, $w_j^R = MIE$, where MIE is the maximum insurable earnings; ρ is the benefit replacement rate for unemployment insurance; $MINWKS$ is the number of weeks of benefits that an individual with $MXYR$ weeks of insurable employment is entitled to receive during the year; and $\overline{SA_j}$ is the maximum full-time, yearly social assistance benefit in location j. Note that unemployment insurance income itself does not appear explicitly in these equations because it is instead expressed as a function of the variables MIN, $MXYR$, and $MINWKS$. Again we note that the definitions of all variables are listed for the reader's convenience in table 4.1. In making the model operational all of these variables must be and are measured in order to define income net of measurable moving costs for each of the four states in each location.

Equation (4.7′) indicates why the incentive to move embedded in the unemployment insurance system, or in any policy, cannot be captured by a single index variable, as we noted earlier. Differences in the probability weighted log-incomes and probability weighted log-leisure times, not individual policy parameters, are what matter to the utility-maximizing individual in the present framework. This is an important point. We examine the nature of these broader measures in some detail in the next chapter.

Three additional features of equations (4.7) and (4.8) are worth noting. First, the variable *INCOME* multiplying α_1 in equation (4.7′) in fact represents expected consumption. It is the sum of the real value of consumption in each state of the world, multiplied by the probability that the state will occur. Since labour supply is assumed to be fixed in each state, utility maximization requires that individuals spend all their income on the consumption good X. Similarly, the components of the variable *LEISURE* that multiply α_2 represent the quantities of leisure or non-work time that individuals consume in each of the four states of the world, also multiplied by their respective probabilities. The expressions multiplying the parameter vectors α_3 and α_4 are less complex because neither real fiscal benefits nor amenities are assumed to vary with the state of the world.

Second, the fact that the incomes and leisure times corresponding to the different states of the world enter equation (4.7) with the same coefficient is a consequence of the assumption that the same direct utility function applies to all states of the world. The utility function is not state-dependent. Similarly, since the direct utility function is assumed to be the same for all alternatives, the coefficients of the model do not vary across alternatives either, with the exception of an alternative-specific constant term that is not included in (4.7).

Third, since equation (4.7) is derived from the direct utility function (4.5), it provides a simple utility-related interpretation of the signs of the coefficients. In the direct utility function, a "good" (that is, a commodity that provides positive utility) will have a positive sign, and a "bad" will have a negative sign. Thus because they are the coefficients of consumption and leisure time in the direct utility function, both of which are generally considered to be "goods," one would expect the estimates of both α_1 and α_2 in equation (4.7) to be positive. Similarly, any fiscal variable or amenity whose estimated coefficient is positive (negative) can be interpreted as providing positive (negative) utility to individuals.

Extensions to Deal with Risk Aversion, Moving Costs, and Extraordinary Events

Our basic model of utility maximization needs to be extended in several ways for empirical application. First, to allow for more risk aversion than the Cobb-Douglas form of (4.5) implies, we will add to expected utility (4.7) the probabilities of the less than full employment states. This also allows for the possibility that individuals value employment in and of itself.

Second, we also add to (4.7) two variables to reflect non-monetary moving costs that are not incorporated in the variable C_{ij}. The distance between the province of origin and the province of destination is added to capture non-monetary costs of moving that increase with distance, while a dummy variable equal to one if the choice involves a move and zero otherwise is included to account for fixed costs of moving, such as the psychic cost of leaving family and friends behind and re-establishing one's home in a new location, the costs of selling a home, and the costs of finding a new place to live. The inclusion of this dummy variable in the model ensures that the utility associated with staying, EU_{ii}, will differ from the expected utility associated with all moves (EU_{ij}, $j \neq i$) even if the attributes of all regions are identical. We also note that this dummy variable does not identify stayers. Rather, it adds an extra term to the utility associated with the staying option for all individuals, whether movers or stayers.

Third, we add dummy variables to allow a consideration of extraordinary events related to the public sector, the effects of which are probably not adequately captured by the other private and public sector variables of the model – the events in Quebec in the early 1970s associated with the October crisis, the election of a separatist government in Quebec in 1976 and the subsequent introduction of language legislation in 1977, and the closing of the cod fishery on the East Coast in 1992. These extraordinary events may create migration incentives that are substantial relative to the fixed costs of moving, compared to year-to-year changes in other public sector-related policy variables. Separate dummy variables are used to distinguish the effects of these events on gross inflows and outflows. The timing of the dummy variables representing the events in Quebec corresponds to a pronounced peak in net outflows from Quebec also identified by Vachon and Vaillancourt (1999).

What we are investigating by including the dummy variables is the extent to which all of the (ordinary) private and public sector determinants of migration that we are so careful to include in our model can account for migration flows occurring before, at the time of, and after the occurrence of these unusual events. The migration that cannot be explained by the usual explanatory variables may reasonably be regarded as extraordinary, that is, as a result of the unusual events themselves rather than as a result of the kind of changes that occur from year to year in the private and public sectors.

Finally, we include dummy variables to control for the effects of language and province-specific amenities. The possibility that the predominance of French in Quebec might deter in-migration to Quebec from other provinces is accounted for by including a dummy variable that is equal to one if the alternative under consideration is a move to Quebec and the province of origin is not Quebec, and zero otherwise. Amenities such as climate, which do not change much over time, are dealt with by including alternative-specific dummy variables for all provinces except British Columbia; that province is excluded to avoid the equivalent of a dummy variable trap.

The Likelihood Function

Once the expected utility function is fully specified by (4.7), (4.10), and the extensions of the model discussed above, it can be used in (4.4) to define the probabilities of moving and staying. These probabilities in turn then permit us to construct a likelihood function for our sample, assuming that all individuals in any particular age-income-gender group of individuals are identical. This likelihood function is the basis for our maximum likelihood estimation of the parameters in the expected utility function.

If we define h to be an index of the specific group to which an individual belongs, where n_{ijh} (possibly equal to zero) is the number of individuals in group h going from region i to region j, the log-likelihood function for a sample of H groups in J regions is

$$\ln L \ = \ \sum_{h=1}^{H}\sum_{i=1}^{J}\sum_{j=1}^{J} n_{ijh} \ln P_{ijh} \, , \tag{4.11}$$

where P_{ijh} represents the probability of moving from i to j, given by equation (4.4), for individuals in group h. In our empirical work, groups are defined by income class, age, and gender, as described in detail in the next chapter. Maximization of (4.11) provides our estimates of the parameter vector α.

Since expected utility (4.7) has been derived using the direct utility function (4.5), it is straightforward to predict the signs of the estimated coefficients α_j. As previously mentioned, the estimated coefficient should be positive for any variable that is a "good" that provides positive utility to individuals. But while their signs can be predicted, in a conditional logit model the coefficients α_j do not directly tell us what the effect of changes in the explanatory variables on the probability of migrating will be because of the nonlinearity of equation (4.4). We explore the effects of changes in the explanatory variables through the calculation of marginal effects in chapter 7 and with simulations in chapter 8.

A FINAL NOTE ON MODELLING MIGRATION WITH INTERTEMPORAL OPTIMIZATION

Since labour migration involves a high fixed cost and a payoff that accrues over a number of years rather than immediately, migration decisions share some of the characteristics of investment decisions and should ideally be modelled using an intertemporal framework (Sjaastad 1962; Polachek and Horvath 1977). Typically this has been acknowledged in the migration context by the use of the discounted value of future income as an explanatory variable rather than current income. Discounted incomes arise in the present framework if expected utility in region j in (4.7) is replaced by discounted expected utility over some time horizon. For a time horizon extending from t_0 to t_1, the latter is

$$EU_{ij} = \sum_{t=t_0}^{t=t_1} \beta^t \sum_{s=1}^{s=4} \pi_{jst} U_{ijst} \, , \tag{4.12}$$

where $\beta^t = [1/(1+\eta)]^t$ and η is the individual's subjective discount rate, assumed to be constant over time and the same for all individuals. Since expected utility (4.7) is linear in parameters, discounted utility (4.12) is as well, giving rise to an equation in which the present values of the income, leisure, and fiscal variables replace the current values in (4.7).

Note that if we use (4.12), the relevant definitions of income in (4.10) above apply prior to a move. If the time horizon includes periods after a move is made, then migration costs C_{ij} equal 0 for those periods, and other components of net income after the move would have to be measured according to what the migrant thinks will happen in the destination rather than in the initial location.

In principle, extending the framework to allow explicitly for intertemporal optimization also involves allowing for the optimal planning of a sequence of moves over an individual's life (Polachek and Horvath 1977). This is a difficult issue to deal with, something that to our knowledge has not been accomplished elsewhere, and we shall not try to do so here. Instead, we allow for the fact that the horizon for the payoff to any migration decision can be expected to vary with the age of the migrant, by using data aggregated into three age groups –20–24, 25–44, and 45–64. To allow for the possibility that the calculation of the payoff to migration, or the response to a given expected income differential, may vary systematically by gender, we disaggregate the data by the gender of the tax filer. These disaggregations also allow for the possibility that costs of moving vary systematically with age and gender.[11]

With these last remarks, we are ready to turn to the construction of the data and related matters in the next chapter, to be followed by the presentation of our estimation results in chapter 6.

5

From Theory to Measurement

Anyone who wants to study interregional migration must invest substantial amounts of time and money. In the first place, data must be collected for each possible destination-origin pair for each year of the sample. Further complicating matters is the fact that for our study we constructed new inter-provincial migration series rather than relying on data prepared by Statistics Canada. This resource-intensive exercise was necessary because of our desire to work with a long time series, extending back into the 1960s, on migration flows that are related to labour force participation and that are disaggregated not only by origin and destination but also by income class as well as by age and sex.

The construction and measurement of the explanatory variables of the empirical model is no less important and also poses challenges. It is difficult to find data that correspond exactly to the definitions used in the theoretical model presented in chapter 4. In some cases, data from a variety of different sources were needed to construct a single variable, and assumptions (discussed below) had to be made in constructing others.

Since the validity of the empirical results rests in part on the suitability of the data, it is important to be clear about assumptions we make in the construction of data. In this chapter we carefully outline the most important assumptions and procedures we used, focussing on the migration data and on the explanatory variables *INCOME* and *LEISURE* introduced in the previous chapter. In addition to discussing the construction of these variables, we explore their behaviour over the sample period we examine. Further details are provided in the appendixes.

USING TAX DATA TO MEASURE MIGRATION

Until recently, researchers interested in interprovincial migration in Canada had only two types of data to choose from for their empirical analyses:

aggregate population flow data derived from either Family Allowance or income tax records, and Census data. The latter consists of microdata files that since 1976 have become available every five years. However, until the 1991 Census, the information they provided on geographic mobility was restricted to a question asking individuals where they had lived five years previously.[1]

Neither of these data sources has been ideal for economic research. The aggregate data are not available on a consistent basis for the entire 1961–96 period we study, and they are for the population as a whole, not the labour force. Similarly, during the five-year interval covered by the Census question individuals could have moved multiple times.

Among the new microdata sets that have more recently become available to Canadian researchers, the one that seems to offer the most potential for interesting analyses of geographic mobility in Canada is the Longitudinal Administrative Database (LAD). The LAD is a longitudinal microdata base compiled from the T1 personal income tax forms submitted to Revenue Canada each year. It now follows 20 percent of Canadian tax filers and contains much detail about family structure and incomes. It has already been used to study various aspects of interprovincial migration by Finnie (1998a, 1998b, 2004). At the time we began this project it covered the period from 1981 to 1996.

For those interested in the effects of fiscal structure on migration, the LAD has a limitation: it does not extend back beyond 1982. Yet some of the most important changes in Canada's unemployment insurance system occurred in the 1970s, years that are not included in the LAD. The political events in Quebec in the mid-1970s are also excluded. Unfortunately, difficulties in matching tax records prior to 1982 make it very difficult to extend the LAD any further back in time. However, using the original tax tapes, it is possible at some cost to construct a data set that goes further back in time and to do so for a subset of tax filers that corresponds closely to the labour force, as is required by our theoretical model, as well as to disaggregate by the income of individuals.

For these reasons, we created a new migration data set from the personal income tax files covering quite a long period of time. Since our focus is on the migration of labour rather than of the population as a whole, we restricted our attention to those tax filers who are attached or potentially attached to the labour force. In addition, our new data are disaggregated by age and sex. Although Statistics Canada produces estimates of migration flows by age and sex from 1977, they cover the entire population and are not available by income class. The latter two characteristics are particularly useful in modelling the role of the public sector. The primary data set we constructed covers the period from 1974 to 1996, while an alternative data set that we constructed with the help of a 10 percent sample of tax files extends back to 1968.

There are some disadvantages, as well as advantages, associated with working with individual income tax files to construct these migration flows. The principal drawback is that only data that meet the stringent confidentiality requirements imposed by Statistics Canada can be publicly released. These requirements dictate that any migration flows consisting of fewer than fifteen individuals must be suppressed. Since many cells in a data set disaggregated by age, sex, income class, province of origin, and province of destination do not meet this criterion, especially when an origin or destination is one of the smaller provinces, the basic data we constructed cannot be publicly released. Only summary data on total inflows and outflows for each province are publishable. We could have worked with releasable data, but then many cells in our migration matrices would have been empty since they do not have the requisite number of cases Statistics Canada requires in order to insure absolute confidentiality. Any researcher who wished to make use of the data constructed for our research could do so after the completion of the technical paper in 2001, as also announced in our journal article of 2006, provided they obtained permission from Statistics Canada and the data did not leave Statistics Canada's premises. Statistics Canada agreed to this arrangement for a period of ten years from 2001, and this period has now expired. No one to our knowledge inquired about access, just as no one inquired about the use of the migration series based on tax data that were constructed by Winer and Gauthier in the early 1980s. We think this is a reflection of the full costs of the time and money involved and the restrictions that (appropriately) apply to use of such data. We are happy that we are at least able to present the results of our work using the tax data in this book.

Readers who are interested in the detailed assumptions underlying the construction of the migration data can find the relevant details in the next subsection. Those who are more interested in the characteristics of the data set we constructed are invited to jump ahead to the two subsections after that, where they will find a brief discussion of some of the general trends in migration revealed by the data.

Construction of the Migration Data

Our migration data are constructed from the tax returns known as the T1 tax forms, which each Canadian who is liable to pay taxes must file on an annual basis. The data contained in these tax forms has for many years been stored by Statistics Canada in an electronic format, without which it would have been impossible for us to construct new migration series. For each year, the entire set of tax returns was read, and tax filers were excluded if one of the following conditions was met:

1 As of December 31st of the tax year, the tax filer did *not* reside in one of the ten Canadian provinces.
2 The tax filer was an immigrant to or an emigrant from Canada in that tax year.[2]
3 The tax filer had no income.
4 The tax filer's only source of income was rentals or investments.
5 The tax filer's age was less than 20 years and greater than 64 years.
6 The tax filer was a full-time student. Tax filers were deemed to be full-time students if they were less than thirty years old and they had claimed a deduction (or tax credit, depending on the year) for tuition fees in excess of a specified amount that varied with the province.[3]

The exclusion of tax filers with no income or whose only source of income is rentals or investments, ensures that only individuals with income from wages and salaries, self-employment, unemployment insurance, or social assistance are included. These exclusions are required since the model we employ is based on the assumption that every individual has some current or prospective attachment to the labour force. For the same reason, tax filers less than twenty and over sixty-four years of age, as well as full-time students over twenty years of age (insofar as they can be identified by the tuition deduction), are excluded.[4]

For each tax filer, interprovincial migration is assumed to occur sometime during the second of two adjacent tax years if the individual tax filer reports a province of residence on 31 December that differs between the two years. Because of confidentiality restrictions, only counts of the total number of migrants were retained for each origin-destination pair and each province. Non-movers – individuals for whom the province of origin and the province of destination were identical – were also counted.

These migration flows were further disaggregated by age, sex, and income class. For the purposes of this project, three age groups (20–24, 25–44, and 45–64) and three income classes were defined. The three income classes used to group individuals in each age/sex category are based on total income as reported in the T1 tax files. The income classes used are

• $0 < \text{total income} \leq 0.5 \cdot \text{median total income}$;

- $0.5 \cdot$ median total income $<$ total income $\leq 1.25 \cdot$ median total income; and
- total income $> 1.25 \cdot$ median total income.

The median total income used was the median total income of all tax filers included in the data set for each year.[5] These groupings allow the construction of migration flows for what can reasonably be thought of as low income, middle income and higher income individuals, while still ensuring that each "cell" – defined by province of origin, destination, income class, age group and sex – of the resulting migration data contains a substantial number of tax filers.

After grouping individuals by income class, age, and sex, it turns out that many of the migration "cells" with an origin and a destination in one of the smaller provinces are quite small.[6] Consider, for example, the 1995–96 data. After excluding tax filers as outlined earlier, the merged 1995 and 1996 tax tapes from which migration during the 1996 calendar year is derived contain approximately 13 million individual tax filers between the ages of 20 and 64. But after disaggregation into three income classes, three age groups, and two genders, about 35 percent of the resulting migration cells for 1996 have less than twenty individuals in them. The percentage of cells with less than twenty individuals is similar for other years.[7] But although confidentiality prevents the release of the actual migration series constructed for this project, except in unusual cases it does not prohibit the publication of estimation results based on the data after they have been carefully vetted by Statistics Canada. Thus for our estimation we were in fact able to use the uncensored, grouped migration data.

Once the process of compiling the migration data was completed, we had two different migration data sets to work with. The first covers the years 1974 to 1996. For these years, the migration data are based on complete (or 100 percent) tapes of T1 personal income tax files for the years 1973 to 1996. The second data set covers the period 1968 to 1996. While it might seem obvious that the longer data set would be the more desirable one to work with, in fact the choice between the two is not so clear because of difficulties encountered in extending the sample period backwards from 1973 to 1968. Although tapes containing the T1 records of all tax filers exist for the years from 1970 to 1972, the record layouts for these tapes have been lost, and so we could not use the original data tapes. (We searched everywhere we could for these layouts, to no avail.) For the years 1968 to 1973, only a tape consisting of a random 10 percent sample of all tax records was available.[8] Furthermore, while total income, age, and sex can be used to define migration flows before 1974, the 10 percent tape does not contain information about types of income or the nature of deductions, so that the same exclusions could not be applied to the pre-1974 data as were applied to the later period. To combine the pre- and post-1974 data, we scaled the latter by 1/10 and rounded down to the nearest integer.[9] It should be noted that because the pre-and post-1974 data are not fully comparable, in what follows we place greater emphasis on the results obtained using the 1974–1996 data.[10]

Our Migration Data versus the "Official" Statistics Canada Data

Before proceeding further, it is useful to compare the behaviour of our new migration data with official estimates of aggregate migration flows. For the purposes of making such a comparison, we obtained from Statistics Canada special tabulations by age, sex, province of origin, province of destination, and year, of their "official" estimates of aggregate interprovincial migration.[11] The Statistics Canada estimates differ from our own in several respects. First, some tax filers (for example, students) are excluded from our migration counts but not the Statistics Canada numbers. And second, Statistics Canada adjusts the counts of tax filers to produce estimates of the total number of Canadians in a particular age-sex group who have moved, while we do not. Thus for a particular age-sex group, the Statistics Canada estimates of the number of migrants should be larger than our own. However, we should expect the pattern of migration flows – in particular changes in the direction of migration flows – to be generally the same.

Figures 5.1 to 5.10 present, by province, the total out-migration counts for our population of tax filers considered to be potential labour market participants for the period 1974–96, together with the corresponding Statistics Canada estimates. Because of differences in the definition of age groups, it was not possible to derive from the Statistics Canada data a set of migration flows that cover exactly the same age group we used to construct our own data. Instead, it is necessary to compare our data for ages 20–64 with Statistics Canada data for individuals aged 18–64. In addition, the Statistics Canada series are available only from 1977.

The figures show that as expected, our count of out-migrants is usually less than the Statistics Canada estimate, except in the case of Prince Edward Island. For that province our counts seem to exceed the Statistic Canada estimates in several years. Also, while changes in the direction of flows do not always occur in precisely the same year in the two data sets, many of these differences in the timing of changes in the direction of flows are

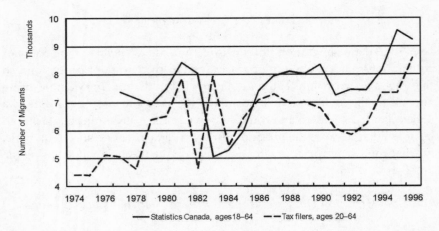

Figure 5.1 Total outflows, NFLD, 1974–96, comparison of tax filer and Statistics Canada data

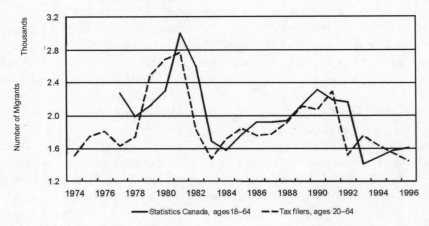

Figure 5.2 Total outflows, PEI, 1974–96, comparison of tax filer and Statistics Canada data

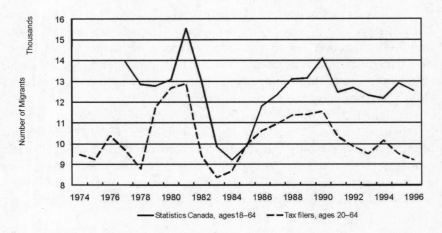

Figure 5.3 Total outflows, NS, 1974–96, comparison of tax filer and Statistics Canada data

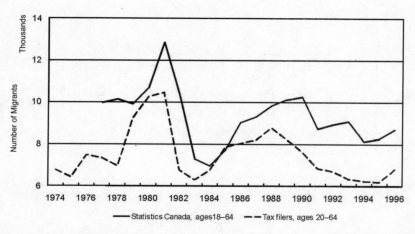

Figure 5.4 Total outflows, NB, 1974–96, comparison of tax filer and Statistics Canada data

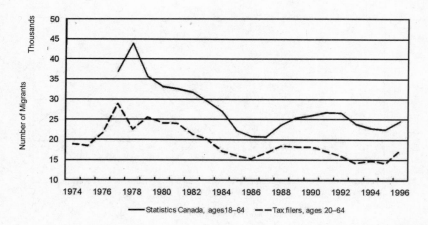

Figure 5.5 Total outflows, QUE, 1974–96, comparison of tax filer and Statistics Canada data

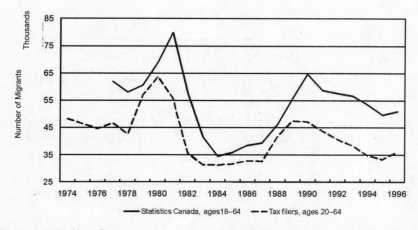

Figure 5.6 Total outflows, ONT, 1974–96, comparison of tax filer and Statistics Canada data

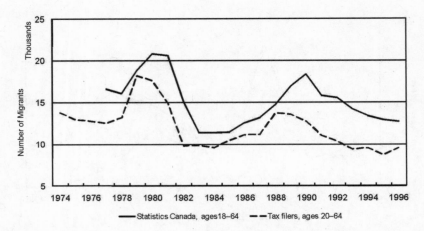

Figure 5.7   Total outflows, MAN, 1974–96, comparison of tax filer and Statistics Canada data

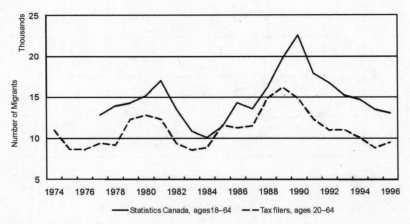

Figure 5.8   Total outflows, SASK, 1974–96, comparison of tax filer and Statistics Canada data

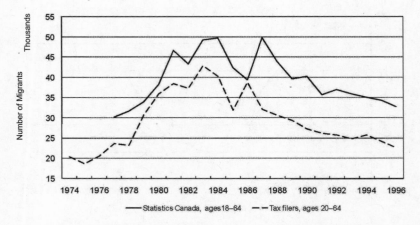

Figure 5.9   Total outflows, ALTA, 1974–96, comparison of tax filer and Statistics Canada data

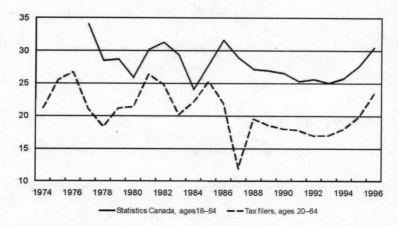

Figure 5.10   Total outflows, BC, 1974–96, comparison of tax filer and Statistics Canada data

relatively minor, so that the overall patterns in the two data sets appear to be quite similar.

Nonetheless, there are a few differences in the time pattern of flows that do stand out. Our data show a drop in the number of out-migrants from Newfoundland in 1981, from 7,833 to 4,654 people, followed by an equally large increase in out-migrants in 1982, with yet another large drop from 7,925 out-migrants to only 5,434 in 1983.[12] In the Statistics Canada estimates, one observes a drop in out-migration from Newfoundland in 1982, from 8,031 to 5,048 people, followed by only a small increase to 5,278 people in 1983. Similarly, our data show an 84 percent decrease in out-migration from British Columbia in 1987, followed by a 64 percent increase in 1988, while the Statistics Canada estimates show relatively small decreases of 9 percent and 6 percent in the same two years. These differences between the two series seem to us too large to be explained by the differences in the coverage of the two sets of migration data, but we have been unable to explain them in another way. The fact that the patterns are similar for other provinces in these periods indicates that computer programming is not an issue, and we are using the original tax tapes. Nor do differences in the patterns indicate anything in particular. Year-to-year migration flows are highly variable, which is one reason why migration models are hard to estimate. In any event, these are the only major unexplained differences between our data and that provided by Statistics Canada. Our view is that these features of the data do not have any important effect on the estimated models.

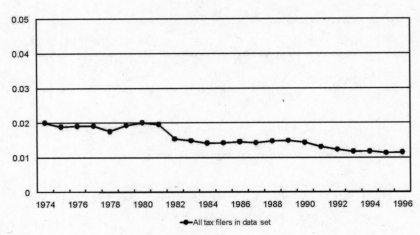

Figure 5.11   Overall mobility rate, all tax filers, 1974–96

In light of our interest in the effect of extraordinary events on migration flows, before moving on to an examination of differences between income classes, age groups, and men and women, it is worth taking a closer look at figures 5.1 and 5.5. Do these figures show any important changes in migration flows after the closure of the cod fishery in 1993 or the election of a separatist government in Quebec in 1976? As far as the cod fishery closure is concerned, in figure 5.1 both our own data and the Statistics Canada series show an increase in outflows from Newfoundland after 1993. Similarly, both the series plotted in figure 5.5 suggest that outflows from Quebec were relatively high in the years immediately following the election of the PQ. What the figures do not tell us, however, is the extent to which these increases in outflows can be explained by market forces, such as changes in wages and unemployment rates that might have accompanied the extraordinary events. The simulations to be carried out in chapter 8 will help us determine what proportion of the observed changes can be explained by the variables included in our model.

Trends in Interprovincial Migration Flows by Age, Sex, and Income Class

To complete our examination of the migration data, we consider some trends in interprovincial mobility that are revealed by graphical inspection of our tax filer data. First, consider the general mobility of tax filers. Figure

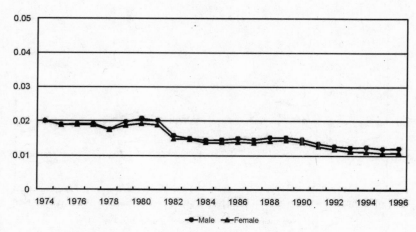

Figure 5.12   Mobility rates by sex, all tax filers, 1974–96

5.11 shows the overall mobility rate, defined as the number of tax filers who left their province of origin in a given year divided by the total number of tax filers in our data set. Consistent with Vachon and Vaillancourt's (1999) observation that there has been a decline in the mobility of Canadians over the period we are studying, figure 5.11 clearly displays a downward trend in the rate of mobility, from a high of 2 percent in 1974 to a low of 1.1 percent in 1995. This fall represents a 45 percent decrease in the overall rate of mobility between 1974 and 1996. A particularly large drop in the overall mobility rate, from about 2 percent to 1.5 percent, occurred in 1982 during the serious recession that hit the Canadian economy at that time. After this shock, the mobility rate never really picked up again before the end of our sample period, continuing to fall throughout the early 1990s.

In figure 5.12 we see the same secular decline in the mobility rates of both men and women, which suggests that gender differences have nothing to do with the overall decline in mobility. Furthermore, there is only a tiny difference between the mobility rates of men and women, with men being slightly more mobile than women after 1978. In figure 5.13 we see that the secular decline in mobility is also evident in all three income classes, though there are marked differences in mobility rates between the three groups. The lowest income group is the most mobile, followed by the middle and then the highest income group.

Differences in mobility rates across income classes may be due to differences in their age composition. Figure 5.14 confirms that mobility rates

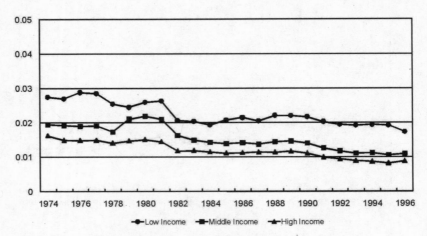

Figure 5.13   Mobility rates by income class, all tax filers, 1974–96

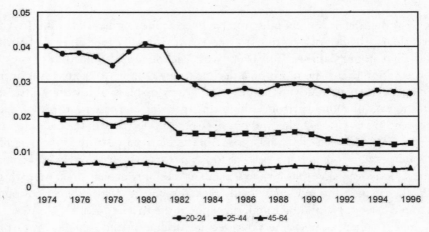

Figure 5.14   Mobility rates by age group, all tax filers, 1974–96

do decrease markedly with age. The mobility rate of the 20–24 age group is almost double that of the 25–44 age group, which is in turn more than double that of the 45–64 age group. However, the aging of the population cannot be the only factor underlying the decline in overall mobility observed in figure 5.11, since in figure 5.14 the mobility rates of both the 20–24 and 25–44 age groups also decrease somewhat between 1974 and 1996.

To obtain a clearer idea of the extent to which the demographic composition of the population is responsible for the observed differences in mobility rates across income classes, we carried out the following hypothetical calculation. First, the share of each of the six age-sex groups in the total population of tax filers in our data set was computed. Next, mobility rates were computed for each of the eighteen age-sex-income class groups in the data set. Finally, *for each income class*, a hypothetical mobility rate was computed using the aggregate age-sex group population shares, rather than the shares specific to that income class. More precisely, let s_{ij} be the population share of age group i and sex j, and let r_{ijk} be the mobility rate of the sub-population consisting of individuals of age i and sex j in income class k. Then the *hypothetical* mobility rate for income class k can be written as

$$r_k^H = \sum_{i=1}^{3} \sum_{j=1}^{2} s_{ij} r_{ijk} \, ,$$

while the *actual* mobility rate for income class k is given by

$$r_k = \sum_{i=1}^{3} \sum_{j=1}^{2} s_{ijk} r_{ijk} \, ,$$

where s_{ijk} is the share of the sub-population belonging to age group i, sex j, and income class k.

The synthetic mobility rates resulting from this calculation are displayed in figure 5.15. The figure shows that controlling for differences in demographic structure across income groups, that is, controlling for age and sex, almost eliminates the differences between the mobility rates of the middle and high income groups. However, the mobility rate of the low income group is not greatly affected. Thus we may conclude that there are important differences between the migration behaviour of individuals in the low income group and that of the other individuals in the data set.

Thus far this examination of our tax filer migration data confirms that it is important to disaggregate by income class and age group when analyzing interregional migration in Canada. But what about the direction of interprovincial migration flows? Does it seem to be consistent with the migration incentives examined in chapter 2? Figures 5.16a,b and 5.17a,b help to answer this question by presenting rates of out-and in-migration by province. Interestingly, the two most populous provinces – Ontario and Quebec – which together constitute more than 60 percent of the population of Canada, have the lowest rates of both out- and in-migration. In the case

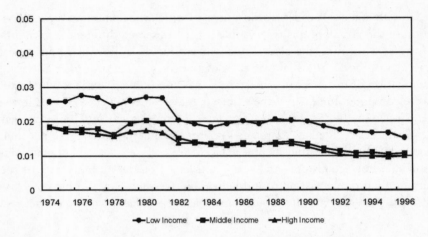

Figure 5.15   Mobility rates by income class if identical demographic structure, 1974–96

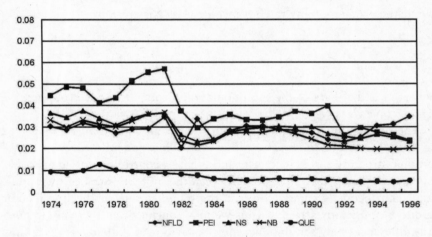

Figure 5.16a   Out-migration rates by province, all tax filers, 1974–96

of Quebec this finding can perhaps be explained by the barrier to mobility that language poses to both out-migrants from and in-migrants to the province, but the results for Ontario are more difficult to understand. While its relatively low out-migration rate may be related to the fact that during the 1974–96 period Ontario enjoyed relatively high average wages and relatively high government spending on health and education, these attributes should also have made Ontario more attractive than most other provinces to in-migrants. Yet this does not seem to have been the case.

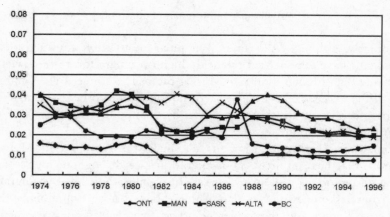

Figure 5.16b Out-migration rates by province, all tax filers, 1974–96

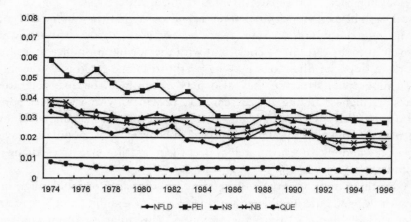

Figure 5.17a In-migration rates by province, all tax filers, 1974–96

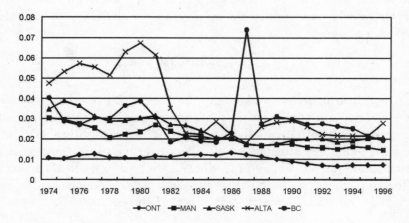

Figure 5.17b In-migration rates by province, all tax filers, 1974–96

Similarly, although Alberta is a popular destination for migrants, it appears to have experienced relatively high out-migration rates as well as relatively high in-migration rates during the period studied. The combination of the two is a classic sign of return migration to other provinces. The boom and bust of an economy driven by commodity prices is the likely culprit in the Alberta case.

Somewhat surprisingly, it is Canada's smallest province – Prince Edward Island – that has the highest out-migration rate throughout much of the 1974–96 period, as well as a high rate of in-migration. The out-migration rate from Saskatchewan was also relatively high. British Columbia, with its attractive climate and above-average wages, experienced relatively high in-migration and relatively low out-migration.[13]

Looking back to the patterns of provincial differences in market and fiscal variables examined in chapter 2, it is clear that the observed trends in in- and out-migration rates over the 1974–96 period do not always appear at first glance to be consistent with them. Migration incentives that work in opposite directions may be partly to blame for this. Differences in demographic structure may also play a role here. Because migration rates are highest among 20–24 year-olds, provinces with a younger population are likely to exhibit higher rates of out-migration. Finally, it must be remembered that the data examined in chapter 2 are population averages only and may not accurately reflect the migration incentives facing all population subgroups.

One thing we can say with certainty is that interregional migration flows in Canada are highly variable over time and exhibit complicated and time-variable patterns across the provinces. This volatility of interregional migration flows makes the econometric analysis of the causes of migration challenging, a fact not often acknowledged in migration studies. In the next chapter we will, among other things, evaluate the ability of our estimated models to capture this volatility.

Measuring INCOME and LEISURE

Our model of interregional migration in chapter 4, like other models in the literature, implies that incomes and employment prospects are important determinants of migration. But it goes beyond most other models by imposing additional structure on the manner in which different types of incomes, and the probability of receipt of each type of income, interact in influencing migration flows. This additional structure is found in equations (4.8) and (4.9), which define the composite variables INCOME and LEISURE as the probability-weighted sums of the logs of income and leisure time in the four possible states of the world.

These two variables are particularly important to our empirical model since they embody three key policy influences on migration: unemployment insurance, taxation, and social assistance. They also incorporate earnings, one of the traditional determinants of labour mobility in previous studies, and other components of income. Because so many variables are involved in the construction of INCOME and LEISURE, the necessary data had to be retrieved from a wide range of sources. Although ideally all the components of INCOME and LEISURE should vary with age, sex, and income class like our migration data, in practice it proved impossible to find data sources that provided this level of disaggregation for many of them. The exceptions to this general rule are highlighted in this section.

Although data construction issues are important to the validity of empirical analysis, it would take far too much time and space to outline in detail every step required to construct INCOME and LEISURE, and the source of every variable. To keep the discussion from becoming overwhelming, most of the details regarding specific data sources for particular variables are relegated to the appendices. Here we concentrate on the most important assumptions we made. The discussion is organized according to the key steps involved in constructing INCOME and LEISURE: first, the relevant unemployment insurance benefits have to be computed; second, after-tax incomes in the four states of the world have to be constructed; third, the probabilities of the four states of the world must be measured; and fourth, all the elements have to be substituted into equations (4.8) and (4.9) in order to construct the variables INCOME and LEISURE for all possible origin-destination pairs and all years. After each of these steps has been briefly described, we will take a quick look at the behaviour of our measures of INCOME and LEISURE.

The Unemployment Insurance Variables

Since the period covered by our analysis is 1968 to 1996, the "new" Canadian Employment Insurance program that was not fully implemented until January of 1997 had only a minor effect on the explanatory variables we constructed.[14] Our study thus constitutes an empirical analysis of the impact on migration of the Unemployment Insurance program that existed prior to 1997, not of its successor Employment Insurance. However, we think it important to point out that it is likely possible to predict the effects of some of the changes brought in under the Employment Insurance Act using our parameter estimates, for two reasons. In the first place, regional variation in entrance requirements and weeks of benefits remain a feature of the new program. Moreover, as table 1.1 indicates, observed variation in these aspects of the insurance system after 1996 are not qualitatively much different from what went on before.

It is this explicit regional differentiation of Canada's unemployment insurance system during the 1971–96 period that raises the possibility that it may have substantially affected migration incentives. In our model of interprovincial labour migration, we assume that migration decisions are influenced by the level of unemployment insurance benefits available to individuals in four possible states of the world. Migration decisions are thus regarded as being dependent on those parameters of the unemployment insurance system that determine the level of insurance benefits in the four states. However, in the model, individuals are actually deemed eligible to receive unemployment insurance benefits in only two of the four states, which henceforth will be referred to as the "unemployment insurance states."

As outlined in chapter 4, in one of these two states the individual works just enough weeks to spend the remainder of the year collecting unemployment insurance benefits, while in the other the individual works only the minimum weeks of work required to qualify for unemployment insurance benefits in a given year. These definitions of the two unemployment insurance states imply that insurance benefits in the two states, and thus migration decisions, are dependent on the minimum number of weeks required to qualify for benefits, the relationship between weeks of work and weeks of benefits, the benefit replacement rate, the weekly maximum insurable earnings, and regional extended benefits. All of these variables thus need to be computed for each province.

As table 2.1 demonstrates, many of the relevant features of the unemployment insurance program changed a number of times over the 1966–96 period.[15] For example, maximum weekly insurable earnings were fixed at $69 in 1959, raised to $100 in 1968, and then indexed in 1971. Similarly, the benefit replacement rate fell from $66^2/_3$ percent in 1976 to 60 percent in 1979, with a further drop to 57 percent in 1993. The formula used to calculate benefits also changed considerably over time. The 1955 UI Act's simple provision that every two weeks of insurable employment entitled the individual to one week of benefits was replaced by a complicated five-phase benefit schedule in 1971.

While all of these changes are relevant to the construction of our data, the two changes that are the most important to our analysis are the introduction of regional extended benefits in 1971 and the variable entrance requirement

(VER) in 1977. These two features of the unemployment insurance system affect the values of MIN, the minimum number of weeks or work required to qualify for benefits, and MXYR, the number of weeks of work that entitle the individual to collect unemployment insurance benefits for the remainder of the year, as well as the weeks of benefits associated with MIN. Changes in the first of these provisions, regional extended benefits, during our sample period are summarized in table 2.2 and were discussed in chapter 2. Changes in the variable entrance requirement, which are summarized in table 2.3, were also discussed in chapter 2.

In translating these policy features into variables for our empirical model, one encounters several problems. The first is that changes to insurance parameters often occurred in the middle of a calendar year. This requires us to make various assumptions regarding how the change affected the value of the affected policy parameter for a particular year. The second problem is that the VER and regional extended benefits apply to unemployment insurance regions, but there is no direct correspondence between administrative unemployment insurance regions and provinces. Furthermore, the number of such regions does not remain fixed over time. Every high-unemployment region receives the same treatment, regardless of the province in which it is located, and virtually all provinces included at least one high-unemployment region at some point in time. A third problem is the existence of different classes of benefits (e.g., regular, seasonal, fishing) and beneficiaries (e.g., with and without dependents). Because it is impossible to take all of these factors explicitly into account in the empirical model, we necessarily made a number of (we think, reasonable) simplifying assumptions about the operation of the insurance system in order to construct the variables required.

In total, we constructed five unemployment insurance-related variables. The first three are MIN, the minimum number of weeks of insurable employment required to qualify for insurance benefits; MXYR, the number of weeks of work such that additional weeks of work will not increase the individual's unemployment insurance entitlement during a 52-week period; and MINWKS, the maximum weeks of benefits that an individual with MIN qualifying weeks can receive. All three of these variables appear in equations (4.9) or (4.10). The remaining two variables are MXYRWKS, the weeks of unemployment insurance benefits that an individual with MXYR qualifying weeks can receive, which is expressed as 50-MXYR in equations (4.10), and WUI, the weekly rate of benefit, which is expressed as expressed as ρw_j^R in equations (4.10). The following general assumptions apply to the construction of all five variables:

1 The individual's time horizon is assumed to be one year, i.e., 52 weeks.
2 For the purposes of calculating MIN and regional extended benefits, each province is treated as a single unemployment insurance region. Changes in the actual number of unemployment insurance regions over time are ignored.
3 Calculations that require unemployment rates as inputs use annual average rates.
4 In years in which legislative changes occurred, variables are computed as a weighted average of the values that would have prevailed had each regime been in effect the entire year. The weights are given by the proportion of months during the year that each benefit regime was in effect.
5 We restrict our attention to the category of benefits that was labelled "regular benefits" under the Unemployment Insurance Act of 1971. The extension of the 1971 definition of benefits backwards in time requires us to incorporate the "seasonal" category of benefits as well as "regular" benefits in our calculations for the 1966 to 1971 period.

More specific assumptions made in the construction of each of the variables are discussed in appendix C. This appendix also includes a series of data tables containing the constructed values of MIN, MXYR, MINWKS, MXYRWKS, and WUI, as well as some additional variables used in the calculation of WUI, all by province for the period 1966–96.

Provincial differences in MIN and MXYR have already been examined in chapter 2. What we did not examine there, though, was the difference between MIN and MXYR in each province and how this difference has changed over time. Table 5.1 shows that in all provinces except Ontario, Manitoba, and Saskatchewan this difference was zero for at least one year during the 1971–96 period, meaning that the average unemployment rate in each of the other provinces was so high that working the minimum number of weeks necessary to qualify for benefit payments in one of those provinces was sufficient to entitle one to receive benefits for the remainder of the year. In terms of our model, this means that in these provinces and years there is no distinction between states 2 and 3, so that unemployment insurance incomes in the two states are identical. Not surprisingly, this situation arose most frequently in the four Atlantic provinces.

After-Tax Incomes Net of Moving Costs

While they are particularly important to our empirical model, the income-related unemployment insurance variables discussed in the previous subsec-

Table 5.1
Difference between MIN and MXYR (MXYR − MIN)

Year	NFLD	PEI	NS	NB	QUE	ONT	MAN	SASK	ALTA	BC
1966	19	19	19	19	19	19	19	19	19	19
1967	19	19	19	19	19	19	19	19	19	19
1968	19	19	19	19	19	19	19	19	19	19
1969	19	19	19	19	19	19	19	19	19	19
1970	19	19	19	19	19	19	19	19	19	19
1971	11	15	15	15	14	15	15	15	15	14
1972	0	0	12	12	9	12	12	12	12	9
1973	0	12	12	4	9	12	12	12	12	9
1974	0	12	9	4	9	12	12	12	12	12
1975	0	12	12	4	9	12	12	12	12	9
1976	0	4	4	0	9	12	12	12	12	9
1977	1	8	4	1	4	12	11	12	12	11
1978	0	3	2	0	1	6	7	9	9	5
1979	0	0	2	0	3	7	8	10	11	5
1980	0	1	3	0	3	6	8	10	11	6
1981	0	0	2	0	2	6	3	9	11	6
1982	0	0	0	0	0	3	5	7	5	0
1983	0	0	0	0	0	2	4	6	1	0
1984	0	0	0	0	0	4	5	5	0	0
1985	0	0	0	0	0	5	5	5	2	0
1986	0	0	0	0	1	6	5	5	3	0
1987	0	0	0	0	2	7	6	6	3	0
1988	0	0	2	0	4	9	5	6	5	2
1989	0	0	3	0	4	8	5	6	6	4
1990	0	0	0	0	0	6	5	6	5	3
1991	1	2	4	2	4	9	7	7	7	6
1992	1	1	4	2	3	5	6	7	6	5
1993	1	1	3	2	3	3	4	4	4	2
1994	4	4	7	7	7	9	9	10	9	9
1995	4	7	9	9	9	10	10	11	10	10
1996	4	7	9	9	9	10	10	11	10	10

Source: Authors' calculations.

tion represent only a subset of the components of income that appear in equations (4.10). Other important components of income that appear in these equations are the wage rate (w), nonwage income (B), personal transfer payments other than unemployment insurance benefits or social assistance (TR), and annual social assistance benefits ($\overline{SA}_j$). For the first three of these variables we use data obtained from Statistics Canada's CANSIM database, and the corresponding series identifiers can be found in appendix A. In all three cases provincial per capita averages are used. In the case of social assistance benefits, however, we do not simply use per capita provincial social assistance benefits, because doing so would tend to underestimate the magnitude of benefits received in state 4 due to the fact that social assistance recipients constitute a small proportion of each province's population. Instead, we use data on the benefits available to a single parent with two children, kindly provided to us by Pierre Lefebvre. Although our migration data do not pertain specifically to single parents, these data have the advantage of being consistent across provinces and across time, and they are likely to provide an accurate reflection of the overall generosity of social assistance benefits in each province in a particular year. Regional variation in this variable (after controlling for inflation) has already been explored in figures 2.2 and 2.9.

The monetary costs of moving, C_{ij}, constitute another important element of equations (4.10). Moving costs can be divided into two components: the actual cost of moving oneself and one's belongings from one province to another and the foregone wage cost resulting from having to take time off work to move. The details of the calculation of these two variables are left to appendix A. Here it suffices to say that the actual cost of moving is based on average airfare and average costs of shipping goods by rail, while the foregone wage cost is constructed from the same average weekly earnings data used to compute employment income and an estimate of the amount of time required to move. Both components of C_{ij} depend on the distance between the provinces of origin and destination.

The most difficult task we faced in constructing appropriate income variables, however, was not measuring the components of before-tax income but rather computing the amount of income tax owed. Since it is after-tax income, not before-tax income, that is relevant to migration decisions, we must model the role of taxation as it affects individual incomes. Of course the tax structures of Canada and the provinces have changed considerably since 1965 (see Gillespie 1991 for a history), making it very difficult to include or capture all aspects of the tax system over the period from 1968 to 1996. Instead, in measuring after-tax incomes, we utilize a stylized version of the income tax system that allows income taxes to vary both across provinces and across states of the world within a given province. In keeping with our approach to modelling the role of public policy, our treatment highlights the importance of specific tax policy parameters, most importantly the marginal personal income tax rates applying to taxable incomes in each location for each state of the world. The basic marginal (federal plus provincial) tax rate applying to the taxable income of an individual in each state in each location is used in computing tax liabilities, and, thus, variation across provinces and over time in this marginal tax rate is explicitly incorporated in calculated after-tax incomes.

Other studies of interprovincial migration have typically dealt with provincial differences in income taxes in a less satisfactory manner. For example, Day (1992) restricts her attention to average tax rates. While easy to compute, average tax rates have at least two drawbacks. They depend in part on income levels within a province, and it would be impossible to construct different average tax rates for the different states of the world in our model of migration. The use of average tax rates would thus make it impossible to capture the interaction between the different levels of income in the different states of the world within a province and interprovincial variation in income taxes that is relevant to potential migrants.

Our stylized tax system consists of a simplified definition of taxable income, the basic rate structure imposed by the federal and provincial governments, and the personal exemption or tax credit. The definition of taxable income in each location in each state of the world also allows for the change in the tax treatment of moving costs and transfer payments such as unemployment insurance after 1972, when moving costs became deductible and transfers became taxable. It also incorporates the general shift from the use of deductions to the use of tax credits following the 1987 tax reforms.

In our stylized tax system, prior to 1972 taxable income is defined as the sum of wage income and interest income, less the foregone wage cost of moving and the personal exemption. After 1972, it includes income from unemployment insurance and government transfer payments other than social assistance, with a deduction equal to the monetary cost of moving. There is a further change in the definition of taxable income in 1988, when the personal exemption was replaced by a tax credit. The statutory rates used to compute Basic Federal Tax are then applied to taxable income in order to compute federal income tax. In all of these calculations, a single individual with no children forms the basis for our work, since each "cell" in the migration data set aggregates over individuals whose personal characteristics and family structures are largely unknown to us.

The only deductions or tax credits that are incorporated in our tax calculations are moving costs and the basic personal exemption or tax credit. For the latter, we use the basic amount for a single individual. The fact that the federal and Quebec values of the personal exemption and tax credit have differed since 1973 is also taken into account.

Our stylized tax system also incorporates changes in the computation of the provincial share of income taxes that were introduced in 1972. Prior to

1972, basic provincial taxes for all provinces except Quebec were computed by applying each province's income tax rate to basic federal tax. Then an individual's total basic tax liability, TOTALTAX in equations (4.10), is computed as the sum of the federal (FEDTAX) and provincial (PROVTAX) income tax liabilities:

$$TOTALTAX = FEDTAX + PROVTAX \qquad (5.1)$$
$$= FT[(1 - ABATEMENT) + PROVRATE],$$

where FT is federal tax before the abatement, ABATEMENT is the federal abatement in favour of the provinces, and PROVRATE is the provincial tax rate.[16] Beginning in 1972, the federal abatement was replaced by a lower federal rate structure, and provincial taxes for all provinces except Quebec were computed as a percentage of basic federal tax (BFT). The individual's total basic tax liability thus is computed as

$$TOTALTAX = BFT(1 + PROVRATE). \qquad (5.2)$$

Quebec maintained its own income tax system throughout the 1966–96 period, with its own rate structure.[17] We assume that the definition of taxable income is the same in Quebec as in the rest of Canada but apply Quebec's basic rate structure to that definition of taxable income in order to compute Quebec income taxes. Total basic taxes in the case of Quebec are thus computed as follows:

$$TOTALTAX = FEDTAX + QUETAX \qquad (5.3)$$
$$= BFT(1 - ABATEMENT) + QUETAX,$$

where QUETAX is Quebec income tax and all other variables are defined as before. Quebec is the only province for which a federal tax abatement remained in existence after 1971. Quebec income tax is computed by applying the statutory rates imposed by Quebec to the stylized definition of taxable income.

Once the stylized tax system was defined, the first step in computing after-tax incomes net of moving costs was to compute taxable income for each state of the world. Because moving costs vary with both province of origin and province of destination, and because some components of income, such as interest income and non-insurance transfers from government, are determined by the province of origin, taxable income also varies with origin and destination.

Letting TI represent taxable income, and the subscripts 1, 2, and 3 the state of the world, taxable incomes in states 1 to 3 are given by the following equations:

$$TI_{ij1} = \begin{cases} 50w_j + B_i - C1_{ij} - P & t \le 1971 \qquad (5.4) \\ 50w_j + B_i + TR_i - C1_{ij} - C2_{ij} - P & 1972 \le t < 1988 \\ 50w_j + B_i + TR_i - C1_{ij} - C2_{ij} & t \ge 1988, \end{cases}$$

$$TI_{ij2} = \begin{cases} w_j MXYR_j + B_i - C1_{ij} - P & t \le 1971 \quad (5.5) \\ w_j MXYR_j + B_i + TR_i + UI_{j2} - C1_{ij} - C2_{ij} - P & 1972 \le t < 1988 \\ w_j MXYR_j + B_i + TR_i + UI_{j2} - C1_{ij} - C2_{ij} & t \ge 1988, \end{cases}$$

$$TI_{ij3} = \begin{cases} w_j MIN_j + B_i - C1_{ij} - P & t \le 1971 \quad (5.6) \\ w_j MIN_j + B_i + TR_i + UI_{j3} - C1_{ij} - C2_{ij} - P & 1972 \le t < 1988 \\ w_j MIN_j + B_i + TR_i + UI_{j3} - C1_{ij} - C2_{ij} & t \ge 1988, \end{cases}$$

where C1 is the foregone wage cost of moving, C2 is the monetary cost of moving, P is the personal income tax exemption, UI is unemployment insurance income, and all other variables are defined in table 4.1. Taxable income is zero in state 4 since in this state individuals receive only social assistance income and other transfer income, which are not taxable.

It should be noted that although the variables in these taxable income definitions should in principle vary across population subgroups (e.g., by income classes, or age-sex groups), we were unable to obtain data that does so. Therefore, the same incomes, both before and after tax, must be used for all the population subgroups for which migration functions were estimated, with the relevant estimated coefficients being required to take up the task, so to speak, of allowing for variation across the various subgroups. Our taxable income variables do vary, however, with province of origin, province of destination, state of the world, and with time.

The second step in the calculations is to compute the marginal tax rate and total income tax liability for each state of the world. For the nine provinces that are party to the tax collection agreement with the federal government, these variables are combined federal-provincial quantities, but as discussed above, for Quebec separate federal and provincial variables had to be constructed. Again, like taxable incomes the tax variables vary with province of origin, province of destination, state of the world, and year. The final step in the calculation of after-tax incomes net of moving costs is to substitute everything into equations (4.10).

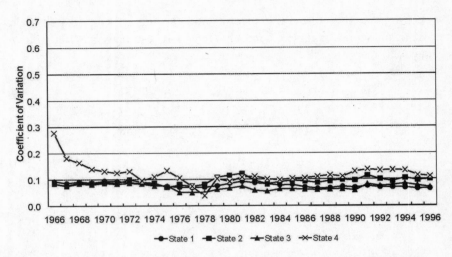

Figure 5.18   Regional dispersion of after-tax real incomes in the four states of the world

Taxes computed using this stylized tax system may over- or under-esti-
mate actual income tax liabilities since several deductions and tax rate
reductions, as well as surtaxes, have been ignored in their calculation.
However, what is most crucial for our empirical analysis is that there be
regional variation in the tax system and that taxes vary across states of
the world in a reasonable approximation to such variations in the real
world. We think that this stylized tax system does capture the most important aspects of provincial income tax differentials that are relevant in the
present context.

Figures 2.2 and 2.10 in chapter 2 provide some insight into how the computed tax liability varies across provinces, but none of the figures in chapter
2 show how after-tax incomes in the different states of the world vary across
provinces. To do so visually, we ignore moving costs and consider only stayers; incorporating moving costs would cause the composite income variable
to vary with both origin and destination, and there would then be too many
possible combinations to consider. Moving costs are of course fully incorporated in the empirical work in the following chapter.

Figure 5.18 presents the coefficients of variation across provinces of real
after-tax incomes in each of the four states of the world. Note that the
vertical axis in this figure has been restricted to the same range as in figures
2.1 to 2.3 so as to facilitate comparisons between the levels of dispersion
of the four incomes and the variables examined in chapter 2. The figure
shows that although there is definitely some regional variation in incomes

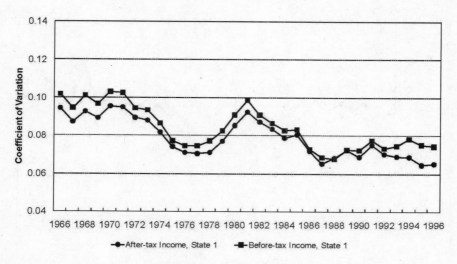

Figure 5.19   Regional dispersion of before-tax and after-tax income, state 1

in the four states of the world, it is of the same order of magnitude as regional dispersion in average weekly earnings (shown in figure 2.1). Also, the extent of regional dispersion is similar for the four different incomes. Regional dispersion is highest in state 4, in which income depends primarily on social assistance benefits, while the coefficients of variation of the other four incomes are clustered together. The slightly higher level of dispersion of state 4 income is not surprising, given that figure 2.2 shows that social assistance benefits do indeed exhibit slightly greater regional dispersion than average weekly earnings.

Since some studies of regional differences in Canada have noted that the tax-transfer system seems to have the overall effect of reducing regional differences in Canada, it is worthwhile to see if the same is true of our stylized tax system. To this end, figures 5.19–5.21 compare regional dispersion of before-tax and after-tax income in states 1 to 3 (recall that in state 4 individuals do not pay taxes, so there is no difference between before- and after-tax income in this state). In the first two figures we can clearly see that the coefficient of variation of before-tax income is greater than that of after-tax income, confirming that the tax system does tend to reduce regional disparities in incomes in these two states. In state 3, however, regional dispersion of after-tax income remains consistently below that of before-tax income only up to 1978. After that year the stylized tax-transfer system does *not* consistently reduce regional dispersion of income in state 3.

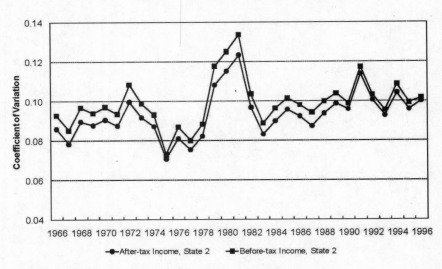

Figure 5.20   Regional dispersion of before-tax and after-tax income, state 2

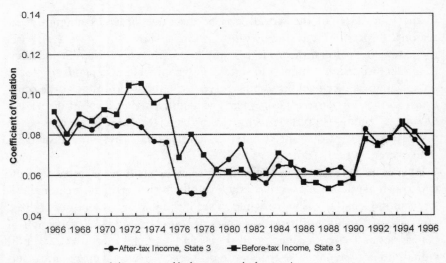

Figure 5.21   Regional dispersion of before-tax and after-tax income, state 3

The simplicity of the stylized income tax calculation may provide one possible explanation for the apparent failure of the tax-transfer system to consistently reduce regional dispersion of incomes in state 3. However, the introduction of regionally extended benefits in 1977, coupled with the fact that unemployment insurance benefits became taxable in 1972, likely plays

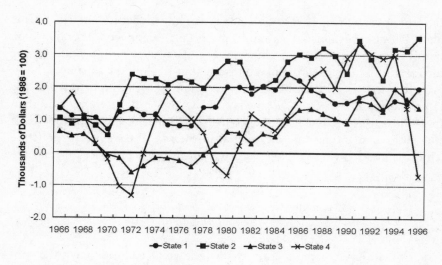

Figure 5.22   Difference in after-tax real incomes, Ontario minus Newfoundland, states 1 to 4

a greater role. By its very nature, the regionally extended benefit provision of the unemployment insurance system created greater regional dispersion in unemployment insurance incomes, an effect that is most pronounced for those weakly attached to the labour force because they rely the most heavily on UI as a source of income. In the absence of such extended benefits it is likely that regional dispersion of before-tax income in state 3 would always have been greater than that of after-tax income.

Thus far we have considered only the degree of regional dispersion in the constructed income variables, not the pattern of dispersion. Although it would be of interest, a complete examination of regional differences in the four income measures would require a great deal of space, so rather than showing how each province compares to the Canadian average for each real after-tax income measure, in figure 5.22 we present the difference between two provinces, Ontario and Newfoundland, for each measure. Once again the values in the figures compare stayers, who incur no moving costs. Ontario has traditionally been considered a high-income province, at least as far as employment income is concerned, and this figure confirms that in the full-year employment state (state 1) Ontario always has the highest income. In most of the years shown the measured real after-tax income differential between the two provinces exceeded $1,000.

In addition, although unemployment insurance benefits are considered to be more generous in Newfoundland due to the VER and the regional extended benefit, figure 5.22 shows that in state 2 (strongly attached to the labour force) real after-tax income is actually higher in Ontario. This is likely because wage income is still an important component of total income in this state, and as we saw in chapter 2 average wages were generally higher in Ontario than in Newfoundland throughout this period. In state 3, however, the story is a little different. In this state of weak attachment to the labour force, after-tax real income is actually higher in Newfoundland than in Ontario through most of the 1970s. Finally, there are relatively large fluctuations in the income differential in the social assistance state (state 4), most likely owing to policy changes in the two provinces during the 1966–96 period.

Measuring the Ex Ante Probabilities of the Employment-Unemployment States

One of the biggest data creation challenges we faced, aside from the construction of the migration data itself, was measuring the ex ante probabilities of the four states of the world, the variables π_{j1}, π_{j2}, π_{j3}, and π_{j4} of chapter 4. These probabilities do not correspond very closely to published data on the unemployment rate, which simply measure the stock of people who meet Statistics Canada's definition of the unemployed (people who are not currently working but who are actively seeking work). One obvious way to measure these probabilities would be to calculate the observed relative frequency of being in each of the states. For the purpose of such calculations, the relevant total population consists of those individuals between the ages of 20 and 64 who have in any year received income from at least one of the following sources: employment (including self-employment), unemployment insurance, or social assistance.

Recall that in our theoretical model, the four states of the world are defined by the number of weeks that each individual expects to work, where weeks of work are assumed for simplicity to have four possible values. In state 1, the individual is employed for at least 50 weeks per year. In state 2, the individual works between MXYR and 50 weeks, and receives unemployment insurance benefits the rest of the year. In state 3, individuals work between MIN and MXYR weeks, and receive unemployment insurance benefits for the remainder of the year. Finally, in state 4 the individual is assumed to receive social assistance for the entire year.

Since data on the empirical distribution of weeks of work that would enable us to compute these relative frequencies simply are not available for most of the years in our sample period, we rely instead on data on the average stock of people who fall into each of the four groups in each province in each year to approximate the probabilities. Specifically, we approximate the probabilities using data on the number of individuals who are employed, receiving unemployment insurance, or receiving social assistance in a given year. Let $n(E_j)$ be employment in region j, $n(U_j)$ the number of recipients of regular unemployment insurance benefits in region j, and $n(SA_j)$ be the number of social assistance recipients. In addition, let $p^j_{<20}$ be the proportion of recipients of regular unemployment benefits with less than 20 qualifying weeks in region j, and let p^j_{20+} be the proportion of recipients of regular benefits who have at least 20 qualifying weeks in region j. Note that $p^j_{<20}$ can be viewed as the proportion of unemployment insurance recipients who are weakly attached to the labour force, while p^j_{20+} is the proportion of recipients who are considered to be strongly attached to the labour force. By construction, $p^j_{<20}$ and p^j_{20+} sum to one. Then we approximate the ex ante probabilities of the four states of the world as follows:

$$\pi_{j1} = \frac{n(E_j)}{n(E_j) + n(UI_j) + n(SA_j)}, \tag{5.7}$$

$$\pi_{j2} = \frac{p^j_{20+} \cdot n(UI_j)}{n(E_j) + n(UI_j) + n(SA_j)},$$

$$\pi_{j3} = \frac{p^j_{<20} \cdot n(UI_j)}{n(E_j) + n(UI_j) + n(SA_j)},$$

$$\pi_{j2} = \frac{n(SA_j)}{n(E_j) + n(UI_j) + n(SA_j)}.$$

In our implementation of these formulae, employment figures from the Labour Force Survey (LFS) are used to measure $n(E_j)$. However, we do not use the LFS estimate of the number of unemployed to measure $n(UI_j)$. Instead, we used the number of people receiving regular unemployment insurance benefits, which is also available from Statistics Canada sources. We do so for two reasons. First, it is the expected receipt of income in each state that matters for migration, including the receipt of unemployment insurance. Second, the number of unemployed people is not always a good measure of the number of people receiving unemployment insurance payments. In some provinces in some years, for example in Newfoundland, Prince Edward Island, and New Brunswick in adverse economic times, the number of unemployment insurance recipients can exceed the number of unemployed as recorded by the Labour Force Survey by a substantial amount.

The third component of our total population, the number of social assistance recipients, $n(SA_j)$, is approximated by the number of social assistance cases reported in each province. The general procedure used to arrive at this number consisted of several steps, the first of which was to compute the number of social assistance cases of all ages on a fiscal year basis. This number was then converted to a calendar year basis. A special compilation of social assistance recipients by age and province derived from all available computerized Surveys of Consumer Finances (SCF) was then used to reduce this to a number of cases for ages 20–64. These aggregate figures are then distributed across age-sex categories using the proportions of cases in each age-sex group given by the SCF data. Note that the total number of social assistance cases is not the same as the number of beneficiaries. We use data on the former since the latter includes children, who are not attached to the labour force and therefore not part of the population we wish to study.

Finally, $p^j_{<20}$ and p^j_{20+} in (5.7) were derived from special tabulations of unemployment insurance beneficiaries by age, sex, and qualifying weeks provided by Marcel Bédard of Human Resources Development Canada. However, these tabulations covered only the period 1972–96. For the period prior to 1971, when only two types of insurance benefits were available, recipients of seasonal benefits were assumed to have less than 20 qualifying weeks of work, while recipients of regular benefits were assumed to have 20 or more qualifying weeks. Further details regarding the exact data sources used to construct these and the other components of the probabilities are provided in appendix D.

As formulae for approximating the theoretical variables π_{j1} to π_{j4}, the definitions in (5.7) do have some limitations. Because they measure the stock of employed people during a particular week (averaged over weeks surveyed during the year), not the number of people who are employed all year long, the Labour Force Survey measure of employment used to measure $n(E_j)$ will include individuals who are in the middle of short- or medium-term employment spells as well as those who are in the midst of a long spell of 50 or more weeks, and thus may tend to overestimate the number of individuals in state 1. The choice of 20 weeks of work as the dividing line between those in states 2 and 3, rather than $MXYR_j$ weeks, is also an approximation that will be more accurate for some regions than others. However, it does coincide with many economists' notion of the dividing line between workers who are "strongly attached" and "weakly attached" to the labour force. In addition, some social assistance recipients may not be labour force participants, and thus the total number of social assistance cases may overestimate the number of individuals in state 4. It should also be noted that the method of defining and recording social assistance cases differs somewhat across provinces.

Nonetheless, our definitions in (5.7) represent the best feasible method of approximating the four probabilities, and we used to it compute not only aggregate probabilities of the four states of the world for the 20–64 age group in each province but also probabilities for each of the six age-sex groups covered by our data. Doing so required an age/sex breakdown of all the elements in the formula, which was not easy to obtain except in the case of employment and the number of unemployment insurance recipients.

Because of the large number of assumptions required to disaggregate the probabilities by age and sex, care should be taken in drawing conclusions from the results based on these data. For this reason, in the chapters that follow we place more emphasis on the results of estimation using aggregate probabilities for each province and migration data disaggregated by income class.

Although we do attempt to compute age- and gender-specific measures of the probabilities of being in each of the four employment states in each province, we did not attempt to compute probabilities specific to each income class, since data on the components of equations (5.7) are simply not available by income class. While in general one would expect that those in the highest income class would have a low probability of being in any of the three states of the world that involve unemployment, it should be remembered that here we are trying to measure ex ante probabilities of unemployment. Even high-income individuals, depending on their occupation, may face a high probability of unemployment as a result of a move. Unfortunately, in the absence of any data that allow us to approximate these probabilities we have no choice but to use the same probabilities for all three income classes.

Since we employ a broader measure of unemployment for the purposes of our empirical analysis than does the Labour Force Survey (LFS), it is helpful to take a quick look at the differences between our measures of the employment and unemployment rates and the official LFS measures. Figure 5.23 displays these measures for two provinces, Newfoundland and Ontario. Panel (a) of the figure shows that with the exception of the last two years of the sample period, the gap between the LFS probability of employment and our own is quite large, with the LFS measure being higher. The mirror image of this gap appears in panel (b), where the LFS unemployment rate lies well below the sum of the probabilities of being in any one of the three unemployment states of our model. This gap can be attributed to two factors, the first of which is the inclusion of people on social assistance in our unemployment total. A large proportion of these people would be counted

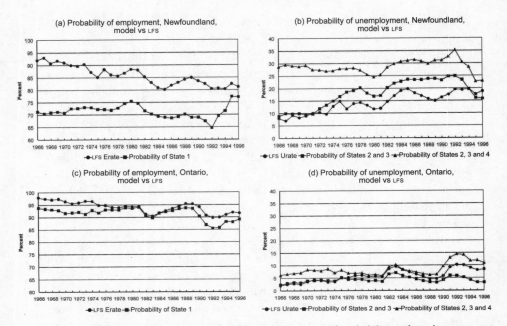

Figure 5.23   Comparison between LFS and model measures of probabilities of employment and unemployment

Source: Statistics Canada and authors' calculations

as "not in the labour force" rather than "unemployed" by the LFS, since they may not be actively looking for work. Indeed, it can also be seen in panel (b) that when the probability of state 4 is excluded from the sum (look at the line labelled "probability of states 2 and 3") the resulting model-based "unemployment rate" tracks the official LFS rate much more closely.

The second factor is that our measures are based on the stock of people in each state at any time during the course of a year, while the LFS measures are the annual average of monthly snapshots. In any particular month, the number of people in states 2, 3, and 4 is likely to be less than the total number of people captured by our measures $p_{<20}^{j} \cdot n(UI_j)$, $p_{20+}^{j} \; n(UI_j)$, and $n(SA_j)$. Consequently, the numerators and denominators of our measures differ from those of the LFS measures, with the increase in the numerator being larger than the increase in the denominator.

Panels (c) and (d) of the figure show that the story is somewhat different for Ontario. In this province, too, the official probability of employment is higher than our own estimate, but the difference between the two series is much smaller. Similarly, in panel (d) one can see that the gap between the model and LFS unemployment rates is small relative to that for Newfound-

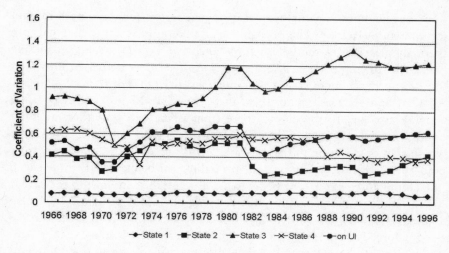

Figure 5.24   Regional variation in probabilities of employment states

land. In fact, up to 1975 the sum of the probabilities of states 2 and 3 was almost equal to the LFS unemployment rate. While the gap between the LFS measures and our own is attributable to the same factors, the smaller total gap for Ontario can be explained by its higher employment rate and smaller proportions of the working-age population on social assistance or working less than twenty weeks. The relative importance of seasonal employment (including fishing) in Newfoundland as compared to Ontario is responsible for the much higher probability of state 3 in that province.

We have seen already in chapter 2 (see figure 2.1) that regional variation in the official LFS unemployment rate was quite high during the 1966 to 1996 period. Is the same true of our constructed probabilities? Figure 5.24 presents the coefficients of variation across provinces of the probabilities of the four states of the world. For purposes of comparison, the coefficient of variation of the probability of receiving unemployment insurance, which is the sum of the probabilities of states 2 and 3, denoted "on UI" in the figure, is also included.

The figure shows that there is relatively little regional dispersion in the probability of state 1, full-year employment. The only year during the 1966–96 period in which the coefficient of variation of this probability exceeds 1.0 is 1992, when the country began to pull out of its deepest postwar recession. However, the probability of state 3, in which individuals are weakly attached to the labour force but spend part of the year receiving insurance benefits, varies widely across the Canadian provinces during the entire period. Furthermore, this probability increased fairly steadily after the introduction of unemployment insurance reforms in 1970 until the end of our sample period. The probability of state 2, in which individuals are strongly attached to the labour force and have at least twenty qualifying weeks for unemployment insurance, also differs more across regions than does the probability of state 1, but much less than that of state 3.

What figure 5.24 does not show directly is that the probability of being weakly attached to the labour force (that is, in state 3) varies far more across provinces than does the official unemployment rate. In figure 2.1 the coefficient of variation of the unemployment rate exceeds 0.5 only in 1974 and 1975, while in figure 5.24 the probability of being weakly attached to the labour force never falls below 0.5. More often than not the coefficient of variation of the probability of receiving unemployment insurance also exceeds 0.5. Only the probability of state 2 being strongly attached to the labour force is frequently below 0.5, but it never falls below 0.2 in magnitude. Overall, then, we can say that differentiating between three different unemployment states tends to increase the amount of regional variation in our data.

Because the probabilities of the states of the world play such an important role in our model, it is worth looking at the absolute differences between provinces as well as at the regional dispersion of the probabilities. Since it would be overwhelming to look at all ten provinces, figures 5.25a to 5.25d compare the probabilities of a high-employment province, Ontario, to those of the low-employment province Newfoundland. These figures show that although the gap between the full-year employment probabilities (state 1) of the two provinces was relatively constant up to 1992, after that year the gap began to decline as a result of an increase in the probability of state 1 in Newfoundland. This increase in the measured probability of employment in Newfoundland is somewhat surprising given that it coincides with the closure of the cod fishery, but recall that figure 5.1 showed an increase in outflows from Newfoundland after the fishery shutdown. Furthermore, we can see in figures 5.25c (and 5.25b) that the probability of state 3 (and to a lesser extent state 2) decreased at the same time. Taken together, these figures suggest that the outflow from Newfoundland after the shutdown of the cod fishery consisted largely of individuals who would have been unemployed and receiving insurance benefits had they remained.

We can also see some signs of the impact of unemployment insurance on the probabilities in figure 5.25. The probabilities of both unemployment insurance states (states 2 and 3) rose after the introduction of unemployment insurance reforms in 1970, reforms that introduced regionally differentiated benefits, with an especially large increase in the proportion of

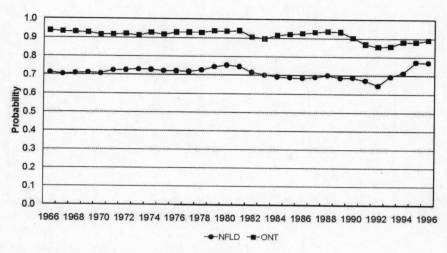

Figure 5.25a   Ontario versus Newfoundland, probability of state 1

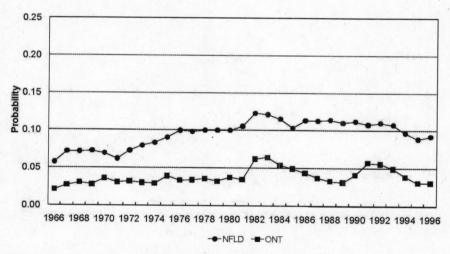

Figure 5.25b   Ontario versus Newfoundland, probability of state 2

those weakly attached to the labour force (state 3) in Newfoundland. The corresponding increase in the probability of being on unemployment insurance in Ontario was small and short-lived.

Interestingly, in Newfoundland the increase in the probability of receiving insurance payments in the early seventies was accompanied by a decrease in the probability of receiving social assistance. This increase may reflect a

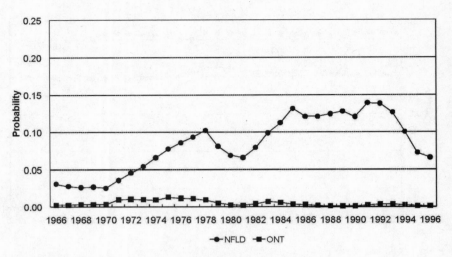

Figure 5.25c   Ontario versus Newfoundland, probability of state 3

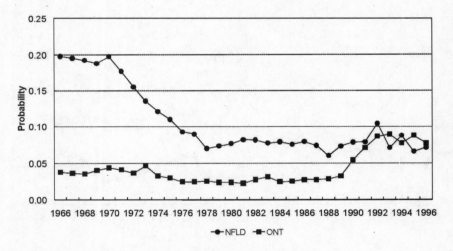

Figure 5.25d   Ontario versus Newfoundland, probability of state 4

substitution from social assistance to unemployment insurance during the 1970s, which we hinted at in chapter 1. This possibility reinforces our decision to include social assistance as one of the states of the world in our modelling. By the mid-nineties, the probability of receiving social assistance was roughly the same in Ontario and Newfoundland, although there remained a substantial gap of more than five percentage points between the two provinces in the probabilities of each of the two unemployment insurance states.

These graphs are interesting because they provide an illustration of the regionally differentiated consequences of unemployment insurance that some economists have pointed to with some alarm. In addition, there is a suggestion in the data here of substitution from social assistance to unemployment insurance, a matter that has not often been considered. While this phenomenon is not the topic of our study, later on we will compare the impacts of unemployment insurance and social assistance on interprovincial migration flows.

The End Result: INCOME and LEISURE

Once MXYR, MIN, and the incomes and probabilities of the four states of the world had been constructed, they were substituted into equations (4.8) and (4.9) to construct the explanatory variables INCOME and LEISURE. Like the state-specific incomes from which it is constructed, INCOME varies with origin and destination, but LEISURE depends only on the destination province. Consequently, as in the case of after-tax real incomes we restrict our examination of provincial differences in INCOME to stayers in order to keep the discussion manageable. Note that the inclusion of moving costs would reduce the value of INCOME in the province of destination, but leave the value in the origin unchanged.

First, consider the regional dispersion of INCOME in figure 5.26. In this figure we present both the standard deviation and the coefficient of variation of INCOME, measured on the left and right axes respectively. To this point we have used the coefficient of variation as our measure of dispersion for all variables, but one can see in figure 5.26 that despite the fact that INCOME is based on the income measures we have constructed for the four states of the world, its coefficient of variation is much smaller in magnitude than the coefficients of variation of the real after-tax incomes that were presented in figure 5.18. The magnitude of the standard deviation of INCOME, however, is very similar to that of the variables in that figure. This is because the standard deviation of a variable transformed by taking logs is comparable to the coefficient of variation of the untransformed variable, since just as changes in units of measurement do not affect the coefficient of variation, they do not affect the standard deviation of the natural log of a variable. Therefore the standard deviations of INCOME and LEISURE are arguably more comparable to the coefficients of variation presented earlier than are their own

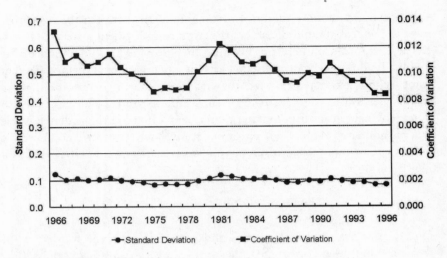

Figure 5.26   Regional dispersion of INCOME (stayers)

coefficients of variation. In fact, the standard deviation of INCOME is almost identical to the coefficient of variation of expected income (that is, the probability weighted sum of the untransformed incomes). To facilitate comparisons with variables examined earlier, the range of the left-hand vertical axis for the standard deviation has been constrained to be identical to that in figures 2.1 to 2.3 and 5.18. The coefficient of variation is measured on the right-hand vertical axis.

It is clear from figure 5.26 that regardless of which measure of dispersion one relies on, the extent of regional dispersion in the composite income variable is relatively small. The standard deviation of INCOME hovers around 0.1 throughout the 1966–96 period, which is very close in magnitude to the coefficients of variation of real average weekly earnings and of the probability of state 1. This observation suggests that variation in INCOME is dominated by that of state 1, in which individuals are employed throughout the year. This is not surprising because the probability of state 1 is much larger than that of the other states – it is rarely less than 0.7 (or 70 percent), even in Newfoundland, and often above 0.9 in low-unemployment provinces. Figure 5.26 also shows that the regional dispersion of INCOME is somewhat cyclical, with peaks reached in 1971, 1981, and 1991. Each peak precedes several years of decline, as if regional dispersion tended to fall slightly during the recessions of the early 1970s, the early 1980s, and the early 1990s.

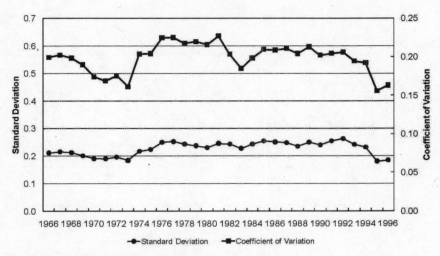

Figure 5.27   Regional dispersion of *LEISURE*

Figure 5.27 shows that regional dispersion of *LEISURE*, the probability-weighted sum of the logs of leisure times in the four states of the world, is slightly higher than that of *INCOME*. In most years during the sample period its standard deviation is close to 0.25 However, its behaviour is a little different from that of the standard deviation of *INCOME*. After declining for most years up to 1973, its direction changed, resulting in an increase in its regional dispersion during the recession of the mid-seventies. Between 1977 and 1992 there was little change in the standard deviation of *LEISURE*, but after 1992 it started to decrease again. If we compare figures 5.26 and 5.27, we can see that the standard deviations of *INCOME* and *LEISURE* tended to move in opposite directions between 1973 and 1977, but in the same direction between 1992 and 1996.

Earlier, while examining both after-tax real incomes and probabilities of the four states of the world, we singled out Ontario and Newfoundland, two provinces that have often been considered to be at opposite ends of the Canadian economic spectrum. Figures 5.28 and 5.29 continue this comparison, once again displaying differences between Ontario and Newfoundland that reveal the migration incentives embodied in the variables *INCOME* and *LEISURE*.[18] When one compares the two graphs, it is immediately obvious that the differentials in *INCOME* and *LEISURE* tend to move in opposite directions. During the first few years of the sample period the difference in

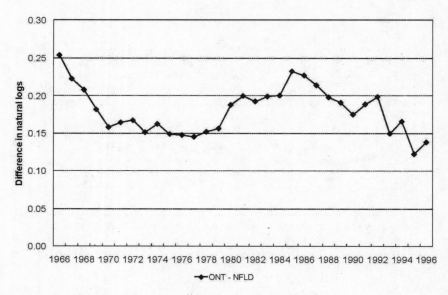

Figure 5.28   Difference in *INCOME*, Ontario minus Newfoundland, stayers

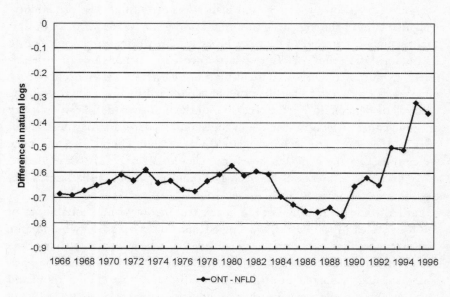

Figure 5.29   Difference in *LEISURE*, Ontario minus Newfoundland, stayers

INCOME is falling, while the difference in LEISURE is rising. This means that as Ontario was becoming less attractive relative to Newfoundland in terms of INCOME, its attractiveness relative to Newfoundland in terms of LEISURE was increasing. During the early 1980s, though, the reverse appears to be true. Ontario was then becoming more attractive relative to Newfoundland with respect to INCOME, and less attractive relative to Newfoundland with respect to LEISURE.

Exactly what is driving these changes is not clear, but it is perhaps noteworthy that there is no indication that the introduction of the variable entrance requirement in 1971 or regional extended benefits in 1977 made Newfoundland relatively more attractive to potential migrants. In fact, both the INCOME and LEISURE differentials actually rose in favour of Ontario for several years after 1977. The effects of changes in unemployment insurance policies as measured by INCOME and LEISURE are apparently more subtle than one might guess by looking only at the insurance parameters themselves.

The most striking feature of figures 5.28 and 5.29, however, is not that the two differentials often move in opposite directions. Rather, it is that throughout our sample period the differential in INCOME is always positive and the differential in LEISURE is always negative. In other words, the variable INCOME, and thus the expected utility arising from the consumption opportunities it represents, is always greater in Ontario than in Newfoundland, providing individuals with a strong incentive to prefer Ontario to Newfoundland. At the same time, the variable LEISURE, and the expected utility arising from the leisure time associated with it, is always greater in Newfoundland than in Ontario, providing individuals with an equally strong incentive to choose Newfoundland over Ontario. Which effect dominates in the end will depend on how individuals value consumption relative to leisure time.

Because LEISURE and INCOME are so important to our model, before moving on to other things it is worthwhile to look more closely at the migration incentives they imply. How do they rank the provinces in terms of their attractiveness? First, figures 5.30a,b plot each province's value of INCOME (once again for stayers) relative to the ten-province average. Comparing the two figures, one can see that the five easternmost provinces almost always have below-average values of INCOME during our sample period, while the five westernmost provinces almost always have above-average values of INCOME. Perhaps the biggest change occurred during the late seventies, when Quebec slipped below the Canadian average, to be replaced by Saskatchewan above the average. However, the deviations from the Canadian

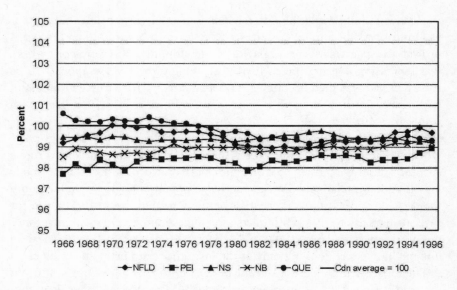

Figure 5.30a *INCOME* relative to 10-province average (stayers)

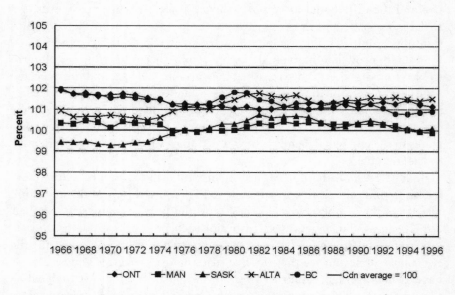

Figure 5.30b *INCOME* relative to 10-province average (stayers)

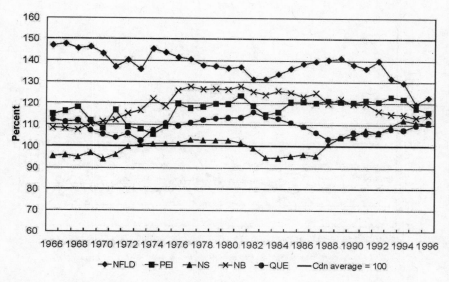

Figure 5.31a   *LEISURE* relative to 10-province average

average value of INCOME are always small – between two percentage points above the Canadian average and three percentage points below.

Although the relative positions of the ten provinces in figures 5.30a,b seem consistent with the general view that the eastern provinces are the "have-not" provinces of Canada, when we compare this figure to figure 2.4, we can see that the ranking of the provinces with respect to INCOME is not as consistent with their ranking with respect to average weekly earnings as one might expect. In figure 2.4 we can see that during the 1966–96 period earnings are generally above the average in Quebec and Newfoundland and below the average in Manitoba and Saskatchewan, while the reverse is true for INCOME. This observation suggests that looking at earnings alone may provide a misleading impression of the income-related incentives to migrate between provinces. Because it incorporates more types of income, as well as uncertainty with respect to the receipt of different types of income, the INCOME composite provides a more accurate measure of those incentives.

Just as we found that relative differences in unemployment rates were more pronounced than those in wages, relative differences in LEISURE are more pronounced than those in INCOME. We can see this simply by comparing the ranges of the vertical axes in figures 5.30a,b and 5.31a,b. Figure 5.31a also reveals that the five easternmost provinces, which tended to have below-average values of INCOME, tend to have above-average values

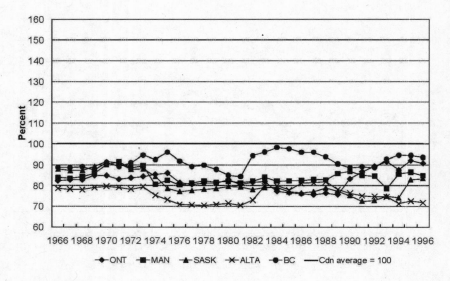

Figure 5.31b   *LEISURE* relative to 10-province average

of *LEISURE*, while the reverse is true for the five westernmost provinces. In this case the correspondence between the ranking of provinces with respect to the standard indicator of employment opportunities, the unemployment rate (in figure 2.5), and *LEISURE* is stronger than was the case for wages and *INCOME*. The five provinces that generally have the lowest unemployment rates also have the lowest values of *LEISURE*; similarly, Newfoundland has both the highest unemployment rate and the highest value of *LEISURE* during our sample period. This correspondence between unemployment rates and *LEISURE* is not surprising, since through the workings of the unemployment insurance system increases in a province's unemployment rate decrease *MIN* and *MXYR*, which in turn raises *LEISURE*.

However, our model of migration attaches a different interpretation to the variable *LEISURE* than to the unemployment rate. In our model leisure time is a "good," which means that increases in *LEISURE* make a province more attractive. But this does not mean that our model should be interpreted as implying that higher unemployment makes a province more attractive. Instead, we must bear in mind that in the context of the model, we are looking at the effect of increasing one variable, in this case *LEISURE,* while holding all other variables constant. Thus the model implies that increases in *LEISURE*, regardless of how they come about, should increase individual welfare and make a destination more attractive, *as long as INCOME remains constant in that destination.* In contrast, in the real world unemployment is usually accompanied by a decrease in income for the individual who is now unemployed, because unemployment insurance benefits replace less than 100 percent of wage income. This is in fact what happens in our model too, when we compare any one of the unemployment states to the full-year employment state, state 1. But our model enables us to go beyond this simple trade-off between income and unemployment by combining the effects of the changes in incomes and leisure times with the probability that each state will occur, so as to create two new summary measures INCOME and LEISURE that show how these components of individual welfare will be affected ex ante. Since migration decisions must often be made ex ante, that is, before the individual knows which state of the world will materialize, if our model is correct, INCOME and LEISURE are better indicators of the migration incentives perceived by individuals than are variables such as wages and unemployment rates. While the migration incentives embodied in INCOME and LEISURE point in opposite directions, in principle our estimation results should help us sort out the separate effects on migration of each of them.

FROM MEASUREMENT TO ESTIMATION

Although INCOME and LEISURE constitute only two of over twenty explanatory variables in our estimating equations, they and the migration series account for most of the data that had to be collected for this project. Most of the remaining variables are dummy variables whose exact definitions are provided in the next chapter along with the expected signs of their coefficients. But before moving on to that chapter, it is useful to return momentarily to the real fiscal benefit measures included in the vector F in equation (4.5). As we mentioned in chapter 4, in the face of serious data limitations we decided that the best course of action was to rely on fiscal aggregates to represent these variables, despite their many limitations. Hence the elements of the vector F are represented by real per capita government spending as measured by Statistics Canada.[19] To capture the mix effect of government spending, we divide spending by provincial and local governments into three categories and also include real per capita federal spending. As indicated in equation (4.5), it is the natural log of each of these variables that actually appears in the estimating equations.

As for the migration incentives implied by these measures of real fiscal benefits, they have already been examined in chapter 2.[20] There we saw that of these four variables, it is actually real per capita federal spending that seems to vary most across provinces, not provincial/local government spending, and that have-not provinces such as Nova Scotia and Prince Edward Island have been the primary beneficiaries of this federal largesse. If individuals place a high enough value on these federally provided public services, these relatively high fiscal benefits may help to encourage in-migration to these provinces in spite of their relative low values of *INCOME*. But if individuals instead place a higher weight on expected consumption possibilities, then we may find that even enjoying a much higher level of federal spending is not enough to encourage greater in-migration to a province in which *INCOME* is relatively low. The estimation results presented in the following chapters will help us to determine whether public policies or private market conditions are more important to potential migrants in Canada.

6

Estimation

Our discussion of the descriptive data in chapter 2, as well as the review of the statistical literature that follows it, together suggest to us that there are in fact links between public policy and interprovincial migration to be uncovered and that further investigation is warranted. In this chapter we consider the parameter estimates of our own conditional logit model of migration and in later chapters use these estimates to assess the nature and quantitative importance of fiscally induced migration in Canada.

Although the model we presented earlier is well defined, it does leave us with some room to experiment with alternative specifications. The principal difference between the alternative specifications we consider is the manner in which the risk aversion of migrants is incorporated in the model. Later in this chapter we explore the impact on the parameter estimates of altering this aspect of our empirical model.

We also present and assess estimates for different disaggregations of our migration data. Initially we consider estimates by income class and then examine some of the differences between age- and gender-specific subgroups within each income class. Most of the estimation results are for the 1974 to 1996 period, for which 100 percent of tax files were available, but we also discuss some results that extend the sample backwards to 1968, prior to the 1971 unemployment insurance reforms.

Although most issues related to the choice of explanatory variables have already been addressed in chapter 4, before turning to the parameter estimates themselves, we define clearly all the variables that are included in the empirical models, as well as our expectations regarding the signs of their coefficients. We then discuss the parameter estimates by income class in section 6.2. Both the statistical significance and the within-sample predictive power of the estimated models are examined. In section 6.3 we look at how the parameter estimates vary when the data are disaggregated by age and sex as well as by income class. Discussions of the economic importance of the parameter estimates, however, is left to the next two chapters, in which we consider the effects on migration flows of small or marginal changes in policy-related migration incentives and then simulate the consequences of some counterfactual policy scenarios.

SUMMARY OF EXPLANATORY VARIABLES

Table 6.1 lists all the variables included in our principal empirical models of migration, together with their definitions. As shown in the table, these variables can be divided into seven categories: basic variables, variables measuring additional risk aversion, moving cost variables, public expenditure variables, a dummy variable identifying inflows to Quebec, extraordinary event variables, and a series of dummy variables that account for other locational attributes. Many of these variables are related to the extensions of the model discussed in the section of chapter 4 titled "Extensions to Deal with Risk Aversion, Moving Costs, and Extraordinary Events."

The first two variables in table 6.1, *INCOME* and *LEISURE*, are called "basic" variables because they are related to the two primary sources of individual welfare in the model of chapter 4, consumption and leisure time. As we noted in chapter 4, economic theory predicts that the coefficients of both *INCOME* and *LEISURE* will be positive, since both consumption and leisure usually provide individuals with positive utility. In other words, holding *LEISURE* and all other variables constant, individuals prefer destinations with higher levels of *INCOME*. Similarly, holding *INCOME* and all other variables constant, individuals prefer destinations that offer higher levels of *LEISURE*.

Next, as discussed in the section of chapter 4 on extensions of the model, we include the probabilities of states 2, 3 and 4 to reflect the possibilities that individuals are more risk averse than the expected utility function (4.7) implies and suffer a loss of well-being if they are unemployed. Economic theory provides us with little guidance as to exactly how these probabilities should enter into the model. For this reason we experimented with different ways of incorporating them in the empirical model. The table shows how we did so. In Model 1, the probabilities of the three unemployment states, denoted $P2$, $P3$, and $P4$ in table 6.1, enter directly into the model. Note that $P2$, $P3$, and $P4$ correspond to the theoretical variables π_2, π_3, and π_4 of table 4.1. In Model 2, the natural log of the sum of the three probabilities, denoted $LP234$, enters instead. The difference between the two specifications is that the first allows each of the different unemployment states to affect utility

Table 6.1
Definitions of Variables: Empirical Model

Variable Name	Definition
Basic variables	
INCOME	Probability-weighted log income variable – see equation (4.8)
LEISURE	Probability-weighted log leisure variable – see equation (4.9)
Additional risk aversion	
P2 (Model 1 only)	Probability of state 2
P3 (Model 1 only)	Probability of state 3
P4 (Model 1 only)	Probability of state 4
LP234 (Model 2 only)	ln $(P2+P3+P4)$
Moving costs	
DISTANCE	Road distance in kilometres between major cities in each province
DSTAY	Dummy variable equal to 1 for stayers and 0 for movers
Public expenditure	Natural log of real per capita non-interest current and capital spending:
HEALTH	By provincial and local governments on health
EDUCATION	By provincial and local governments on education
OTHER SPENDING	By provincial and local governments on other functions
FEDERAL SPENDING	By federal government on all functions
Locational amenities	
NFLD	1 if destination is Newfoundland, 0 otherwise
PEI	1 if destination is Prince Edward Island, 0 otherwise
NS	1 if destination is Nova Scotia, 0 otherwise
NB	1 if destination is New Brunswick, 0 otherwise
QUE	1 if destination is Quebec, 0 otherwise
ONT	1 if destination is Ontario, 0 otherwise
MAN	1 if destination is Manitoba, 0 otherwise
SASK	1 if destination is Saskatchewan, 0 otherwise
ALTA	1 if destination is Alberta, 0 otherwise
Migration to Quebec	
QUEBEC	1 if migration flow *to* Quebec from *outside* Quebec, 0 otherwise
Extraordinary events	
OCT	1 if migration flow *from* Quebec to elsewhere, 1969–71, 0 otherwise
OCT2	1 if migration flow *to* Quebec from elsewhere, 1969–71, 0 otherwise
PQ	1 if migration flow *from* Quebec to elsewhere, 1977–80, 0 otherwise
PQ2	1 if migration flow *to* Quebec from elsewhere, 1977–80, 0 otherwise
FISH	1 if migration flow *from* NFLD to elsewhere, 1993–96, 0 otherwise
FISH2	1 if migration flow *to* NFLD from elsewhere, 1993–96, 0 otherwise

differently, which would be appropriate if the three unemployment states were not equally undesirable. The second specification implies that what matters most when making migration decisions is the overall probability of unemployment, not the probabilities of particular unemployment states. If individuals are indeed more risk averse than the basic model implies or care about employment per se, then individuals should be less likely to migrate to regions with high probabilities of unemployment, which means that the coefficient of each additional risk aversion variable should be negative.

While there is no particular theoretical reason to take the log of the sum of probabilities, in Model 2 we do so simply because in the Cobb-Douglas functional form we have adopted for the direct utility function all variables are measured in logs. In the case of Model 1, we do not use the log form of individual probabilities. Because the probabilities of states 2, 3, and 4 are small, the log transformation may give a larger weight to them.[1] This problem is avoided in Model 2 by using a sum of probabilities. We also note that regardless of the manner in which the probabilities enter the model, likelihood ratio tests indicate that the null hypothesis that they belong there cannot be rejected.[2]

Properly accounting for moving costs in any empirical model of migration is difficult because an important part of the cost of moving is likely a psychic cost that is not directly observable or measurable. Foregone earnings and the monetary cost of moving, which are measurable, are included in the variable INCOME, but the psychic costs should not be ignored. Such costs of leaving family and friends behind may depend on distance, so we include DISTANCE, the road distance between major cities in each province, in the set of explanatory variables. Since the psychic costs of moving likely increase with the distance from one's original place of residence, we expect the coefficient of DISTANCE to be negative. In addition, as discussed earlier, we include DSTAY, a dummy variable equal to one for a staying choice (i.e., when $i = j$), and zero otherwise. DSTAY represents unmeasured fixed costs of moving, some of which may be psychic costs, including the costs of selling a home and of finding a new place to live, neither of which are likely to vary with distance. Note that the inclusion of DSTAY in the model ensures that the expected utility associated with staying, EU_{ii}, will differ from the expected utility associated with all moves ($EU_{ij}, j \neq i$) even if the attributes of all regions are identical. If there are indeed fixed costs associated with moving, then we should expect the coefficient of DSTAY to be positive.[3]

Because they directly reflect public policies that benefit individuals, the public expenditure variables are important to our empirical model. As discussed previously, we divide provincial government spending into several components in order to capture the mix effects associated with public spending. These components include real per capita current and capital spending by provinces and municipalities on health (HEALTH), education (EDUCATION), and all other non-interest provincial and local spending except for social services (OTHER SPENDING). Social service spending is excluded to avoid double-counting – recall that social assistance benefits are already incorporated in INCOME. We also include federal spending on goods, services, and capital (FEDERAL SPENDING). We expect the effect of each type of public expenditure to be positive; in other words, the higher is public spending in region j, the higher should be in-migration to that province, holding all else constant. A negative coefficient for any of these four variables would imply that the corresponding services reduce individual welfare.

The next nine variables in table 6.1 are provincial dummy variables that represent provincial attributes or locational amenities that do not change much over time, including climate and cultural factors. They correspond to the vector A in equation (4.5). These variables also allow to some extent for unmeasured components of variables already included in the model that vary systematically across provinces. Each variable is defined to equal one if the destination is the province identified, regardless of the province of origin.[4] Since there is no variable for British Columbia, the coefficients of these variables measure the difference between the effect on utility of unmeasured locational attributes of the specified province and the effect in British Columbia. A positive and significant coefficient for one of these variables would indicate that the overall effect of the unmeasured locational attributes of the province in question outweighs those of British Columbia, while a negative and significant coefficient would imply that holding all else constant, British Columbia is more attractive than the other province.

It should be noted that when alternative-specific constants are included in the model, the conditional logit framework ensures that the total number of people in the data set (summing over years and provinces of origin) who are predicted to choose a particular province will equal the actual number of people who chose that province. This in turn ensures that the total predicted *net* migration flow over the entire estimation period for any province of origin will equal the actual net flow.[5]

Following previous studies of interprovincial migration in Canada (see, for example, Winer and Gauthier 1982a), we also include in our empirical models a dummy variable that allows for the general effect of language and culture in Quebec on the pattern of internal migration in Canada. This variable, called QUEBEC, is defined to be 1 if migration is to Quebec from a province other than Quebec, and zero otherwise. While it would have been preferable to include a variable that distinguished between potential migrants who speak English and those who speak French, our data do not distinguish between the two.[6] QUEBEC is expected to have a negative sign, since, ceteris paribus, migration between provinces other than Quebec is expected to be higher than that between the rest of Canada and Quebec.

The remaining variables in table 6.1 are included in order to capture the effects on interprovincial migration of certain extraordinary events associated with the public sector that may not be allowed for by the other variables already included in the model. The investigation of these events is somewhat preliminary in nature because the timing of them for estimation purposes is based on ex-post identification of the relevant dates and because we have not explicitly included these events in our theoretical model of individual migration decisions. Nonetheless, as noted earlier, such events may have had effects on internal migration that are easier to distinguish than those of normal, day-to-day policies. Furthermore, ignoring them is likely to result in a misspecified model because these events are probably not adequately captured by changes in the other included variables, such as wages or unemployment rates.

Here we focus on three extraordinary events that occurred during our sample period. The first covers the period 1969 to 1971, which includes both the large demonstration associated with Bill 63 (an early language law) that occurred in 1969 and the kidnapping crisis of October 1970. This period of unrest in Quebec is reflected in the variables OCT, which equals 1 for outflows from Quebec and 0 otherwise and allows for increased out-migration from Quebec during the 1969-71 period, and OCT2, which equals 1 for inflows to Quebec and 0 otherwise and allows for the possibility that these events also reduced in-migration to Quebec. Because not all of our migration data extend back to 1968, these two variables can be included only when the longer ten percent data set is employed.

Similarly, PQ and PQ2 are included to capture the net outflow from Quebec during the 1977–80 period, over and above what can be explained by all other variables in the model, that may have followed the election of the Parti Québécois in 1976, our second extraordinary event.[7] Anecdotal evidence suggests that the election of the Parti Québécois caused many anglophones to leave Quebec, and it may also have reduced inflows to the province. Finally, FISH and FISH2, defined in a fashion analogous to the other dummy variables, are included to test for the extent to which the closing of the cod fishery in 1992 affected migration to and from Newfoundland over the period from 1993 to 1996.

Statistically significant coefficients for these extraordinary event dummy variables indicate that the effects of these important policy changes are not fully captured by rest of the model. In other words, such results imply that any changes in wages, unemployment probabilities, and other variables that might have been caused by the extraordinary events cannot fully explain the changes in migration flows that accompanied them. Since the events in question had negative consequences for substantial groups living in the immediately affected provinces and appear to have made the affected regions less attractive at least for some people, we expect the coefficients of OCT, PQ, and FISH to be positive and the coefficients of OCT2, PQ2, and FISH2 to be negative, implying that outflows increased and inflows decreased in each case. Anecdotal evidence surrounding the events in question suggests these patterns, which remain to be confirmed by our statistical analysis.

ESTIMATES BY INCOME CLASS

As we saw in figure 5.13, throughout our sample period rates of interprovincial mobility in Canada differed across income classes, with low-income individuals being almost twice as mobile as high-income individuals. Therefore, even though it is impossible to construct income class-specific data on the explanatory variables of our model, it is desirable to estimate migration models for each income class separately. Differences in the estimated coefficients for each income class compensate to a large extent for the lack of income class-specific data on the explanatory variables.

All estimates were generated by maximizing the likelihood function defined by equation (4.11). Estimates of migration functions by income class were carried out using data for both the 1974–96 period and the extended 1968–96 period. We discuss each of these sample periods in turn.

1974–1996

Table 6.2 presents estimates of the parameters of Models 1 and 2 for the three different income classes for the 1974–96 period. The migration counts for these models were derived from the 100 percent income tax tapes discussed in chapter 5. The first three columns present the results for Model 1, in which the probabilities of states 2, 3, and 4 (P2, P3, and P4) are included as explanatory variables. The last three columns present estimates for Model 2, in which the three probabilities are replaced by LP234, the natural log of the sum of the three probabilities. The sample used to generate each set of

Table 6.2
Parameter estimates by Income Class, 1974–96

Variable	Model 1			Model 2		
	Low Income	Middle Income	High Income	Low Income	Middle Income	High Income
INCOME	1.806	2.391	1.507	0.748	1.200	0.416
	(41.79)	(63.93)	(35.07)	(18.35)	(34.23)	(10.29)
LEISURE	2.832	7.105	4.887	0.571	0.904	-0.010***
	(12.61)	(36.29)	(21.10)	(26.87)	(46.70)	(-0.44)
HEALTH	-0.471	-0.414	-0.300	0.169	0.149	0.192
	(-28.24)	(-29.33)	(-18.57)	(11.19)	(11.57)	(12.93)
EDUCATION	0.388	-0.007***	-0.161	0.662	0.327	0.054
	(26.35)	(-0.521)	(-10.93)	(45.04)	(25.22)	(3.62)
OTHER SPENDING	-0.198	-0.341	-0.419	-0.357	-0.494	-0.547
	(-22.91)	(-45.05)	(-48.78)	(-41.89)	(-66.51)	(-64.72)
FEDERAL SPENDING	0.229	0.493	0.514	-0.429	-0.214	-0.137**
	(22.95)	(59.61)	(52.36)	(-52.02)	(-31.05)	(-1.66)
DSTAY	1.576	1.848	1.378	1.496	1.761	1.290
	(155.60)	(207.18)	(133.47)	(149.42)	(199.67)	(126.24)
DISTANCE	-0.502	-0.504	-0.599	-0.517	-0.521	-0.616
	(-349.25)	(-398.90)	(-409.63)	(-365.71)	(-419.18)	(-427.42)
P2	-28.979	-42.977	-30.780			
	(-40.50)	(-69.11)	(-41.82)			
P3	-13.396	-26.861	-21.103			
	(-18.53)	(-42.61)	(-28.25)			
P4	-9.890	-23.780	-17.150			
	(-13.11)	(-36.09)	(-22.03)			
LNP234				-0.748	-0.842	-0.477
				(-127.85)	(-158.58)	(-79.98)
QUEBEC	-2.243	-2.351	-2.065	-2.240	-2.348	-2.066
	(-407.27))	(-487.53)	(-399.05)	(-406.51)	(-486.77)	(-399.20)
PQ	0.232	0.405	0.486	0.294	0.460	0.545
	(29.48)	(64.73)	(73.27)	(37.61)	(74.28)	(83.36)
PQ2	0.151	0.156	0.076	0.076	0.095	0.013***
	(15.87)	(19.12)	(8.39)	(8.08)	(11.69)	(1.50)

Table 6.2 (continued)

	Model 1			Model 2		
Variable	Low Income	Middle Income	High Income	Low Income	Middle Income	High Income
FISH	0.105	−0.142	−0.267	0.003 ***	−0.291	−0.361
	(10.47)	(−13.08)	(−17.97)	(0.316)	(−26.83)	(−24.41)
FISH2	−0.883	−1.168	−1.084	−0.790	−1.030	−0.995
	(−60.65)	(−83.23)	(−64.56)	(−54.54)	(−73.62)	(−59.48)
NFLD	0.354	0.469	−0.054	−0.572	−0.641	−0.903
	(27.45)	(41.11)	(−3.87)	(−56.85)	(−71.78)	(−86.85)
PEI	−0.883	−0.835	−1.521	−0.992	−1.049	−1.738
	(−66.57)	(−73.32)	(−110.37)	(−78.46)	(−97.81)	(−136.26)
NS	−0.491	−0.661	−1.069	−0.211	−0.378	−0.890
	(−40.99)	(−66.12)	(−90.12)	(−17.93)	(−39.23)	(−75.75)
NB	−0.052	−0.041	−0.539	−0.335	−0.428	−0.842
	(−5.41)	(−4.97)	(−54.72)	(−37.89)	(−56.57)	(−94.78)
QUE	1.577	1.897	1.505	1.319	1.554	1.274
	(204.72)	(285.40)	(198.91)	(180.53)	(248.98)	(178.52)
ONT	−0.252	−0.342	−0.263	0.120	0.050	0.039
	(−41.76)	(−66.31)	(−44.42)	(24.06)	(11.57)	(7.78)
MAN	−1.046	−1.177	−1.377	−0.721	−0.839	−1.138
	(−156.59)	(−208.97)	(−212.09)	(−112.50)	(−153.21)	(−180.63)
SASK	−1.136	−1.083	−1.212	−1.010	−0.971	−1.127
	(−176.52)	(−194.70)	(−194.34)	(−159.85)	(−177.33)	(−183.35)
ALTA	−0.543	−0.541	−0.542	−0.595	−0.589	−0.538
	(−90.62)	(−103.05)	(−91.09)	(−99.59)	(−112.58)	(−91.72)
Log L	−7213435	−9794318	−8019435	−7216434	−9806258	−8022762
Log L_0	−92028900	−165821900	−163142600	−92028900	−165821900	−163142600
McFadden's R^2	0.922	0.941	0.951	0.922	0.941	0.951
No. of observations	2300	2300	2300	2300	2300	2300

Notes: The values in parentheses under the parameter estimates are t-statistics. All coefficients are statistically significant at the 1% level of significance unless otherwise indicated. One asterisk (*) indicates significance at the 5% level, two asterisks (**) indicate significance at the 10% level, and three asterisks (***) indicate that the coefficient is not statistically significant at a level of significance less than or equal to 10%. Log L is the value of the log of the likelihood function at the parameter estimates, while Log L_0 is the maximum value of the log of the likelihood function for a model with only alternative-specific constants. McFadden's (1974b) pseudo R^2 is given by $1-(\text{Log } L/\text{Log } L_0)$. Finally, although the test statistic is not included in the table, the likelihood ratio test always indicates that the model with alternative-specific constants can be rejected at the 1% level.

estimates consisted of 2,300 observations – 100 origin-destination flows observed over a period of 23 years.

A quick glance at the summary statistics for the six sets of estimation results shows that the pseudo R^2 values are all in excess of 0.9, indicating that on average the model fits well. In addition, likelihood ratio tests of the overall significance of each model compared to one that includes *only* the alternative-specific constants indicate that the latter can always be rejected at the 1 percent significance level. So the models appear to have a high degree of explanatory power. The table also shows that nearly all the coefficient estimates have high *t* statistics; only five are not significant at the 1 percent level and of those, one is in fact significant at the 10 percent level. These results with respect to the individual significance of the coefficients seems to confirm the conclusions implied by the pseudo R^2 and likelihood ratio tests.

But what of the interpretations of the coefficient estimates? Are they consistent with our expectations? Consider first the coefficients of the two basic variables, *INCOME* and *LEISURE*. The coefficient of *INCOME* is positive and significant in all six equations, suggesting that individuals do indeed value positively the prospect of higher expected income, although the magnitude of the coefficient does vary across income classes. Interestingly, in both Models 1 and 2 it is highest for the middle-income class. With one exception – the high-income class in Model 2 – the coefficient of *LEISURE* is positive and significant as well, indicating as expected that individuals also value the prospect of more leisure time positively. For the high-income class the coefficient is not significant.

One notable difference between the results for Models 1 and 2 involves the size of the coefficients on *INCOME* and *LEISURE*: the coefficients on these two variables are smaller in Model 2 than in Model 1. Moreover, the ratio of the coefficient of *INCOME* to the coefficient of *LEISURE* is larger in Model 2. For example, for the low income class it is 0.6 for Model 1 and 1.3 for Model 2. What this means is that *LEISURE* plays a more important role relative to *INCOME* in determining migration decisions in the Model 1 estimates.

Note that because *INCOME* is a function of several policy and market variables, the positive coefficient for *INCOME* also provides us with insights into the effects on migration of these component variables. For example, it implies that holding all else constant, an increase in wages or social assistance benefits in province *i* will increase in-migration to and decrease out-migration from that province. A decrease in the income tax rate imposed by province *i* will have the same effect. Increases in the monetary cost of moving, which reduce after-tax income, will have the reverse effect.

Like the coefficient of *INCOME*, the coefficients of the additional risk aversion variables in both models are statistically significant, and all have the expected negative sign in both models. Combined with the results for *INCOME* and *LEISURE*, the negative coefficients for the probabilities of the unemployment states imply not only that individuals tend to avoid regions where employment prospects are relatively poor but also that they do not like additional leisure in the form of unemployment. While additional leisure time does increase welfare, a higher probability of unemployment evidently has the reverse effect, holding *LEISURE* constant.

The fact that *INCOME* has a statistically significant coefficient ensures that the monetary costs of moving will have an impact on migration, as they are among the components of net income. But the significant coefficients of *DSTAY* and *DISTANCE* in all the equations of table 6.2 show that moving costs have additional effects on interprovincial migration flows. Specifically, the positive coefficient of *DSTAY* implies that there do exist fixed costs associated with moving that serve as a deterrent to migration, while the negative coefficient of *DISTANCE* implies that people are more likely to move to nearby provinces than far away ones, holding all else constant. Again, these results are consistent with our prior expectations.

As far as the alternative-specific constants are concerned, we had no prior expectations regarding their sign because they are omnibus variables that account for many different factors. However, they are all statistically significant, and though their magnitudes vary across income classes and models, for all provinces except Newfoundland and Ontario the signs are the same in all equations. The negative signs of the coefficients for Prince Edward Island, Nova Scotia, New Brunswick, Manitoba, Saskatchewan, and Alberta suggest that on average these provinces are considered less attractive than British Columbia, while the positive coefficients for Quebec (*QUE*) imply that it is the one province that is preferred to British Columbia by individuals in all three income classes, holding all else constant. At the same time, the negative coefficient for the dummy variable *QUEBEC* indicates that in-migration to Quebec from other provinces declined over the 1974–96 period even after controlling for other possible determinants of migration. These two apparently conflicting results can be reconciled by noting that *QUEBEC* is equal to o for flows from Quebec to Quebec, while *QUE* is 1 for such flows. Thus the positive coefficient of *QUE* may largely reflect a strong preference on the part of Quebec residents to remain there, perhaps for linguistic reasons.

For the remaining two provinces, the results appear to be sensitive to the model specification. The alternative-specific constant for Ontario has a negative coefficient for all income classes in Model 1, and a positive coefficient for all income classes in Model 2. In the case of Newfoundland, the coefficient is positive for the low- and middle-income classes in Model 1 and negative for all income classes in Model 2 and for the high-income class in Model 1. These inconsistencies in sign make it difficult to draw any general conclusions regarding Canadians' preferences with respect to these two provinces.

Like the coefficients of NFLD and ONT, the coefficients of three of the four public spending variables – HEALTH, EDUCATION, and FEDERAL SPENDING – differ across models, and their signs are frequently inconsistent with our expectations. Although the coefficients of all three were expected to be positive for all income classes, the coefficient of HEALTH is positive only in Model 2, while the coefficient of FEDERAL SPENDING is positive only in Model 1. The coefficient of EDUCATION, meanwhile, appears to be positive for all income classes in Model 2 and positive for the low-income class in Model 1. For the middle-income class in Model 1 it is not statistically significant.

OTHER SPENDING, as it turns out, is the only government spending variable whose coefficient has a consistent sign across all equations estimated. Its negative sign is unexpected but easier to explain than the negative signs of some of the coefficients of the other government spending variables. This category of provincial government spending includes many different government functions – provincial recreation and culture, protection of persons and property, transportation, industrial development, and regional planning, among others – some of which will have a more direct impact on individuals' well-being than others. The negative coefficient on this variable could simply indicate that on balance, individuals do not directly benefit from the components of OTHER SPENDING. [8]

How can we explain the unexpected signs and magnitudes of some coefficients, and the inconsistencies in some of the results across models? The most likely explanation is correlation between explanatory variables, a possibility that was first raised in section 4.2. In fact, the coefficient of correlation between $LP234$ and LEISURE is 0.9575.[9] LEISURE is also highly correlated with $P2$, $P3$, and $P4$ – the R^2 from the regression of LEISURE on these three variables is 0.9992. This correlation arises not only because the probabilities are used as weights in the construction of LEISURE but also because leisure times in states 2 and 3 depend on the variables MIN and MXYR, which in turn are directly related to provincial unemployment rates through the workings of the unemployment insurance system. In high-unemployment provinces, MIN and MXYR will be lower, and expected leisure higher, than in low-unemployment provinces. Since $P2$, $P3$, and $P4$ (as well as $LP234$) are all highly correlated with the provincial unemployment rates used in the construction of MIN and MXYR, it is not surprising that they are also correlated with LEISURE.[10]

In the case of the coefficients of the government spending variables, the nature of the correlation involved appears to be complicated. Simple correlations between the probabilities of unemployment in either form and the fiscal spending variables in the data as a whole are low (see appendix E, table E1). As discussed in chapter 4, collinearity between the additional risk aversion variables, the government spending variables, and possibly also INCOME and LEISURE can arise as a consequence of structural relationships between private market and public sector variables.

Although multicollinearity may affect the coefficients of INCOME, LEISURE, the additional risk aversion variables, the alternative specific dummy variables, and especially the four government spending variables, the coefficients of most of the remaining variables are not greatly affected. The coefficients of DSTAY and DISTANCE differ more across income classes than across model specifications, as do the coefficients of the dummy variables representing extraordinary events.[11] As anticipated, the coefficient of PQ has the expected positive sign. Events in Quebec during the 1977–80 period appear to have led to gross out-migration of adults between the ages of 20 and 64, as shown by the positive coefficients on PQ for all income classes and both models. This is what one should expect of events that create uncertainties about the future for large groups in a province. On the other hand, gross in-migration also increased during this period, as indicated by the positive and significant coefficient on PQ2 for all income classes in Model 1 and the two lowest income classes in Model 2.

The results also indicate that the closing of the cod fishery led to smaller gross in-flows to Newfoundland, since the coefficient on FISH2 is negative in all equations in table 6.2. But the fishery closing is not clearly associated with increased gross out-migration except in the case of the low-income group in Model 1, since the coefficient on FISH is negative for the middle- and high-income groups. As with other variables, simulations are required to sort out the relative strength of the countervailing tendencies indicated by the coefficient estimates on the extraordinary event dummy variables.

Summarizing, we may say that our results for the 1974–96 period appear to be broadly consistent with our expectations. In our results thus far, income and leisure are positive goods, people avoid places where employment prospects are poor, and moving costs discourage migration.

The high pseudo R^2 values also suggest that the model fits the data well. To further assess the fit of the model, we computed the correlation between the actual and fitted values of each of the 100 migration rates, for each

Table 6.3
Summary Statistics for Correlations between Actual and Fitted Migration Rates, 1974–96

	Minimum	Maximum	Mean
Model 1			
Low Income	−0.5134	0.9597	0.3132
Middle Income	−0.4372	0.9002	0.3615
High Income	−0.4582	0.8641	0.3612
Model 2			
Low Income	−0.7648	0.9163	0.2570
Middle Income	−0.7749	0.8862	0.3231
High Income	−0.6287	0.8603	0.3396

Note: See table E2 of appendix E for the correlation coefficients for individual origin-destination pairs.

income class and both models, instead of relying only on the summary R^2 statistic. Table 6.3 summarizes the results of these calculations by presenting the maximum, minimum, and average correlation coefficient for each model and income class.[12] As the table shows, although the largest correlation coefficient in each case exceeds 0.8, the average coefficient of correlation is smaller, between 0.2 and 0.4 in each of the six cases examined. These values are not high, given that time-series data have been used to produce the estimates. Furthermore, as the first column of the table indicates, negative correlations between actual and fitted values, which imply that the actual and predicted migration rates are moving in opposite directions over time, also occur. Thus the model does not predict all 100 migration rates equally well. For example, for the low-income class, Model 1 predicts the rate of migration from Quebec to Alberta quite well for all income classes (the corresponding correlation coefficients are all greater than 0.85), but it predicts the rate of migration from Manitoba to Quebec quite poorly for all income classes (the correlation coefficients are all negative).

The Model 2 estimates do an even worse job of predicting the rate of migration from Manitoba to Quebec, with correlation coefficients less than −0.5 for both the low- and middle-income classes. However, Model 2 does a better job than Model 1 of predicting the rate of migration from Newfoundland to Alberta for all three income classes. It is evidently difficult to construct a conditional logit model of internal migration that predicts time series migration data well, a problem that has been noted before (e.g., see Day 1989).

Although neither model seems to do a good job of predicting all 100 individual migration rates, it is possible that they might do a better job of predicting migration aggregates such as in-, out-, or net in-migration. To see if this is the case, we computed correlation coefficients for these three aggregate migration measures for each income class in each province of origin, for both models. These correlation coefficients are presented in table 6.4. It can be seen that the models predict migration of low-income people best. For this income class, there are no negative correlation coefficients in table 6.4, and of the 30 correlation coefficients for each model, most are above 0.6. Model 1 predicts all three migration measures slightly better than Model 2 for this income class, as its correlation coefficients are higher for most flows in the table. Model 1 also yields slightly higher correlation coefficients than Model 2 for the middle- and high-income classes.

Further information on the nature of the prediction errors for in-, out-, and net in-migration is provided in table 6.5, which shows the difference between the 1974–96 average of the actual and predicted values of each flow for each model and income class, and for all income classes combined. The table shows that the average predicted net flows for each province closely resemble the actual net flows over the period. This result is a by-product of the use of alternative-specific constants, as noted earlier. A better test of the model is given by the pattern of gross in- and out-migration flows. The predicted average gross flows are clearly closer to the actual for some provinces than for others. Both models appear to over-predict gross flows for the Atlantic provinces, especially Prince Edward Island, for all income classes. The predicted gross flows for Quebec for each income class are also above actual averages, while those for Ontario are below actual averages. Both models also under-predict in- and out-migration to Alberta and British Columbia by a wide margin, especially for the high-income class.

These explorations of within-sample predictive power indicate that the models do not explain all 100 interprovincial migration flows equally well, no doubt owing in part to the volatility of year-to-year migration flows that was observed in the first section of chapter 5. Our models do a better job of predicting flows averaged over time. Finally, it should be noted that it is difficult to compare the within-sample forecasting performance of our models with that of the models in other studies because of the limited information provided in the literature on this matter.

1968–1996

Thus far we have not discussed any estimates derived from the 1968–96 data set, constructed by combining migration counts from the 10 percent sample for 1968–73 with the 100 percent tapes for 1974–96. Recall that

Table 6.4
Correlations between Actual and Fitted Values of In-, Out-, and Net In-migration 1974–96

	Model 1			Model 2		
Province	Out-migration	In-migration	Net In-migration	Out-migration	In-migration	Net In-Migration
Low Income						
NFLD	0.7056	0.6714	0.6036	0.6532	0.7167	0.5091
PEI	0.7502	0.2045	0.5733	0.5497	0.3454	0.3309
NS	0.6840	0.7480	0.2486	0.7421	0.6861	0.3229
NB	0.7649	0.3106	0.3382	0.8438	0.2871	0.5312
QUE	0.6736	0.5995	0.6930	0.5967	0.3994	0.3480
ONT	0.5265	0.7879	0.7365	0.3549	0.8222	0.6954
MAN	0.4195	0.1050	0.3837	0.3141	0.1904	0.2390
SASK	0.9149	0.6417	0.9251	0.7459	0.2377	0.4511
ALTA	0.7215	0.8640	0.9224	0.6774	0.8715	0.9120
BC	0.6746	0.7744	0.7183	0.7166	0.7058	0.6563
Min	0.4195	0.1050	0.2486	0.3141	0.1904	0.2390
Max	0.9149	0.8640	0.9251	0.8438	0.8715	0.9120
Middle Income						
NFLD	0.2356	0.5605	0.5172	0.3172	0.5461	0.6137
PEI	0.3663	-0.3435	0.6796	0.1264	-0.4364	0.5920
NS	0.2530	-0.3374	0.3818	0.4873	-0.5146	0.4161
NB	0.2237	-0.4951	0.3329	0.5579	-0.5301	0.4997
QUE	0.6163	-0.2996	0.8291	0.4902	-0.3059	0.6249
ONT	0.3532	0.2037	0.5916	0.0886	0.3694	0.5168
MAN	-0.0794	-0.3160	0.3911	-0.3990	-0.1169	0.0384
SASK	0.6212	0.2966	0.9063	0.4983	-0.6436	0.4091
ALTA	0.3013	0.6468	0.9081	0.2399	0.6939	0.8917
BC	0.2496	0.5823	0.7315	0.2931	0.4002	0.6684
Min	-0.0794	-0.4951	0.3329	-0.3990	-0.6436	0.0384
Max	0.6212	0.6468	0.9081	0.5579	0.6939	0.8917

Table 6.4 (continued)

	Model 1			Model 2		
Province	Out-migration	In-migration	Net In-migration	Out-migration	In-migration	Net In-Migration
High Income						
NFLD	0.3743	0.6574	0.5172	0.4324	0.6526	0.2887
PEI	0.2214	-0.0985	0.6796	0.1965	-0.1708	0.3040
NS	0.6598	0.6096	0.3818	0.7070	0.5084	0.1657
NB	0.4530	-0.2934	0.3329	0.5555	-0.3366	0.0978
QUE	0.6253	0.3086	0.8291	0.5645	0.2288	0.7139
ONT	0.2221	0.6598	0.5916	0.1615	0.7378	0.6437
MAN	-0.0017	-0.1079	0.3911	-0.1648	-0.0663	0.0085
SASK	0.8495	0.1958	0.9063	0.7610	-0.2086	0.1088
ALTA	0.7960	0.5533	0.9081	0.7684	0.5103	0.9423
BC	0.3954	0.6371	0.7315	0.4146	0.5284	0.6614
Min	-0.0017	-0.2934	0.3329	-0.1648	-0.3366	0.0085
Max	0.8495	0.6598	0.9081	0.7684	0.7378	0.9423

Table 6.5
Difference between 1974–96 Averages of Actual and Predicted Migration Flows

Province	Model 1			Model 2		
	In-Migration	Out-Migration	Net in-migration	In-migration	Out-migration	Net in-migration
Low income						
NFLD	-740	-786	46	-754	-797	42
PEI	-1428	-1442	14	-1453	-1442	-11
NS	-1279	-1340	61	-1325	-1340	15
NB	-2122	-2058	-64	-2119	-2057	-62
QUE	-177	-319	142	-149	-357	208
ONT	1550	1824	-275	1661	1762	-101
MAN	-1637	-1745	108	-1615	-1780	165
SASK	-1495	-1463	-31	-1535	-1380	-155
ALTA	3310	3279	31	3254	3263	-9
BC	2331	2363	-31	2285	2378	-94
Middle Income						
NFLD	-941	-927	-14	-983	-920	-63
PEI	-1946	-2009	62	-1971	-2008	37
NS	-2031	-2009	-22	-2094	-2013	-80
NB	-3014	-2813	-202	-3030	-2795	-235
QUE	-344	-547	204	-301	-626	324
ONT	1297	1449	-152	1453	1289	163
MAN	-2057	-2213	156	-2025	-2258	233
SASK	-1758	-1706	-52	-1838	-1558	-280
ALTA	4719	4755	-36	4616	4728	-111
BC	3089	3035	54	3051	3043	8

Table 6.5 (continued)

Province	Model 1			Model 2		
	In-Migration	Out-Migration	Net in-migration	In-migration	Out-migration	Net in-migratiion
High Income						
NFLD	-572	-585	13	-302	-574	272
PEI	-1052	-1063	11	-998	-1069	71
NS	-902	-925	23	-981	-943	-37
NB	-1858	-1727	-131	-1710	-1725	14
QUE	-260	-514	253	-516	-576	60
ONT	1227	1335	-108	1704	1243	462
MAN	-1394	-1462	68	-1331	-1480	149
SASK	-1659	-1544	-115	-1444	-1478	34
ALTA	2556	2547	8	4410	2606	1804
BC	1749	1771	-23	2195	1767	428
All income classes						
NFLD	-2253	-2298	45	-2338	-2292	-46
PEI	-4426	-4513	87	-4489	-4519	30
NS	-4212	-4273	61	-4344	-4297	-47
NB	-6995	-6598	-397	-7008	-6576	-432
QUE	-781	-1380	599	-670	-1558	888
ONT	4074	4609	-535	4399	4294	105
MAN	-5087	-5420	332	-5021	-5518	497
SASK	-4911	-4715	-196	-5076	-4417	-659
ALTA	10585	10581	4	10381	10596	-215
BC	7169	7169	0	7069	7189	-120

in combining data from the two sources, we divided migration flows from the 100 percent sample by 10 to obtain migration estimates of comparable magnitude for both periods. The combination of data from these two sources allows us to increase our sample size to 2,900 observations from 2,300 and to include the 1971 reforms to unemployment insurance in our sample period. The extension of the sample period backwards in time also allows us to include the variables OCT and OCT2 that account for the effects on migration from and to Quebec of language legislation introduced in 1969 and of the kidnappings by the FLQ in 1970.

Table 6.6 presents the parameter estimates obtained using these 1968–96 data, for Model 1 only. For the most part, the qualitative results are the same as those for the 1974–96 period; all statistically significant coefficients have the same sign as before. The only coefficients that are significant for the 1974–96 period but not the 1968–96 period are those of EDUCATION and PQ2 for the high-income class. One may note that the coefficients of INCOME and LEISURE are higher for the 1968–96 sample than for the 1974–96 sample, although this difference is less pronounced for the middle-income group. The coefficients of the probabilities of the three unemployment states are also higher for the low- and middle-income groups.

For all three income classes, the coefficient of the variable OCT is positive and statistically significant, indicating that the events of the 1969 to 1971 period did lead to increased outflows from the province, just as did the events after 1976. However, the effects of these two episodes on inflows to Quebec appear to have been different. While inflows of low- and middle-income individuals to Quebec increased during the 1977–80 period, only inflows of high-income individuals increased between 1969 and 1971. Moreover, the results suggest that the events during the earlier period reduced inflows of low-income migrants to Quebec while leaving inflows of middle-income individuals unaffected.

Finally, we note that the coefficients of DSTAY, DISTANCE, QUEBEC, and the extraordinary event dummy variables do not change much when the sample period is extended further back in time. We also recall our caution that whatever the difference in results between the two samples may be, it is impossible to tell how important a variable is without calculating marginal effects or carrying out simulations. These investigations are presented in the next two chapters.

ESTIMATES BY AGE, SEX, AND INCOME CLASS

Many previous studies of migration have suggested that age and sex are important determinants of migration flows. It is difficult to test for such

Table 6.6
Parameter Estimates by Income Class, Model 1, 1968–96

Variable	Low Income	Middle Income	High Income	Variable	Low Income	Middle Income	High Income
INCOME	2.345 (22.51)	2.671 (30.67)	1.652 (15.89)	PQ	0.242 (10.03)	0.381 (20.24)	0.456 (22.87)
LEISURE	7.261 (13.76)	8.327 (18.87)	7.188 (12.95)	PQ2	0.111 (3.78)	0.108 (4.27)	-0.001 (-0.03)
HEALTH	-0.287 (-7.35)	-0.349 (-10.83)	-0.272 (-7.06)	FISH	0.074 (2.36)	-0.174 (-5.08)	-0.308 (-6.46)
EDUCATION	0.182 (5.26)	-0.041 (-1.40)	0.009 (0.268)	FISH2	-0.897 (-19.06)	-1.211 (-26.55)	-1.155 (-21.15)
OTHER SPENDING	-0.145 (-6.76)	-0.253 (-13.84)	-0.341 (-16.17)	NFLD	0.105 (3.03)	0.182 (6.10)	-0.325 (-8.87)
FEDERAL SPENDING	0.123 (4.63)	0.469 (21.64)	0.630 (24.25)	PEI	-0.878 (-23.93)	-0.999 (-32.52)	-1.791 (-47.64)
DSTAY	1.505 (51.12)	1.648 (65.02)	1.181 (39.59)	NS	-0.382 (-11.44)	-0.682 (-24.86)	-1.255 (-38.61)
DISTANCE	-0.510 (124.09)	-0.529 (-149.54)	-0.624 (-149.83)	NB	-0.080 (-2.96)	-0.144 (-6.39)	-0.684 (-25.19)
P2	-40.430 (-23.28)	-45.046 (-31.05)	-36.624 (-20.24)	QUE	1.633 (78.22)	1.859 (107.45)	1.438 (72.28)
P3	-24.239 (-13.82)	-28.167 (-19.09)	-26.346 (-14.20)	ONT	-0.124 (-7.83)	-0.299 (-22.57)	-0.298 (-19.32)
P4	-24.764 (-14.07)	-28.245 (-19.16)	-25.372 (-13.68)	MAN	-0.903 (-48.72)	-1.134 (-73.87)	-1.414 (-78.66)
QUEBEC	-2.228 (-133.40)	-2.324 (-163.11)	-2.014 (-130.44)	SASK	-0.981 (-57.74)	-1.034 (-71.83)	-1.205 (-71.73)
OCT	0.694 (19.93)	0.763 (30.67)	0.890 (32.49)	ALTA	-0.538 (-33.70)	-0.590 (-43.25)	-0.630 (-39.42)

Table 6.6 (continued)

Variable	Low Income	Middle Income	High Income	Variable	Low Income	Middle Income	High Income
OCT2	−0.123	−0.042	0.285				
	(−3.04)	(−1.44)	(8.84)				
				Log L	−814376	−1157840	−915571
				Log L_0	−10469370	−19539870	−18456370
				McFadden's R^2	0.922	0.941	0.950
				No. of observations	2900	2900	2900

See notes to Table 6.2.

effects in most time-series studies of migration since time-series data on migration are usually not disaggregated by age and sex. Our ability to disaggregate migration data by age and sex as well as by income class thus provides us with an excellent opportunity to examine the magnitude of the effect of age and sex on interprovincial migration flows over time. Recall that in constructing these data, individual tax filers were divided into three age groups: young (20–24 years old), middle aged (25–44 years old), and older (45–64 years old) people. Disaggregating by age, sex, and three income classes thus gives us eighteen different samples. In this section we examine the parameter estimates for these eighteen different samples for the 1974–96 period for both Model 1 and Model 2.

As in the case of the previous estimates, most of the explanatory variables are exactly the same for each sample of migration data because it was impossible to obtain data that differed by age, sex, *and* income class. However, as discussed in chapter 5, we were able to construct age- and sex-specific probabilities of the four states of the world. Thus in the models discussed here, the variables $P1$, $P2$, $P3$, and $LP234$ do vary with age and sex. In addition, *INCOME* and *LEISURE* vary with age and sex because we used the age- and sex-specific probabilities as weights in their construction. Other variables that entered into the construction of *INCOME* and *LEISURE*, such as wages, UI benefits, and income taxes, remain the same for all age, sex, and income groups.

Because the presentation of eighteen additional sets of parameter estimates would be overwhelming, tables containing estimates of all the parameters for the eighteen age/sex/income class groups for Models 1 and 2 have been relegated to appendix E. Here we focus on how just a few important coefficients vary across the eighteen groups. A general comment before we turn to details is that the coefficients of *INCOME* and *LEISURE* still vary across Models 1 and 2, as was the case when the data were disaggregated by income class only. The same is true of the coefficients of the public spending variables.

We begin by looking at the coefficients of *INCOME* and *LEISURE*, among others, to see if there are any patterns in their variation with age, sex, and income class. As table 6.7 shows, in at least eleven of the eighteen cases (nine age/income-class groups, two models) the coefficient of *INCOME* is higher for men than for women, suggesting that the migration behaviour of men may be more sensitive than that of women to expected log income differentials. For men, the highest values of the coefficient for both models tend to be those for young men, the only exception arising in the middle-income class, where older men have the highest coefficient. For women, the reverse is true – the coefficient of *INCOME* is actually lowest for young women, in all income classes and both models. Thus for men income appears to lose some of its importance as a determinant of migration with age, while for women income considerations seem to gain importance with age. It is harder to discern any patterns in the coefficients of *LEISURE*, other than that they are frequently negative for women in Model 1. This unexpected sign is likely a consequence of multicollinearity, since the coefficient of *LEISURE* is almost always positive for both men and women in Model 2.

Although the problem of collinearity makes it difficult to draw strong conclusions regarding age/sex/income-class differences in many of the coefficients, as we saw in the previous section, not all the coefficient estimates are afflicted by this problem. Among those that are not, it is particularly interesting to look at the coefficients of *DSTAY*, *DISTANCE*, and the extraordinary event dummies. The coefficients of the first two of these variables, for all age/sex/income-class groups and both models, are presented in table 6.8. As the table shows, these coefficients differ less across models for each subgroup than do those of *INCOME* and *LEISURE*, have the expected signs, and are statistically significant except in the case of high-income older women in Model 2.

Furthermore, because *DSTAY* and *DISTANCE* represent unmeasurable costs of moving, their coefficients can tell us something about the importance of such costs to different subgroups of the population. In general, one would expect younger Canadians to be more mobile, since they are less likely to be tied down by a family. For men, the coefficient of *DSTAY* does unambiguously increase with age, implying that fixed costs become a bigger deterrent to migration as men age. A similar pattern is observed for women, with one interesting exception: the coefficient of *DSTAY* is smaller for older high-income women than for middle-aged high-income women. This decrease in the coefficient suggests that higher-income women 45 and older, whose children (if any) are likely to be older and may already have left home, face lower fixed costs of moving than middle-aged women, who are more likely to have younger children who are still in school.[13]

On balance the estimates of the coefficient of *DSTAY* suggest that the fixed costs of moving tend to increase with age for both men and women. Can the same be said of distance-related moving costs? A look at the coefficients of *DISTANCE* in the lower panel of table 6.8 helps to answer this question. Here it can be seen that the magnitude of the (always-negative) coefficient generally increases with age, with a few exceptions. For men the exception is high income-earners in the middle-aged group, who appear to be slightly

Table 6.7
Coefficients of INCOME and LEISURE by Age, Sex, and Income Class, 1974–96

| | Coefficient of INCOME | | | |
| | Men | | Women | |
	Model 1	Model 2	Model 1	Model 2
Low Income				
Young	2.26	1.88	1.72	0.43
Middle aged	1.54	0.59	1.86	0.83
Older	1.89	0.70	1.77	1.57
Middle Income				
Young	2.87	2.50	1.58	0.32
Middle aged	2.16	1.05	1.58	0.37
Older	2.89	1.91	1.95	1.60
High Income				
Young	2.47	1.78	0.63^x	−0.75
Middle aged	0.85	0.07^x	1.33	0.20^x
Older	0.56	0.06^x	1.24	0.81

| | Coefficient of LEISURE | | | |
| | Men | | Women | |
	Model 1	Model 2	Model 1	Model 2
Low Income				
Young	1.70	0.77	−1.60	0.80
Middle aged	1.90	0.47	−3.38	0.70
Older	1.18^x	0.38	−9.10	0.16^x
Middle Income				
Young	4.21	0.63	0.13^x	0.55
Middle aged	6.81	0.51	−2.62	1.04
Older	5.84	0.75	−8.21	−0.06^x
High Income				
Young	4.20	−0.26	−0.019^x	0.019^x
Middle aged	3.49	−0.23	−0.47^x	0.51
Older	−1.93	0.17	−7.86	−0.51

Note: Superscript x indicates that estimated coefficient is not significant at the 5% level. "Young" are aged 20–24, "Middle aged" are 25–44, and "Older" are 45–64.

Table 6.8
Coefficients of DSTAY and DISTANCE by Age, Sex, and Income Class, 1974–96

| | Coefficient of DSTAY | | | |
| | Men | | Women | |
	Model 1	Model 2	Model 1	Model 2
Low Income				
Young	1.52	1.50	0.99	0.88
Middle aged	1.64	1.58	1.61	1.53
Older	1.87	1.76	1.74	1.72
Middle Income				
Young	1.63	1.60	0.65	0.55
Middle aged	2.04	1.97	1.72	1.62
Older	2.30	2.22	1.86	1.83
High Income				
Young	0.46	0.40	0.27	0.15
Middle aged	1.20	1.15	1.59	1.49
Older	1.23	1.19	1.29	1.25[x]

| | Coefficient of DISTANCE | | | |
| | Men | | Women | |
	Model 1	Model 2	Model 1	Model 2
Low Income				
Young	−0.43	−0.43	−0.52	−0.54
Middle aged	−0.47	−0.49	−0.53	−0.55
Older	−0.60	−0.62	−0.63	−0.64
Middle Income				
Young	−0.43	−0.43	−0.59	−0.61
Middle aged	−0.47	−0.49	−0.54	−0.56
Older	−0.59	−0.60	−0.65	−0.66
High Income				
Young	−0.61	−0.62	−0.63	−0.66
Middle aged	−0.59	−0.60	−0.57	−0.59
Older	−0.73	−0.73	−0.75	−0.76

Note: Superscript x indicates that estimated coefficient is not significant at the 5% level. "Young" are aged 20–24, "Middle aged" are 25–44, and "Older" are 45–64.

less sensitive to distance than young high-income men. For women the exceptions are middle-aged women in both the middle- and the high-income classes. Perhaps for middle-aged women it is the fixed costs of moving that are the most important, so that moves farther away, while more costly, do not impose as great a cost on them as on younger women.

Another question one can answer with the help of the estimates in table 6.8 is whether men and women respond differently to the unmeasurable costs of moving. Interestingly, the coefficient of DSTAY is generally higher for men than for women, except for high-income individuals aged twenty-five and over. However, the coefficient of DISTANCE is generally lower for men than for women in the low-income and middle-income classes; for high-income individuals, the differences between men and women in this coefficient appear to be much smaller. These findings suggest that in the low- and middle-income groups, men are more sensitive to the fixed costs of moving than are women, while women are in general more sensitive to the distance between their provinces of origin and destination. In other words, women are less likely than men to move far away from their original location, but more likely to make a move, holding all else constant.

One can also ask whether responses to the election of a separatist government in Quebec in 1976 differed by age and sex as well as by income class. Table 6.9 presents the estimates by age, sex, and income class of the coefficients of PQ and PQ2, the two dummy variables associated with this extraordinary event. The predominantly positive coefficients of PQ that appear in the upper panel of the table imply that this event led to increased out-migration from Quebec of all age/sex/income class-groups except young, high-income men. Furthermore, in the middle- and high-income classes the effect clearly increased with age. The rate of out-migration of low-income women also increased with age. The only group in which there was no tendency for out-migration from Quebec to increase with age during the 1977–80 period was that of low-income men.

Although this extraordinary event led to an increase in out-migration from Quebec, as was noted in the previous section, it also led to increased in-migration to Quebec in all income classes when Models 1 and 2 were estimated using 1974–96 data for the three income classes. The negative coefficients for PQ2 in the lower panel of table 6.9 show that this phenomenon was not present in all age/sex/income-class groups. The most striking result in the lower panel of the table is that young, high-income individuals, both men and women, were less likely to move to Quebec during the 1977–80 period. On the other hand, holding all else constant the in-migration rate of young, low-income men increased.

Table 6.9
Coefficients of PQ and PQ2 by Age, Sex, and Income Class, 1974–96

| | Coefficient of PQ | | | |
| | Men | | Women | |
	Model 1	Model 2	Model 1	Model 2
Low Income				
Young	0.39	0.45	0.18	0.28
Middle aged	0.42	0.44	0.25	0.34
Older	0.42^x	0.43	0.31	0.36
Middle Income				
Young	0.28	0.30	0.15	0.22
Middle aged	0.39	0.38	0.53	0.63
Older	0.50	0.48	0.67	0.73
High Income				
Young	−0.04	−0.01	0.10	0.17
Middle aged	0.48	0.49	0.50	0.58
Older	0.62	0.61	0.73	0.77

| | Coefficient of PQ2 | | | |
| | Men | | Women | |
	Model 1	Model 2	Model 1	Model 2
Low Income				
Young	0.31	0.25	0.14	0.04^x
Middle aged	0.14	0.12	0.09	−0.01^x
Older	0.02^x	0.02	0.29	0.24
Middle Income				
Young	−0.02^x	−0.04	0.05	−0.03^x
Middle aged	0.03^x	0.43	0.16	0.05
Older	−0.03^x	−0.01^x	0.14	0.08^x
High Income				
Young	−0.26	−0.29	−0.15	−0.23
Middle aged	0.01	0.01	0.16	0.08
Older	0.01	0.24	0.15	0.11

Note: Superscript x indicates that estimated coefficient is not significant at the 5% level. "Young" are aged 20–24, "Middle aged" are 25–44, and "Older" are 45–64. A positive coefficient for PQ implies an increase in outflows *from* Quebec during the 1977–80 period, while a positive coefficient for PQ2 implies an increase in inflows *to* Quebec during the same period.

Together the results in table 6.9 suggest that the election of a separatist government in Quebec and the subsequent introduction of legislation to promote the use of French in the province altered not only the size of the province's population but also its demographic structure. High-income and older individuals appear to have been more affected by the change. The end result was likely a population that was on average younger and had lower average income.

The last extraordinary event included in the model is the shutdown of the cod fishery in 1992. The coefficients of FISH and FISH2, the two explanatory variables associated with this event, are presented in table 6.10. Our earlier results presented in table 6.2 indicate that the effect of the shutdown was to increase out-migration from Newfoundland of low-income individuals and reduce out-migration of middle- and high-income individuals. The estimated coefficients of FISH in table 6.10 show that young men in all three income classes were more likely to leave Newfoundland as a result of this policy shock. In contrast, women of all ages and men aged 25 and over in all income classes (with the sole exception being older middle-income men in Model 1) were less likely to leave Newfoundland in the years following the fishery shutdown. The most likely explanation for this phenomenon is that older individuals were more likely to either qualify for, or take advantage of, government compensation and retraining programs for those affected by the shutdown, and hence that they decided to stay rather than leave.

In the second panel of table 6.10, which presents the estimated coefficients of FISH2, all the estimates are negative and statistically significant. In other words, holding all else equal all subgroups were *less* likely to move *to* Newfoundland during the 1993–96 period. This negative effect appears to have been largest for high-income women under age 45 and middle-aged men and women in the middle-income group. Within the low- and middle-income classes the effect tends to be smallest for individuals aged 45 and older and the same is true for high-income women. Strangely, the deterrent effect of the fishery closure appears to have been smaller for young high-income men than for young men in the other two income classes. Overall though, the results suggest that the proportion of young men in the New-foundland population decreased as a result of the closure of the fishery.

Taken together, the estimates presented in tables 6.7 to 6.10 suggest that there are some interesting differences in the migration behaviour of men and women and of different age groups, as well as different income classes. One should note that in an aggregate study of this nature the impossibility of obtaining age-, sex-, and income class-specific data on all the explanatory variables makes these estimates less reliable than we would like. For this

Table 6.10
Coefficients of FISH and FISH2 by Age, Sex, and Income Class, 1974–96

| | Coefficient of FISH | | | |
| | Men | | Women | |
	Model 1	Model 2	Model 1	Model 2
Low Income				
Young	0.10	−0.10	−0.04	−0.08
Middle aged	0.02^x	−0.02^x	−0.47	−0.15
Older	−0.09^x	−0.17	−0.15	−0.09^x
Middle Income				
Young	0.30	0.13	−0.12	−0.13
Middle aged	−0.07	−0.13	−0.40	−0.53
Older	0.11	−0.02^x	−0.40	−0.35
High Income				
Young	0.30	0.17^x	−0.20^x	−0.19^x
Middle aged	−0.31	−0.31	−0.46	−0.58
Older	−0.17	−0.24	−0.31	−0.22

| | Coefficient of FISH2 | | | |
| | Men | | Women | |
	Model 1	Model 2	Model 1	Model 2
Low Income				
Young	−0.82	−0.64	−0.74	−0.69
Middle aged	−0.94	−0.92	−0.84	−0.74
Older	−0.72	−0.66	−0.46	−0.51
Middle Income				
Young	−0.95	−0.80	−0.91	−0.90
Middle aged	−1.03	−0.98	−1.12	−0.98
Older	−0.59	−0.48	−0.76	−0.82
High Income				
Young	−0.70	−0.60	−1.05	−1.03
Middle aged	−0.91	−0.92	−1.15	−1.02
Older	−0.73	−0.66	−0.69	−0.77

Note: Subscript x indicates that estimated coefficient is not significant at the 5% level. "Young" are aged 20–24, "Middle aged" are 25–44, and "Older" are 45–64. A positive coefficient for FISH implies an increase in outflows *from* Newfoundland during the 1993–96 period, while a positive coefficient for FISH2 implies an increase in inflows *to* Newfoundland during the same period.

reason, most of the marginal effects and simulations discussed in subsequent chapters are carried out using data disaggregated by income class only.

CHOOSING AMONG MODELS AND RESULTS

The lack of complete consistency across Models 1 and 2 with respect to the coefficients on INCOME, LEISURE, and the public expenditure variables is probably partly due to a collinearity problem involving not only LEISURE and the additional risk aversion variables but also INCOME and the public expenditure variables. [14] This correlation arises because migrants are, realistically, assumed to be concerned with the riskiness of employment in alternative locations, an aspect of behaviour that probably does not go away even in large samples.

The variability of the estimated coefficients of INCOME and LEISURE in the different models we have estimated means that the effect on migration flows of a change in MIN, the minimum weeks to qualify for UI, may differ across population subgroups. More precisely, as we will see in the next chapter, the effect of a change in MIN depends not only on the coefficients of INCOME and LEISURE but also on several model variables, so that numerical calculations in the form of marginal effects and simulations are required to assess the direction as well as the absolute size of the effect. Looking ahead for a moment, we will find in chapter 8 that the direction of the effect of a change in MIN turns out to be the same regardless of the model used as a basis for our simulations.

Because the direction of the effect of many variables included in the model is determined by the sign of the coefficient on INCOME, which is consistently positive when the data are disaggregated by income class only, the direction of the effect of changes in these variables is easier to predict before simulations are conducted. Here too, however, simulation will be needed to assess the quantitative consequences of policy counterfactuals. We can also be confident about the direction of the effect of changing the costs of moving and about the direction of the effects on migration of the extraordinary events, since neither the sign nor the magnitude of their coefficients seems to be greatly affected by collinearity. Finally, with respect to the effects of public expenditure, we do not think it wise to draw firm conclusions even after conducting simulations, since the only such variable whose coefficient consistently has the same (negative) sign is OTHER SPENDING.

Whenever one estimates different versions of a model, it is tempting to pick one variant and say that it is the best. The within-sample forecasting ability of the model using different aggregations and our observations concerning multicollinearity suggests caution, however. For this reason, in the next two chapters we compute marginal effects and carry out simulations with both Models 1 and 2, using mainly data aggregated by income class and averaging the results over a substantial period, since the forecasting properties of our models are better over long time periods. We will on a few occasions use results produced using the estimates for all eighteen subgroups as a check on the results. In the end, we will draw conclusions that are robust with respect to the results of both models and different disaggregations of migration flows.

7

Exploring the Effects of Marginal Policy Reforms

In this and the next chapter we explore the quantitative implications of the models we have estimated. Here we use the models to consider the likely consequences of small or marginal changes in selected policy parameters and market conditions. In chapter 8 we use simulation to investigate more comprehensive policy reforms and the consequences of extraordinary policies like the closing of the cod fishery.

To investigate the marginal effects of changes in one policy parameter by itself, we need more than the estimated coefficients in our migration equations. In the conditional logit model of migration, each estimated coefficient by itself does not tell us much because of the mathematical form of the expression for the probability of migrating from one region to another. The marginal effect of a change in a policy parameter depends on the relative size of various estimated coefficients, along with the levels of various private market and public sector variables. Fortunately the calculations required to compute these effects are not difficult, and looking closely at them leads to interesting insights about policy-induced migration.

In view of the migration probabilities given by equation (4.4), the general formula for the marginal effect on the probability of migration from province i to another province j of a change in some explanatory variable or policy parameter X in province j is:

$$\frac{\partial P_{ij}}{\partial X_j} = P_{ij}(1 - P_{ij})\frac{\partial EU_{ij}}{\partial X_j}.$$ (7.1)

Since expected utility is defined by (4.7), this marginal effect calculation is completed by appropriately differentiating the utility function and substituting the result into this formula. A change in x in other provinces k will also affect migration from provinces i to j, since individuals in principle optimize over all locations. The formula for this second marginal effect is similar to (7.1) and is given in appendix F along with a summary of all marginal effect calculations.

The number of specific marginal effects that can be computed in a study such as ours is large. There are 100 (10 × 10) different gross migration flows to be considered. Each flow can be expected to respond differently to a change in a particular location-specific factor. Each location-specific factor included in the model takes on ten distinct values, one for each alternative destination, and the effect of changing the value of some variable or parameter in one province, such as the wage rate or the tax rate, is not the same as the effect of changing the value of the same factor in any other province. In addition, because separate coefficients can be estimated for various income classes and age and sex groups, each marginal effect can also be computed separately for each of these groups. A final complication is that the derivatives of the migration rates in (7.1) clearly depend on the data and thus vary from year to year.

Since the volume of material to absorb would otherwise be too great, we compute marginal effects only for selected variables and policy parameters based on the estimates obtained for Models 1 and 2 using the 100 percent tax data set for the period 1974–96. These marginal effects are presented in tables 7.1 and 7.2. For the benefit of the reader, in these tables the results of the incremental changes in predicted migration rates are translated into flows of persons, which are easier to understand.

As a further step towards making the results more manageable, we will consider only net in-migration for each province, computed by aggregating across provinces of origin and destination, and present only average marginal effects for the nineteen-year period 1978–96. Since our models do not predict year-to-year fluctuations in origin-destination specific flows particularly well, the annual values of the marginal effects are unlikely to be accurate, especially for specific origin-destination pairs. Average effects are more reliable. The 1978–96 period, rather than the estimation period 1974–96, is used here to make the results we discuss in this chapter comparable to the simulations presented in the next. We will return to the choice of the simulation period in chapter 8.

In the following discussion we also emphasize own-province effects, that is, the effect on net in-migration to a province of a change in the value of some key variable in *that* province. We do so in part to keep the discussion brief and in part because this own-province effect is always much larger than the effects on net migration to other provinces.[1]

Accordingly, tables 7.1 and 7.2 present the average own-province marginal effects on net in-migration of changes in seven variables: average weekly earnings (in current dollars); MIN, the minimum weeks of work required to qualify for unemployment insurance benefits; MINWKS, the maximum weeks of benefits that an individual with MIN qualifying weeks may receive; the provincial ("piggy-back") income tax rate that is applied to basic federal tax; provincial social assistance benefits (current dollars per case per year); real per capita federal spending; and real per capita provincial spending on education. The first of these tables reports results using Model 1, while the second uses Model 2. Each entry in the tables can be interpreted as the change in the number of net in-migrants resulting from a one unit increase in the variable in question. A minus sign in these tables means that the policy or other change considered reduces net in-migration or, equivalently, that it increases net out-migration.

One should note that while the magnitude of the effects can be compared across income classes and provinces within a single column of each table, it is not appropriate to compare them across columns of each table. The impact of a one-dollar increase in average weekly earnings, for example, is not comparable to the effect of a one-week increase in the minimum weeks of work required to qualify for unemployment insurance benefits, or a one-dollar increase in *annual* social assistance benefits. Each individual marginal effect can of course be compared across models (i.e., tables) – a quick comparison of tables 7.1 and 7.2 reveals that the migration flows calculated using Model 1 are usually larger than those that rely on the second model.

To provide a basis for comparisons between the incremental effects of changes in different variables, tables 7.3 and 7.4, corresponding to Models 1 and 2 respectively, record the change in each variable or policy parameter that is required to produce the same own-province change in net in-migration (in absolute value) that would occur if the average weekly wage in the province increased by one dollar.[2] The quantities in these tables are thus ratios of the marginal effect of a one-dollar increase in average weekly earnings to that of a one-unit change in each of the other variables.

The last piece of information needed to interpret the marginal effects in the tables is contained in table 7.5. This table shows the historical average values, by province, of all of the variables for which marginal effects are presented. By comparing the values in tables 7.3 and 7.4 to the historical average values of the variables in question given in table 7.5, we can develop

Table 7.1
Average Own-Province Marginal Effects on Net In-migration of Changes in Selected Variables, 1978–96, Model 1 (number of persons)

Province	Average Weekly Wage (nominal) (1)	MIN (2)	MINWKS (3)	Provincial Income Tax Rate (4)	Annual Social Assistance Benefits (nominal) (5)	Real Per Capita Federal Spending (6)	Real Per Capita Education Spending (7)
Low Income							
NFLD	40	-32.553	0.363	-1613	0.112	1.486	2.124
PEI	14	-17.523	-1.545	-1027	0.064	0.563	1.537
NS	32	-15.036	-0.698	-2579	0.098	0.986	3.690
NB	29	-25.398	2.012	-2435	0.185	1.769	3.739
QUE	78	-6.215	0.078	-1087	0.222	3.314	3.262
ONT	125	-4.004	-0.008	-6727	0.134	5.290	7.661
MAN	34	-2.112	0.042	-2778	0.075	2.104	3.773
SASK	32	-1.721	-0.089	-2656	0.025	3.054	3.465
ALTA	91	-2.350	-0.002	-3880	0.000	4.383	4.098
BC	127	-5.802	-0.036	-3355	0.142	3.696	4.475
Middle Income							
NFLD	52	-96.505	0.629	-2186	0.155	3.278	-0.038
PEI	23	-61.871	-2.693	-1739	0.108	1.549	-0.034
NS	51	-49.960	-1.063	-4067	0.163	2.548	-0.077
NB	46	-89.990	3.256	-3872	0.296	4.588	-0.079
QUE	145	-25.784	0.150	-1795	0.378	9.087	-0.072
ONT	213	-14.275	-0.009	-11309	0.235	14.507	-0.169
MAN	55	-7.433	0.076	-4525	0.121	5.593	-0.081
SASK	53	-5.865	-0.143	-4345	0.041	8.140	-0.075
ALTA	151	-8.738	0.000	-6551	0.000	12.012	-0.091
BC	215	-21.380	-0.032	-5693	0.239	10.219	-0.100

Table 7.1 (continued)

Province	Average Weekly Wage (nominal) (1)	MIN (2)	MINWKS (3)	Provincial Income Tax Rate (4)	Annual Social Assistance Benefits (nominal) (5)	Real Per Capita Federal Spending (6)	Real Per Capita Education Spending (7)
High Income							
NFLD	21	-41.564	0.242	-859	0.061	2.133	-0.562
PEI	9	-24.870	-0.997	-639	0.040	0.937	-0.476
NS	23	-25.500	-0.513	-1891	0.073	1.953	-1.352
NB	20	-43.752	1.432	-1703	0.129	3.331	-1.302
QUE	81	-16.985	0.084	-1051	0.224	8.966	-1.629
ONT	114	-8.705	-0.014	-6334	0.128	13.411	-3.576
MAN	27	-4.071	0.036	-2274	0.058	4.630	-1.535
SASK	27	-3.298	-0.074	-2251	0.019	6.947	-1.456
ALTA	90	-5.685	-0.004	-3734	0.000	11.247	-1.940
BC	128	-13.896	-0.027	-3317	0.137	9.756	-2.198

Table 7.2
Average Own-Province Marginal Effects on Net In-migration of Changes in Selected Variables, 1978–96, Model 2 (number of persons)

Province	Average Weekly Wage (nominal) (1)	MIN (2)	MINWKS (3)	Provincial Income Tax Rate (4)	Annual Social Assistance Benefits (nominal) (5)	Real Per Capita Federal Spending (6)	Real Per Capita Education Spending (7)
Low Income							
NFLD	17	-4.569	0.151	-671	0.046	-2.800	3.643
PEI	6	-2.939	-0.643	-428	0.027	-1.063	2.640
NS	13	-2.392	-0.291	-1073	0.041	-1.858	6.329
NB	12	-3.195	0.832	-1008	0.077	-3.315	6.378
QUE	32	-0.494	0.032	-451	0.092	-6.220	5.572
ONT	51	-0.625	-0.003	-2782	0.055	-9.897	13.046
MAN	14	-0.314	0.017	-1152	0.031	-3.949	6.445
SASK	13	-0.283	-0.037	-1096	0.010	-5.706	5.893
ALTA	38	-0.323	-0.001	-1617	0.000	-8.273	7.041
BC	53	-0.829	-0.016	-1393	0.059	-6.954	7.657
Middle Income							
NFLD	27	-7.431	0.319	-1104	0.078	-1.429	1.843
PEI	12	-6.017	-1.358	-878	0.054	-0.675	1.663
NS	26	-4.520	-0.537	-2054	0.082	-1.110	3.749
NB	23	-5.990	1.632	-1943	0.149	-1.987	3.790
QUE	72	-1.007	0.075	-903	0.190	-3.947	3.504
ONT	107	-1.276	-0.005	-5681	0.118	-6.283	8.180
MAN	27	-0.619	0.038	-2273	0.062	-2.424	3.923
SASK	26	-0.560	-0.071	-2171	0.019	-3.508	3.595
ALTA	76	-0.658	0.000	-3315	0.000	-5.247	4.439
BC	107	-1.680	-0.019	-2861	0.121	-4.438	4.847

Table 7.2 (continued)

Province	Average Weekly Wage (nominal) (1)	MIN (2)	MINWKS (3)	Provincial Income Tax Rate (4)	Annual Social Assistance Benefits (nominal) (5)	Real Per Capita Federal Spending (6)	Real Per Capita Education Spending (7)
High Income							
NFLD	6	1.500	0.067	−238	0.017	−0.057	0.188
PEI	2	0.563	−0.277	−177	0.011	−0.025	0.160
NS	7	0.695	−0.142	−524	0.020	−0.053	0.453
NB	6	1.869	0.394	−470	0.036	−0.089	0.434
QUE	22	1.039	0.023	−290	0.062	−0.240	0.544
ONT	32	0.239	−0.004	−1750	0.035	−0.359	1.192
MAN	8	0.129	0.010	−627	0.016	−0.124	0.512
SASK	7	0.075	−0.020	−620	0.005	−0.186	0.484
ALTA	25	0.207	−0.001	−1028	0.000	−0.301	0.646
BC	35	0.485	−0.008	−916	0.038	−0.262	0.733

Table 7.3
Policy Changes Equivalent to a $1 Change in Average Weekly Earnings, 1978–96, Model 1 (units indicated in parentheses)

Province	MIN (weeks) (1)	MINWKS (weeks) (2)	Provincial Income Tax Rate (percentage points) (3)	Annual Social Assistance Benefits (current $) (4)	Real Per Capita Federal Spending (constant $) (5)	Real Per Capita Education Spending (constant $) (6)
Low Income						
NFLD	-1.2	109.0	-0.02	353	27	19
PEI	-0.8	-9.0	-0.01	218	25	9
NS	-2.1	-46.3	-0.01	330	33	9
NB	-1.1	14.4	-0.01	157	16	8
QUE	-12.6	1003.7	-0.07	353	24	24
ONT	-31.2	-15599.8	-0.02	931	24	16
MAN	-15.9	798.1	-0.01	447	16	9
SASK	-18.7	-361.3	-0.01	1286	11	9
ALTA	-38.5	-45262.5	-0.02	*	21	22
BC	-21.9	-3534.3	-0.04	896	34	28
Middle Income						
NFLD	-0.5	83.1	-0.02	337	16	-1376
PEI	-0.4	-8.7	-0.01	216	15	-686
NS	-1.0	-47.9	-0.01	313	20	-662
NB	-0.5	14.1	-0.01	156	10	-583
QUE	-5.6	965.6	-0.08	383	16	-2012
ONT	-14.9	-23707.8	-0.02	908	15	-1263
MAN	-7.3	718.3	-0.01	451	10	-674
SASK	-9.0	-368.4	-0.01	1285	6	-702
ALTA	-17.3	*	-0.02	*	13	-1663
BC	-10.0	-6706.0	-0.04	898	21	-2146

Table 7.3 (continued)

Province	MIN (weeks) (1)	MINWKS (weeks) (2)	Provincial Income Tax Rate (percentage points) (3)	Annual Social Assistance Benefits (current $) (4)	Real Per Capita Federal Spending (constant $) (5)	Real Per Capita Education Spending (constant $) (6)
High Income						
NFLD	-0.5	86.1	-0.02	342	10	-37
PEI	-0.3	-8.6	-0.01	213	9	-18
NS	-0.9	-45.8	-0.01	322	12	-17
NB	-0.5	14.0	-0.01	156	6	-15
QUE	-4.8	964.2	-0.08	362	9	-50
ONT	-13.1	-8162.9	-0.02	893	9	-32
MAN	-6.7	757.0	-0.01	470	6	-18
SASK	-8.2	-366.8	-0.01	1429	4	-19
ALTA	-15.8	-22405.5	-0.02	*	8	-46
BC	-9.2	-4746.5	-0.04	935	13	-58

* The calculated marginal effect is approximately zero, so it is impossible to compute the equivalent policy change.

Table 7.4
Policy Changes Equivalent to a $1 Change in Average Weekly Earnings, 1978–96, Model 2 (units indicated in parentheses)

Province	MIN (weeks) (1)	MINWKS (weeks) (2)	Provincial Income Tax Rate (percentage points) (3)	Annual Social Assistance Benefits (current $) (4)	Real Per Capita Federal Spending (constant $) (5)	Real Per Capita Education Spending (constant $) (6)
Low Income						
NFLD	−3.6	110.2	−0.02	362	−6	5
PEI	−2.0	−9.0	−0.01	215	−5	2
NS	−5.6	−46.2	−0.01	328	−7	2
NB	−3.8	14.4	−0.01	156	−4	2
QUE	−65.0	1002.8	−0.07	349	−5	6
ONT	−82.4	−17162.7	−0.02	936	−5	4
MAN	−44.2	817.1	−0.01	448	−5	2
SASK	−46.9	−358.5	−0.01	1327	−2	2
ALTA	−116.5	−37633.0	−0.02	*	−5	5
BC	−63.7	−3300.8	−0.04	895	−8	7
Middle Income						
NFLD	−3.6	83.2	−0.02	340	−19	14
PEI	−2.0	−8.7	−0.01	218	−17	7
NS	−5.7	−47.9	−0.01	314	−23	7
NB	−3.9	14.2	−0.01	155	−12	6
QUE	−71.8	964.1	−0.08	381	−18	21
ONT	−83.9	−21405.2	−0.02	907	−17	13
MAN	−44.3	721.1	−0.01	442	−11	7
SASK	−47.0	−370.6	−0.01	1385	−8	7
ALTA	−115.7	*	−0.02	*	−15	17
BC	−64.0	−5654.7	−0.04	888	−24	22

Table 7.4 (continued)

Province	MIN (weeks) (1)	MINWKS (weeks) (2)	Provincial Income Tax Rate (percentage points) (3)	Annual Social Assistance Benefits (current $) (4)	Real Per Capita Federal Spending (constant $) (5)	Real Per Capita Education Spending (constant $) (6)
High Income						
NFLD	3.8	86.0	-0.02	339	-101	31
PEI	4.2	-8.6	-0.01	216	-95	15
NS	9.4	-45.8	-0.01	325	-123	14
NB	3.0	14.1	-0.01	154	-62	13
QUE	21.4	967.4	-0.08	359	-93	41
ONT	132.0	-7884.5	-0.02	901	-88	26
MAN	58.3	751.6	-0.01	470	-61	15
SASK	99.6	-373.6	-0.01	1494	-40	15
ALTA	118.6	-24540.0	-0.02	*	-82	38
BC	72.9	-4418.4	-0.04	930	-135	48

* The calculated marginal effect is approximately zero, so it is impossible to compute the equivalent policy change.

Table 7.5
Means of Selected Explanatory Variables, 1978–96, by Province

Province	Average Weekly Earnings (Current dollars)	Real Per Capita Federal Spending (1986=100)	Real Per Capita Spending on Education (1986=100)	Annual Social Assistance Benefits (Current dollars)	Provincial Income Tax Rates	MIN (weeks)	MINWKS (weeks)
NFLD	417.65	904.67	1,063.10	9,029.60	0.619	10	39
PEI	362.72	1,629.00	998.23	9,614.20	0.551	10	38
NS	391.49	2,142.70	964.64	9,631.90	0.568	11	35
NB	397.19	1,165.90	935.25	7,445.40	0.585	11	36
QUE	429.29	670.10	1,151.90	8,640.60	0.854[1]	11	34
ONT	452.89	929.96	1,091.30	11,289.00	0.509	13	26
MAN	400.57	1,021.70	966.62	8,770.40	0.532	14	25
SASK	395.56	665.72	995.01	10,059.00	0.508	15	22
ALTA	445.50	646.10	1,174.50	9,804.50	0.433	14	25
BC	457.57	688.39	944.96	10,555.00	0.488	13	31
Average	415.04	1,046.42	1,133.19	9,483.96	0.565	12.2	31.1

[1] The value for Quebec is an approximation obtained by computing an implicit Quebec tax rate comparable in definition to that for the other provinces, for stayers in Quebec in states of the world 1, 2, and 3 in each year. These values are then averaged across states of the world and years for the period 1978–96. The formula for the implicit Quebec tax rate is

$$\tau_Q = \frac{TOTALTAX_Q - FT_{BA}}{FT_{BA}},$$

where $TOTALTAX_Q$ is total tax owed and FT_{BA} is federal tax owing before the Quebec abatement is applied. FT_{BA} is computed as

$$FT_{BA} = \frac{FT_Q}{1 - a_Q},$$

where FT_Q is actual federal tax owed and a_Q is the federal abatement rate.

an impression of the actual sensitivity of Canadians to various types of market and policy changes.

THE MARGINAL EFFECT OF CHANGES IN AVERAGE WEEKLY WAGES

We begin by computing the marginal effect of changing weekly before-tax wages. This is useful as a foil to the effects of changes in policy parameters. A comparison of the effects of small changes in market wages with those of a small policy reform leads to a better understanding of the quantitative importance of marginal changes in policy parameters.

The sign of the derivative of the migration rate with respect to weekly wages depends on the sign of the coefficient on the expected income variable, among other factors. The exact form of this marginal effect is somewhat complicated and is safely relegated to appendix F. Because the estimated value of the coefficient of INCOME is positive for all income classes, we know from the formulas for marginal effects that an increase in the wage rate in any province j will increase in-migration to and decrease out-migration from that province, while having the opposite effect on all other regions. It is harder to predict which province's wage rate will have the greatest effect on migration flows. The formula in appendix F indicates that the effect on P_{ij} will be larger, the larger are the probabilities of states 1 to 3. The marginal migration flows will also depend on the size of provincial populations, which are used to convert changes in probabilities into flows of persons.

Taking all this into account, column (1) of table 7.1 indicates that marginal changes in average weekly earnings in Quebec, Ontario, Alberta, and British Columbia have larger effects on net in-migration to those provinces than does a change in average weekly earnings in the Atlantic region or in the Prairie provinces. For each income class, the biggest effects are found in Ontario and British Columbia, followed by Alberta and Quebec. For all provinces, the effects rise and then decline with income.

Column (1) of table 7.2 displays a similar pattern, although the magnitude of the marginal effects is smaller for all provinces and income classes, no doubt because the estimated coefficient of the composite INCOME variable is smaller for Model 2. As a comparison of tables 7.1 and 7.2 shows, the difference between Models 1 and 2 in the magnitude of the coefficient of INCOME leads to large differences in the magnitude of the marginal effects. For example, the tables suggest that a one-dollar increase in average weekly earnings in British Columbia would increase net in-migration to that province by a total of 470 people if computed using Model 1, but only by 195 people if Model 2 is used. Similarly, the predicted increase in the net inflow of individuals to Prince Edward Island in response to a one-dollar increase in nominal average weekly earnings in that province ranges from 46 people for Model 1 to 20 people for Model 2.

MINIMUM WEEKS REQUIRED TO QUALIFY FOR UNEMPLOYMENT INSURANCE

The effect on migration of a marginal increase in MIN, the minimum weeks of work required for UI qualification, is of ambiguous sign theoretically speaking. Assuming that weeks of unemployment insurance *entitlement* are unchanged, the marginal effect on migration from origin i to destination j of a small increase in MIN_j by one week is

$$\frac{\partial P_{ij}}{\partial MIN_j} = P_{ij}(1 - P_{ij})\left\{\frac{\alpha_1 \pi_{j3}}{INC_{ij3}}\left[w_j(1 - \tau_{ij3}) - \frac{\overline{SA_j}}{52}\right] - \frac{\alpha_2 \pi_{j3}}{(T - MIN_j)}\right\}. \qquad (7.2)$$

Here we see that a marginal change in MIN in region j has two effects that tend to offset each other. First, since individuals must now work longer to qualify for unemployment insurance benefits in state 3 – that is, when weakly attached to the labour market – in location j after the policy change has taken place, their wage income in that state will be higher and their social assistance (SA) income will be lower. Consequently, as long as the after-tax wage exceeds average weekly SA benefits, and the coefficient α_1 in expected utility (4.7) is positive, a small increase in MIN will tend to increase inflows to province j. Second, a marginal increase in MIN means that the individual's leisure time will be lower in state 3. If α_2 is also positive, this effect tends to reduce inflows to province j. A similar argument applies to a change in MIN in a third region k.

The nature of the change in migration will depend on which of the two effects is largest. The smaller is α_2 relative to α_1 or, in other words, the weaker is the individual's preference for leisure relative to consumption, the more likely it is that the net effect will be positive. And if it is positive, increases in MIN_j will result in larger inflows to (and smaller outflows from) region j as individuals optimize over alternative locations.

Note also the interesting interaction between the generosity of unemployment insurance, represented in (7.2) by the parameter MIN, and the generosity of social assistance, represented by SA. We saw a hint of this interaction in table 1.1, where it appeared that provinces with a high qualifying threshold for unemployment insurance also tended to provide higher than average social assistance. Equation (7.2) implies that the more generous are social assistance benefits SA in province j, the smaller will be the effect of a change in MIN_j.

The results for a small increase in MIN in column (2) of tables 7.1 and 7.2 suggest that on average the leisure effect of a change in MIN outweighs the income effect, except for the high-income group under Model 2. With the exception of the latter case, the marginal effect of a change in MIN is always negative. Thus Models 1 and 2, when estimated using migration and other data disaggregated according to income, age, and sex, imply that the average Canadian would prefer an additional week of leisure time (or non-wage activity) and less income to an additional week of wage income and less leisure time.

Although once again the magnitude of the effect is smaller for Model 2, both models suggest that the impact of a change in the generosity of unemployment insurance as reflected by MIN will be largest in the four Atlantic provinces. Model 1 suggests that a one-week decrease in MIN in Newfoundland would result in a decrease in net in-migration of 171 people. With the Model 2 parameter estimates, the decrease in the net inflow is only 6 percent of that amount, or 11 people. Similarly, for Saskatchewan, whose residents appear to be the least sensitive to changes in MIN, the predicted decrease in net in-migration ranges from 11 for Model 1 to only 1 person for Model 2. For all provinces, the effect of a change in MIN is largest for middle-income taxpayers, a result likely due to the fact that the coefficient of $INCOME$ is largest for this group.

Even though the marginal effects of changes in MIN are biggest in the Atlantic provinces, the first columns of tables 7.3 and 7.4 indicate that the change in MIN required to produce the same net in-migration as a one-dollar increase in the weekly wage is the largest in Ontario and Alberta and the smallest in the Atlantic region and Quebec for all income classes. For example, for low-income individuals the equivalent change in MIN in Ontario is a decrease of 31 weeks according to Model 1, and 82 weeks according to Model 2. By way of contrast, MIN would have to decrease by only 1 to 4 weeks (depending on the model) to achieve the same increase in net in-migration of low-income individuals to Newfoundland as a one-dollar increase in average weekly earnings in that province. Note that these differences across provinces in the "standardized" marginal effects are not simply the consequence of smaller marginal effects with respect to wages in the Atlantic provinces. In fact, as tables 7.1 and 7.2 indicate, the marginal effect of a change in the wage is actually larger in Newfoundland than in the Prairie provinces.

To help put the magnitude of the changes in column (1) of tables 7.3 and 7.4 into perspective, it should be noted that the average value of MIN in the 1978–96 period in the country as a whole was 12.2 weeks (see table 7.5). Thus a reduction of, say, 31 weeks, as in the case of the low-income group in Ontario for Model 1, is probably far from anything that might be introduced. From this point of view, net migration to Ontario appears to be more sensitive to changes in wages in Ontario than it is to changes in the unemployment insurance system. On the other hand, a change in MIN of less than two weeks is likely a feasible policy change. So these results suggest that net migration to the Atlantic provinces is more sensitive to this parameter of the insurance system than is migration to Ontario or, as the tables indicate, to the Western provinces.

The Model 1 results indicate that the decrease in MIN required to produce the same effect as a one-dollar change in weekly wages also declines with income for each province, suggesting that higher-income people derive more utility from an increment to leisure or non-work time and, thus, require a smaller decrease in MIN to compensate for a given reduction in income. However, the results using Model 2 do not support Model 1 in this respect.

It should be emphasized that the negative signs in column (2) of tables 7.1 and 7.2 do not imply that during the sample period, people have deliberately altered their behaviour to increase the likelihood that they will have just enough work to qualify for unemployment insurance benefits. While some individuals may in fact do so, the model we are using is not capable of testing for such behaviour because it assumes that province-wide employment probabilities as well as weeks of work in each state of the world are fixed independently of individual decision making. However, our results do suggest that on average, Canadians tend to prefer provinces where benefits are more generous. That is, people tend to prefer locations where their expected leisure time will be greater, holding all else constant, because they seem to have a relatively strong preference for leisure. In this respect, the Model 2 estimates for the low- and middle-income classes lead to the same conclusion, even though the ratio of the coefficients on INCOME and LEISURE is considerably different than it is using Model 1.

MAXIMUM WEEKS OF UNEMPLOYMENT BENEFITS WITH MINIMUM QUALIFICATIONS

If MINWKS increases, an individual in state 3 spends more time on unemployment insurance and less time on social assistance, with the total amount of leisure time available remaining constant. This effect is different from that for a change in MIN, as the following formula indicates:.

$$\frac{\partial P_{ij}}{\partial MINWKS_{j}} = P_{ij}\left(1-P_{ij}\right)\alpha_1 \frac{\pi_{j3}}{INC_{ij3}}\left[\rho w_j^R\left(1-\tau_{ij3}\right)-\frac{\overline{SA_j}}{52}\right], \ t > 1971. \quad (7.3)$$

If we compare (7.3) with (7.2), we see that the consequences of a change in MIN depend on the after-tax wage rather than on the legislated replacement wage for insurance claimants and, in contrast to the effect of a change in MINWKS, it also depends on the effect on leisure time, since someone without the minimum weeks of insurance eligibility must give up leisure or non-wage activity to gain eligibility for benefits. When the estimated income coefficient α_1 in (7.3) is positive, the sign of the derivative of migration rates with respect to MINWKS depends on the size of the after-tax weekly unemployment insurance benefit or replacement wage ρw_j^R relative to the weekly social assistance payment $\overline{SA_j}/52$, which people in state 3 are assumed to receive if not eligible for unemployment insurance. As long as the after-tax weekly unemployment insurance payment is greater than the weekly social assistance payment, an increase in MINWKS in province j will lead to an increase in net in-migration to that province.

The reference to 1971 in (7.3) signifies that this is the year when unemployment insurance benefits became taxable. For prior years we must drop the tax rate from the formula, which is otherwise the same. Since we are examining marginal effects for the 1978–96 period only, however, only equation (7.3) needs to be used in their calculation.

Column (3) of tables 7.1 and 7.2 displays the change in net in-migration resulting from a one-week increase in MINWKS. Variation across provinces in the level of social assistance payments relative to insurance benefits is responsible for the variation in the sign of the marginal effect. Only in Newfoundland, New Brunswick, Quebec, and Manitoba have after-tax unemployment insurance benefits tended to be larger than weekly social assistance benefits, resulting in a positive effect for an increase in MINWKS in those provinces. The magnitude of the response to a one-week increase in MINWKS ranges from an increase in net in-migration to New Brunswick of 3–7 individuals, depending on the model used, to a decrease in net in-migration to Prince Edward Island of 2–5 individuals.

As a whole, these results indicate that the interaction of the unemployment insurance system and the social assistance system is important in determining the effect of the MINWKS parameter of the insurance system on migration behaviour.[3] They also show that for nearly all provinces and income classes, the effect of marginal changes in MINWKS is small. The consequences of the insurance system combined with social assistance for income and leisure time apparently make migration insensitive to marginal changes in MINWKS when compared to the effect of marginal changes in MIN.

Column (2) of Tables 7.3 and 7.4 presents the changes in MINWKS that would have the same migration effect as a one-dollar increase in average weekly earnings. These numbers are considerably larger than those for MIN, for all provinces and income classes. For example, both the Model 1 and Model 2 results suggest that MINWKS would have to decrease by over 22,000 weeks in order to induce the same increase in net in-migration of high-income individuals to Alberta as a one-dollar increase in average weekly earnings in Alberta!

The large numbers in column (2) for Ontario, British Columbia, and Alberta reflect the fact that the insurance payment and the social assistance payment are similar in these cases, causing the marginal effect with respect to MINWKS to be extremely small. The absence of a number for Alberta for the middle-income group reflects the approximately zero value of the derivative in this case.

The numbers for Prince Edward Island are smaller, however. MINWKS would have to decrease by only about 9 weeks in Prince Edward Island to generate the same effect as a one-dollar increase in average weekly earnings. The numbers are also relatively small in absolute value for the other Atlantic provinces, again suggesting that unemployment insurance is more important there than it is in Central and Western Canada.

THE PROVINCIAL "PIGGY BACK" TAX RATE

We turn now to the marginal effects of a one-unit change in the provincial tax rate applied to basic federal income tax. Today provinces levy their income taxes directly on taxable income. But during our sample period, with the exception of Quebec, which has long had its own income tax, the provinces made use of a piggy-back income tax levied as a percent of the federal income tax. Accordingly, the effect on migration to province j of a change in the income tax rate in j is

$$\frac{\partial P_{ij}}{\partial \tau_j^P} = P_{ij}\left(1 - P_{ij}\right)\alpha_1\left[\frac{\pi_{j1}}{INC_{ij1}}FT_{ij1} + \frac{\pi_{j2}}{INC_{ij2}}FT_{ij2} + \frac{\pi_{j3}}{INC_{ij3}}FT_{ij3}\right], \quad (7.4)$$

where FT_{ijs} is income tax payable to the federal government in state s. The formula for Quebec is slightly more involved. See appendix F for the details.

The calculations are presented in column (4) of tables 7.1 and 7.2. The effects of a small change in this tax rate are similar for the two models. The negative sign of the marginal effect implies that an increase in the tax rate in a province reduces net in-migration to that province. As the formula for the marginal effect confirms, this result is simply a consequence of the positive sign of the coefficient of expected income.

In comparison to the other numbers in the tables, the marginal tax effects are very large, and well over 1,000 people in most cases. However, as table 7.5 indicates, the average over the 1978–96 period of the provincial tax rates that are applied to the basic federal income tax for the purposes of determining provincial tax under the tax collection agreements is just 0.564.[4] Thus an increase of 1 in provincial tax rates would be enormous. A more realistic amount is a tax rate increase of 0.01, and the effect of such a change can be approximated by multiplying the values in column (4) by 0.01. Numbers that are closer in magnitude to those in column (1) result from this calculation. For example, the approximate total effect of a 0.01 percentage point increase in the Manitoba tax rate on net in-migration to Manitoba would be a decrease of 96 people according to Model 1, and a decrease of 41 people according to Model 2.

For all income classes and both models, Ontario is the province where the marginal effect of income tax changes is largest in magnitude. Models 1 and 2 predict declines of approximately 244 or 102 people in total net inflows to Ontario as a result of an increase of 0.01 in the Ontario piggy-back tax rate. By way of contrast, the predicted decrease in net inflows to Prince Edward Island would be much smaller: only 15 people for Model 2 and only 34 people for Model 1.

In column (3) of tables 7.3 and 7.4 one can find the change in provincial tax rates required to replicate the effect on net in-migration of a one-dollar change in weekly wages. The changes in column (3) are small relative to the average provincial tax rate of 0.564, and from the perspective of someone interested in public policy reform, these results can be read as indicating that migration is generally sensitive to changes in provincial income tax rates, just as it is to wage changes. This should not be surprising, since taxes affect migration by altering after-tax wages.

It is interesting to note that for Quebec, which is the province with by far the highest average tax rate over the 1978–96 period (0.854), the tax rate change required to replicate the effect of a one-dollar change in weekly wages is the largest of all the provinces – a decrease of 0.07 to 0.08 percentage points. This result is not apparent if one looks at the marginal migration flows directly instead of at the calculations in tables 7.3 and 7.4. The next largest response, which is half of the Quebec one, is for British Columbia.

One intriguing possibility suggested by the calculations in column (3) is that the government of Quebec takes advantage of the relative insensitivity of out-migration from Quebec to tax changes in order to increase income tax rates above those in other parts of the country. Whether such an explanation is in fact the main or the correct one is an issue that lies outside the scope of the present study.

SOCIAL ASSISTANCE

We have seen that the level of social assistance payments relative to the generosity of unemployment insurance affects the consequences of changing unemployment insurance parameters. But what about the consequences of a change in the level of social assistance by itself? The exact formula for this marginal effect (in j, on migration to j) is given by the following:

$$\frac{\partial P_{ij}}{\partial SA_j} = P_{ij}\left(1 - P_{ij}\right)\alpha_1 \left[\frac{\pi_{j3}}{INC_{ij3}} \frac{\left(50 - MIN_j - MINWKS_j\right)}{52} + \frac{\pi_{j4}}{INC_{ij4}}\right]. \quad (7.5)$$

Column (5) of tables 7.1 and 7.2 shows that for both models and all income classes, the effect of a one-dollar increase in yearly social assistance payments is small. We should expect such a result, since a one-dollar increase in annual social assistance benefits is a minuscule amount. However, multiplying these marginal effects by 52, so as to obtain a change more comparable to that of a one-dollar increase in average weekly earnings, would still result in numbers that are smaller in magnitude than those in column (1), suggesting that migration flows are much less sensitive to changes in social assistance benefits than they are to changes in weekly wages. For example, the numbers in table 7.1 imply that a $52 increase in annual social assistance benefits in Quebec leads to an increase in total net in-migration to that province of about 43 people, which is far less than the 304-person increase that the same model predicts would result from a comparable change in average weekly earnings.

The change in the yearly social assistance payment required to produce the same effect as a one-dollar change in the weekly wage, shown in column (4) of table 7.3 for Model 1, varies from about $160 in New Brunswick to over \$1,400 in Saskatchewan, depending on the income class. For Model 2, the range is similar. For both models, and as we saw for the marginal effect of changing MIN, there is a distinct difference in tables 7.3 and 7.4 between the Atlantic provinces and Quebec on the one hand, and Ontario and the West on the other. The smaller figures in the former case indicate that social assistance is generally more than twice as important in Quebec and the Eastern provinces, though Manitoba is closer to the Atlantic region than the other Western provinces.

To assess the relevance or feasibility of the marginal changes in policy required to generate flows equal to that from a small change in wages, we note that the average yearly social assistance payment for a single person with two children in the 1978–96 period is about \$9,484 current dollars (see, again. table 7.5). Thus \$1,400 is a large change that is unlikely to be introduced. One may also note that since a one-dollar change in weekly wages is equivalent to a change in yearly social assistance benefits of \$52, a \$1,400 change in social assistance in the case of Saskatchewan is equivalent to a change in the weekly wage there of about \$27, or 7 percent of the 1978–96 average weekly wage in that province. These figures reflect the fact that while social assistance is more important in the East than in the West (in our sample period), generally migration is not very sensitive to marginal changes in the level of social assistance payments.

GOVERNMENT SPENDING

Finally, we consider the effects of marginal changes in federal current and capital spending, and of provincial and local spending on education. The formula for the marginal effect of public spending variable F_h in province j is

$$\frac{\partial P_{ij}}{\partial F_{hj}} = P_{ij}(1 - P_{ij})\frac{\alpha_{3h}}{F_{hj}}, \tag{7.6}$$

which is simpler than the formulas for the other variables examined. As this formula indicates, the signs of these marginal effects are determined entirely by the signs of the corresponding coefficients, α_{3h}. Thus table 7.1 shows that for Model 1, where the coefficient of real per capita federal spending is positive, the marginal effects of changes in spending are positive, while table 7.2 for Model 2, where the coefficient is negative, shows that the marginal effect is negative. The signs of the marginal effects of real per capita spending on education for the middle- and high-income groups also change when one switches from Model 1 to Model 2. As far as the magnitude of these effects is concerned, it seems to be lowest for the Atlantic provinces, regardless of the direction of the effect.

Of course the changes in the signs of the coefficients also affect the direction of the changes equivalent to a one-dollar change in average weekly earnings, reported in the last two columns of tables 7.3 and 7.4. In the case of federal spending, the figures are all small – ranging from a high of about $14.50 to a low of about $0.56 for Model 1, depending on the income class – when compared to the average level of per capita federal spending in each province over the 1978–96 period, about $1,046. The same can be said of the education spending numbers, except for the middle class under Model 1; however, the very large values for this group in column (6) of table 7.3 can be explained by the fact that the estimated coefficient of education spending in this case is close to zero.

CONCLUSIONS

At this point it would be nice to compare our estimated marginal effects to those of other studies. Unfortunately, few other studies report marginal effects, and those that do report numbers that are not directly comparable to ours. For example, although Bahkshi et al. (2009) report results relating to flows of migrants measured in numbers of people between an origin i and a destination j, their results with respect to wage rates are reported in the form of elasticities that measure the percentage change in each migration flow associated with a 1 percent change in the ratio of the origin real wage to the destination real wage. Not only are our marginal effects for wages not reported in elasticity form, they also pertain to current dollar wages rather than real wages, and to the wage in the destination, not the ratio of origin and destination wages. Similarly, other studies either do not include unemployment insurance parameters that are directly comparable to MIN and MINWKS or do not compute marginal effects as such, or report marginal effects for migration rates rather than migration flows.

To summarize our calculations briefly, we can say that the marginal effects presented in this chapter indicate that unemployment insurance and social assistance reduce interprovincial mobility. In our study, we find that these effects are strongest (relative to the effect of marginal changes in market wages) for the Atlantic region and Quebec. The role of taxation also appears to be a significant determinant of mobility at least for Quebec and British Columbia, though in most cases, the effects of changes in average weekly wages appear to be more important than policy changes, judging by the substantial size of the marginal policy changes (if we can call them that) that are required to replicate the consequences of a change in weekly wages.

In the next chapter we present simulations of more complex counterfactuals regarding market conditions and public policies. The reason we do so is that neither statistical significance nor the calculation of the effects of marginal policy changes give us a complete picture of the quantitative importance of public policy. For example, the marginal effect calculations for MIN and MINWKS are only suggestive of the effects of changes in the regionally extended entrance and benefit provisions of unemployment insurance. This is because changes in these aspects of the insurance system will only occasionally have the effect of changing the values of MIN and MINWKS in one province alone, as the marginal effect calculations assume. Instead, changes in regional aspects of the system may affect the values of MIN and MINWKS in more than one province at the same time, and the values of MXYR and MXYRWKS may be affected as well. The simulations in the next chapter take all these changes into account simultaneously.

8

Simulating Counterfactual Policy Regimes and Other Scenarios

How different would Canadian migration patterns be if the variable entrance requirement for unemployment insurance benefits was eliminated, or if the Parti Québécois had not won the election in Quebec in the mid-1970s? These are just two examples of the kind of questions we can ask using simulation. Constructing such counterfactuals provides insight into which factors matter most to interprovincial migrants and what the consequences for migration flows might be if public policy had been altered in specific ways or if some extraordinary events had not occurred. While marginal effects constitute a useful way of looking at the implications of our estimated models, they are limited by the fact that only small changes in one policy affecting specific migration flows can be considered. Simulations allow the investigation of alternative policy regimes that involve simultaneous changes in all provinces and in all origin-destination pairs.

The range of possible policy changes that can be explored through simulation is large, so we need to place some limits on the scope of our analysis. The general focus of the counterfactual simulations we discuss in this chapter is on the effects of removing regional variation in fiscal policies, since this variation is at the heart of the debates about policy-induced migration. To provide some perspective on the results of these policy simulations, we also consider the effects of eliminating regional variation in two important features of labour markets, namely average weekly earnings and the probabilities of the states of the world, as well as moving costs. Comparing the effects of eliminating regional variation in policy to the effects of eliminating regional variation in these market or non-policy variables will provide more insight into the relative importance of all of these factors in the migration decisions of Canadians.

Before turning to the simulation results themselves, in the next section we explain how the results are reported and discuss some of the limitations of the simulation procedure. Then we discuss the simulations in two parts. First we consider regional variation in fiscal policies and in selected market conditions and moving costs. We also investigate the implications for provincial unemployment rates of the complete elimination of regional variation in the unemployment insurance system. Although our discussion of labour market consequences is of necessity speculative because we have not actually modelled the relationship between migration and labour markets, it turns out that these counterfactuals provide an important perspective on fiscally induced migration in Canada. Finally, we turn to the extraordinary events and explore their impact on net migration to Quebec and Newfoundland.

INTERPRETING THE SIMULATION RESULTS

All the simulation results are reported as changes from a base case defined by the fitted values of the model being simulated. The reason for drawing comparisons with the fitted values of migration flows rather than the historical values is that we do not want to colour our simulations with mistakes the models make in replicating history. We want the simulations to reflect the structure of things as we have estimated it.

As in the case of the marginal effects, and for the convenience of the reader, we translate the changes in predicted migration rates to changes in migration flows by multiplying each origin/destination-specific migration flow by the appropriate provincial population. Then the origin/destination-specific flows are summed to obtain the changes in total in-, out-, and net in-migration for each province. We do this here, as in the last chapter, because there are simply too many gross flows between provinces to examine the effect of each simulation on each flow individually. Furthermore, to the extent that total in-, out-, and net in-migration are the most important from a labour market perspective, changes in these aggregates are of greater interest than changes in origin-destination flows. In addition, we report only the average change over the 1978–96 period. This period is chosen because prior to 1978, as we pointed out in chapter 2, there was no regional variation in MIN, one of the key unemployment insurance parameters we wish to examine.

To aid us in evaluating the magnitude of the simulated changes in migration flows, table 8.1 presents the actual and predicted flows averaged over the simulation period of 1978–96. The predicted flows in this table are generated using the Model 1 and 2 estimates in table 6.2. For example, Model 1 predicts that average annual net in-migration to Ontario over the 1978–96 period was 928 individuals, while Model 2 predicts it to have been only 288 individuals. The actual value was 393.

Before continuing it is also important to note that although the simulations cover a nineteen-year period, they are not dynamic. Rather, in each year the same policy change is treated as if it were being introduced that year for the first time. The average changes reported can thus be viewed as the average impact effect of introducing the policy change. While it would have been possible, though difficult, to make the simulations dynamic by treating each province's population as an endogenous variable whose value is altered by the predicted change in net migration flows, we chose not to carry out this type of dynamic simulation. Our models do a mediocre job of explaining year-to-year fluctuations in migration flows, as we have noted, so that the annual forecast errors may at times be large. (We recall that we cannot compare these forecasts with those in the literature because no one else presents comparable details.) These forecast errors would then be compounded from year to year as the predicted change in net migration flows was used to adjust the provincial population in each year of the simulation. Moreover, theory suggests that changes in migration flows may change the state of labour markets, but we do not also model these responses. For these reasons, it is better if we restrict our attention to the impact effects of policy changes. Conclusions must be drawn in the light of these characteristics of our simulations.

The assumptions underlying each of the simulations that follow are described briefly as the simulation is discussed. All the simulations are carried out using the parameter estimates by income class for Models 1 and 2 obtained using data for the period 1974–96 (see table 6.2). Only one simulation, discussed in section "Regional Variation in the Unemployment Insurance System," below, is carried out using the estimates in table 6.6, which were derived from the 10 percent sample for 1968–96. To help the reader assimilate the large volume of data generated by the simulations, where possible the results are reported graphically rather than in tabular form, with detailed numerical results and some additional information regarding the assumptions underlying the simulations relegated to appendix G. While the graphical presentation of the results blurs differences between models in the precise magnitudes of the flows generated, it has the advantage of making patterns easier to identify. At the outset, we note that a careful comparison of the ranges of the vertical axes in the figures, as well as the discussion that accompanies the figures, will reveal that Model 2 usually generates smaller

Table 8.1
Actual and Predicted Values of Average Annual Migration Flows, 1978–96

	Model 1 Predicted Average Flows[1]			Model 2 Predicted Average Flows[1]			Actual Average Flows		
	In-migration	Out-migration	Net In-migration	In-migration	Out-migration	Net In-migration	In-migration	Out-migration	Net In-migration
Low Income									
NFLD	2307	3698	-1391	2321	3709	-1387	1567	2912	-1345
PEI	2040	2228	-188	2065	2228	-163	612	786	-174
NS	4320	5140	-820	4366	5140	-774	3041	3800	-759
NB	4320	5008	-688	4317	5007	-690	2198	2950	-752
QUE	3905	5840	-1935	3877	5878	-2001	3728	5521	-1793
ONT	11456	10230	1227	11345	10292	1053	13006	12054	952
MAN	4303	5369	-1066	4281	5404	-1123	2666	3624	-958
SASK	4133	5043	-911	4173	4960	-787	2638	3580	-942
ALTA	7433	5027	2406	7489	5043	2446	10743	8306	2437
BC	7183	3817	3365	7229	3802	3428	9514	6180	3334
Middle Income									
NFLD	2788	3298	-510	2830	3291	-461	1847	2371	-524
PEI	2650	2684	-33	2675	2683	-8	704	675	29
NS	5618	5574	44	5681	5578	102	3587	3565	22
NB	5597	5498	100	5613	5480	133	2583	2685	-102
QUE	5120	7254	-2135	5077	7333	-2255	4776	6707	-1931
ONT	13627	13825	-198	13471	13985	-513	14924	15274	-350
MAN	5165	6675	-1510	5133	6720	-1587	3108	4462	-1354
SASK	5111	6139	-1028	5191	5991	-800	3353	4433	-1080
ALTA	8252	7584	668	8355	7611	743	12971	12339	632
BC	9336	4734	4602	9374	4726	4648	12425	7769	4656

Table 8.1 (continued)

	Model 1 Predicted Average Flows[1]			Model 2 Predicted Average Flows[1]			Actual Average Flows		
	In-migration	Out-migration	Net In-migration	In-migration	Out-migration	Net In-migration	In-migration	Out-migration	Net In-migration
High Income									
NFLD	1830	1950	−120	1859	1939	−80	1258	1365	−107
PEI	1609	1514	95	1622	1520	102	557	451	106
NS	4298	3920	378	4322	3938	383	3396	2995	401
NB	4025	3698	327	4026	3696	331	2167	1971	196
QUE	4956	6751	−1795	4916	6813	−1897	4696	6237	−1542
ONT	12109	12210	−101	12051	12302	−252	13336	13545	−209
MAN	4205	5179	−974	4193	5197	−1004	2811	3717	−906
SASK	4263	4901	−638	4309	4835	−526	2604	3357	−753
ALTA	6453	7758	−1305	6498	7699	−1201	9009	10305	−1297
BC	8527	4395	4133	8543	4399	4144	10276	6166	4110
All Income Classes									
NFLD	6925	8945	−2020	7010	8939	−1929	4672	6647	−1975
PEI	6299	6425	−126	6362	6431	−69	1873	1912	−39
NS	14236	14633	−397	14368	14657	−289	10024	10360	−336
NB	13943	14204	−261	13956	14182	−226	6948	7606	−658
QUE	13981	19846	−5865	13870	20024	−6154	13200	18466	−5266
ONT	37192	36264	928	36867	36579	288	41266	40873	393
MAN	13672	17223	−3550	13606	17321	−3715	8585	11803	−3218
SASK	13507	16084	−2577	13672	15786	−2114	8596	11369	−2773
ALTA	22138	20369	1769	22342	20354	1988	32723	30950	1773
BC	25046	12946	12100	25146	12926	12220	32215	20115	12100

[1] Parameter estimates from table 6.2.

changes in migration flows than does Model 1, as was the case for the marginal effects. This is another feature of our results that we need to take into account in reaching conclusions.

The last set of simulations to be presented are those that deal with the extraordinary events. These are set out at the end of the chapter because the procedure for simulating the effects of the three extraordinary events included in our empirical model is different from that used for the other simulations. Each extraordinary event is assumed in the estimation to have had an effect for a distinct period of time only. Therefore we need only to compute the migration flow that would be predicted under the contrary-to-fact assumption that the event did not occur in the years during which the event is assumed to have had an effect, by setting the associated dummy variables equal to zero and all other explanatory variables equal to their actual values. To compute the change due to the event, we compare this predicted flow to the base case predicted flow for each year of the simulation, the base case here being represented by the predicted flow in the presence of the event. Then we report the total cumulated change in migration over the relevant period of each counterfactual.

REGIONAL VARIATION IN THE UNEMPLOYMENT INSURANCE SYSTEM

As we have documented in previous chapters, regional variation in unemployment insurance benefits arises through the variable entrance requirement (VER) and the regional extended benefit. To explore the separate and combined effects of these two provisions, we carry out three simulations. In the first, the variable entrance requirement is eliminated. In the second, the dependence of benefits on regional unemployment rates is eliminated. And in the third, regional variation in entrance requirements and benefits are eliminated simultaneously. We discuss each of these simulations in turn. Further details about these simulations are provided in appendix G.

Elimination of Regional Variation in Entrance Requirements

Under the VER, which came into effect in December 1977, fewer weeks of employment were required to qualify for benefits in high-unemployment regions. We eliminate the VER by setting the variable MIN, the minimum number of weeks of work required to qualify for insurance benefits, to 13 in all provinces and all years of the simulation. This value is the average value of MIN for Ontario over the period 1978 to 1996. As a consequence of this change in *MIN*, the values of the insurance parameters *MINWKS, MXYR, MXYRWKS* (see again table 4.1 for definitions), and weeks of social assistance benefits in employment state 3 all change as well. Consequently, both income and leisure time in states 2 and 3 change, resulting in changes to the variables *INCOME* and *LEISURE*.

The effect of this change on net in-migration for all three income classes using Model 1 can be found in figure 8.1a, while analogous results using Model 2 are presented in figure 8.1b. The corresponding numerical results for both models can be found in table G11 of appendix G. To read these and the following figures, first note that bars to the left of the zero line represent decreases in net inflows to a province, and bars to the right represent increases in net inflows. The length of the bars is proportional to the actual changes in the number of migrants, which are provided in tables in appendix G. The reader should also be aware that the range of the scale at the top of each figure is not the same for each figure.

Now by comparing the range of the horizontal axes in figures 8.1a and b, we can see immediately that the magnitude of the changes in net migration (and the in- and out-migration flows that underlie them) is greater for Model 1 than for Model 2. This difference is due to differences in the relative size of the coefficients on the variables *INCOME* and *LEISURE*, as well as those on other variables.

Figure 8.1a shows that the overall effect of the elimination of the VER is to move people out of the Atlantic region and Quebec, and to a much smaller extent, from British Columbia. Net in-migration to Ontario increases substantially as a result. Gross flows to and from Ontario and Newfoundland show the biggest changes. To understand these results, recall that an increase in *MIN* has two effects: in the region in which *MIN* is changed, leisure is reduced when people are weakly attached to the labour market (in state 3). At the same time, their income is higher because people with *MIN* weeks of employment are working more. The simulations thus tell us that the consequences for migration decisions of the reduction in leisure that results from the increase in *MIN* in higher-unemployment regions outweigh the income effect associated with additional weeks of work.

The effects using Model 2 shown in figure 8.1b are about one-tenth as big as those using Model 1. Note also that for the high-income group, *and for this group only*, Model 2 indicates that migration would flow in a direction opposite to that predicted by Model 1, that is, towards the Atlantic region. This latter difference stems from the negative sign of the estimated coefficient of *LEISURE* for high-income individuals in Model 2.

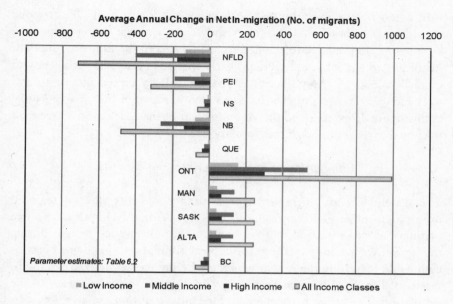

Average Annual Change in Net In-migration (No. of migrants)

-1000 -800 -600 -400 -200 0 200 400 600 800 1000 1200

NFLD
PEI
NS
NB
QUE
ONT
MAN
SASK
ALTA
BC

Parameter estimates: Table 6.2

■ Low Income   ■ Middle Income   ■ High Income   ▢ All Income Classes

Figure 8.1a   No variable entrance requirement, model 1

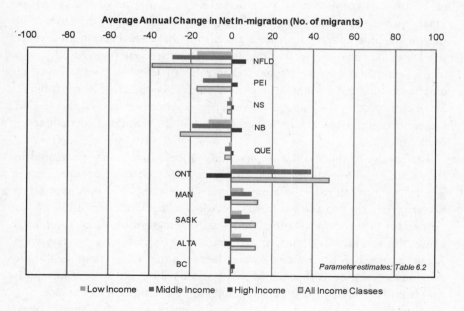

Average Annual Change in Net In-migration (No. of migrants)

-100 -80 -60 -40 -20 0 20 40 60 80 100

NFLD
PEI
NS
NB
QUE
ONT
MAN
SASK
ALTA
BC

Parameter estimates: Table 6.2

■ Low Income   ■ Middle Income   ■ High Income   ▢ All Income Classes

Figure 8.1b   No variable entrance requirement, model 2

In assessing the importance of the changes shown in the figures, one should keep in mind that the flows shown are average changes over the 1978–96 period relative to the predicted flows from the estimated models. According to Model 1, the average yearly change in the total net in-flow to Ontario over the 1978–96 period is 992 adults between the ages of 20 and 64, which is 107 percent of the base case predicted net in-flow. Using Model 2, this figure drops to 48 adults, or 17 percent of the base case average over the nineteen-year period of the simulation.

Elimination of Regionally Extended Benefits

The dependence of unemployment insurance benefits on the regional unemployment rate, first introduced in 1971, is another important source of interregional variation in the unemployment insurance system during the period we are investigating. In the next simulation, this dependence is eliminated by setting the rate at which qualifying weeks are translated into weeks of benefits (θ) equal to 2 weeks in all provinces in all years of the simulation. This value is the average for Ontario during the 1978–96 period. While two weeks of benefits for each week of employment may seem generous, it is consistent with the actual implementation of the system in Ontario over the 1978–96 period. It is quite possible that in the absence of the various unemployment-related provisions that have been in effect over the years, the basic entitlement might have been this generous. Modifying θ in this manner results in changes in the value of MXYR, MXYRWKS, MINWKS, and weeks of social assistance benefits in state 3, as discussed in appendix G. Since both INCOME and LEISURE change as a result, the effects of this second unemployment insurance simulation depend on the estimated coefficients of both variables.

The results of the simulation involving θ for Model 1 are presented in figure 8.2a, and for Model 2 in figure 8.2b.[1] The pattern of changes here is generally similar to that observed in figures 8.1a and b. Net in-migration to Ontario rises by 250 percent (2,329 persons) using Model 1, and by about 50 percent (139 persons) using Model 2. Net migration to Newfoundland using Model 1 falls by about 50 percent, but by only about 4 percent when Model 2 is used. A difference between the two models that is not seen in the previous simulation is that the Model 1 results show heavy net out-migration from Prince Edward Island (an increase of 318 percent of the base case prediction), while Model 2 predicts a modest increase in net in-migration to Prince Edward Island of about 12 percent.

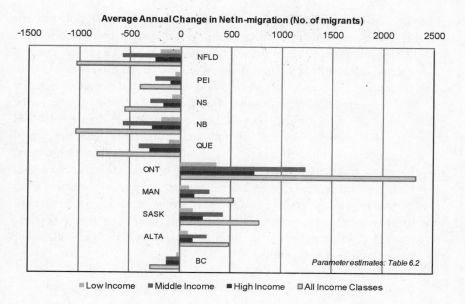

Average Annual Change in Net In-migration (No. of migrants)

-1500 -1000 -500 0 500 1000 1500 2000 2500

NFLD
PEI
NS
NB
QUE
ONT
MAN
SASK
ALTA
BC

Parameter estimates: Table 6.2

■ Low Income ■ Middle Income ■ High Income ▢ All Income Classes

Figure 8.2a   No regional extended benefit, model 1

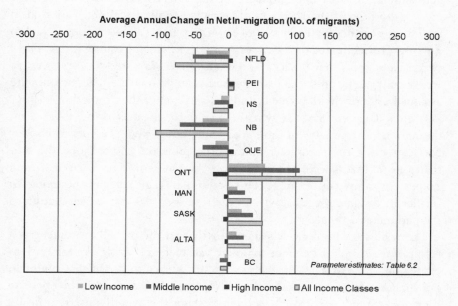

Average Annual Change in Net In-migration (No. of migrants)

-300 -250 -200 -150 -100 -50 0 50 100 150 200 250 300

NFLD
PEI
NS
NB
QUE
ONT
MAN
SASK
ALTA
BC

Parameter estimates: Table 6.2

■ Low Income ■ Middle Income ■ High Income ▢ All Income Classes

Figure 8.2b   No regional extended benefit, model 2

Before examining what happens when we combine these two policy changes, it is interesting to compare our results with respect to the effect of eliminating regional extended benefits to those of Winer and Gauthier (1982a).
They carried out a similar simulation in which they computed the change in
1977 migration rates under the assumption that regional extended benefits
had not been introduced, for out-migration from the Atlantic provinces (see
tables 5–2 and 5–4 of Winer and Gauthier 1982a). While their model was
different – they used the index of unemployment insurance generosity given
in equation (3.5) – and their definitions of income classes differ from ours,
the objective of the simulation is the same.[2] Their estimates implied that
had there been no regional extended benefits in 1977, out-migration from
the Atlantic provinces (mostly to Ontario) would have been higher than
it actually was for low-income individuals, but lower than it actually was
for all other (higher-income) individuals. For low-income individuals our
results are consistent with theirs.

Elimination of All Regional Variation in the Employment Insurance System

This simulation is a combination of the previous two and is in our view the
most important of the three simulations concerning regional variation in
insurance parameters. The value of MIN is 13 weeks, while θ is set equal to
2 weeks of benefits for one week of work, as in previous simulations. These
two choices imply that $MINWKS$ = 26 weeks, $MXYR$ = 17 weeks, $MXYRWKS$ = 33
weeks, and weeks on social assistance in state 3 equal 11. These values are
assumed to apply in all provinces and in all years of the simulation.

Figures 8.3a and 8.3b present the results for Models 1 and 2 based on
the parameter estimates in table 6.2, while figure 8.3c presents results for
Model 1 using the parameter estimates in table 6.6.[3] Recall that the estimates in table 6.6 were obtained using the 1968–96 data derived from a
10 percent sample of tax filers. This additional set of results is presented to
further investigate the sensitivity of the results of this critical simulation to
the parameter estimates.

The results for both models show clearly that the overall movement as a
result of the simulated change in policy parameters is away from the Atlantic region, and, to a lesser extent, out of Quebec and British Columbia.
For higher-income adults only, the effects using Model 2 go in the opposite
direction, though not strongly enough to shape the overall pattern of flows.
The results in figure 8.3c using the Model 1 estimates for the longer period,
which includes the 1971 changes in the UI Act, are qualitatively the same as

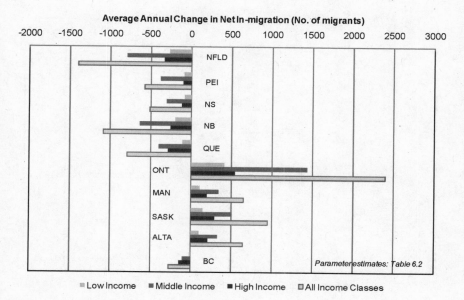

Average Annual Change in Net In-migration (No. of migrants)

Figure 8.3a   No regional variation in UI, model 1

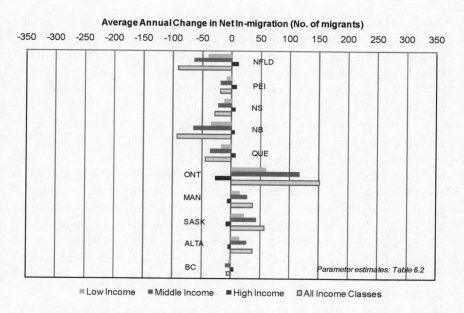

Average Annual Change in Net In-migration (No. of migrants)

Figure 8.3b   No regional variation in UI, model 2

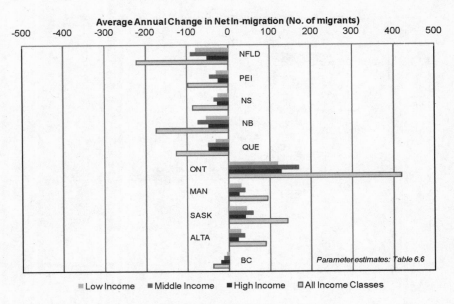

Figure 8.3c   No regional variation in UI, model I (10% sample)

those in figure 8.3a, but smaller in magnitude. As a percentage of average predicted flows, however, they tend to be larger. Net migration to Ontario rises by about 260 percent (2,395 persons) using the 1974–96 estimates of Model 1, by about 296 percent (419 persons) using the 1968–96 estimates of Model 1, and by about 50 percent (151 persons) using the 1974–96 estimates of Model 2.

To further assess these magnitudes and the corresponding gross flows, we can compare the simulation effects with the average *predicted outflows* in table 8.1. Gross average total predicted outflows from Newfoundland, for example, are about 9,000 per year using either model, and for Ontario are about 36,000 per year. For Newfoundland, considering the Model 1 simulation figures in table G13, the overall change in gross outflow is about 9 percent, or roughly 810 adults per year on average over the period. Using Model 2, the gross outflow changes by about 0.1 per cent, or about 50 people per year. For Ontario, Model 1 implies a change of about 0.02 of the gross predicted outflow, while Model 2 implies a change that is less than 1/10 of that.

To summarize at this point, what we see is a consistent general pattern of movement away from regions where the insurance system has in the simulations become less generous. We also see that predicted magnitudes vary quite a bit depending on the model and sample that are used.

Another means of investigating the sensitivity of the results to the coefficient estimates is to repeat this simulation using the estimates by income class, age, and sex obtained for the 1974–96 period, which appear in tables 6.7 to 6.10 and table E4 of appendix E. Rather than presenting all these results, we show only those for Model 1 in figures 8.4a to 8.4f, but differences between the two models are described in the text.[4]

Two aspects of these simulations stand out. First, for each income class and age group, the direction of the simulated flows is different for men and women. The only exception is high-income older men, whose behaviour is similar to that of women. This difference in behaviour can be traced to the signs of the estimated coefficients on the variable *LEISURE* in table 6.7, which are negative (or small and statistically insignificant) for high-income older men and for women in all age groups and income classes. This negative sign implies that a decrease in leisure time will increase the welfare of these groups. As a result, we see that the net outflow of men in all age groups and income classes (except for high-income older men) from the Atlantic region, Quebec, and British Columbia to Ontario and the three Prairie provinces increases as a result of the elimination of regional variation in the unemployment insurance system, while women move in the opposite direction. By way of contrast, the analogous results using Model 2 (not shown, but available in Day and Winer 2001), show that young and middle-aged women in all three income classes move out of the Atlantic region in greater numbers as a result of the simulated policy change, while young and middle-aged high-income men and young middle-income men do the opposite.

Second, one can also see that the changes in the flows of men resulting from the elimination of regional variation in unemployment insurance are generally greater than those of women. Consequently, even though men and women are moving in opposite directions, when the changes are summed across the eighteen groups, the overall effects of the simulation are in the same direction as noted previously – on balance, people leave the Atlantic region and Quebec. However, *even for Model 1*, the overall effects are small in percentage terms when compared to those in figure 8.3a, reaching no higher than 1.3 percent of base case predicted gross out-flows for Newfoundland (as compared to 9.3 percent in the figure 8.3a results).

The age/sex patterns in figures 8.4a–f and their analogue for Model 2 suggest that the age/sex-specific results should not be considered unambiguously better than those in which the data are disaggregated by income class

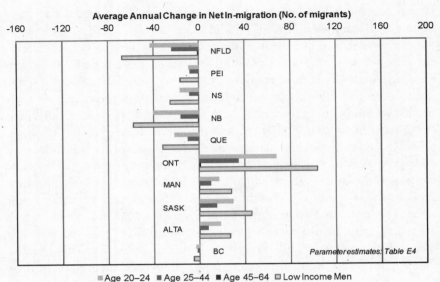

Average Annual Change in Net In-migration (No. of migrants)

■ Age 20–24   ■ Age 25–44   ■ Age 45–64   ☐ Low Income Men

Figure 8.4a   No regional variation in UI, model 1, low income men

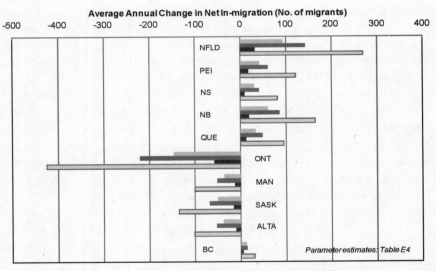

Average Annual Change in Net In-migration (No. of migrants)

■ Age 20–24   ■ Age 25–44   ■ Age 45–64   ☐ Low Income Women

Figure 8.4b   No regional variation in UI, model 1, low income women

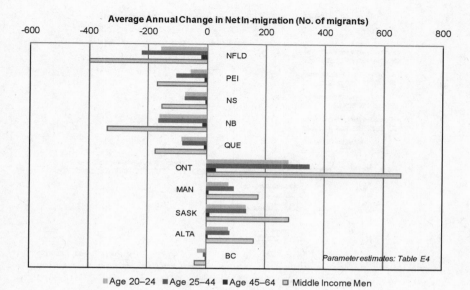

Average Annual Change in Net In-migration (No. of migrants)

■ Age 20–24   ■ Age 25–44   ■ Age 45–64   □ Middle Income Men

Figure 8.4c   No regional variation in UI, model 1, middle income men

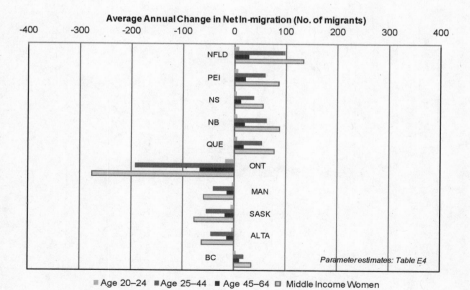

Average Annual Change in Net In-migration (No. of migrants)

■ Age 20–24   ■ Age 25–44   ■ Age 45–64   □ Middle Income Women

Figure 8.4d   No regional variation in UI, model 1, middle income women

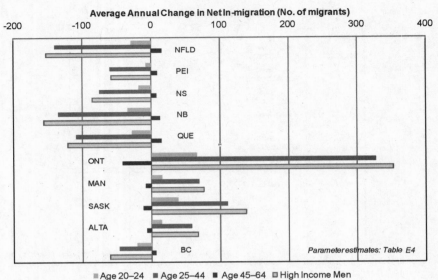

Figure 8.4e   No regional variation in UI, model 1, high income men

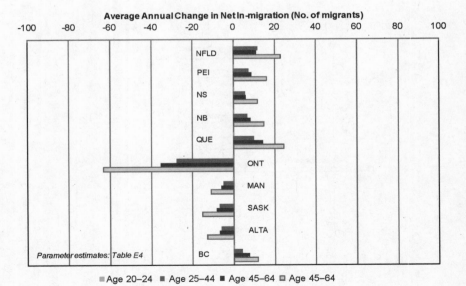

Figure 8.4f   No regional variation in UI, model 1, high income women

only. It is possible that the correlation between the leisure variable and the employment probabilities noted in chapter 6 has more severe consequences when the data are disaggregated by age and sex as well as by income class. Also, it is quite difficult to measure age/sex-specific probabilities for all of the employment states in the model for the long time period used in the estimation, though we tried hard to do so. The probabilities of states 2 and 3 are especially difficult to calculate because of the nature of the available data. As a result, a higher level of aggregation may yield more reliable results, though we point out again that all of the results for the simulation under consideration reveal a similar pattern.

REGIONAL VARIATION IN PROVINCIAL TAX RATES

The marginal-effect calculations of chapter 7 indicate that interprovincial migration flows are sensitive to provincial differences in income tax rates, with Quebec standing out as the province in which income tax rates had the most substantial effect. Under this simulation, the personal income tax rate in each province in each year is set equal to the average rate imposed by the nine provinces that participated in the tax collection agreements with the federal government during our sample period. Consequently, the average rate in the country as a whole evolves as it actually did over the simulation period. Thus, in contrast to the previous simulations, under this simulation the value of the variable affected – the provincial tax rate – changes from year to year. To simplify a complex situation, we pretend that Quebec is a signatory to the federal government's tax collection agreement with the provinces during the simulation period. Note that the rate used in the simulations underestimates the actual average rate, since Quebec's income taxes have tended to be higher than those imposed by the other provinces. The tax rate values used for the simulation are shown in appendix G, table G9. The effect of the simulation is to alter the level of after-tax income in states 1, 2, and 3 of the model. In state 4, social assistance recipients do not pay tax, and thus after-tax income in this state does not change.

It should also be noted that the simulation is not equivalent to an investigation of what happens when one province reduces its rate unilaterally. That sort of experiment was conducted using marginal effects in chapter 7. Here we assume that the provinces either relinquish the right to set their own tax rates to the federal government, or come to an agreement to set identical tax rates, which are unlikely but still interesting scenarios.

Figures 8.5a and 8.5b illustrate the effects of this simulation on net in-migration for Models 1 and 2 respectively.[5] The figures suggest that if all

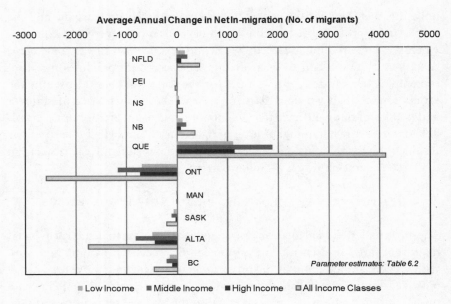

Figure 8.5a Equal income tax rates, model 1

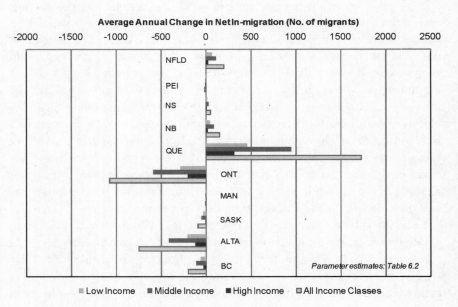

Figure 8.5b Equal income tax rates, model 2

provinces levied the same tax rate, the predominant movement would be towards Quebec and the higher-tax Atlantic region (with the exception of Prince Edward Island), and away from Ontario and the Western provinces, generally for all income classes. Flows to and from Quebec are the most greatly affected. Model 1 predicts an average increase in net inflows to Quebec of 4,124 people, while Model 2 predicts an average increase of 1,726 people. By way of comparison, average net inflows to Manitoba decrease by only 2 to 4 individuals, depending on the model.

What is happening here is that provinces with relatively low tax rates, like Alberta and Ontario, are moved upwards in terms of the level of their tax rate, while the rates in high-tax provinces like Quebec and the Atlantic provinces are averaged downwards. Manitoba, which has an average rate over the 1978–96 period that is close to the average for all provinces, is among the least affected, while Quebec, which is subjected to a much larger reduction in tax rates, experiences substantial percentage changes in gross flows, especially for middle-income people.

REGIONAL VARIATION IN SOCIAL ASSISTANCE PAYMENTS

Since there is some rough evidence that social assistance may be a substitute for unemployment insurance for some people, it is useful to consider what would happen if the variable used in our empirical analysis, annual social assistance benefits for a single mother with two children, was in each year of the simulation set equal to the ten-province average for all provinces in that year. This change affects social assistance incomes in states 3 and 4 of the model. The values used for the simulation, which vary from year to year, are given in table G9. The simulation results themselves are presented in figures 8.6a and b.[6]

Since the range of the horizontal axis is exactly the same in the two figures, it is easy to see that the magnitude of the effects is once again greater for Model 1. The pattern of the changes in net migration, however, is exactly the same for Models 1 and 2. In this simulation, changes in gross flows are small in percentage terms for all income classes, regardless of which model is used. In percentage terms, the biggest Model 1 effects are observed for the middle-income group in Nova Scotia (−73 percent or −32 people) and New Brunswick (69 percent or 68 people). Overall, we can see that this change in social assistance benefits would cause net inflows to New Brunswick, Quebec, Alberta, and Saskatchewan to increase, while net inflows to the other provinces, especially Ontario, Nova Scotia, and British Columbia, decrease. Somewhat surprisingly, the gaining provinces did not all offer below-

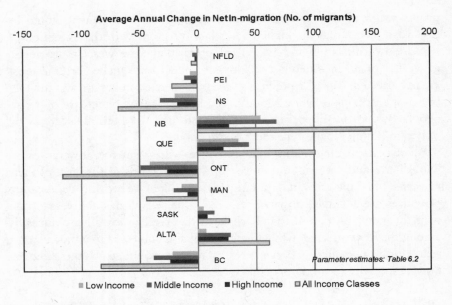

Figure 8.6a   Equal social assistance benefits, model 1

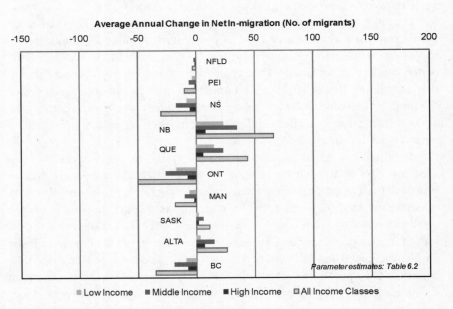

Figure 8.6b   Equal social assistance benefits, model 2

average social assistance benefits during the simulation period, as a quick look at table 7.5 reveals, nor did the losing provinces all offer above-average benefits. This result is likely due in part to the fact that a change in social assistance benefits will have less of an effect in provinces where the probabilities of states 3 and 4 are relatively low during the simulation period.

REGIONAL VARIATION IN EDUCATION AND FEDERAL SPENDING

The simulations discussed so far all involve policy variables that directly affect individual budget constraints. We now turn to simulations of the effects of eliminating regional variation in fiscal aggregates that do not enter individual budget constraints directly, including real per capita provincial and local spending on education (current and capital), and real per capita federal (non-interest) spending on goods, services, and capital goods. Owing to the form of equation (4.4) for the probability of migrating from i to j and the manner in which the government spending variables are assumed to enter the expected utility function (4.7), the results of these simulations will be the same regardless of the particular value chosen for real per capita spending. We therefore carry out the simulation in the simplest possible manner, assuming that the natural log of real per capita spending is zero everywhere in all years.

The simulated effects of this change in per capita spending on education for Models 1 and 2 are given in figures 8.7a and 8.7b respectively.[7] Both models indicate that the elimination of regional variation in education expenditure would result in increased net outflows from Ontario, Alberta, Quebec, and Newfoundland (listed here by order of magnitude of the percentage change in net flows). The remaining provinces would gain population. The province that would benefit the most in percentage terms is New Brunswick.

Although for all the simulations examined thus far the Model 1 results have tended to be larger in magnitude than the Model 2 results, this is not the case for this particular simulation. Instead, it is Model 2 that predicts the largest effects, except for the high-income group. For instance, Model 2 suggests that eliminating regional variation in per capita spending on education would on average increase total annual net inflows to New Brunswick by about 489 percent (1,106 people), while Model 1 predicts an average increase of only 91 percent (237 people) in total annual net inflows to New Brunswick. Model 2 also exhibits greater uniformity across income classes

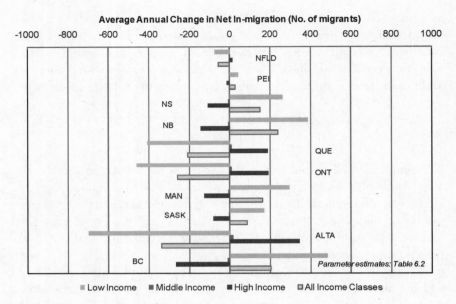

Figure 8.7a   Equal spending on education, model 1

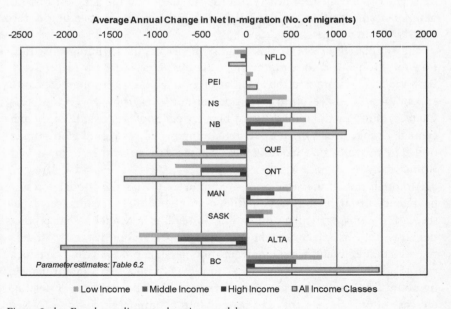

Figure 8.7b   Equal spending on education, model 2

in terms of the direction of the effects, because the sign of the coefficient of education spending is the same for all income classes for that model.

Figures 8.8a and b give the results for federal spending.[8] The elimination of regional variation in per capita federal spending generally has a much larger impact on gross and net flows than did the elimination of regional variation in education spending. Since regional variation in education spending is much lower than that of federal spending, as shown in chapter 2, it is not surprising that the elimination of regional variation in the former will have smaller migration effects than the elimination of regional variation in the latter. It is also not surprising that the effects are largest in magnitude in Nova Scotia, because as figures 2.15a and 2.15b illustrate, it is the province in which actual per capita federal spending was highest during the simulation period.

Finally, the fact that figures 8.8a and 8.8b are mirror images of each other can be explained by the fact that the signs of the federal spending coefficients are different in Models 1 and 2. As has already been noted in chapter 6, this change in the signs of the coefficients is hard to explain other than as the consequence of multicollinearity between the explanatory variables of the two models. The end result is that Model 1 predicts that on average, Nova Scotia would *lose* 10,126 net in-migrants per year as a result of eliminating regional variation in real per capita federal spending, while Model 2 predicts that it would instead *gain* 5,528 net in-migrants. Thus no clear conclusions regarding the effects of eliminating regional variation in this variable can be drawn. All one can say is that both models imply fairly substantial migration effects related to federal spending.

ELIMINATION OF REGIONAL VARIATION IN ALL POLICY VARIABLES

The final policy experiment we conduct involves simultaneously eliminating regional variation in all policy parameters and variables previously considered. In addition, we eliminate regional variation in the two government expenditure variables not considered so far: health spending and other spending. This simulation helps us to assess the overall effect of regional variation in public policy in Canada. Since the different policies do not all have the same effects, it is possible that the undesirable migration consequences of some policies may be cancelled out by the more desirable consequences of others.

The effects of this experiment on net migration are shown in figure 8.9a for Model 1 and in figure 8.9b for Model 2.[9] Both figures show that when

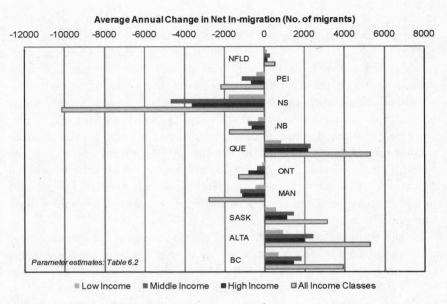

Figure 8.8a   Equal federal spending, model 1

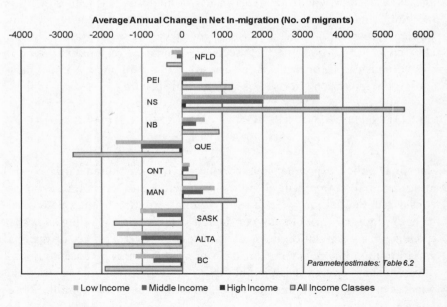

Figure 8.8b   Equal federal spending, model 2

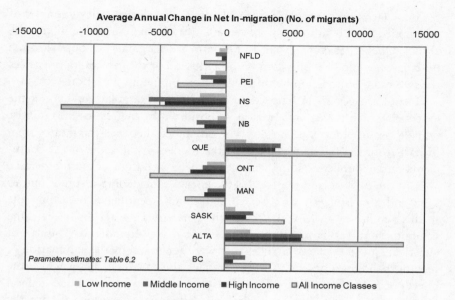

Average Annual Change in Net In-migration (No. of migrants)

-15000 -10000 -5000 0 5000 10000 15000

NFLD
PEI
NS
NB
QUE
ONT
MAN
SASK
ALTA
BC

Parameter estimates: Table 6.2

▨ Low Income   ▨ Middle Income   ■ High Income   ▨ All Income Classes

Figure 8.9a   No regional variation in policies, model 1

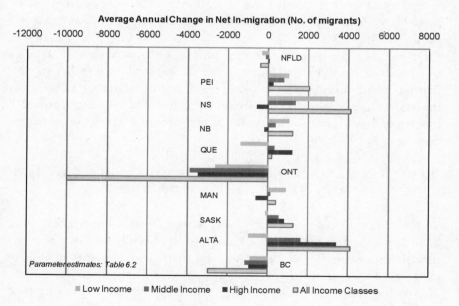

Average Annual Change in Net In-migration (No. of migrants)

-12000 -10000 -8000 -6000 -4000 -2000 0 2000 4000 6000 8000

NFLD
PEI
NS
NB
QUE
ONT
MAN
SASK
ALTA
BC

Parameter estimates: Table 6.2

▨ Low Income   ▨ Middle Income   ■ High Income   ▨ All Income Classes

Figure 8.9b   No regional variation in policies, model 2

regional variation is simultaneously eliminated in all the policy variables of our model, there is substantial movement away from Ontario for all income classes. Quebec, Saskatchewan, and Alberta are net gainers of population in both cases, while Newfoundland is a net loser. For the remaining provinces the two models predict quite different effects on net in-migration.

Overall, the results in figure 8.9a accord with a popular view about the extent to which the Atlantic region is subsidized by the rest of the country, while those in figure 8.9b do not. The differences between the figures stem in part from the differences between the models in the signs of the coefficients on the public spending variables, as well as differences in the relative sizes of the *INCOME* and *LEISURE* coefficients. A quick comparison of figures 8.8a and 8.9a suggests that per capita federal spending plays a big role in this simulation in Model 1, since the pattern of the results is the same for both simulations for all provinces except Newfoundland. This is not surprising given the large changes that were generated by the elimination of federal spending differentials in that model. But in Model 2, for which the effects of federal spending differentials were smaller in magnitude, federal spending seems to play a somewhat less influential role, especially for the high-income class. In the case of Ontario, the positive effects of eliminating federal spending differentials are clearly offset by other policy changes, since Model 2 predicts a relatively large average annual net loss of almost 10,000 people in figure 8.9b.

Despite the differences between the models, Ontario remains a net loser of population using either model. Hence the simulations together suggest that on balance during the 1978–96 period, regional variation in policy in the country as a whole was *not* harmful to the interests of Ontario, provided that we assume Ontario's interests are isomorphic to the direction of migration flows.

REGIONAL VARIATION IN WAGES, PROBABILITIES OF THE FOUR STATES, AND MOVING COSTS

To help place the policy simulations in perspective, it is important to look at analogous results for non-policy variables, specifically weekly wages, the probabilities of employment, and moving costs. The graphical analysis in chapter 2 demonstrated that regional variation in public policy is comparable to that in average weekly earnings and the probabilities of the states of the world. Now we will be able to see if this variation matters as much to migration flows as that of market variables. We shall also consider moving costs because Canadian geography guarantees that such costs are not trivial. Each of these cases is considered in turn.

We begin with average weekly wages (or earnings). The elimination of regional variation in wages affects the model in three ways. First, it alters wage income in states 1, 2, and 3. Second, it alters unemployment insurance income in states 2 and 3, because the rate of benefits, WUI_j, depends on the wage in each region. And third, it alters the foregone wage cost of moving, $C1_{ij}$. Thus for the purposes of the simulation not just w_j, but also WUI_j and $C1_{ij}$, must be redefined. The Canadian industrial composite average weekly wage is used as the new value of w_j, and the other two variables are re-computed using this value. The simulation values of both w_j and WUI_j are given in table G9. The changes in net in-migration resulting from this simulation are presented in figures 8.10a and 8.10b for Models 1 and 2 respectively.[10]

Comparing these two figures, one can see that the pattern of changes is the same for both models: Quebec, Ontario, Alberta, and British Columbia lose people, while the remaining provinces gain. As can be seen from figures 2.4a and 2.4b, all of the losing provinces enjoyed above-average average weekly earnings during the 1978–96 period; thus the simulation is giving us an idea of how that wage advantage affected movements of people during the 1978–96 period. Model 1 implies that net in-migration to Ontario decreases on average by over 8,000 people, owing to a reduction in in-migration and an even larger increase in out-migration (2,706 in versus 5,466 out). Once again the magnitudes of the changes are smaller for Model 2 (1,170 in versus 2,204 out), but the percentage changes in inflows and outflows are fairly large – the increase in out-migration from Ontario amounts to 15 percent using Model 1 and 6 percent using Model 2.

Like the average weekly earnings simulation, the simulation that involves removing regional variation in the probabilities is also complex because it results in changes to so many variables: *MIN*, *MINWKS*, *MXYR*, *MXYRWKS*, and weeks on social assistance in state 3, in addition to the probabilities of the four states of the world. All these variables must be changed to compute the counterfactual because it is not reasonable to allow unemployment insurance benefits to continue to vary with the old regional unemployment rates when the probabilities of the various unemployment states of the world are assumed to be the same everywhere. In implementing the simulation, we use the Canadian average unemployment rate to reconstruct *MIN*, *MINWKS*, *MXYR*, *MXYRWKS*, and weeks on social assistance in state 3. We also construct average probabilities for the four states of the world by first summing across provinces the number of people in each state of the world in each year,

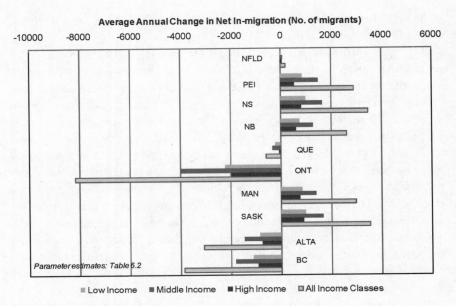

Average Annual Change in Net In-migration (No. of migrants)

Parameter estimates: Table 6.2

▨ Low Income ■ Middle Income ■ High Income ▨ All Income Classes

Figure 8.10a   No regional variation in earnings, model 1

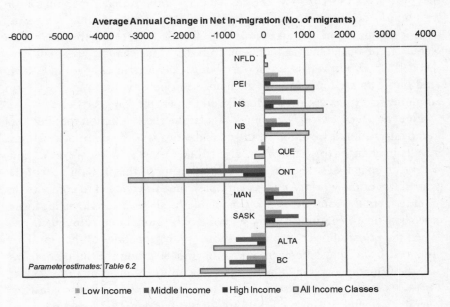

Average Annual Change in Net In-migration (No. of migrants)

Parameter estimates: Table 6.2

▨ Low Income ■ Middle Income ■ High Income ▨ All Income Classes

Figure 8.10b   No regional variation in earnings, model 2

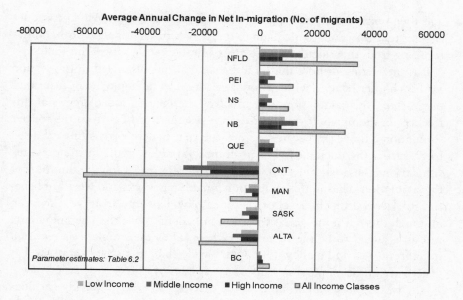

Figure 8.11a   No regional variation in probabilities, model 1

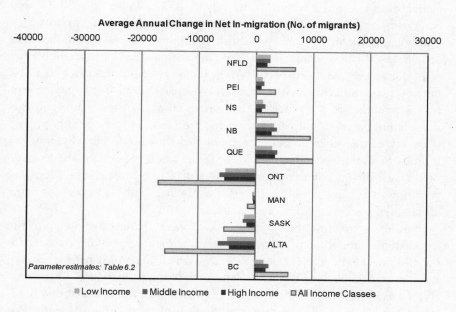

Figure 8.11b   No regional variation in probabilities, model 2

and then constructing new probabilities using these sums. This procedure ensures that the probabilities sum to one across provinces. The probabilities resulting from this calculation are given in table G10 in appendix G.

It is interesting to note that like the simulations discussed in the section of this chapter dealing with regional variation in unemployment insurance parameters, this simulation also involves the elimination of regional differences in the unemployment insurance system. It differs from the former simulations, however, because here the actual benefit provisions are used to construct the unemployment insurance variables, while in the previous simulations these variables are fixed at arbitrary levels for the duration of the simulation. Thus in this simulation, qualifying weeks and weeks of benefits still depend on the level of the unemployment rate from year to year, although there is no regional variation in benefits since the unemployment rate is assumed to be the same everywhere. Thus the simulations reported in figures 8.11a and b allow for country-wide changes in the overall level of generosity of the employment insurance system over time.[11]

The two figures show that as in the case of the average weekly earnings simulation, the pattern of the effects is the same using both models. Only the magnitude of the changes is different, with the largest changes once again being registered when Model 1 is used. The figures also show that equalizing employment probabilities results in large movements towards Quebec, the Atlantic region, and British Columbia and away from the other provinces – this is of course a result of eliminating what have been historically poor employment prospects in these regions (see figures 2.5a and 2.5b). However, a comparison with the results of earlier simulations (paying particular attention to the range of the horizontal axes in the figures) reveals that eliminating regional variation in the probabilities has a greater impact than any of the other simulations conducted thus far. Using Model 2, net inflows to Ontario decrease by 16,978, or 5,894 percent of the average predicted flow, as compared to decreases of 1,171 percent when regional variation in average weekly earnings is eliminated and 3,471 percent when all regional policy variation is eliminated.

In order to examine the extent to which these changes are owing to the associated elimination of regional variation in unemployment insurance benefits, we also conduct a simulation in which unemployment insurance benefits remain at their historical values while the probabilities of the four states are assumed to be the same in all provinces. The results of this simulation for Model 1 are not provided, because they are almost identical to those in figure 8.11a.[12] So it appears that interaction between the probabilities and unemployment insurance is not important in shaping migration patterns. Furthermore, we observe that the effect of eliminating regional variation in unemployment insurance benefits (see figure 8.3a) appears to be quite small in comparison with the effect of eliminating regional variation in the probabilities (in figure 8.11a).

The last simulation we carried out involves the elimination of moving costs. Although it is difficult to measure all aspects of moving costs, they are widely acknowledged to be an important determinant of interprovincial moves. Our model includes four variables that relate to moving costs: $C1_{ij}$, the foregone wage cost of moving; $C2_{ij}$, the monetary cost of moving; DSTAY, the dummy variable intended to capture the fixed costs of moving; and DISTANCE, which is included to capture other non-monetary costs associated with moving. The elimination of moving costs from the model thus requires that all of these variables be set to zero in all provinces in all years. As a result, after-tax incomes in all four states of the world change, as do DSTAY and DIST, the two variables that enter the model independently of after-tax incomes.

The results of this simulation are presented in figures 8.12a and 8.12b for Models 1 and 2 respectively.[13] Because the coefficients of DIST and DSTAY were very similar for the two models, the simulation results are as well. But the most striking feature of these results is that the effects are enormous. They also tend to increase with income class in most provinces. The movement in the simulation is away from Ontario and Quebec and towards the peripheries of the country, as we should expect. Most people live in the two central provinces, so when moving costs are eliminated, there is a large flood of people moving out (compared to those moving in) to the eastern and western regions of the country. On average, Quebec and Ontario would lose 1.3 million and 1.6 million more people respectively each year, with the gains distributed relatively equally across the other provinces. Moving costs likely are the single most important factor determining migration behaviour in our model.

OVERALL EFFECTS ON MIGRATION BY VARIABLE

In our discussion thus far we have focused on the implications of our simulations with respect to the pattern of migration flows and hence the distribution of tax filers across the country. In passing we have also commented on the magnitudes of the changes in the flows, but a closer look at the effect of each simulation on the overall *volume* of migration in the country as a whole is also warranted. Tables 8.2a and 8.2b summarize the effects of the various simulations on the volume of migration for Models 1 and 2, based

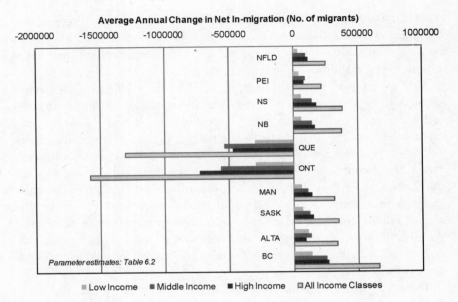

Figure 8.12a   No moving costs, model 1

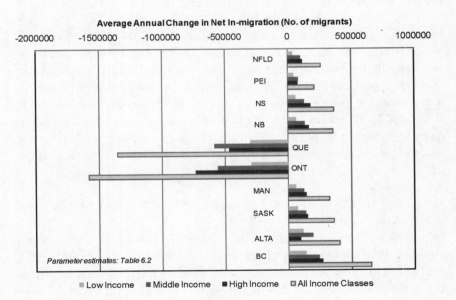

Figure 8.12b   No moving costs, model 2

Table 8.2a
Predicted Effect on Mobility of Eliminating Regional Variation, Model 1[1]

Elimination of regional variation in	Low Income	Middle Income	High Income	Total
Change in number of interprovincial migrants[2]				
VER under UI	59	63	–2	120
Regional extended benefit under UI	143	248	46	437
VER and regional extended benefit	176	328	649	1,153
Per capita federal spending	727	2,040	1,175	3,941
Per capita education spending	61	–5	–164	–108
Provincial income tax rates	–307	–176	–43	–527
Social assistance benefits	–142	–227	–127	–496
All policy variables	1,455	4,159	2,428	8,042
Average weekly earnings	1,087	2,888	1,588	5,563
Probabilities of states of the world	14,102	26,779	15,104	55,984
Moving costs	1,773,054	3,120,010	3,378,924	8,271,988
Change in number of interprovincial migrants as percentage of base case migrants[3]				
VER under UI	0.12	0.10	–0.00	0.07
Regional extended benefit under UI	0.28	0.39	0.09	0.26
VER and regional extended benefit	0.34	0.52	1.24	0.69
Per capita federal spending	1.41	3.22	2.25	2.36
Per capita education spending	0.12	–0.01	–0.31	–0.06
Provincial income tax rates	–0.60	–0.28	–0.08	–0.32
Social assistance benefits	–0.28	–0.36	–0.24	–0.30
All policy variables	2.83	6.57	4.65	4.82
Average weekly earnings	2.12	4.56	3.04	3.33
Probabilities of states of the world	27.44	42.33	28.89	33.54
Moving costs	3449.48	4931.71	6463.77	4955.07

[1] Parameter estimates from table 6.2. All numbers reported in the table relate to the average annual change over the simulation period of 1978–96.
[2] The number of migrants is the sum across provinces of gross out–migration flows.
[3] The base case number of migrants is the average annual predicted out–migration for Model 1, calculated using table 6.2 estimates.

on the parameter estimates in table 6.2 for the 100 percent data set for the 1974–96 period. The change in the volume of migration is computed by summing gross outflows across provinces for each income class.[14] Both the change in the total number of interprovincial migrants and the percentage change relative to the base case are presented.

A comparison across simulations of the percentage change in the number of migrants, shown in the lower panels of the tables, confirms that moving costs are by far the single most important determinant of migration behaviour in Canada, easily dominating the role of the probabilities by two or three orders of magnitude. The simulation with the next largest effect on

Table 8.2b
Predicted Effect on Mobility of Eliminating Regional Variation, Model 2[1]

Elimination of regional variation in	Low Income	Middle Income	High Income	Total
Change in number of interprovincial migrants[2]				
VER under UI	8	4	2	14
Regional extended benefit under UI	19	10	1	30
VER and regional extended benefit	22	13	1	37
Per capita federal spending	302	217	9	528
Per capita education spending	218	323	62	603
Provincial income tax rates	−153	−148	−29	−331
Social assistance benefits	−59	−115	−35	−209
All policy variables	368	197	27	592
Average weekly earnings	369	1,262	386	2,016
Probabilities of states of the world	812	2,828	2,816	6,455
Moving costs	1,774,272	3,155,662	3,382,173	8,312,106
Change in number of interprovincial migrants as percentage of base case migrants[3]				
VER under UI	0.02	0.01	0.00	0.01
Regional extended benefit under UI	0.04	0.02	0.00	0.02
VER and regional extended benefit	0.04	0.02	0.00	0.02
Per capita federal spending	0.59	0.34	0.02	0.32
Per capita education spending	0.42	0.51	0.12	0.36
Provincial income tax rates	−0.30	−0.23	−0.06	−0.20
Social assistance benefits	−0.12	−0.18	−0.07	−0.13
All policy variables	0.72	0.31	0.05	0.35
Average weekly earnings	0.72	1.99	0.74	1.21
Probabilities of states of the world	1.58	4.46	5.38	3.86
Moving costs	3,447.68	4,977.51	6,462.08	4,971.36

[1] Parameter estimates from table 6.2. All numbers reported in the table relate to the average annual change over the simulation period of 1978–96.
[2] The number of migrants is the sum across provinces of gross out–migration flows.
[3] The base case number of migrants is the average annual predicted out–migration for Model 1, calculated using table 6.2 estimates.

mobility of all three income classes is the elimination of regional variation in the probabilities of the various unemployment states, although it has a far smaller impact on mobility than the elimination of moving costs. The policy scenario with the greatest impact on mobility is the elimination of all regional policy variation; its overall effect is slightly larger than that of the elimination of regional dispersion in average weekly earnings in Model 1, but not in Model 2. The differences in results between models likely stem from the role of federal spending, which has a bigger percentage impact on mobility for Model 1 (2.36) than for Model 2 (0.32).

Individually, the various policy variables, including the unemployment insurance variables, play a less important role (except for federal spending in table 8.2a). Provincial tax rates have an effect that, for each income class, is more or less the same in the two tables. It is interesting to note that in the case of tax rates, the overall change in the number of migrants is smallest for the high-income group. The elimination of the variable entrance requirement has a uniformly small effect compared to, say, the overall effect of wages in both models. The effects for the other two unemployment insurance simulations are not uniform across the models, being smaller for Model 2, a finding that mimics the previous comparisons of figures 8.2 and 8.3. Note that the mobility effects of the elimination of the VER and regional extended benefits taken alone are smallest for the highest-income group, but the same is not true for the combined simulation using Model 1. In all cases, however, the gross change in the number of migrants is quite small when compared to that for average weekly earnings or for the probabilities.

What these results indicate is that next to moving costs, uncertainty about employment prospects – which enters the model both through the variables *INCOME* and *LEISURE* and through the additional risk aversion variables $P2$, $P3$, $P4$, or $LP234$ – is the most important determinant of migration flows. Employment income, another labour market variable represented by average weekly earnings, also plays a role. The simulations also suggest that even collectively and for all income classes, policy variables play a far less important role than moving costs and labour market uncertainty.

THE ECONOMIC CONSEQUENCES OF ELIMINATING REGIONAL VARIATION IN FISCAL POLICIES: A PRELIMINARY ASSESSMENT

Despite the fact that the volume of migration attributable to regional variation in policy variables appears to be low, it may still be the case that the resulting reallocation of labour across provinces has a beneficial effect on provincial labour markets. One form that this beneficial effect might take is a reduction in provincial unemployment rates. Because we model only migration behaviour, we cannot say anything conclusive about the impact of migration on unemployment rates. But we can estimate the change in provincial unemployment rates resulting from each simulation if we make some assumptions about the impact of migration on unemployment. In particular, suppose that we assume that all out-migrants from a province were previously unemployed, while all in-migrants to the province will end up employed. Then the change in in-migration will always equal the change in employment, while the change in out-migration will equal the change in unemployment.

This pair of assumptions leads to the most favourable outcome possible in terms of the impact of migration on unemployment rates. In the real world, some interprovincial migrants will simply be moving from one job to another, while others will be unemployed in both province of origin and province of destination. Thus this calculation is likely to over-estimate any reduction in unemployment rates that might result from the elimination of regional variation in policy and other variables.

The results of these calculations of the impact of eliminating regional variation in selected variables on provincial unemployment rates are presented in table 8.3. As in the case of the simulations, only the average unemployment rate for the 1978–96 period – computed using average employment and average unemployment data for the period for individuals of both sexes aged 20–64 – is presented. The calculations are carried out using the simulation results for Models 1 and 2 derived from the coefficient estimates in table 6.2 for the 1974–96 estimation period, summed over all income classes. The actual average unemployment rate for each province during the period is also presented.

The hypothetical unemployment rate calculations for both models indicate that the elimination of moving costs has by far the largest impact on unemployment rates. Indeed, the hypothetical unemployment rates for this simulation are actually negative, reflecting the fact that the increase in the volume of out-migration under this simulation far exceeds the actual level of unemployment in all provinces. One interpretation of this result is that the elimination of moving costs would encourage many individuals not currently included in Statistics Canada's measure of the labour force (but included in our data) to make interprovincial moves.

Turning to the other ten simulations, it can be seen that their effects on average unemployment rates are generally not big, even for Model 1 which leads to larger changes in migration flows than does Model 2. One simulation which seems to have a larger impact on average unemployment rates than most of the others is that in which regional variation in the probabilities of the states of the world is eliminated, but the effect is different for different provinces. Both Models 1 and 2 predict increases in average unemployment rates for all the Atlantic provinces except Nova Scotia under this scenario, with the largest increase being 1.5 percentage points for Prince Edward Island in the case of Model 1. Both models also predict that this

Table 8.3
Hypothetical Unemployment Rates Resulting from Elimination of Regional Dispersion (average 1978–96)[1]

Simulation	NFLD	PEI	NS	NB	QUE	ONT	MAN	SASK	ALTA	BC
Model 1										
VER under UI	16.7	13.7	11.3	12.0	10.8	7.4	7.2	6.4	7.4	9.6
Regional extended benefit under UI	16.6	13.6	11.2	11.9	10.8	7.4	7.2	6.4	7.4	9.6
VER and regional extended benefit	16.5	13.4	11.2	11.9	10.8	7.4	7.2	6.4	7.4	9.6
Per capita federal spending	16.8	12.1	9.9	11.7	10.9	7.4	6.8	6.6	7.5	9.6
Per capita education spending	16.8	13.9	11.3	12.1	10.8	7.4	7.2	6.3	7.4	9.6
Provincial income tax rates	16.9	13.9	11.3	12.1	10.9	7.4	7.2	6.3	7.3	9.6
Social assistance benefits	16.8	13.9	11.3	12.1	10.8	7.4	7.2	6.3	7.4	9.6
All policy variables	16.4	10.6	9.5	11.3	10.9	7.3	6.8	6.7	7.7	9.6
Average weekly earnings	16.7	15.0	11.5	12.2	10.8	7.3	7.3	6.6	7.2	9.5
Probabilities of states of the world	17.1	15.4	11.3	13.1	10.9	6.5	5.6	4.2	6.3	9.5
Moving costs	-37.9	-8.1	-56.3	-47.2	-82.9	-87.6	-46.3	-40.9	-52.4	-39.0
Model 2										
VER under UI	16.8	13.9	11.3	12.0	10.8	7.4	7.2	6.3	7.4	9.6
Regional extended benefit under UI	16.8	13.9	11.3	12.0	10.8	7.4	7.2	6.3	7.4	9.6
VER and regional extended benefit	16.8	13.9	11.3	12.0	10.8	7.4	7.2	6.3	7.4	9.6
Per capita federal spending	16.7	14.6	11.8	12.1	10.8	7.4	7.3	6.1	7.3	9.5
Per capita education spending	16.8	14.0	11.4	12.2	10.8	7.4	7.2	6.4	7.3	9.6
Provincial income tax rates	16.8	13.9	11.3	12.0	10.8	7.4	7.2	6.3	7.4	9.6
Social assistance benefits	16.8	13.9	11.3	12.0	10.8	7.4	7.2	6.3	7.4	9.6
All policy variables	16.7	15.0	11.7	12.2	10.8	7.3	7.2	6.5	7.6	9.5
Average weekly earnings	16.8	14.4	11.4	12.1	10.8	7.4	7.2	6.4	7.3	9.5

Table 8.3 (continued)

Simulation	NFLD	PEI	NS	NB	QUE	ONT	MAN	SASK	ALTA	BC
Probabilities of states of the world	17.6	15.3	11.6	12.9	10.9	7.2	7.0	5.6	6.8	9.7
Moving costs	−37.4	−7.9	−55.6	−46.5	−87.5	−87.8	−45.5	−40.1	−49.7	−39.3
Actual average unemployment rate[2]	16.8	13.9	11.3	12.0	10.8	7.4	7.2	6.3	7.4	9.6

[1] Hypothetical unemployment rates were computed under the assumptions that all out-migrants from a province were unemployed prior to moving, and that all in-migrants would be employed after moving. Total employment and unemployment for both sexes aged 20–64, obtained from CANSIM (see data appendix), were used as the basis for the calculations. For each simulation average employment over the 1978–96 period was computed as actual average employment plus the change in in-migration, while average unemployment was computed as actual average unemployment less the change in out-migration. The average unemployment rate was then computed as the ratio of average unemployment to the sum of average employment and average unemployment. The calculations were done using the simulation results for Model 1 and Model 2, based on the parameter estimates for income classes for 1974–96 in table 6.2.

[2] The actual average unemployment rate was constructed using the average annual values of employment and unemployment over the 1978–96 period. It is very similar in magnitude to the average of annual unemployment rates over this period.

scenario will lead to decreases in unemployment rates in Ontario, Manitoba, Saskatchewan, and Alberta, with the largest decrease being 2.1 percentage points for Saskatchewan under Model 2.

The only other simulations that result in changes of more than one percentage point in average unemployment rates are the elimination of regional variation in per capita federal spending and the elimination of regional variation in all policy variables. However, the relatively large negative effect of the latter simulation on unemployment rates in Nova Scotia and Prince Edward Island under Model 1 (a decrease of 1.8 percentage points for Nova Scotia and 3.3 percentage points for Prince Edward Island) appears to be related to the positive coefficients on per capita federal spending for Model 1. For Model 2, where the coefficients on per capita federal spending are negative, the elimination of regional variation in all policy variables actually increases unemployment rates in these provinces, rather than reducing them.

Although it is the result one should expect for a variable whose estimated coefficient is positive, in the case of per capita federal spending the result that the elimination of regional variation leads to decreases in unemployment rates in the provinces in which the level of the variable is highest (Nova Scotia, Prince Edward Island, and New Brunswick) seems somewhat surprising. After all, federal spending is presumably one tool that the federal government uses to create employment in different regions, and the simulation results for Model 1 suggest that a better way to reduce unemployment in the three Maritime provinces might be to reduce per capita federal spending in these provinces. In general, a reduction in the level of a variable that enters the expected utility function with a positive coefficient will tend to reduce in-migration to and increase out-migration from the province in which the reduction occurs. Under the assumptions used to compute the hypothetical unemployment rates in table 8.3, these changes in migration flows will tend to reduce both employment and unemployment, with the resulting effect on the unemployment rate depending on the relative magnitudes of the changes in employment and unemployment. The simulation results for Model 1 thus imply that the effect on unemployment outweighs the effect on employment in the three Maritime provinces, and particularly in Nova Scotia and New Brunswick.

If the parameter estimates for Model 1 are to be believed, then, per capita federal spending in Nova Scotia and Prince Edward Island may be so high relative to levels in the other provinces that it no longer has a beneficial effect on unemployment rates. On the other hand, if the parameter estimates for Model 2 are closer to the truth, per capita federal spending is viewed by individuals as a "bad," and the effects are reversed. Although in-migration and thus employment increase when per capita federal spending falls, the increase in employment is not enough to outweigh the increase in unemployment that results because fewer people leave. Once again the unemployment effects of the elimination of regional variation in per capita federal spending outweigh the employment effects, and unemployment rates rise in the four Atlantic provinces (although the effects are less dramatic in this case). Thus the common denominator in the results of this simulation for the two models is that when regional variation in per capita federal spending is eliminated, the unemployment effects (i.e., the effects on out-migration) outweigh the employment effects (i.e., the effects on in-migration).

Finally, returning to the consequences of eliminating variation in unemployment insurance generosity, it is important to note that even in the case of Model 1, which yielded the largest changes in migration flows when regional variation in the insurance system was eliminated, the impact on average unemployment rates of the elimination of this policy variation is small. Model 1 involves changes in unemployment rates only in the four Atlantic provinces, with the largest decrease in unemployment rates being half a percentage point in Prince Edward Island. With Model 2, average unemployment rates in all ten provinces are completely unaffected by the elimination of regional variation in unemployment insurance.

We cannot rule out the possibility that the interprovincial migration of labour has beneficial effects at a more micro level that we cannot observe in this study. For example, interprovincial migration may boost overall labour productivity if migrating individuals end up in jobs where their marginal productivity of labour is higher. Therefore the results presented here, while suggesting that fiscally induced migration may be much less important in determining unemployment rates at the macro level than some economists have feared, should not be construed as implying that policy-induced migration is economically unimportant in all respects. On the other hand, our results indicate that regional variation in the public policy variables we have examined does not have much impact on migration. In particular, our experiments indicate that eliminating regional variation in the unemployment insurance system does not lead to migration flows that are substantial in terms of absolute numbers or in magnitudes that are likely to alter the nature of provincial labour markets, at least in the short run.

Of course, it is possible that over a longer period the cumulative effect of the relatively small changes in annual migration flows our models predict might lead to more noticeable changes in provincial labour markets. Wilson (2003), for example, suggests that the long-run effect on migration flows resulting from the 1974 changes to the equalization system was large enough to yield a large welfare gain for Canadians. However, in the absence of a more complete dynamic model that incorporates changes in wages and unemployment rates as well as migration flows, any attempt on our part to predict longer-run effects would be highly speculative. If such a model existed, one would likely find that at some point feedback from labour market variables to migration would dampen the size of the annual migration response. Our simulation results suggest that even in the absence of such feedback effects it would take many years for most of the policy changes we consider to have a large impact on provincial unemployment rates, since as table 8.3 demonstrates, even policy changes with relatively large migration responses are unlikely to have much impact on provincial unemployment rates.

SIMULATING THE EFFECTS OF EXTRAORDINARY EVENTS

Many of the policy simulations conducted so far are, in our view, within the realm of possibility. This includes eliminating explicit regional variation in the unemployment insurance system, a reform often discussed during recessions. Other simulations, such as eliminating all regional variation in every policy variable we considered, are less feasible. But we can still conduct them, we think, because we are making use of estimates made on the basis of a history that includes the relevant variation in the data.

What we have not simulated, and cannot using our models, is a counterfactual like ending all publicly provided unemployment insurance of any kind. Such a sea change in policy regimes may have substantial migration consequences despite the results we report above. But we cannot simulate such a policy shock because nothing like it is in the data that are available for estimation of our models.

However, there are some big events that we can in a broad sense classify as policy shocks and that did occur in the sample period we are investigating: language legislation (Bill 63) and the October kidnapping crisis in Quebec in the late 1960s and early 1970s; the election of a separatist government in Quebec and its immediate aftermath, including more language legislation (Bill 101), in the mid- to late 1970s; and the closing of the cod fishery on the East Coast in 1992. In this last section of the chapter we present simulations of what would have happened in the absence of these extraordinary events, and we do so for two reasons. First, the events in question are certainly interesting in their own right. Second, such simulations serve as a reminder that although the policy reforms, taken one at a time, that we have investigated earlier do not appear to induce important changes in migration patterns, we cannot infer from such results that "large" policy shocks, should they occur, will have similar (small) migration consequences.

Although flows to and from the other provinces would also have been affected by these events, we restrict our attention to the impacts on inflows to and outflows from Quebec and Newfoundland, since these are the two provinces that were most affected by the events we consider.

The general implications of the estimated coefficients of OCT, OCT2, PQ, PQ2, FISH, and FISH2, representing the extraordinary shocks, have already been discussed in chapter 6. There we saw that the signs and magnitudes of the coefficients of the extraordinary events are generally consistent across models, and more so than the coefficients of some of the other explanatory variables of our model. What remains to be done here is to look at the migration precipitated by or associated with these events by constructing counterfactuals in which these events are assumed away.

Of course the calculations we are about to look at do not tell us the full story of the impact of each event on migration flows, because it is unlikely that events of this magnitude would have left variables such as average weekly earnings or the probabilities of the unemployment states unaffected. What we are measuring here with the simulations is the impact each event had, over and above all other determinants of migration included in the models.

The effects of the three extraordinary events on in-, out-, and net in-migration are presented in table 8.4. The top panel of the table shows the estimated overall impact of the language of school instruction legislation known as Bill 63 and of the October kidnapping crisis on inflows to and outflows from Quebec during the 1969–71 period, calculated by setting the variables OCT and OCT2 equal to zero and subtracting the predicted migration flows that result from the predicted flows when OCT and OCT2 equal 1. Here only the Model 1 estimates obtained using the 10 percent sample for 1968–96 (from table 6.6) can be used for the calculation. The table shows that both inflows to and outflows from Quebec increased during this period, but the increase in outflows far exceeds the increase in inflows in all income classes. In total, the model predicts a net outflow of almost 25,500 persons (or tax filers), of whom almost 47 percent belonged to the middle-income class.

The middle panel of the table contains three sets of estimates of the effect on inflows to and outflows from Quebec during the period 1977–80, after the election of the separatist Parti Québécois and the passing of language legislation known as Bill 101. These are derived from the estimated coefficients of the variables PQ and PQ2. In addition to the 10 percent sample

Table 8.4
Change in Migration Flows Due to Extraordinary Events in Quebec and Newfoundland[1]

Event	Model 1[2] (10% sample)			Model 1[3] (100% sample)			Model 2[3] (100% sample)		
	In-migration	Out-migration	Net In-migration	In-migration	Out-migration	Net In-migration	In-migration	Out-migration	Net In-migration
Bill 63, October Crisis, 1969–71[4]									
Low Income	912	5028	−5940						
Middle Income	594	11270	−11872						
High Income	2870	10510	−7648						
All Income Classes	4376	26808	−25460						
Election of PQ, Bill 101, 1977–80[4]									
Low Income	1514	4898	−3383	2049	4754	−2705	1074	5844	−4770
Middle Income	1990	12633	−10640	2858	13340	−10482	1788	14775	−12987
High Income	−12	13515	−13527	1152	14314	−13162	210	15625	−15415
All Income Classes	3492	31046	−27550	6059	32408	−26349	3072	36244	−33172
Closing of Cod Fishery, 1993–96[5]									
Low Income	−7213	925	−8137	−7553	1314	−8867	−6411	41	−6452
Middle Income	−12235	−1868	−10366	−12457	−1536	−10922	−10128	−3376	−6752
High Income	−7928	−1764	−6164	−7727	−1580	−6147	−6738	−2245	−4493
All Income Classes	−27376	−2707	−24667	−27737	−1802	−25936	−23277	−5580	−17697

[1] Values in table are differences between predicted flows when the event occurs and predicted flows when it does not occur, measured in numbers of people.
[2] Parameter estimates from table 6.6. Numbers are multiplied by 10 to ensure comparability with results for other sets of estimates.
[3] Parameter estimates from table 6.2.
[4] Values for Quebec only.
[5] Values for Newfoundland only.

estimates of Model 1, we also use the 100 percent sample estimates of Models 1 and 2 (from table 6.2) to simulate the effect of these events. Although both inflows and outflows once again increase (with only one exception), again the increase in out-migration far exceeds the increase in in-migration, resulting in a net outflow that is substantial regardless of the set of estimates used to compute it. The predicted total net outflow ranges from about 26,350 to over 33,000, depending on the estimates used. In comparison, the actual net outflow in our data during this four-year period was 50,600 people (including those who left as a result of the event in question). Our estimates thus suggest that a large proportion of these migrants left Quebec for reasons not related to wage differentials or employment prospects, or other factors included in our model.

It is also noteworthy that for this shock the highest-income class accounts for 49 percent of the total net outflow due to the shock, even though it constitutes only 34 percent of our sample of migrants at the beginning of 1976.[15] The loss of disproportionately large numbers of high-income tax-payers is an undesirable outcome for any sending province but a potential gain for the receiving provinces, especially if these individuals are able to find jobs without too much difficulty after their move.[16]

Finally, the bottom panel of the table shows the effect on flows to and from Newfoundland during the 1993 to 1996 period, after the closure of the cod fishery on the East Coast. These effects are computed using the estimated coefficients of FISH and FISH2. We have already discovered in chapter 6 that both inflows and outflows were negatively affected by this event, with larger coefficients on the variable related to inflows to Newfoundland, FISH. Table 8.4 shows us how those larger coefficients translate into considerably larger *decreases* in inflows to than in outflows from the province. That there should have been larger reductions in inflows than in outflows seems somewhat counterintuitive, but it may reflect the effect of the TAGS income subsidy program for fishers that was instituted when the fishery closed.[17] Only current residents at the time of the closure were eligible for these subsidies, so that return migrants would not benefit. In this case, the reduction in inflows may reflect a large reduction in return migration.

The total effect of the closing of the fishery as we calculate it was substantial, amounting to a decrease in net in-migration of 25,000–26,000 persons using Model 1. For Model 2, the predicted decrease in net in-migration is smaller – less than 18,000 people – but compared to the sorts of responses to the "normal" policy reforms we investigated in previous sections, still large. Both predictions are greater than the actual net outflow over the period, which was about 14,500 tax filers. The discrepancy between the actual and predicted figures may simply be a prediction error, or it may be a sign that there were offsetting changes in other variables in the model that reduced the net outflow below what it would otherwise have been.

The results of these three simulations demonstrate that extraordinary events can have big effects on migration flows, likely because the consequences of these shocks are substantial enough to overcome even high costs of moving. It should not be forgotten that these are cumulative effects over a period of several years, and of course the average annual effect would be smaller. Even so, these effects remain large relative to the average annual effects of the other policy changes that we considered in the earlier parts of this chapter

9

What We Have Learned

Over the past four decades empirical researchers have repeatedly tried to find evidence that regionalized aspects of fiscal policy in Canada blunt the tendency for people to move from economically disadvantaged to relatively more advantaged places in Canada. The main argument behind this search for policy-induced migration is that the (overly) generous subsidization of people living in less prosperous parts of the country that is built into public policy in the Canadian federation short-circuits the tendency for migration to lead to more efficient regional allocations of labour and to less regional disparity in earned incomes.

From this perspective, it is particularly easy to indict the unemployment insurance system, because since 1971 it has explicitly and consistently discriminated in favour of people who live in relatively high-unemployment regions by requiring shorter periods of work to qualify for benefits and offering more weeks of benefits once qualified. Moreover, while the precise characteristics of the insurance system have been adjusted in various ways since benefit periods were regionalized in 1971, the basic nature of the regional differentiation, or discrimination, in the insurance system remains in place today.

The matter does not rest there, however, even in principle. In one contrary view, public policy is not regarded as arising exogenously, or prior to migration, as it is in the transfer dependency view expressed above. Rather, it is precisely because governments must respond to migration induced by their actions that fiscally induced migration acts as a constraint on their behaviour, forcing provincial governments (especially) to take the national consequences of their actions more fully into account.

On balance it seems to us fair to say that the negative view – that fiscally induced migration leads to adverse consequences for the country as a whole – still has the upper hand, theoretically speaking. In either case though, and whatever the theoretical balance, the matter comes down to the empirics. The costs of moving away from home are substantial relative to the wage gains from moving, especially for middle-aged and older people. Thus, regional differences in the generosity of, or net benefits from, the public sector resulting from the operation of the unemployment insurance system and other aspects of public policy, whatever the level of government involved or why, have to be substantial to induce a quantitatively large and economically significant change in migration patterns. Moreover, for many people the unemployment insurance system (which was relabelled Employment Insurance in 1996) is not relevant, either because the prospect that they will become unemployed is consistently low or because they are more concerned with the riskiness of employment prospects in alternative locations as opposed to the level of insurance benefits if unemployed there. In the end, it *is* an empirical question as to whether and to what extent the regionalized nature of insurance generosity, or of any other aspect of public policy that favours some places or provinces over others, has in fact created incentives large enough to induce a substantial number of people to change their migration decisions.

The model we have used to search for policy-induced internal migration is based on the view that migration decisions are shaped importantly by differences in the comprehensive income (or welfare) that individuals expect to experience if they move. Of course what individuals think might happen to them in alternative locations in various states of the world is difficult, if not impossible to measure directly. But we can observe key factors upon which systematic regional differences in expected well-being are likely to depend and then use them along with migration data to estimate a model of interregional migration in which public policy is well represented.

Our model of migration decision making by a risk-averse individual who maximizes expected utility over all possible locations and states of the world led us to the construction of composite variables INCOME and LEISURE for each origin-destination pair for each year and subgroup in the migration data series we constructed from tax files for the 1968 to 1996 period. These variables, the main explanatory factors in our empirical models, are defined with respect to four states of the world: full employment, strong and weak attachment to the labour market, and on social assistance. They represent expected income and expected leisure in each location and for each of the eighteen income-class, age, and sex groups in the migration data we constructed from income tax data.

In addition to the usual market-related conditions in origin and destination that are the major determinants of economic migration in normal times, we measured as carefully as possible the policy-related factors that may create incentives to move between provinces in Canada over the 1968 to 1996 period, including unemployment insurance, federal and provincial tax systems, provincial social assistance, and other aspects of federal and provincial spending. Along with wages and employment probabilities, unemployment insurance parameters, tax rates, and social assistance played important roles in the measurement of *INCOME* and to a lesser extent of *LEISURE*, and so appear in the model through the effect of these composites. Other factors, such as public expenditure and location-specific attributes appear in our migration equations separately from the composites. We also allowed for the consequences of some extraordinary events in Quebec in the early 1970s and in the mid- to late 1970s, and on the East Coast after the closing of the coast cod fishery in 1992.

The public sector data we used exhibit considerable variability in the regional dimension even when compared to variability in market conditions. This observation is important. It implies that if our empirical models indicate that there is little or no fiscally induced migration, we cannot ascribe such a result to a lack of action in the data we use to represent public policy.

So, what have we learned from using a data set with this considerable policy-related action in it? To answer that question, we proceed in three steps. We first provide a general overview of our results from chapters 6, 7, and 8 concerning the role of fiscal policy in internal migration in the 1968–96 period. Then we reflect on our results in conjunction with the past four decades of research we reviewed in chapter 3. Our intention here is to reach an overall, state-of-the-art assessment concerning fiscally induced migration in "normal" times. Finally, we turn to our results concerning the consequences for migration of extraordinary events.

A GENERAL SUMMARY OF RESULTS CONCERNING FISCALLY INDUCED MIGRATION

The volatile nature of year-to-year migration flows and the multiple factors affecting migration decisions – including wages if employed, employment prospects, and moving costs, in addition to various aspects of public policy – combine to make an empirical search for policy-induced migration challenging. What follows is an overview of what we think we have learned from answering the challenge on this occasion.

The implications of the parameter estimates from the two migration models we estimated were explored by calculating marginal effects and, most interestingly, by doing simulations. We summarize only two of the main features of the marginal effect calculations in chapter 7 here, as other aspects of the results are best revealed by simulation. First, these calculations reveal that the interaction of the unemployment insurance system and of provincial social assistance matters, especially when a change in the weeks of insurance benefits accruing to minimal qualifiers (MINWKS) is considered. This may be obvious once one thinks about what people without jobs do after losing entitlement to insurance, but it is comforting to see this logic reflected in the calculations. Increases in MINWKS, holding all else constant, lead to increases in net in-migration only in Newfoundland, New Brunswick, Quebec, and Manitoba, because it is only in those provinces that after-tax weekly insurance benefits in our sample periods have tended to be larger than social assistance benefits. In the remaining provinces, increases in MINWKS lead to decreases in net in-migration, regardless of the model.

Second, the marginal change in the Quebec income tax rate that is required to produce the same effect on net in-migration as would a one-dollar change in average weekly earnings (a decrease of at least 0.07) is much larger than that for other provinces (a decrease of 0.01 to 0.04), indicating that out-migration from Quebec is less responsive to personal tax changes than that from the other provinces. Since Quebec has the highest personal income tax rate of all the provinces in our sample, this result suggests that Quebec has taken advantage of, or made appropriate use of, a relatively sluggish response of migration to personal tax increases. In assessing these results, it is noteworthy that marginal effects with respect to a change in provincial taxation are approximately the same for the two versions of the basic model we estimated.

Simulations are the primary method we use to explore the implications of the estimation results. The simulations in chapter 8 are designed to uncover the consequences for migration of eliminating all regional variation in policy variables. Such simulations have not before been conducted in the migration context except, to a limited extent, in Winer and Gauthier (1982a).

The unemployment insurance simulations we conducted indicate that eliminating regional variation in the generosity of the insurance system would lead to more net out-migration from the Atlantic region, Quebec, and British Columbia and more net in-migration to Ontario. In other words, these simulations show that the unemployment insurance system has on balance led to more migration towards regions where employment prospects are relatively poor, especially for lower- and middle-income people. This is seen most clearly in simulations of the effects of eliminating regional variation in weeks of regionally extended benefits.

Our insurance simulations as a whole also indicate that the magnitude of the effects on migration patterns of regional variation in the unemployment insurance system is small when compared to the consequences of regional variation in wages or in employment prospects. For Newfoundland and other small provinces, results using Model 1 are larger than in other simulations, but these are not obviously to be preferred to other estimates. Using Model 2, the effect is about one-tenth as big. One should note that for both models, the overall effects based on summing over the eighteen income/age/sex groups in the migration data are smaller than the results based on data aggregated by income class only. In the fully disaggregated results, the change over all groups in gross migration flows never rises above 1.3 percent of the base case for any province.

The differences between the two models stem in part from the treatment of the role of the probabilities of the four states of the world as indicators of risk aversion. Each way of representing aversion to the riskiness of employment opportunities leads to a different pattern of correlation between the probability-weighted leisure term and the probabilities themselves, and leads to changes in the magnitudes and/or signs of the coefficients of expected income and leisure. This feature of our results occurs because labour market choices and hence expected income and leisure are correlated with the riskiness of alternatives, something that would be unlikely to disappear even if our sample were to grow in size.

Simulations concerning the effects of eliminating regional variation in provincial income tax rates indicate that Quebec would gain the most in terms of net in-flows if tax rates everywhere were reduced to the national average. No doubt this reflects the fact that Quebec tax rates historically have been the highest, as well as estimated behavioral responses. Ontario would lose the most in this scenario.

Regional variation in social assistance appears to have only small effects on migration patterns in all provinces, but the consequences of eliminating regional variation in some fiscal aggregates, especially federal spending, are substantial in comparison with the effects of eliminating regional variation in other policy variables. We regard the latter results with caution though, because they depend on the nature of correlation between fiscal policy variables and the probabilities of the employment states of the world. It seems likely to us that the estimated coefficients of the fiscal variables depend on unobserved and omitted factors.

To put the foregoing results into better perspective, we conducted analogous simulations with all policy variables together, and with weekly wages, employment prospects, and moving costs. Not surprisingly, eliminating all policy variation – an unlikely policy scenario in a federal country like Canada – has more substantial consequences for the regional distribution of population than the individual policy simulations. Using either of our models, Ontario is a net loser of population in this simulation, while the pattern across other provinces varies with the model employed. The implication here is that regional variation in public policy in the country as a whole over the 1968 to 1996 period has not been accomplished at Ontario's expense.

Generally speaking, however, the effects of the policy simulations are dominated by the elimination of regional variation in wages, states of the world, and moving costs. In comparison to most of the policy variables taken one at a time, these three variables have much larger consequences for the volume of gross migration flows. Moving costs are by far the most important influence on internal migration, by at least two orders of magnitude, with the probabilities next in order of influence.

While the models we estimate do not tell us what economic impacts would result from the migration flows generated in the simulations, we can make an informed guess at how provincial unemployment rates would be affected. To do so, we assumed that all out-migrants in any simulation were previously unemployed and that all in-migrants are fully employed, assumptions that lead to highly favorable outcomes in terms of the impact of migration on unemployment rates. The corresponding calculations showed that even if we use the estimates that lead to the largest simulated effects from regional variation in employment insurance generosity, average provincial unemployment rates are hardly affected by policy variables, except for federal spending, and even then the effect is quite modest.

FISCALLY INDUCED MIGRATION IN THE LIGHT OF FOUR DECADES OF RESEARCH

Because it allows the researcher to include more policy parameters than other approaches, the structural approach adopted by us in this book, and earlier by Day (1992), provides more precise information about the migration effects of the design of unemployment insurance systems, taxes, and social assistance than do the other approaches. With respect to unemployment insurance, we have focused directly on regular benefits, the category of benefits that does involve regional variation in both qualifying requirements and generosity of benefits, and our basic framework is grounded in microeconomic theory.

No one study is perfect of course. Our models exhibit a collinearity problem that can be traced in part to the dependence of the unemployment insurance parameters on regional unemployment rates, which makes it difficult to empirically distinguish the effects of higher unemployment rates from the effects of a more generous unemployment system given the unemployment rate. All time-series studies suffer to some extent from this problem, although most don't report correlations between explanatory variables, making it impossible to determine the severity of the problem. We have addressed this issue by carrying out simulations using more than one version of our model, rather than relying on just one set of estimates.

What then is our bottom line concerning the nature and strength of fiscally induced migration in Canada? In what we follows, we divide our answer to this question into two parts, dealing first with unemployment insurance and then with other fiscal policies.

Unemployment Insurance

Concerning unemployment insurance, we think that the following general conclusions can be drawn on the basis of the new work presented in this book, along with the four decades of empirical research we reviewed in chapter 3. First, the work of Winer and Gauthier (1982a), of Audas and McDonald (2003), and in this book suggests that only a subset of the population is influenced by unemployment insurance benefits when making migration decisions. This subset of the population consists of individuals who are more likely to make use of the unemployment insurance system because they are not strongly attached to the labour force (Audas/McDonald), or are lower-income and middle-income tax payers (Winer/Gauthier, and this study).[1] This is intuitively reasonable.

Second, the marginal effect calculations and the simulation results provided here (and to a limited extent in previous work) suggest that where a statistically significant effect exists, it is too small to have much of an effect on provincial economies. Even using the model that is most likely to yield large effects, we find that a simulation in which *both* the variable entrance requirement and regional extended benefits are eliminated would only reduce Newfoundland's average unemployment rate over the 1978–96 period to 16.5 percent as compared to an actual average unemployment rate over that period of approximately 16.8 percent. Marginal effects reported by other authors are also small, when they are reported, and no one has found large impact effects. So while there does exist empirical evidence that Courchene's (1970) argument about the direction of the effect of the variable entrance requirement and regional differences in weeks of benefits is correct, the magnitude of the effect appears to be too small to have serious consequences for economic efficiency. We conclude that neither our results nor the literature as a whole are supportive of the view that the regional subsidization built into the unemployment insurance system plays an important role in maintaining regional disparities by inducing too many people to stay in relatively poorer parts of the country.

One could cumulate the small retarding effect of the regionalized insurance system we think exists, such as it is in the literature, over many decades, or a century, *holding all other factors constant including labour market developments that might alter the balance between the public and private sector determinants of migration behaviour*, and it would then be larger.[2] But dynamic, fully empirically estimated models of migration behaviour are not available,[3] and in the light of the empirical research that has been conducted here and over the last forty years, the burden falls heavily on those who want to extend their predictions to the very long run.

Taxation, Social Assistance, Public Services, and Grants

Conclusions in the literature as a whole about the role of fiscal policies other than unemployment insurance are more difficult to arrive at. We consider here in turn results concerning taxation, social assistance, public services, and intergovernmental grants.

Our own results concerning taxation are definite – high taxation discourages in-migration. But there have been few studies where the role of taxation has been examined independently of labour income. If one is prepared to accept the view that disposable or after-tax income is what matters (the basis for the treatment of taxation in our models), then the evidence in the literature becomes clearer, since taxation then has effects that are essentially the same as those of wages, provided that we are considering tax changes that are expected to be as permanent as changes in wages.

The argument that social assistance benefits are equivalent to a change in wages is not as easily defended since the state of the labour market plays a more important role in this case than it does in the case of taxes. We are not aware of other studies that have looked directly at the consequences of variation in social assistance as we have, and none so far as we know have considered the interaction of social assistance and unemployment insurance that we observe. Researchers using microdata who include receipt of social assistance as a dummy variable are not really looking at the consequences of variation in the generosity of assistance payments. Rather, they are in effect classifying people and asking if the classification matters. Our conclusion about the role of general transfer programs is that their effects on migration are subject to clarification in future work.

The same conclusion is appropriate when we consider the role of public services as it has been revealed in the literature as a whole so far. While measuring transfer payments for individuals is difficult but not impossible, measuring the net individual benefits from public services – the theoretically correct variable one wants to use in a migration equation – is still not possible. The consequent reliance on actual per capita fiscal aggregates as a substitute for individual benefits from public services, in our own work as in the literature as a whole, is not satisfactory. The use of such proxies is probably a source of confounding correlation between the fiscal aggregates and labour market factors. As we noted earlier, we are suspicious of the results using the public spending variables for this reason.

Finally, we come to the role of intergovernmental grants like equalization, which explicitly subsidize governments in less prosperous parts of the country. The only way to look directly at the role of grants in a migration equation is to use a reduced-form approach, one that we have explicitly decided not to implement, preferring instead to develop a formulation that emphasizes the role of public policies as they enter an individual's budget constraint. Grants allow the recipient government to lower taxes and raise expenditures, thereby altering individual comprehensive incomes and migration decisions, in principle anyway. There is some evidence in Courchene (1970), Winer and Gauthier (1982a) and in Bahkshi et al. (2009) that grants matter in the expected way, retarding out-migration from poorer provinces. But there is no solid evidence that the effect on migration of the variation in grants that has occurred over the past four decades is quantitatively substantial in some sense.

To summarize, the literature over the past four decades provides us with some reasonably definite results concerning unemployment insurance and individual income taxation. Social assistance, public services, and grants also appear to influence migration in a predictable fashion, but with quantitative effects that are not well established.

EXTRAORDINARY EVENTS AND THE STUDY OF INTERNAL MIGRATION

The preceding assessment of our own results and of those in the literature as a whole must be tempered with the observation that studies based on historical data can evaluate only the kind of policy changes that are reflected in the data. Since truly big shocks originating in the public sector rarely occur, simulations of such shocks using data from "normal" times may produce inaccurate results. If the complete elimination of regional variation in the unemployment insurance system constitutes such a big shock, the simulation results we report in chapter 8 could underestimate its consequences.

Similarly, no one could infer from the data what would happen if the system of equalization grants was completely eliminated.

The fact that the part of the public budget in the poorest provinces that is financed from federal grants can be well above 25 percent – and even double that – leads one to guess that if these grants ceased completely, life with one-quarter to one-half of the schools, hospitals, and roads would be sufficiently unpleasant that out-migration from some provinces would increase substantially. But as an empirical matter, we do not know.

As for the elimination of all regional variation in the unemployment insurance system, in our sample covering the 1974 to 1996 period there was substantial variation in the generosity of the insurance system, and the counterfactual is in fact not so far removed from the historical experience underlying our estimates. Moreover, we have found that the calculated effect of this often proposed reform on migration is smaller when we base our simulation on estimates derived from a data set for the years from 1968 to 1996, a period that includes at least three years before the initial introduction of regional variation in unemployment insurance in 1971. Together, these considerations suggest that the elimination of regional variation in the system is not so large a change that we need to be concerned that its effects have been grossly underestimated.

It seems safe to conclude then that while changing regionalized incentives in the insurance system may have allocative effects, for example by influencing work-leisure decisions in particular locations, the degree of regional variation in unemployment insurance is unlikely to have serious allocative (i.e., efficiency) consequences *resulting from policy-induced migration*. In other words, if changes in the degree of regional variation in the current Employment Insurance system are contemplated – a system that our discussion in chapters 1 and 2 shows is not very different in its regional variability from the system that existed before 1997 – the principal justification for such changes should be equity considerations and possibly allocative effects that are not related to policy-induced migration.

On the other hand, all bets are off concerning reforms that are truly historically extraordinary. We have shown that the unusual events that occurred in our sample period – political events in Quebec in the early and in the mid-1970s and the closing of the East Coast cod fishery in 1992 – all had after-effects on migration patterns that were substantial relative to average annual migration flows. This is common knowledge perhaps, though the magnitudes of the resulting changes in gross migration flows have not before been carefully estimated. These shocks originating in the public sector (in a broad sense) created incentives to move out of Quebec that were substantial relative to the costs of moving and that did, in the case of the fishery, substantially depress incentives to move to Newfoundland, as income support was available only for those thrown out of work in the directly affected areas. We can expect such rare events, if they occur, to again have substantial effects on internal migration patterns, though predicting what those effects might be will always be a risky business.

FINAL WORDS

Migration is a significant and fascinating part of the human experience. There is much more to be said about it and about policy-induced internal migration in Canada in particular, though we are at the end of what we have to say on this occasion. It remains only for us to express the hope that our contribution to the study of internal migration will serve as a stimulus for further research in Canada and elsewhere.

Appendices

APPENDIX A

Data Sources

The principal challenges we faced in assembling the data set for this project were discussed in chapter 5, but many details regarding data sources were omitted from that chapter in an attempt to avoid overwhelming readers with tedious details. Because they are important, however, especially to those who might want to embark on a similar investigation in the future, these details are provided in this and several other data appendices. Readers who are interested in our data sources should begin with this data appendix, which will direct them to other appendices as necessary. The first section of this appendix indicates where to find information regarding the source of the variables examined in chapter 2.

As in the text, the subscripts i, j, and s refer, respectively, to province of origin i, province of destination j, and state of the world s ($=1,2,3,4$). Time subscripts apply to all variables but have been omitted for convenience. For precise definitions of the variables that appear in the theoretical and empirical models, readers should consult tables 4.1 and 6.1 respectively, as the focus of this appendix is on the data used to represent these variables in the empirical models, not their definitions.

THE FIGURES IN CHAPTER 2

Most of the variables presented in the figures in chapter 2 were constructed for our empirical model, and thus their construction is discussed later in this appendix. For the convenience of the reader, table A1 indicates where information about the sources of each variable discussed in chapter 2 can be found.

Table A1
Data Sources for Variables Used in Figures in Chapter 2

Variable	Formula	Sub-section Describing Sources
Real average weekly earnings	$(100\, w_j)/q_j$	After-Tax Incomes
Real social assistance benefits	$(100\, \overline{SA}_j)/q_j$	
Real income tax burden	$(100\ TOTALTAX_{jj1})/q_j$	
Unemployment rate, both sexes, 15+	$100\,(LF_j - EMP_j)/LF_j$	TABLE A2
Real per capita health spending	$\exp(HEALTH_j)$	Public Spending Variables
Real per capita education spending	$\exp(EDUCATION_j)$	
Real per capita other spending	$\exp(OTHER\ SPENDING_j)$	
Real per capita federal spending	$\exp(FEDERAL\ SPENDING_j)$	
Minimum qualifying weeks	MIN_j	Unemployment Insurance Variables
UI benefits for minimal quali-fiers	UI_{j3}	

Note: Since the base year value of the price index q_j is 100, nominal variables are multiplied by 100 when deflated to ensure that the unit of measurement remains dollars. Also, as indicated in the table, it is the antilogs of the model's government spending variables that are used in the construction of the figures.

Table A2
CANSIM Numbers for Labour Force and Employment Data Used to Compute Unemployment Rate, 15 and over

Province	Employment (EMP) 15 and over (1976–96)	Labour Force (LF) 15 and over (1976–96)
NFLD		D985139
PEI	D985458	D985421
NS	D985740	D985703
NB	D986022	D985985
QUE	D986304	D986267
ONT	D986586	D986549
MAN	D986868	D986831
SASK	D987150	D987113
ALTA	D987432	D987395
BC	D987714	D987677
Canada	D984670	D984598

All provinces, 1966–75	Unpublished data from Statistics Canada	

MIGRATION DATA

The migration data are discussed in the first section of chapter 5. Additional details regarding their construction are provided in appendix B.

UNEMPLOYMENT INSURANCE VARIABLES

The variables MIN_j, $MXYR_j$, and UI_{js} all depend on the unemployment insurance system. Since the definition of unemployment insurance income was provided only implicitly in chapter 4, for clarity we provide it explicitly below. In state 2, in which individuals are employed for $MXYR$ weeks, unemployment insurance income is

$$UI_{j2} = WUI_j \cdot MXYRWKS_j \tag{A1}$$

where

$$WUI_j = \rho w_j^R , \tag{A2}$$

and $MXYRWKS$ is the number of weeks of benefits that an individual with $MXYR$ weeks of insurable employment is entitled to receive during the year. In state 3, in which individuals are employed for MIN weeks, unemployment insurance income is

$$UI_{j3} = WUI_j \cdot MINWKS_j . \tag{A3}$$

In the other two states of the world individuals receive no unemployment insurance income. For further details regarding how MIN, $MXYR$, $MINWKS$, $MXYRWKS$, and WUI were computed, see appendix C.

AFTER-TAX INCOMES

After-tax incomes in the four states of the world, which are defined in equations (4.10), have many components.

Weekly Wages: w_j

For this variable we use average weekly earnings (including overtime), industrial composite/aggregate, by province, in current dollars. These data

Table A3
CANSIM Numbers for Average Weekly Earnings Data

Province	Old Series (1966M01–1983M03)	New Series (1983M01–1996M12)
NFLD	D703300	L661222
PEI	D703350	L663101
NS	D703360	L664926
NB	D703410	L667585
QUE	D703460	L670290
ONT	D703660	L673960
MAN	D704010	L677569
SASK	D704060	L680500
ALTA	D704160	L683346
BC	D704316	L686578
Canada	D703000	L657711

were obtained from CANSIM. In 1983 the survey upon which these data are based was modified considerably, resulting in a break in the series. (For further details regarding this change, see "Note to Users" in Statistics Canada catalogue 72–002, *Employment, Earnings and Hours*, 1983.) To convert them to the same basis as the new data, the data for 1966–82 were adjusted using a scale factor equal to the average over the first three months of 1983 of the ratio of the new series to the old series. The monthly data were then converted to annual data by taking annual averages. The CANSIM numbers for both the old and new series are given in table A3.

Nonwage Income: B_{is}

Nonwage income in current dollars is assumed to be the same in states 1 to 3 of the world (B_{i4} is zero in state 4) and to depend only on the province of origin. It is measured as per capita interest, dividend, and miscellaneous investment income: INT_i / POP_i, where INT_i is interest, dividend, and miscellaneous investment income in province i, and POP_i is the population of province i. Data on both variables were obtained from CANSIM, as indicated in table A4.

Transfers from the Federal Government, excluding UI: TR_i

Transfers from the federal government, excluding UI, which depend only on the origin province, are measured as the per capita value of the sum of spending in current dollars on three categories of federal transfers to

Table A4
CANSIM Numbers for Nonwage Income and Population Data

Variable	INT_i	POP_i
NFLD	D43205	D2
PEI	D43221	D3
NS	D43237	D4
NB	D43252	D5
QUE	D43269	D6
ONT	D43285	D7
MAN	D43301	D8
SASK	D43317	D9
ALTA	D43333	D10
BC	D44454	D11

Table A5
CANSIM Matrix and Series Numbers for Data on Government Transfer Payments to Persons, Old Basis

Province	Matrix	Family and youth allowances	Adult occupational training allowances	Miscellaneous and other transfers
NFLD	5068	D42646	D42654	D42655
PEI	5069	D42671	D42679	D42680
NS	5070	D42696	D42704	D42705
NB	5071	D42721	D42729	D42730
QUE	5072	D42746	D42754	D42755
ONT	5073	D42771	D42779	D42780
MAN	5074	D42796	D42804	D42805
SASK	5075	D42821	D42829	D42830
ALTA	5078	D42846	D42854	D42855
BC	6961	D44344	D44352	D44353

persons: family and youth allowances, adult occupational training payments, and miscellaneous and other payments. After total federal expenditure on these three types of transfers had been summed for each province, the result was divided by the provincial population (POP_i) to obtain the per capita value

Note that although the Provincial Economic Accounts published by Statistics Canada include many other categories of transfers to persons, only those federal non-pension transfer payments that directly supplement the incomes of labour force participants were included in TR_i. For the years 1968–95, the necessary data were obtained from CANSIM; the CANSIM series and matrix numbers are given in table A5. Data for 1996 on the same basis as the 1968–95 data were supplied by Dan Finnerty, Income and Expenditure Accounts Division, Statistics Canada.

Moving Costs: $DIST_{ij}$ and C_{ij}

For $DIST_{ij}$, the distance between province i and province j, we use the distance in kilometers between the major city in province i and the major city in province j. The major cities selected were St John's, Newfoundland; Charlottetown, Prince Edward Island; Halifax, Nova Scotia; Saint John, New Brunswick; Montreal, Quebec; Toronto, Ontario; Winnipeg, Manitoba; Regina, Saskatchewan; Calgary, Alberta; and Vancouver, British Columbia. The distances were obtained from the AAA *Road Atlas* (1992), page 127. The distance between PEI and BC was computed as the sum of the distances between PEI and NB and NB and BC.

As discussed in chapter 5, moving costs C_{ij} are the sum of two components: $C1_{ij}$, the foregone wage cost of moving from i to j; and $C2_{ij}$, the monetary cost of moving from i to j. The foregone wage cost is computed as the average weekly wage in the province of origin multiplied by the number of weeks required to move, where the latter is assumed to take on only three possible values that depend on the distance travelled. Thus

$$C1_{ij} = \begin{cases} w_i & \text{if } DIST_{ij} < 1600\,km \\ 1.5w_i & \text{if } 1600\,km < DIST_{ij} < 3200\,km \\ 2w_i & \text{if } DIST_{ij} > 3200\,km \end{cases} \tag{A4}$$

The monetary cost of moving from i to j is defined as the airplane travel cost for one person for the distance moved plus the rail cost of moving one ton of freight for the same distance:

$$C2_{ij} = AC \cdot DIST_{ij} + RC \cdot DIST_{ij}, \tag{A5}$$

where AC is passenger revenue per passenger kilometre for air travel and RC is railway operating revenue per revenue ton-kilometre. Statistics Canada provided us with unpublished data on AC, passenger revenue per passenger kilometre, air, for the period 1966–77, while the corresponding data for the period 1978–96 can be found in Statistics Canada catalogue 51–206. RC was computed as railway operating revenue freight divided by revenue ton-miles converted to kilometres. Data on both of these variables were obtained from Statistics Canada catalogue 52–216, *Rail in Canada*. All dollar values are in current dollars.

Income Taxes: $TOTALTAX_{ijs}$

The stylized tax system used to compute the tax liability that each individual faces in each state of the world has already been discussed at length in

Table A6
Sources of Tax System Parameters

Tax Parameter	Source
Personal exemption for a single individual	1966–70, *The National Finances*, various editions
Personal tax credit (Basic)	1971–87, table 7.2, *The National Finances*, 1988–89
	1988–89, table 7.3, *The National Finances*, 1990
	1990–92, table 7.6, *The National Finances*, 1992
	1993, table 3.6, *Finances of the Nation*, 1995
	1994–96, table 3.6, *Finances of the Nation*, 1996
Quebec personal exemption for a single individual	1972–84, table 7.7, *The National Finances*, 1984–85
	1985–87, table 7.10, *The National Finances*, 1987–88
	1988–90, table 7.11, *The National Finances*, 1990
Quebec personal tax credit (basic)	1985–87, table 7.10, *The National Finances*, 1987–88
	1988–90, table 7.11, *The National Finances*, 1990
	1991–92, table 7.10, *The National Finances*, 1992
	1993–96, table 3.11, The Finances of the Nation, 1996
Federal income tax schedule (thresholds, infra-marginal amounts, and marginal rates)	1966–96: *Taxation Statistics*, 1968–96 editions
Federal abatements in favour of the provinces	1966–71 (1966–96 in case of Quebec only): *The National Finances*, various issues
Quebec income tax schedule (thresholds and marginal rates)	1966–96: *The National Finances*, various editions
	Note: Infra-marginal amounts for Quebec were computed by the authors.

the section of chapter 5 titled "After-Tax Incomes Net of Moving Costs." All that remains here is to list the sources from which we obtained information on personal exemptions, personal tax credits, and income tax schedules. Our sources for these tax system parameters were various editions of Revenue Canada's publication *Taxation Statistics* and the Canadian Tax Foundation's publications *The National Finances* and *The Finances of the Nation*. The editions of each publication used for each parameter are indicated in table A6.

Social Assistance Income: SA_{js}

In our model, individuals in both states 3 and 4 receive income from social assistance. In fact, in state 4 it is the only source of income other than transfers from the federal government. As noted in chapter 5, the only measure of social assistance benefits we were able to obtain that was comparable across time and across provinces was the amount payable to a single parent with two children. For this type of family we obtained data on the maximum full-time, yearly social assistance benefit in each province (in current dollars) for the years 1966–94 from Pierre Lefebvre, which we call $\overline{SA}_j$. Two series, one for 1950 to 1992 and one for 1973 to 1994, were spliced together by

regressing the log of the newer series on the log of the older one and then
predicting values for 1968–72 comparable to the newer series. Figures for
1995 and 1996 were derived using the figure for "couple with 2 children"
from *Welfare Incomes* (National Council of Welfare, 1995, 1996). These figures for 1995 and 1996 were adjusted downwards by removing the premium
paid when there are two spouses. The difference between payments with one
as opposed to two spouses was calculated using the Lefebvre data for 1994.

Given these data on maximum full-time benefits, which are used as state
4 social assistance income (i.e., $SA_{j4} = \overline{SA_j}$), we computed social assistance
benefits in state 3 as follows:

$$SA_{j3} = \frac{\overline{SA_j}}{52} \cdot (50 - MIN_j - MINWKS_j),$$ \hfill (A6)

where the term in parentheses represents the weeks remaining after working *MIN* weeks and receiving unemployment insurance benefits for *MINWKS*
weeks. (Recall that the maximum possible value of weeks of work plus
weeks of benefits in our model is 50, due to the two-week waiting period
for unemployment insurance benefits.)

Price of Consumption Goods: q_j

The variable q_j is used in the construction of the composite variable *LEISURE*
to convert the nominal value of all dollar incomes into a real value. In addition, as will be seen below, we also use it to deflate our nominal data on fiscal aggregates to produce measures of real fiscal benefits. Ideally we would
like to have a price measure that compares price levels across provinces
and across time, but such price indices for the Canadian provinces do not
exist for all the years of our sample. Instead, we use the all-items regional
city consumer price index (CPI) for one major city in each province, with
1986=100. The cities chosen were St John's, NL; Charlottetown, PE; Halifax,
NS; St John, NB; Montreal, QC; Toronto, ON; Winnipeg, MB; Saskatoon, SK;
Edmonton, AB; and Vancouver, BC. For all cities other than Charlottetown,
the price index data were obtained from Winer and Gauthier (1982) for
the period 1966–71. For the period 1972–96, the following CANSIM series are used: P816000 (St John's), P816400 (Halifax), P816600 (St John),
P817000 (Montreal), P817400 (Toronto), P817800 (Winnipeg), P818200
(Saskatoon), P818400 (Edmonton), P818800 (Vancouver). In the case of
Charlottetown, we use CANSIM series P816200 for the years 1974–96, and
assume that the CPI for Charlottetown was the same as that for Halifax for

the years 1966–73. Note that the use of regional city CPIs obscures somewhat differences in price levels across provinces, since for all ten provinces the value of the regional city CPI is the same (equal to 100) in the base year, 1986.

PROBABILITIES OF THE STATES OF THE WORLD

See appendix D for further information (in addition to that already provided in chapter 5) regarding the construction of the probabilities π_{js}.

PUBLIC SPENDING VARIABLES

Provincial/Local Government Spending: HEALTH$_j$, EDUCATION$_j$, OTHER SPENDING$_j$

All three provincial/local government spending variables are constructed in the same fashion, using CANSIM data on consolidated provincial and local government spending. However, although these data were readily available from CANSIM for the period 1966–95, in CANSIM they are provided for the fiscal year ending 31 March, not for the calendar year. The spending data were converted to a calendar year basis by taking weighted averages of spending for each pair of years as follows:

$$EXP_t^{CY} = 0.25 EXP_t^{FY} + 0.75 EXP_{t+1}^{FY}, \qquad (A7)$$

where EXP_t is government expenditure in year t, CY indicates calendar year data, and FY stands for fiscal year data. In addition, a change in the definition of the government sector that was introduced by Statistics Canada in 1997 resulted in a break in the fiscal year data in 1996. The 1996 data on the new basis were converted to the old basis by multiplying the 1996 value on the new basis by the ratio of the 1995 value on the old basis and the 1995 value on the new basis, for each series retrieved. The calendar year data were then divided by the provincial population and deflated using regional city CPIs. The provincial CPIs are used as deflators owing to the lack of provincial government spending deflators for the sample period as a whole.

Finally, natural logs were taken. Letting G_HEALTH, G_EDUCATION, and G_OTHER_SPENDING represent consolidated provincial and local government spending on health, education, and other functions respectively, the variables HEALTH, EDUCATION, and OTHER SPENDING are thus defined as follows:

Table A7
CANSIM Matrix and Series Numbers for Consolidated Provincial/Local Government Spending Data

Province	Matrix	Health	Education	Social Services	Debt Charges	Total Spending
Old basis (1966–95)						
NFLD	2808	D465283	D465285	D465284	D465294	D465279
PEI	2809	D465324	D465326	D465325	D465335	D465320
NS	2810	D465365	D465367	D465366	D465376	D465361
NB	2811	D465406	D465408	D465407	D465417	D465402
QUE	2812	D465447	D465449	D465448	D465458	D465443
ONT	2813	D465488	D465490	D465489	D465499	D465484
MAN	2814	D465529	D465531	D465530	D465540	D465525
SASK	2815	D465570	D465572	D465571	D465581	D465566
ALTA	2816	D465611	D465613	D465612	D465622	D465607
BC	2817	D465652	D465654	D465653	D465663	D465648
New basis (1996)						
NFLD	8182	D482602	D482613	D482607	D482627	D482598
PEI	8183	D482667	D482678	D482672	D482692	D482663
NS	8184	D482732	D482743	D482737	D482757	D482728
NB	8185	D482797	D482808	D482802	D482822	D482793
QUE	8186	D482862	D482873	D482867	D482887	D482858
ONT	8187	D482927	D482938	D482932	D482952	D482923
MAN	8188	D482992	D483003	D482997	D483017	D482988
SASK	8189	D483057	D483068	D483062	D483082	D483053
ALTA	8190	D483122	D483133	D483127	D483147	D483118
BC	8191	D483187	D483198	D483192	D483212	D483183

$$HEALTH_j = \ln\left[\frac{G\_HEALTH_j}{POP_j \cdot q_j}\right], \tag{A8}$$

$$EDUCATION_j = \ln\left[\frac{G\_EDUCATION_j}{POP_j \cdot q_j}\right],$$

$$OTHER\ SPENDING_j = \ln\left[\frac{G\_OTHER\_SPENDING_j}{POP_j \cdot q_j}\right].$$

Note that G_OTHER_SPENDING is calculated as total spending less spending on health, education, social services, and debt charges. The CANSIM matrix and series numbers for both the old and the new (post-revisions) series retrieved are given in table A7.

Table A8
CANSIM Matrix and Series Numbers for Federal Government Spending Data

Province	Matrix	Current Expenditure on Goods and Services	Investment in Fixed Capital and Inventories	Capital Consumption Allowances
Old basis (1966–95)				
NFLD	6757	D13233	D13243	D13242
PEI	6758	D13253	D13263	D13262
NS	6759	D13273	D13283	D13282
NB	6760	D13293	D13303	D13302
QUE	6761	D13313	D13323	D13322
ONT	6762	D13333	D13343	D13342
MAN	6763	D13353	D13363	D13362
SASK	6764	D13373	D13383	D13382
ALTA	6765	D13393	D13403	D13402
BC	6766	D13413	D13423	D13422
New basis (1996)				
NFLD	9071	Data provided by	D25804	D25801
PEI	9072	Dan Finnerty, Statis-	D25827	D25824
NS	9073	tics Canada	D25850	D25847
NB	9074		D25873	D25870
QUE	9075		D25896	D25893
ONT	9076		D25919	D25916
MAN	9077		D25942	D25939
SASK	9078		D25965	D25962
ALTA	9079		D25988	D25985
BC	9080		D26011	D26008

Federal Government Spending: FEDERAL SPENDING$_j$

For the purposes of our empirical analysis, total federal spending in current dollars is defined as current expenditure on goods and services plus investment in fixed capital and inventories, less capital consumption allowances. This spending total for each province is then deflated using the regional city CPIs and divided by the provincial population to obtain real per capita federal spending in each province. We then take natural logs to obtain the variable FEDERAL SPENDING, as shown in the equation below:

$$FEDERAL\ SPENDING_j = \ln\left[\frac{G\_FEDERAL_j}{POP_j \cdot q_j}\right], \tag{A9}$$

where G_FEDERAL is total federal current and capital spending in current dollars.

For the years 1966–95, the data needed to construct *FEDERAL SPENDING* were obtained from the Provincial Economic Accounts through CANSIM. As for the provincial government spending variables, a change in the definition of the government sector introduced by Statistics Canada in 1997 resulted in a break in the series in 1996. 1996 data on the old basis were provided by Dan Finnerty of the Income and Expenditure Accounts Division, Statistics Canada, for federal government current expenditure on goods and services. 1996 values for investment in fixed capital and inventories and capital consumption allowances were constructed by multiplying the 1996 value on the new basis by the ratio of the 1995 value on the old basis and the 1995 value on the new basis. The CANSIM matrix and series numbers for both the old and new series used are given in table A8.

Construction of the Migration Data

The migration data are derived by matching personal income tax returns for adjacent years, based on Social Insurance Numbers (SINS) or "RED_ID" numbers, internal identification codes that were used instead of SINS by Revenue Canada until the use of SINS became widespread. Individuals whose province of residence had changed from one year to the next were defined to be migrants. All returns for the years 1973 to 1996 were processed, while only a 10 percent sample of returns was available for the years 1968 to 1973.[1] Machine-readable income tax data for years prior to 1968 do not exist.

The personal income tax files are very large, consisting of about ten to twenty million individual records depending on the tax year. Each record corresponds to a single tax filer. The record layouts for each year are complex. Moreover, many changes have been made over the years in the definition and types of variables recorded on the tapes and in the nature of the computer coding used. The processing of these personal income tax tapes is thus a complicated task.

The procedure used for each tape was generally as follows: the tape for each year (consisting of several reels) was read, and selected types of records were excluded, as described in detail below. The purpose of the exclusions was to restrict the population to one that corresponded as closely as possible to the labour force, where the labour force is broadly defined to include all individuals who are either working or who would like to be working. Those who did not have any income from employment, self-employment, or some form of public assistance were excluded, as were immigrants, emigrants, and students (to the extent that the latter could be identified). People younger than 20 and older than 64 were also excluded. These exclusions allowed us to construct a (still very large) data set of tax filers who were attached to the Canadian labour force in an important manner, or who were on some form of social assistance. The result is called a master data set or master tape for each year from 1967 to 1996.

After the exclusions were implemented, individual records on the master tapes for two adjacent years were matched on the basis of SIN numbers, using the answer to the province of residence question on the T1 form ("what was your province of residence on Dec 31?").[2] A new, merged tape was written consisting of matched pairs of files for each tax filer who was present in both years. Each merged tape of matched files was then used to construct migration flows. If province of residence was different for years t-1 and t, individuals were deemed to have moved in year t.[3]

THE MASTER OR EXTRACTED DATA SETS

A master data set or tape was constructed by excluding certain categories of tax filers from the original tape of tax files. The list of exclusions from the original personal income tax tape is given below, followed by discussion when appropriate. The "positions" referred to in what follows are from the record layout for the 1995 tax tape. Note that for each year prior to 1980, there are two original tapes for each year – an Income tape and a Personal Identification tape. Records were excluded

1 If the tax filer's province of residence as of 31 December (position 329) was *not* one of the following ten provinces: Newfoundland, Prince Edward Island, Nova Scotia, New Brunswick, Quebec, Ontario, Manitoba, Saskatchewan, Alberta, British Columbia. Province of residence was determined by the following: 1988–96 – "PROV-OF-RES" (position 329); 1982–87 – "RESPROV"; 1978–81 – "RESPROV" on Income tape; 1977 and earlier – "PROVCD" (based on discussion with Robert Greenburg of Statistics Canada). Thus we excluded migration to and from the northern territories.

2 If the tax filer was an immigrant or emigrant (position 219), or deceased (position 213).

3 If the sum of T4 earnings (position 357), net business income (position 531), net professional income (position 535), net commission income (position 539), net farming income (position 543), net fishing income (position 547), UI benefits (position 491), and income from social assistance (953) was zero. People whose only source of income was from rentals or investments were therefore excluded.

4 If age < 20 or age > 64. This age range was determined by the availability on a consistent basis from 1966 by province, age, and sex of labour market employment data that we wished to use in our migration model,

Table B1
Tuition Fee Amounts for 1995 and 1996

Province	1995($)	1996($)
NFLD	2,150	2,312
PEI	2,620	2,820
NS	2,800	3,000
NB	2,152	2,190
QUE	1,663	1,665
ONT	2,228	2,451
MAN	1,988	2,087
SASK	2,025	2,550
ALTA	2,279	2,529
BC	2,130	2,198

as well as by our desire to study people whose migration decisions were closely related to the labour market.

5 If full-time students. The decision rule for determining who was a full-time student was age < 30 and tuition fees ≥ 0.75 times the amount given in table B1 for each province for 1995 and 1996 (for earlier years, the figures used were those for 1995 deflated by the CPI). The result was a cut-off for tuition that was conservative, with any bias being towards exclusion of tax files where tuition was paid. The 10 percent tape does not record claims for tuition, so that for the years before 1973 it is not possible to filter out full-time students. Since many students allow their parents to use the tuition deduction on their behalf, many students cannot be identified as such from the tax files.

To give an idea of the size of the tapes before and after exclusions, the full tape for 1995 has 20,242,560 records. Applying the preceding criteria to exclude records results in a master tape for 1995 of 14,612,580 records. For 1996, the corresponding figures are 20,770,719 and 14,863,962 records. The 1973 full tape, to take another example, contains 11,003,446 records on the Income tape and 11,002,133 on the Personal Identification tape before exclusions. After exclusions, there are 8,468,601 individual records.

MERGING MASTER DATA SETS FOR ADJACENT YEARS

After the master tapes had been written, the files on master tapes for adjacent pairs of years were merged using SIN numbers. Tax filers who did not file a return in both years were dropped from the data set. If the province of residence code was not the same in the second year as in the first year, the tax filer was judged to have moved during the last year of the pair of years being considered. Otherwise, the tax filer was judged to have stayed in the original province of residence.

For 1995/96, the merged data set contains 13,369,737 individual records. The difference between this figure and that for the master data set for 1995 is due to the presence in 1996 of new tax filers, including immigrants from the previous year who subsequently filed tax forms, and younger people who entered the labour force or who filed forms to get government transfers, or people who for various reasons did not file a form in 1996 but did file one in the previous year, such as some spouses, and some people with low incomes. There are many other, probably small categories of people not excluded in writing the master tapes that are responsible in part for the difference between the number of files on the master tapes and the number on the merged tapes. For 1973, the merged file contains 7,793,430 records.

OUTPUT DATA SETS

The output data sets were constructed by sorting files on the merged tapes in different ways. The primary characteristics used to aggregate tax files, in addition to province of origin and destination, included various combinations of income, age, gender, receipt of unemployment insurance, language, marital status, and the presence of children. Flags for these characteristics were created and attached to each matched pair of files on the merged data sets when these merged sets were written. A type of income flag (only self-employment income, only employment (T4) income, and all other) was also assigned to each matched pair on the merged tapes but was not used to construct output data sets.

For each set of primary characteristics used to aggregate tax files, confidentiality restrictions made it necessary to return to the merged tapes of individual matched files in order to construct an output data set with the smallest number of empty cells.

In the first output data set, the data were disaggregated by income class, age, sex, province of origin, province of destination, and year. The age groups included in the data set were 20–24 years, 25–44 years, and 45–64 years, while the income classes were defined as follows:

Income class 1: total income $\leq 0.5 \cdot$ median total income
Income class 2: $0.5 \cdot$ median total income $<$ total income $\leq 1.25 \cdot$ median total income
Income class 3: $1.25 \cdot$ median total income $<$ total income .

Table B2
Median Total Income after Exclusions of Tax Filers[1]

Tax year	Median total income (current dollars)	Tax year	Median total income (current dollars)
1967	4449	1982	15160
1968	5016	1983	15391
1969	5227	1984	16554
1970	5671	1985	17488
1971	6034	1986	18092
1972	6651	1987	19060
1973	7395	1988	21109
1974	7892	1989	22384
1975	8894	1990	23243
1976	10028	1991	23208
1977	11024	1992	24420
1978	10439	1993	24525
1979	11369	1994	25553
1980	12566	1995	24144
1981	14184		

[1] Median total income of actual tax filers remaining in sample after exclusions discussed in the text.

The median income used to define the income classes was computed for each year based on the total income reported by tax filers, and is given in table B2 .

As has been previously noted, the data for the period 1967–73 were derived from a 10 percent sample of tax filers. These data were combined with the 1974–96 data derived from the 100 percent T1 tapes by first dividing the data for 1974–96 by 10. All values less than 1 in the scaled data set were set equal to zero, and the remaining values were rounded to the nearest integer.

A second data set in which tax filers were sorted according to whether or not they had received unemployment insurance benefits was also created, but not analysed in this study. Four categories of recipient status were created:

Case 1: No unemployment insurance benefits received in years t and t-1
Case 2: Benefits received in year t-1 only
Case 3: Benefits received in year t only
Case 4: Benefits received in both years t and t-1

Tax filers in this data set were also sorted according to age and sex, using the same three age groups as in the first data set.

TOTAL OUT-MIGRATION BY PROVINCE

Because the various migration data sets produced included so many cells containing very few individuals, they could not be released. However, aggregating over all age and sex groups, income classes, and origin-destination pairs yielded a set of data that did satisfy Statistics Canada's confidentiality restrictions. These data on total in-, out-, and net in-migration by province for the period 1968–96 are presented in tables B3 to B5. To ensure comparability with the later data, the numbers for the years 1968 to 1973 are multiplied by 10.

Table B3
Total Outflows by Province, 1968–96

Year	NFLD	PEI	NS	NB	QUE	ONT	MAN	SASK	ALTA	BC
1968	3040	1010	5580	5080	17380	26980	9800	9980	12910	12580
1969	4230	970	5690	5090	19330	28800	10900	14300	15800	11450
1970	3130	760	5190	4160	15540	25440	9770	11290	12980	11620
1971	2390	650	4690	3630	14400	23850	8980	8840	12840	9740
1972	2800	600	4610	4450	15500	26810	9620	9130	14340	11020
1973	4830	740	4420	4470	12410	28040	8550	8450	12940	9790
1974	4417	1512	9484	6760	18855	48330	13740	10974	20432	21133
1975	4392	1745	9232	6418	18458	46414	12892	8691	18703	25471
1976	5130	1807	10374	7478	21458	44613	12766	8644	20639	26678
1977	5047	1625	9696	7322	28846	46680	12474	9405	23680	20992
1978	4601	1738	8780	6944	22480	42530	13190	9146	23211	18287
1979	6384	2487	11747	9242	25478	56769	18192	12269	30692	21170
1980	6521	2684	12669	10242	24073	63652	17550	12789	35919	21333
1981	7833	2768	12880	10455	23977	55637	14898	12277	38422	26373
1982	4654	1824	9390	6758	21329	35615	9825	9320	37260	24771
1983	7925	1472	8358	6303	19992	31308	9836	8589	42865	20151
1984	5434	1710	8665	6759	17169	31131	9617	8861	40230	22134
1985	6454	1845	9992	7859	15968	31609	10444	11555	31909	25331
1986	7086	1753	10595	8035	15270	32686	11114	11246	38766	21842
1987	7289	1776	10934	8204	16741	32638	11168	11503	32148	11894
1988	6959	1911	11356	8774	18468	41617	13707	14892	30670	19496
1989	7003	2110	11395	8220	18188	47537	13535	16119	29322	18497
1990	6783	2067	11540	7626	18182	47159	12711	14801	27267	17989
1991	6046	2286	10324	6844	17161	43679	10993	12302	26217	17757
1992	5842	1519	9889	6693	15948	40633	10326	10989	25793	16929
1993	6220	1753	9491	6341	14096	38300	9385	11001	24805	17010
1994	7346	1635	10148	6240	14785	34854	9524	10075	25755	18000
1995	7334	1539	9493	6182	14119	33226	8703	8808	24195	19846
1996	8581	1444	9199	6793	17422	36016	9540	9471	22610	23378

Source: Constructed by authors from tax files held by Statistics Canada. These data are counts of out-migrants, after the exclusion of certain tax filers (see text for details). Since the data for 1968–73 were derived from a 10 percent sample rather than a complete set of records that included 100 percent of tax filers, they have been multiplied by 10 to ensure comparability with the 1974–96 data.

Table B4
Total Inflows by Province, 1968–96

Year	NFLD	PEI	NS	NB	QUE	ONT	MAN	SASK	ALTA	BC
1968	2850	930	5740	3820	11260	29050	8030	6400	15770	20490
1969	2410	850	6140	4780	12540	31990	8440	5140	18080	26190
1970	3120	900	5360	4510	10130	26790	7300	4940	15460	21370
1971	3040	980	4500	4330	9670	24300	6330	4820	12900	19140
1972	3530	740	5170	4630	10760	25600	6610	5440	14660	21740
1973	2710	990	5620	4020	11090	21630	6810	4930	14470	22370
1974	4798	1989	9486	7845	16363	33222	10563	9472	27757	34142
1975	4769	1846	9590	8095	15036	33027	10601	10966	32945	25541
1976	3994	1823	9210	7194	14077	39712	10179	10677	37934	24787
1977	4056	2138	9454	7088	12494	42810	9785	9528	39390	29024
1978	3712	1883	8926	6510	11317	36224	7858	8687	37206	28584
1979	5140	2054	10165	7603	13331	41093	9680	10572	54751	40041
1980	5430	2104	10565	7389	13080	40834	10311	11213	62333	44173
1981	5116	2245	11379	7826	13187	45187	11752	11932	60667	36229
1982	5824	1947	10704	8260	10725	43818	10552	10421	36294	22201
1983	4417	2140	11387	7965	12502	49246	9699	10436	24196	24811
1984	4126	1901	10532	6725	14408	49273	9619	9448	23338	22340
1985	3655	1604	9732	6555	14266	48727	9127	8135	29737	21428
1986	4278	1629	9277	6319	14546	54631	9330	8063	23520	26800
1987	4768	1786	9404	6794	14094	51624	8187	6727	17726	23185
1988	5687	2105	11335	7614	15616	49254	7899	6806	27668	33866
1989	5842	1906	11551	8293	15668	43669	8085	7027	30401	39484
1990	5692	1900	10844	7623	14518	39067	8168	7607	31731	38975
1991	5594	1750	10415	7144	13494	34209	7406	7832	29121	36644
1992	4554	1905	9747	6310	12438	31190	7247	7830	25483	37857
1993	3718	1781	9206	5776	12544	29158	6833	7133	25052	37201
1994	3599	1682	8266	5573	11920	31445	7352	7309	24859	36357
1995	3797	1589	8121	5839	11616	31346	7089	7791	24771	31486
1996	3820	1669	8902	5886	11539	34059	6930	8352	32882	30415

Source: Constructed by authors from tax files held by Statistics Canada. These data are counts of in-migrants, after the exclusion of certain tax filers (see text for details). Since the data for 1968–73 were derived from a 10 percent sample rather than a complete set of records that included 100 percent of tax filers, they have been multiplied by 10 to ensure comparability with the 1974–96 data.

Table B5
Total Net Inflows by Province, 1968–96

Year	NFLD	PEI	NS	NB	QUE	ONT	MAN	SASK	ALTA	BC
1968	-190	-80	160	-1260	-6120	2070	-1770	-3580	2860	7910
1969	-1820	-120	450	-310	-6790	3190	-2460	-9160	2280	14740
1970	-10	140	170	350	-5410	1350	-2470	-6350	2480	9750
1971	650	330	-190	700	-4730	450	-2650	-4020	60	9400
1972	730	140	560	180	-4740	-1210	-3010	-3690	320	10720
1973	-2120	250	1200	-450	-1320	-6410	-1740	-3520	1530	12580
1974	381	477	2	1085	-2492	-15108	-3177	-1502	7325	13009
1975	377	101	358	1677	-3422	-13387	-2291	2275	14242	70
1976	-1136	16	-1164	-284	-7381	-4901	-2587	2033	17295	-1891
1977	-991	513	-242	-234	-16352	-3870	-2689	123	15710	8032
1978	-889	145	146	-434	-11163	-6306	-5332	-459	13995	10297
1979	-1244	-433	-1582	-1639	-12147	-15676	-8512	-1697	24059	18871
1980	-1091	-580	-2104	-2853	-10993	-22818	-7239	-1576	26414	22840
1981	-2717	-523	-1501	-2629	-10790	-10450	-3146	-345	22245	9856
1982	1170	123	1314	1502	-10604	8203	727	1101	-966	-2570
1983	-3508	668	3029	1662	-7490	17938	-137	1847	-18669	4660
1984	-1308	191	1867	-34	-2761	18142	2	587	-16892	206
1985	-2799	-241	-260	-1304	-1702	17118	-1317	-3420	-2172	-3903
1986	-2808	-124	-1318	-1716	-724	21945	-1784	-3183	-15246	4958
1987	-2521	10	-1530	-1410	-2647	18986	-2981	-4776	-14422	11291
1988	-1272	194	-21	-1160	-2852	7637	-5808	-8086	-3002	14370
1989	-1161	-204	156	73	-2520	-3868	-5450	-9092	1079	20987
1990	-1091	-167	-696	-3	-3664	-8092	-4543	-7194	4464	20986
1991	-452	-536	91	300	-3667	-9470	-3587	-4470	2904	18887
1992	-1288	386	-142	-383	-3510	-9443	-3079	-3159	-310	20928
1993	-2502	28	-285	-565	-1552	-9142	-2552	-3868	247	20191
1994	-3747	47	-1882	-667	-2865	-3409	-2172	-2766	-896	18357
1995	-3537	50	-1372	-343	-2503	-1880	-1614	-1017	576	11640
1996	-4761	225	-297	-907	-5883	-1957	-2610	-1119	10272	7037

Source: Constructed by authors from tax files held by Statistics Canada. These data are counts of in-migrants, after the exclusion of certain tax filers (see text for details). Since the data for 1968–73 were derived from a 10 percent sample rather than a complete set of records that included 100 percent of tax filers, they have been multiplied by 10 to ensure comparability with the 1974–96 data.

APPENDIX C

Construction of the Unemployment
Insurance Variables

This appendix provides additional details regarding the construction of the unemployment insurance variables MIN, MXYR, MINWKS, MXYRWKS, and WUI, as well as tables presenting the constructed data by province.[1]

MIN

MIN is defined as the minimum number of weeks of insurable employment required to qualify for benefits. Legislative changes affecting MIN occurred on the following dates: 27 June 1971, 4 December 1977, 11 February 1990, 18 November 1990, and 3 July 1994. Prior to 27 June 1971, 30 qualifying weeks of work were required for "regular" benefits, while only 15 qualifying weeks were required for what were known as "seasonal" benefits. Seasonal benefits were payable only during the period 1 December to 15 May and were intended compensate for the fact that unemployment rates were higher and jobs harder to find during this period (Dingledine 1981, 34). Both requirements applied across the country. The UI Act of 1971 eliminated the category of seasonal benefits completely but relaxed the qualifying requirement for regular benefits quite dramatically, to only 8 weeks of insurable employment nationwide. Because the new Act in effect amalgamated the seasonal and regular benefit categories into one, we define MIN to equal the seasonal benefit requirement of 15 weeks prior to 27 June 1971.

On 4 December 1977, the variable entrance requirement, or VER, was introduced; it was defined in table 3 of Schedule A of the 1971 Act, which is reproduced in the first panel of table 2.3 of the text. Between 11 February and 18 November of 1990 the VER was replaced by a uniform entrance requirement of 14 weeks of insurable employment nationwide, owing to the failure of the Senate to pass the legislation required to renew the VER. New legislation that came into force on 18 November 1990 restored the VER, replacing the previous range of 10 to 14 qualifying weeks with one of 10 to 20 weeks. The new VER is summarized in the second panel of table 2.3. On 3 July 1994, yet another modification of the VER, shown in the third panel of table 2.3, came into effect. This VER remained in effect until the beginning of January 1997, when a new VER based on hours, not weeks, of insurable employment was introduced under the Employment Insurance Act of 1996.

For non-transition years from 1971 to 1996, MIN was constructed using table 2.3 and annual unemployment rates for the provinces. For the transition years (i.e., years when the legislation changed), MIN was computed as follows:

1971: Average of old value of 30 weeks and new value of 8 weeks.
1977: 11/12 times 8 weeks plus 1/12 of value under new legislation.
1990: 1/12 of value under 1977 legislation plus 10/12 times 14 weeks plus 1/12 of value under new legislation.
1994: Average of value under 1990 legislation and value under new legislation.

In each case, the value was rounded to the nearest week for the purposes of calculating income and weeks of benefits.

The calculated value of MIN for each province is shown in table C4 at the end of this appendix.

MXYR

MXYR is defined as the number of weeks of work such that additional weeks of work do not increase the individual's entitlement to weeks of benefits during a given 52-week period. Alternatively, it can be viewed as the number of weeks of work during a 52-week period such that the sum of weeks of work, weeks of unemployment insurance entitlement, and weeks in the waiting period is 52. Note that MXYR is an artificial construct resulting from our modelling assumption that individuals face a one-year time horizon, since nothing in the regulations forces individuals to adhere to such a time horizon. Legislative changes affecting MXYR occurred on the following dates: 27 June 1971; 11 September 1977; 18 November 1990; 3 April 1994.

The value of MXYR depends primarily on the benefit structure; i.e., the way in which weeks of entitlement are calculated. In general, MXYR can be viewed as the solution to the following equation, where weeks on Unemployment Insurance (UI WEEKS) depend on the benefit structure in effect:

$$MXYR + UI\ WEEKS + WAITING\ PERIOD = 52. \tag{C1}$$

WAITING PERIOD is also a statutory parameter that has changed only once during the sample period, from six days (or approximately one week) to two weeks in 1971.

Prior to 1971, the benefit structure for regular benefits was relatively simple: one week of benefits for every two weeks of insurable employment, up to a maximum that was raised from 36 weeks to 56 weeks in 1959.[2] For this period, MXYR can thus be computed by solving the following equation:

$$MXYR + 0.5MXYR + 1 = 52, \tag{C2}$$

where the first term on the left-hand side represents weeks of work, the second weeks of benefit entitlement, and the third the one-week waiting period. The solution to the equation is 34 weeks. This value for MXYR applies nationwide.

Since 1971 the benefit structure has included a regional extended benefit component, which introduces a dependence between weeks of entitlement and the regional unemployment rate. The effect of this dependence has been to introduce differences across unemployment insurance regions in the value of MXYR. In the presence of regional extended benefits, UI WEEKS can be regarded as the sum of regional extended benefits (EXT) and the component of benefits that is not dependent upon the regional unemployment rate.

Unfortunately, although MXYR is still defined by equation (C1) after 1971, the complexity of the benefit structure prevailing in some periods means that it is not always possible to solve equation (C1) mathematically. The procedure used to compute MXYR was the following:

1 *1971 to 1977*: Regional extended benefits were computed using the annual values of the provincial and national unemployment rates. First benefits for phases 1, 2, 3, and 4 were computed and summed for weeks of work ranging from 8 to 30 (these quantities were the same for all regions). Then regional extended benefits were estimated as follows: if the regional rate exceeded 4 percent *and* exceeded the national rate by no more than two percentage points, EXT was set equal to 6 weeks; if the regional rate exceeded 4 percent *and* exceeded the national rate by more than two percentage points but no more than three percentage points, EXT was set equal to 12 weeks; and if the regional rate exceeded 4 percent *and* exceeded the national rate by more than three percentage points, then EXT was set equal to 18 weeks. The value of MXYR

corresponding to each of the three values of *EXT* was then determined; it was the *lowest* number of weeks of insurable employment *greater than or equal to MIN* such that the sum of weeks of insurable employment plus weeks of benefits was equal to *at least* 50 weeks. The result of this calculation was that $MXYR = 20$ weeks if $EXT = 0$; $MXYR = 17$ weeks if $EXT = 6$ weeks; $MXYR = 12$ weeks if $EXT = 12$ weeks; and $MXYR = 8$ weeks $= MIN$ if $EXT = 18$ weeks.

2 *1977 to 1990*: During this period, only phases 1 and 3 of the benefit structure are relevant to the calculation of *MXYR*. Also, the relative simplicity of the benefit structure implied that the solution to equation (c1) could be written as follows:

$$MXYR = \frac{(50 - EXT)}{2}.$$

(c3)

First, annual unemployment rates were used to determine the appropriate value of *EXT* for each province in each year. Then *MXYR* was computed for each province and each year using equation (c3). Finally, the value of *MXYR* was set equal to *MIN* in any case in which the value obtained using equation (c3) was found to be less than *MIN*. (In fact, during the 1977 to 1990 period, the value of *MXYR* produced by (c3) was less than *MIN* in 51 out of a total of 140 cases.)

3 *1990 to 1994*: The three-phase benefit structure that had previously been in effect was replaced with a single table, table 2 of the Schedule of the revised UI Act, showing weeks of benefits given the number of qualifying weeks and the regional unemployment rate. This table is reproduced in Lin (1998) as table 3. To determine the value of *MXYR* for each province, each column of the table was examined to determine the value of *MXYR* corresponding to that unemployment rate range. Once again, *MXYR* was defined to be the lowest number of weeks of insurable employment greater than or equal to *MIN* such that weeks of insurable employment plus weeks of benefits was equal to at least 50 weeks. These values are shown in table c1. Then the appropriate value of *MXYR* was assigned to each province in each year using the provincial unemployment rates.

4 *1994 to 1996*: Table 2 of the Schedule of the UI Act was revised. The procedure described in 3 immediately above was once again applied, this time using the revised table of weeks of benefits. The values of *MXYR* corresponding to each unemployment rate range under the new benefit structure are also shown in table c1. For the transition years, *MXYR* was computed as follows:

Table C1
Relationship between MXYR and the Regional Rate of Unemployment

Range of Regional Unemployment rate (percentages)	18 November 1990 to 3 April 1994	3 April 1994 to 31 December 1996
under 6.0	27	31
6.1 to 7.0	25	30
7.1 to 8.0	24	28
8.1 to 9.0	22	27
9.1 to 10.0	20	26
10.1 to 11.0	18	24
11.1 to 12.0	16	23
12.1 to 13.0	15	22
13.1 to 14.0	14	20
14.1 to 15.0	13	19
15.1 to 16.0	12	18
over 16.1	11	16

Source: Authors' calculations and schedules of benefits that came into effect on 18 November 1990 and 3 April 1994.

1971: average of the old value of 34 weeks and the value under 1971 legislation

1977: $2/3$ of the value under 1971 legislation plus $1/3$ of the value under 1977 legislation

1990: $11/12$ of the value under 1977 legislation plus $1/12$ of the value under 1990 legislation, subject to the condition that MXYR be greater than or equal to the weighted average MIN for 1990

1994: ¼ of the value under 1990 legislation plus ¾ of the value under 1994 legislation

The values of MXYR that were produced are presented in table C5 at the end of this appendix.

MINWKS

MINWKS is defined as the maximum weeks of benefits that an individual with MIN weeks of insurable employment is entitled to receive. Legislative changes affecting MINWKS occurred on the following dates: 27 June 1971, 11 September 1977, 4 December 1977, 11 February 1990, 18 November 1990, 3 April 1994, 3 July 1994. In non-transition years, MINWKS was calculated by applying the benefit structure to MIN, i.e., by computing directly the number of weeks of benefits to which a person with MIN weeks of insurable employment was entitled. Because of the model's 52-week time horizon, however, the maximum possible value for MINWKS is 51-MIN prior to 1971, and 50-MIN after 1971. The generosity of the benefit structure was such that it was necessary to impose this ceiling on MINWKS in some provinces in some years. The cases in which the ceiling was imposed were Newfoundland – 1972–90; Prince Edward Island – 1972, 1982–90; Nova Scotia – 1982–87; New Brunswick – 1976–78, 1981–90; Quebec – 1982–85; and British Columbia – 1982–87. The ceiling on MINWKS was always imposed, if necessary, *before* the average values for the transition years were computed.

In transition years, the computation of MIN was complicated by the fact that the benefit structure and the VER (which affects the value of MIN) did not always change on the same date. The transition years were handled as follows:

1971: Average of the old value of 15 weeks and the new value under 1977 legislation

1977: Benefit structure changed before the VER was introduced – used 8/12 of the value under 1971 legislation plus 3/12 of the value under 1977 benefit structure with MIN=8 weeks everywhere plus 1/12 the value under 1977 benefit structure and VER

1990: 1/12 of the value under 1977 benefit structure with VER plus 10/12 of the value under 1977 benefit structure with MIN=14 weeks everywhere plus 1/12 of the value under 1990 VER and benefit structure. To ensure that MINWKS = MXYRWKS for PEI in this year (for which MIN = MXYR), MINWKS was arbitrarily raised by one week. PEI in 1990 was the only case in which MINWKS did not automatically equal MXYRWKS when MIN equalled MXYR, most likely owing to rounding error.

1994: ¼ of the value under 1990 benefit structure plus ¾ of the value under 1994 benefit structure. Note that although the new VER was not effective until July, the new benefit structure became effective in April. According to the transitional provisions of the revisions to the UI Act, between 3 April and July of 1994 all individuals with between 10 and 12 qualifying weeks were deemed to have 12 qualifying weeks for the purposes of determining weeks of benefit entitlement.

The values of MINWKS that resulted from these calculations are presented in table C6 at the end of this appendix.

MXYRWKS

MXYRWKS is defined as the number of weeks of benefits that an individual with MXYR weeks of insurable employment is entitled to receive during the year. Legislative changes affecting MXYRWKS occurred on the following dates: 27 June 1971, 11 September 1977, 18 November 1990, 3 April 1994 (these are the same dates that affect MXYR). For the years 1966 to 1970, MXYRWKS was computed using the formula

$$MXYRWKS = 51 - MXYR. \tag{c4}$$

For the years 1971 to 1996, MXYRWKS was computed using the formula

$$MXYRWKS = 50 - MXYR. \tag{c5}$$

The difference between the two formulas is due to the change in the length of the waiting period that came into effect midway through 1971. Equation (c5) was arbitrarily used for the transition year 1971 to ensure that the values of MXYR and MXYRWKS would be consistent with each other, even though the length of the waiting period changed in the middle of 1971.

The values of MXYRWKS are presented in table c7 at the end of this appendix.

WUI

WUI is defined as the weekly rate of unemployment insurance benefit. It depends on the weekly maximum insurable earnings (MIE), the maximum weekly benefit, and the benefit replacement rate (ρ).

Legislative changes affecting ρ occurred on the following dates: 27 June 1971, 1 January 1979, 4 April 1993, 3 July 1994. Legislative changes affecting the MIE and/or maximum weekly benefit occurred on the following dates: 30 June 1968, 27 June 1971, 30 June 1996. Prior to 1971, the relationship between the weekly rate of benefit and previous weekly earnings depended on the level of average weekly earnings and/or contributions. This relationship was defined by two schedules, one that defined the weekly contribution corresponding to each range of earnings, and another that indicated the weekly rate of benefit corresponding to each range of average weekly contributions. For the purposes of computing a weekly rate of benefit for our model, these two tables were combined to arrive at a relationship between the range of weekly earnings and the weekly rate of benefit. Table c2 shows the relationship that was used for 1966 to mid-1968, while table c3 shows the table of benefits that was used from mid-1968 to mid-1971. The weekly rate of benefit for each province in each year of the 1966 to 1971 period

Table C2
Weekly Rates of Benefit Prevailing under 1959 Revisions to the UI Act

	Weekly rate of benefit	
Range of weekly earnings	Person without dependent	Person with dependent
Less than $15.00	$6.00	$8.00
$15.00 and under $21.00	$9.00	$12.00
$21.00 and under $27.00	$11.00	$15.00
$27.00 and under $33.00	$13.00	$18.00
$33.00 and under $39.00	$15.00	$21.00
$39.00 and under $45.00	$17.00	$24.00
$45.00 and under $51.00	$19.00	$26.00
$51.00 and under $57.00	$21.00	$28.00
$57.00 and under $63.00	$23.00	$30.00
$63.00 and under $69.00	$25.00	$33.00
$69.00 and over	$27.00	$36.00

Source: Schedules entitled "Rates of Contribution" and "Rates of Benefit," section II of S.C. 1959, c. 36, An Act to Amend the Unemployment Insurance Act.

Table C3
Weekly Rates of Benefit Prevailing under the 1968 Revisions to the UI Act

	Weekly rate of benefit	
Range of weekly earnings	Person without dependent	Person with dependent
Less than $30.00	$13.00	$17.00
$30.00 and under $40.00	$16.00	$21.00
$40.00 and under $50.00	$19.00	$25.00
$50.00 and under $60.00	$22.00	$29.00
$60.00 and under $70.00	$26.00	$33.00
$70.00 and under $80.00	$30.00	$38.00
$80.00 and under $90.00	$34.00	$43.00
$90.00 and under $100.00	$38.00	$48.00
$100.00 and over	$42.00	$53.00

Source: Schedules entitled "Rates of Contribution" and "Rates of Benefit," S.C. 1967–68, c. 33, An Act to Amend the Unemployment Insurance Act.

was determined by applying the "Person without Dependent" column to average weekly earnings in each province.

Since the passing of the Unemployment Insurance Act of 1971, the weekly rate of benefit WUI has been a fixed percentage of the individual's average weekly earnings over some period, up to a ceiling related to the weekly maximum insurable earnings (MIE). For this period, the relationship between

WUI, the benefit replacement rate, and maximum insurable earnings (*MIE*) can be expressed as follows:

$$WUI = \begin{cases} \rho w & w < MIE \\ \rho MIE & w \geq MIE \end{cases}, \hspace{2cm} \text{(c6)}$$

where ρ is the benefit replacement rate and w is the average of the individual's previous weekly earnings over some specified period. Under the legislation, the *MIE* changed annually according to a formula based on average weekly earnings in the economy as a whole. The maximum weekly benefit, given by ρMIE, also changed accordingly. Equation (c6) was applied to average weekly earnings data for each province to compute the value of *WUI* for each province in each year. In years where there were different benefit replacement rates for those with and without dependents, the rate for those without dependents was used.

For the transition years when the legislation changed *WUI* was computed as follows:

1968: Average of rate under 1959 schedule and rate under 1968 schedule

1971: Average of rate under 1968 schedule and new value under 1971 legislation

1993: Replacement rate used in equation (c6) is ¼ of 60 percent plus ¾ of 57 percent

1994: replacement rate used is average of 57 percent and the new rate of 55 percent (as for earlier years, the higher rate for low-income individuals with dependents was not used)

1996: *MIE* used is average of old value of $848 and new value under Employment Insurance of $750

Table c8 summarizes the weekly *MIE*, replacement rates, and maximum weekly benefits used in the calculation of *WUI*, while the values of *WUI* themselves are presented in table c9. Both tables can be found at the end of this appendix.

CALCULATION OF INCOMES IN THE UNEMPLOYMENT INSURANCE STATES

The data on *MIN*, *MXYR*, *MINWKS*, *MXYRWKS*, and *WUI* were used to compute wage and unemployment insurance income in states 2 and 3 as follows:

UI income, state 2 = *MXYRWKS* (rounded to nearest week) times *WUI*
UI income, state 3 = *MINWKS* (rounded to nearest week) times *WUI*
Wage income, state 2 = *MXYR* (rounded to nearest week) times average weekly earnings
Wage income, state 3 = *MIN* (rounded to nearest week) times average weekly earnings

Table c4
MIN by Province, 1966–96

Year	NFLD	PEI	NS	NB	QUE	ONT	MAN	SASK	ALTA	BC
1966	15	15	15	15	15	15	15	15	15	15
1967	15	15	15	15	15	15	15	15	15	15
1968	15	15	15	15	15	15	15	15	15	15
1969	15	15	15	15	15	15	15	15	15	15
1970	15	15	15	15	15	15	15	15	15	15
1971	12	12	12	12	12	12	12	12	12	12
1972	8	8	8	8	8	8	8	8	8	8
1973	8	8	8	8	8	8	8	8	8	8
1974	8	8	8	8	8	8	8	8	8	8
1975	8	8	8	8	8	8	8	8	8	8
1976	8	8	8	8	8	8	8	8	8	8
1977	8	8	8	8	8	8	9	9	9	8
1978	10	10	10	10	10	12	13	14	14	11
1979	10	10	10	10	10	13	14	14	14	12
1980	10	10	10	10	10	13	14	14	14	13
1981	10	10	10	10	10	13	14	14	14	13
1982	10	10	10	10	10	10	11	13	12	10
1983	10	10	10	10	10	10	10	12	10	10
1984	10	10	10	10	10	10	11	12	10	10
1985	10	10	10	10	10	11	11	11	10	10
1986	10	10	10	10	10	13	12	12	10	10
1987	10	10	10	10	10	13	12	12	10	10
1988	10	10	10	10	10	14	12	12	11	10
1989	10	10	10	10	10	14	12	12	12	10
1990	13	13	14	14	14	14	14	14	14	14
1991	10	10	14	13	14	16	17	18	17	16
1992	10	10	12	13	13	15	16	17	16	15
1993	10	10	11	13	12	15	16	18	16	16
1994	11	11	12	13	13	16	16	19	17	16
1995	12	12	13	14	14	17	18	19	18	17
1996	12	12	13	14	14	17	18	19	18	17

Source: Authors' calculations.

Table c5

MXYR by Province, 1966–96

Year	NFLD	PEI	NS	NB	QUE	ONT	MAN	SASK	ALTA	BC
1966	34	34	34	34	34	34	34	34	34	34
1967	34	34	34	34	34	34	34	34	34	34
1968	34	34	34	34	34	34	34	34	34	34
1969	34	34	34	34	34	34	34	34	34	34
1970	34	34	34	34	34	34	34	34	34	34
1971	23	27	27	27	26	27	27	27	27	26
1972	8	8	20	20	17	20	20	20	20	17
1973	8	20	20	12	17	20	20	20	20	17
1974	8	20	17	12	17	20	20	20	20	20
1975	8	20	20	12	17	20	20	20	20	17
1976	8	12	12	8	17	20	20	20	20	17
1977	9	16	12	9	12	20	20	21	21	19
1978	10	13	12	10	11	18	20	23	23	16
1979	10	10	12	10	13	20	22	24	25	17
1980	10	11	13	10	13	19	22	24	25	19
1981	10	10	12	10	12	19	17	23	25	19
1982	10	10	10	10	10	13	16	20	17	10
1983	10	10	10	10	10	12	14	18	11	10
1984	10	10	10	10	10	14	16	17	10	10
1985	10	10	10	10	10	16	16	16	12	10
1986	10	10	10	10	11	19	17	17	13	10
1987	10	10	10	10	12	20	18	18	13	10
1988	10	10	12	10	14	23	17	18	16	12
1989	10	10	13	10	14	22	17	18	18	14
1990	13	13	14	14	14	20	19	19	19	17
1991	11	12	18	15	18	25	24	25	24	22
1992	11	11	16	15	16	20	22	24	22	20
1993	11	11	14	15	15	18	20	22	20	18
1994	15	15	19	20	20	25	25	29	26	25
1995	16	19	22	23	23	27	28	30	28	27
1996	16	19	22	23	23	27	28	30	28	27

Source: Authors' calculations.

Table c6
MINWKS by Province, 1966–96

Year	NFLD	PEI	NS	NB	QUE	ONT	MAN	SASK	ALTA	BC
1966	13	13	13	13	13	13	13	13	13	13
1967	13	13	13	13	13	13	13	13	13	13
1968	13	13	13	13	13	13	13	13	13	13
1969	13	13	13	13	13	13	13	13	13	13
1970	13	13	13	13	13	13	13	13	13	13
1971	26	20	20	20	23	20	20	20	20	23
1972	42	42	26	26	32	26	26	26	26	32
1973	42	26	26	38	32	26	26	26	26	32
1974	42	26	32	38	32	26	26	26	26	26
1975	42	26	26	38	32	26	26	26	26	32
1976	42	38	38	42	32	26	26	26	26	26
1977	41	32	37	41	37	24	23	21	22	29
1978	40	34	36	40	38	26	23	18	18	28
1979	40	40	36	40	34	23	20	16	14	25
1980	40	38	34	40	34	25	20	16	14	25
1981	40	40	36	40	36	25	30	18	14	40
1982	40	40	40	40	40	34	29	23	28	40
1983	40	40	40	40	40	36	32	26	38	40
1984	40	40	40	40	40	32	29	28	40	40
1985	40	40	40	40	40	29	29	29	36	40
1986	40	40	40	40	38	25	28	28	34	40
1987	40	40	40	40	36	23	26	26	34	40
1988	40	40	36	40	32	18	28	26	29	36
1989	40	40	34	40	32	20	28	26	26	32
1990	37	37	36	36	36	24	27	25	27	31
1991	39	39	33	34	33	27	24	21	24	27
1992	39	39	35	34	34	30	27	24	27	30
1993	39	39	36	34	35	30	27	21	27	27
1994	34	34	28	27	27	22	22	16	20	22
1995	32	28	24	23	23	18	17	15	17	18
1996	32	28	24	23	23	18	17	15	17	18

Source: Authors' calculations.

Table C7
MXYRWKS by Province, 1966–96

Year	NFLD	PEI	NS	NB	QUE	ONT	MAN	SASK	ALTA	BC
1966	17	17	17	17	17	17	17	17	17	17
1967	17	17	17	17	17	17	17	17	17	17
1968	17	17	17	17	17	17	17	17	17	17
1969	17	17	17	17	17	17	17	17	17	17
1970	17	17	17	17	17	17	17	17	17	17
1971	27	23	23	23	25	23	23	23	23	25
1972	42	42	30	30	33	30	30	30	30	33
1973	42	30	30	38	33	30	30	30	30	33
1974	42	30	33	38	33	30	30	30	30	30
1975	42	30	30	38	33	30	30	30	30	33
1976	42	38	38	42	33	30	30	30	30	33
1977	41	34	38	41	38	30	30	29	29	31
1978	40	37	38	40	39	32	30	27	27	34
1979	40	40	38	40	37	30	28	26	25	33
1980	40	39	37	40	37	31	28	26	25	31
1981	40	40	38	40	38	31	33	27	25	31
1982	40	40	40	40	40	37	34	30	33	40
1983	40	40	40	40	40	38	36	32	39	40
1984	40	40	40	40	40	36	34	33	40	40
1985	40	40	40	40	40	34	34	34	38	40
1986	40	40	40	40	39	31	33	33	37	40
1987	40	40	40	40	38	30	32	32	37	40
1988	40	40	38	40	36	27	33	32	34	38
1989	40	40	37	40	36	28	33	32	32	36
1990	37	37	36	36	36	30	32	31	32	34
1991	39	38	32	35	32	25	26	25	26	28
1992	39	39	34	35	34	30	28	26	28	30
1993	39	39	36	35	35	32	30	28	30	32
1994	35	35	32	30	30	26	26	21	24	26
1995	34	31	28	27	27	23	22	20	22	23
1996	34	31	28	27	27	23	22	20	22	23

Source: Authors' calculations.

Appendix C

Table c8
Maximum Insurable Earnings, Benefit Replacement Rate, and Maximum Weekly Benefit

Year	Weekly MIE ($)	Replacement Rate (%) (No Dependents)	Maximum Weekly Benefit ($) (No Dependents)
1966	69		27
1967	69		27
1968	100		42
1969	100		42
1970	100		42
1971	125		71
1972	150	66.67	100
1973	160	66.67	107
1974	170	66.67	113
1975	185	66.67	123
1976	200	66.67	133
1977	220	66.67	147
1978	240	66.67	160
1979	265	60	159
1980	290	60	174
1981	315	60	189
1982	350	60	210
1983	385	60	231
1984	425	60	255
1985	460	60	276
1986	495	60	297
1987	530	60	318
1988	565	60	339
1989	605	60	363
1990	640	60	384
1991	680	60	408
1992	710	60	426
1993	745	57.75	425
1994	780	56	429
1995	815	55	448
1996	799	55	440

Table C9
WUI by Province, 1966–96 (rounded to nearest dollar)

Year	NFLD	PEI	NS	NB	QUE	ONT	MAN	SASK	ALTA	BC
1966	27	25	27	27	27	27	27	27	27	27
1967	27	27	27	27	27	27	27	27	27	27
1968	33	29	31	31	33	35	33	33	33	35
1969	42	34	38	38	42	42	42	38	42	42
1970	42	34	42	38	42	42	42	42	42	42
1971	61	52	58	56	61	65	63	59	62	66
1972	86	71	80	78	87	95	91	83	89	97
1973	96	78	87	84	94	101	97	89	96	105
1974	108	90	97	97	106	111	104	99	106	113
1975	123	106	112	114	122	123	119	115	123	123
1976	133	121	126	126	133	133	133	132	133	133
1977	147	132	138	139	147	147	144	144	147	147
1978	159	139	145	145	160	160	153	153	160	160
1979	157	133	142	144	157	157	148	152	159	159
1980	167	146	156	160	174	172	162	167	174	174
1981	189	159	173	176	189	189	180	186	189	189
1982	209	177	192	192	210	210	199	206	210	210
1983	220	191	204	210	228	226	213	218	231	231
1984	233	198	217	223	236	237	225	227	255	255
1985	238	207	226	230	243	249	230	232	261	263
1986	245	211	236	239	249	260	239	238	262	264
1987	253	221	242	242	259	272	246	241	265	273
1988	266	232	251	250	271	287	253	246	274	279
1989	276	241	258	263	282	303	267	255	288	297
1990	285	250	272	272	298	316	277	267	302	307
1991	298	258	285	287	310	332	287	278	318	319
1992	305	267	294	295	321	346	294	282	326	328
1993	304	262	285	290	313	340	285	274	319	322
1994	298	254	278	280	306	339	281	273	310	324
1995	294	257	269	281	302	336	278	271	305	327
1996	293	270	272	281	305	344	284	280	318	334

Source: Authors' calculations.

Measuring the Probabilities of the Employment States by Age and Sex

In this appendix we discuss in turn the measurement of each of the probabilities defined in equation (5.7), which vary by age, sex, year, and province. Because of the nature of the data, it is convenient to distinguish between various time periods for which data sources and the method used to calculate various quantities differ substantially. The numbers used are all "snapshots" at a point in time and refer to ranges of weeks of work rather than to specific weeks, as discussed in the main text.

$$n(E_j) = \text{EMPLOYMENT IN PROVINCE } j$$

1 *1966–75*: Age-sex specific employment figures by province for 1966–75 are unpublished Labour Force Survey figures supplied by Mark Levesque of Statistics Canada. In some cases, data for the province of Prince Edward Island are missing. We proxy this missing data by the average for 1976–78 of the ratios of employment in PEI to that in Nova Scotia times employment in Nova Scotia for 1966–75.
2 *1976–1996*: Age-sex specific employment figures are from the Labour Force Survey as published in CANSIM. The CANSIM numbers for these data are given in table D1.

$$n(UI_j) = \text{THE TOTAL NUMBER OF RECIPIENTS OF REGULAR}$$
$$\text{UNEMPLOYMENT INSURANCE BENEFITS}$$

The measurement of the number of unemployment insurance recipients is complicated by several factors: the lack of CANSIM data before 1975, the absence of computerized administrative data before 1972, the change in the

Table D1
CANSIM Numbers for LFS Employment Series

Province	20–24 years	25–44 years	45–64 years
Females			
NFLD	D985197	D985201	D985202
PEI	D985479	D985483	D985484
NS	D985761	D985765	D985766
NB	D986043	D986047	D986048
QUE	D986325	D986329	D986330
ONT	D986607	D986611	D986612
MAN	D986889	D986893	D986894
SASK	D987171	D987175	D987176
ALTA	D987453	D987457	D987458
BC	D987735	D987739	D987740
Males			
NFLD	D985188	D985192	D985193
PEI	D985470	D985474	D985475
NS	D985752	D985756	D985757
NB	D986034	D986038	D986039
QUE	D986316	D986320	D986321
ONT	D986598	D986602	D986603
MAN	D986880	D986884	D986885
SASK	D987162	D987166	D987167
ALTA	D987444	D987448	D987449
BC	D987726	D987730	D987731

unemployment insurance system and associated statistical reporting during 1971, and the absence for 1972 to 1974 of published figures on the number of people actually receiving unemployment insurance as opposed to the number of claims filed or total payments made.

The following discussion of the measurement of $n(UI_j)$ overlaps to some extent with the discussion of $p_{<20}$ and p_{20+}. The reason is that the nature of the available data for some years required that numbers of people in the <20 and 20+ qualifying weeks groups be calculated directly rather than as the product of a proportion and a total as indicated in the formulas given earlier. Moreover, it was necessary for most years to calculate the number of beneficiaries by sex directly.

In the following discussion, the term "regular" beneficiary applied to data before 1971 refers to someone who was not a recipient of seasonal benefits. After the new act in June of 1971, the term "regular" refers to someone who received benefits as a result of unemployment, as opposed to benefits related to maternity or other characteristics.

1   1966–70: Figures on both the number of seasonal and total (seasonal plus regular) beneficiaries (monthly average of weekly figures) are given in monthly issues of Statistics Canada catalogue 73–001, *Statistical Report on the Operation of the Unemployment Insurance Act*. Yearly averages of monthly data are used to compute the number of seasonal and total beneficiaries. The number of regular beneficiaries is calculated as a residual. Seasonal recipients are assumed to have < 20 qualifying weeks of work, and regular beneficiaries are assumed to have 20+ qualifying weeks of work.

2   1971: The derivation of figures for this year is complicated by the change in the unemployment insurance system that occurred in mid-year; in the new system, the category of seasonal beneficiaries no longer exists, and the reporting of data changes in various ways. We proceed as follows. The total number of beneficiaries in the first and the second six months of 1971 are calculated. The total number of beneficiaries in the first six months is calculated as for 1966–70. The total number of beneficiaries in the second six months is obtained using the same method as applied to the 1972–74 data, discussed below. The average number of beneficiaries over these two sub-periods in 1971 is then multiplied by the 1970 monthly average ratio of seasonal to total beneficiaries (for the period before the act changed) to obtain the total number of <20 qualifying-weeks beneficiaries in 1971. The number of 20+ qualifying-weeks beneficiaries in 1971 is obtained as a residual from the above calculation.

3   1972–74: For each year and province, the total number of regular beneficiaries by sex is estimated as the average over twelve months of *Claimants Reporting to District Offices on the Last Working Day of the Month* by sex from Statistics Canada catalogue 73–001 *times* the monthly average of *the regular beneficiary/claimant ratio by sex for 1975*. Note that 1975 is the first year for which such a ratio is available. Data on the number of claimants by sex for 1975 is from Statistics Canada catalogue 73–001, Table IV, Dec. 1975. Claimant data for 1972–74 is from monthly issues of the same publication for these years.

4   1975–1996: The total number of recipients of regular benefits by province by sex is given in CANSIM. These monthly data are averaged over

Table D2
CANSIM Numbers for Number of Recipients of Regular *UI* Benefits

Province	Men	Women
NFLD	D730605	D730606
PEI	D730608	D730609
NS	D730611	D730612
NB	D730614	D730615
QUE	D730617	D730618
ONT	D730620	D730621
MAN	D730623	D730624
SASK	D730626	D730627
ALTA	D730629	D730630
BC	D730632	D730633

the year. The CANSIM numbers for these data series can be found in table D2.

$p^j_{<20}$ = THE PROPORTION OF RECIPIENTS OF REGULAR UNEMPLOYMENT BENEFITS IN PROVINCE *J* WHO HAVE LESS THAN 20 QUALIFYING WEEKS OF WORK

The measurement of p^j_{20+} is derived as $1 - p^j_{<20}$, and only the latter is discussed in detail in this appendix. In what follows, it is convenient to consider directly the calculation of numbers of beneficiaries in each qualifying weeks-age-sex category, that is, to consider the product $p^j_{<20} * n(UI_j)$, rather than to discuss proportions of individuals.

1 *1966–70*: Numbers of beneficiaries by qualifying weeks discussed above are distributed over age-sex categories as follows. The distribution of (seasonal) beneficiaries with less than 20 weeks of work by age-sex category is assumed to be the same as the age-sex distribution of the number of regular benefit periods established given in monthly publications of Statistics Canada catalogue 73–201, *Annual Report on Benefit Periods Established and Terminated under the Unemployment Insurance Act*. The annual average of monthly figures is used. For the years 1966 to 1970, the measured age-sex distribution of those with less than 20 qualifying weeks of work is the same as that for people with 20 or more qualifying weeks.

2 *1971*: The age-sex breakdown of the number of beneficiaries by qualifying weeks discussed above is assumed to be given by the age-sex breakdown in the Bédard data for 1972 that is introduced immediately below.

3 *1972–74*: The numbers of regular beneficiaries by sex discussed earlier are distributed across qualifying weeks and age groups using administrative data on the unemployment insurance system compiled for us by Marcel Bédard of HRDC. These data record the number of beneficiaries who received at least $1 of regular benefits in the current year, and are stratified by qualifying weeks, age, and sex. The age group 20–24 is not defined in the Bédard data, and the value of $p^j_{<20}$ for the youngest age group in our classification scheme (those 20–24) for both males and females refers to the proportion of beneficiaries less than 25 years of age.

4 *1975–1996*: The number of regular beneficiaries by sex discussed above are distributed across qualifying weeks and age categories using the Bédard administrative data.

p^j_{20+} = THE PROPORTION OF RECIPIENTS OF REGULAR UNEMPLOYMENT BENEFITS IN PROVINCE J IN ANY YEAR WHO HAVE 20 OR MORE QUALIFYING WEEKS OF WORK

See the discussion of $p^j_{<20}$ above. The number of individuals with 20+ qualifying weeks, for each age-sex category, is derived using the condition that $p^j_{<20}$ and p^j_{20+} sum to one.

$n(SA_j)$ = THE NUMBER OF SOCIAL ASSISTANCE RECIPIENTS IN REGION J

The general methodology used to measure $n(SA_j)$ is as follows. The number of social assistance cases of all ages on a fiscal year basis is computed and converted to a calendar year basis. A special compilation of social assistance recipients by age and province using all available computerized Surveys of Consumer Finances (SCF) is used to reduce this to a number of cases for ages 20–64. These aggregate figures are then distributed across age-sex categories using the proportions of cases in each age-sex group given by the SCF data.

The total number of social assistance cases is to be distinguished from the number of beneficiaries. We use data on the former, since the latter includes children.

The number of cases under the general assistance component of the Canada Assistance Program, by province on a fiscal year basis from 1981/82 to 1997/98, was supplied by Anne Tweddle of HRDC. Fiscal year data on social assistance beneficiaries by province prior to 1980/81 are from *Social Security Statistics, Canada and Provinces, 1963–64 to 1987–88*, Supply and Services Canada 1989, table 361. The number of cases prior to 1981/82 is constructed by adjusting, for each province, the number of beneficiaries for fiscal 1967/68 to 1979/80 to a case basis using the province-specific average ratio of cases to all beneficiaries for fiscal years 1980/81 and 1981/82. The fiscal year data are then converted to a calendar year basis assuming a uniform distribution over the quarters.

The data on social assistance recipients by age and sex from the Survey of Consumer Finances (SCF) record the number of individuals receiving social assistance in each group. These data are used to reduce total cases to number of cases in each province in the 20–64 age category and then to distribute the resulting figures across our six age-sex groups. We utilize all computerized surveys, for years 1973 to 1975, 1981, 1983, and 1984 to 1996. Data based on these surveys were complied for us by Brian Murphy and Shawna Brown of Statistics Canada.

To compute the age-sex distribution of social assistance recipients for the missing years 1968 to 1972, an average of SCF data for 1973–75 was used. For years 1976–80, an average of SCF data for 1975 and 1981 was used. Age-sex data for 1982 were based on an average of SCF data for 1981 and 1983.

Since the SCF sample sizes varied considerably from year to year, some figures for the percentage of cases in the 20–64 age group (used to reduce data on all cases to that for ages 20–64) appear to be erroneous for some provinces in certain years, probably owing to the smallness of the samples taken in those years. We have made the following adjustments: the proportion of cases in the 20–64 age group in Nova Scotia for 1989 and 1990 was set to the average of the 1988 and 1991 Nova Scotia figures; figures for Ontario for 1986–89 are replaced with an average of the 1985 and 1991 Ontario figures; and the 1989 figure on the proportion of cases in the 20–64 age group for Saskatchewan in 1988 was set to its 1987 value.

THE AGGREGATE PROBABILITIES, 1966–96

Table D3 lists the aggregate probabilities of the four states from 1966 to 1996. The probabilities for the six age-sex groups are available from the authors upon request.

Table D3
Listing of Aggregate Probabilities of the Four States of the World, 1966–96

					Aggregate Probability of State 1					
Year	NFLD	PEI	NS	NB	QUE	ONT	MAN	SASK	ALTA	BC
1966	0.7131	0.8238	0.8878	0.8420	0.8376	0.9379	0.9324	0.9207	0.9520	0.9134
1967	0.7046	0.8146	0.8830	0.8398	0.8382	0.9335	0.9329	0.9217	0.9517	0.9107
1968	0.7093	0.8045	0.8842	0.8398	0.8321	0.9306	0.9265	0.9183	0.9496	0.9062
1969	0.7122	0.8301	0.8819	0.8354	0.8522	0.9280	0.9251	0.9144	0.9500	0.9160
1970	0.7074	0.8312	0.8804	0.8192	0.8443	0.9161	0.8992	0.8954	0.9358	0.8902
1971	0.7249	0.7972	0.8683	0.8112	0.8440	0.9180	0.8889	0.8923	0.9329	0.8950
1972	0.7262	0.8351	0.8622	0.8077	0.8434	0.9206	0.9054	0.9088	0.9410	0.8947
1973	0.7305	0.8257	0.8521	0.7977	0.8479	0.9128	0.8965	0.9022	0.9319	0.8759
1974	0.7292	0.8582	0.8746	0.8061	0.8537	0.9284	0.9462	0.9336	0.9642	0.9029
1975	0.7218	0.8347	0.8634	0.8066	0.8328	0.9178	0.9330	0.9464	0.9652	0.8835
1976	0.7215	0.7948	0.8617	0.7771	0.8310	0.9298	0.9357	0.9472	0.9691	0.8938
1977	0.7185	0.7957	0.8505	0.7652	0.8245	0.9300	0.9283	0.9418	0.9670	0.8989
1978	0.7273	0.7958	0.8523	0.7698	0.8214	0.9293	0.9247	0.9391	0.9680	0.8985
1979	0.7455	0.8067	0.8649	0.7838	0.8318	0.9384	0.9368	0.9476	0.9750	0.9155
1980	0.7546	0.8123	0.8688	0.7906	0.8350	0.9358	0.9381	0.9474	0.9759	0.9285
1981	0.7466	0.7940	0.8678	0.7792	0.8302	0.9405	0.9382	0.9444	0.9761	0.9270
1982	0.7161	0.7651	0.8399	0.7403	0.7782	0.9061	0.9028	0.9182	0.9386	0.8593
1983	0.7025	0.7687	0.8465	0.7337	0.7762	0.8972	0.8885	0.9071	0.9045	0.8435
1984	0.6934	0.7632	0.8482	0.7271	0.7801	0.9159	0.8955	0.9079	0.9060	0.8358
1985	0.6893	0.7516	0.8492	0.7362	0.7927	0.9216	0.8991	0.9197	0.9174	0.8432
1986	0.6864	0.7562	0.8503	0.7486	0.8039	0.9261	0.9021	0.9241	0.9077	0.8535
1987	0.6921	0.7666	0.8597	0.7514	0.8214	0.9337	0.9055	0.9268	0.9126	0.8608
1988	0.7018	0.7740	0.8485	0.7795	0.8407	0.9374	0.9138	0.9271	0.9178	0.8761
1989	0.6887	0.7664	0.8291	0.7632	0.8302	0.9351	0.8968	0.9271	0.9247	0.8807
1990	0.6891	0.7594	0.8214	0.7634	0.8163	0.9035	0.8892	0.9315	0.9277	0.8819
1991	0.6741	0.7342	0.7868	0.7387	0.7944	0.8691	0.8763	0.9242	0.9142	0.8596
1992	0.6471	0.7269	0.7844	0.7416	0.7852	0.8546	0.8719	0.9170	0.9098	0.8557

Table D3 (continued)

| | | Aggregate Probability of State 1 | | | | | | | | |
Year	NFLD	PEI	NS	NB	QUE	ONT	MAN	SASK	ALTA	BC
1993	0.6952	0.7307	0.7851	0.7598	0.7916	0.8578	0.9051	0.9185	0.9202	0.8523
1994	0.7153	0.7460	0.7841	0.7703	0.8030	0.8810	0.8872	0.9280	0.9389	0.8533
1995	0.7729	0.7795	0.8064	0.7935	0.8127	0.8800	0.8983	0.9106	0.9471	0.8693
1996	0.7708	0.7947	0.8160	0.7976	0.8152	0.8908	0.9103	0.9147	0.9558	0.8795

| | | Aggregate Probability of State 2 | | | | | | | | |
Year	NFLD	PEI	NS	NB	QUE	ONT	MAN	SASK	ALTA	BC
1966	0.0576	0.0393	0.0431	0.0500	0.0293	0.0215	0.0213	0.0181	0.0156	0.0319
1967	0.0717	0.0494	0.0495	0.0554	0.0335	0.0272	0.0218	0.0187	0.0170	0.0372
1968	0.0716	0.0546	0.0499	0.0575	0.0404	0.0305	0.0292	0.0226	0.0200	0.0425
1969	0.0724	0.0505	0.0481	0.0552	0.0376	0.0281	0.0262	0.0262	0.0190	0.0366
1970	0.0693	0.0473	0.0495	0.0553	0.0428	0.0360	0.0334	0.0311	0.0284	0.0512
1971	0.0621	0.0420	0.0490	0.0506	0.0378	0.0309	0.0318	0.0239	0.0252	0.0397
1972	0.0728	0.0451	0.0513	0.0572	0.0460	0.0321	0.0230	0.0187	0.0209	0.0474
1973	0.0797	0.0525	0.0519	0.0631	0.0449	0.0302	0.0208	0.0194	0.0192	0.0448
1974	0.0834	0.0506	0.0519	0.0620	0.0476	0.0294	0.0164	0.0168	0.0129	0.0435
1975	0.0905	0.0598	0.0585	0.0706	0.0574	0.0392	0.0169	0.0151	0.0136	0.0529
1976	0.0996	0.0780	0.0651	0.0783	0.0593	0.0336	0.0210	0.0184	0.0122	0.0458
1977	0.0980	0.0745	0.0715	0.0810	0.0639	0.0340	0.0280	0.0235	0.0148	0.0452
1978	0.0998	0.0797	0.0717	0.0808	0.0679	0.0358	0.0354	0.0273	0.0164	0.0489
1979	0.0998	0.0815	0.0714	0.0831	0.0641	0.0326	0.0297	0.0224	0.0123	0.0446
1980	0.0998	0.0886	0.0743	0.0880	0.0668	0.0377	0.0313	0.0233	0.0129	0.0404
1981	0.1053	0.0933	0.0787	0.0915	0.0698	0.0349	0.0348	0.0256	0.0135	0.0398
1982	0.1228	0.0974	0.1031	0.1084	0.0988	0.0620	0.0606	0.0440	0.0444	0.0873
1983	0.1211	0.0949	0.0981	0.1020	0.0886	0.0644	0.0659	0.0496	0.0723	0.0878
1984	0.1150	0.1034	0.0917	0.1008	0.0831	0.0537	0.0589	0.0521	0.0675	0.0847
1985	0.1031	0.0917	0.0895	0.0913	0.0789	0.0492	0.0573	0.0518	0.0582	0.0755
1986	0.1132	0.0932	0.0886	0.0926	0.0754	0.0436	0.0537	0.0527	0.0573	0.0738

Table D3 (continued)

Aggregate Probability of State 2

Year	NFLD	PEI	NS	NB	QUE	ONT	MAN	SASK	ALTA	BC
1987	0.1127	0.0908	0.0852	0.0892	0.0711	0.0370	0.0520	0.0523	0.0608	0.0715
1988	0.1137	0.0893	0.0797	0.0917	0.0735	0.0329	0.0543	0.0527	0.0521	0.0691
1989	0.1101	0.0952	0.0819	0.0924	0.0755	0.0314	0.0541	0.0530	0.0506	0.0634
1990	0.1118	0.0920	0.0870	0.0980	0.0824	0.0413	0.0525	0.0499	0.0483	0.0634
1991	0.1078	0.0947	0.0874	0.0979	0.0867	0.0571	0.0580	0.0537	0.0560	0.0699
1992	0.1099	0.0964	0.0881	0.0970	0.0848	0.0556	0.0539	0.0532	0.0571	0.0632
1993	0.1073	0.0908	0.0828	0.0935	0.0786	0.0493	0.0505	0.0488	0.0528	0.0568
1994	0.0966	0.0815	0.0750	0.0875	0.0678	0.0390	0.0407	0.0395	0.0445	0.0459
1995	0.0887	0.0740	0.0625	0.0776	0.0591	0.0310	0.0345	0.0316	0.0367	0.0391
1996	0.0921	0.0727	0.0610	0.0763	0.0576	0.0308	0.0315	0.0297	0.0315	0.0377

Aggregate Probability of State 3

Year	NFLD	PEI	NS	NB	QUE	ONT	MAN	SASK	ALTA	BC
1966	0.0311	0.0266	0.0131	0.0174	0.0043	0.0026	0.0042	0.0039	0.0023	0.0048
1967	0.0279	0.0258	0.0134	0.0168	0.0036	0.0027	0.0032	0.0030	0.0018	0.0052
1968	0.0265	0.0297	0.0125	0.0162	0.0045	0.0033	0.0037	0.0036	0.0020	0.0058
1969	0.0270	0.0284	0.0124	0.0166	0.0050	0.0032	0.0040	0.0037	0.0022	0.0057
1970	0.0255	0.0274	0.0129	0.0157	0.0055	0.0037	0.0045	0.0054	0.0025	0.0057
1971	0.0359	0.0304	0.0215	0.0283	0.0150	0.0098	0.0112	0.0091	0.0091	0.0156
1972	0.0457	0.0343	0.0237	0.0344	0.0190	0.0105	0.0085	0.0072	0.0076	0.0192
1973	0.0539	0.0380	0.0251	0.0406	0.0188	0.0101	0.0079	0.0072	0.0064	0.0195
1974	0.0659	0.0333	0.0254	0.0434	0.0207	0.0095	0.0058	0.0059	0.0038	0.0186
1975	0.0774	0.0472	0.0286	0.0527	0.0256	0.0133	0.0051	0.0048	0.0040	0.0231
1976	0.0859	0.0682	0.0324	0.0598	0.0277	0.0118	0.0067	0.0061	0.0035	0.0202
1977	0.0936	0.0751	0.0410	0.0693	0.0291	0.0114	0.0091	0.0072	0.0037	0.0206
1978	0.1026	0.0717	0.0411	0.0680	0.0281	0.0094	0.0091	0.0058	0.0027	0.0192
1979	0.0812	0.0553	0.0286	0.0508	0.0183	0.0051	0.0046	0.0030	0.0013	0.0110
1980	0.0688	0.0380	0.0174	0.0409	0.0109	0.0026	0.0019	0.0012	0.0005	0.0038

Table D3 (continued)

Aggregate Probability of State 3

Year	NFLD	PEI	NS	NB	QUE	ONT	MAN	SASK	ALTA	BC
1981	0.0659	0.0431	0.0183	0.0433	0.0108	0.0020	0.0018	0.0011	0.0004	0.0029
1982	0.0794	0.0613	0.0276	0.0544	0.0178	0.0042	0.0037	0.0022	0.0017	0.0089
1983	0.0989	0.0664	0.0328	0.0647	0.0217	0.0070	0.0060	0.0035	0.0059	0.0166
1984	0.1125	0.0765	0.0341	0.0718	0.0201	0.0058	0.0058	0.0041	0.0089	0.0200
1985	0.1318	0.0893	0.0372	0.0742	0.0186	0.0038	0.0048	0.0039	0.0066	0.0199
1986	0.1209	0.0874	0.0333	0.0652	0.0153	0.0028	0.0038	0.0039	0.0125	0.0157
1987	0.1210	0.0838	0.0318	0.0628	0.0127	0.0019	0.0034	0.0037	0.0053	0.0142
1988	0.1243	0.0839	0.0275	0.0617	0.0115	0.0012	0.0034	0.0036	0.0037	0.0119
1989	0.1280	0.0868	0.0241	0.0546	0.0110	0.0009	0.0032	0.0034	0.0031	0.0097
1990	0.1206	0.0796	0.0224	0.0466	0.0087	0.0009	0.0025	0.0025	0.0020	0.0060
1991	0.1393	0.0979	0.0312	0.0590	0.0152	0.0024	0.0041	0.0031	0.0026	0.0080
1992	0.1383	0.0988	0.0330	0.0569	0.0153	0.0034	0.0042	0.0037	0.0033	0.0077
1993	0.1264	0.1060	0.0359	0.0565	0.0164	0.0036	0.0045	0.0039	0.0034	0.0071
1994	0.1004	0.0917	0.0321	0.0513	0.0131	0.0025	0.0035	0.0028	0.0026	0.0055
1995	0.0724	0.0735	0.0230	0.0397	0.0092	0.0014	0.0021	0.0018	0.0017	0.0040
1996	0.0659	0.0620	0.0195	0.0337	0.0084	0.0012	0.0016	0.0014	0.0013	0.0033

Aggregate Probability of State 4

Year	NFLD	PEI	NS	NB	QUE	ONT	MAN	SASK	ALTA	BC
1966	0.1981	0.1103	0.0560	0.0906	0.1288	0.0380	0.0421	0.0574	0.0302	0.0498
1967	0.1957	0.1102	0.0541	0.0881	0.1247	0.0366	0.0421	0.0566	0.0295	0.0469
1968	0.1926	0.1112	0.0534	0.0865	0.1230	0.0355	0.0406	0.0554	0.0283	0.0455
1969	0.1885	0.0910	0.0576	0.0928	0.1052	0.0406	0.0448	0.0556	0.0288	0.0417
1970	0.1978	0.0941	0.0572	0.1098	0.1074	0.0442	0.0629	0.0681	0.0332	0.0529
1971	0.1771	0.1304	0.0612	0.1100	0.1033	0.0413	0.0680	0.0747	0.0328	0.0497
1972	0.1553	0.0855	0.0628	0.1007	0.0916	0.0368	0.0631	0.0653	0.0305	0.0387
1973	0.1359	0.0839	0.0709	0.0986	0.0883	0.0469	0.0749	0.0712	0.0425	0.0597
1974	0.1216	0.0578	0.0482	0.0885	0.0779	0.0327	0.0317	0.0437	0.0191	0.0350

Table D3 (continued)

| | Aggregate Probability of State 2 | | | | | | | | | |
Year	NFLD	PEI	NS	NB	QUE	ONT	MAN	SASK	ALTA	BC
1975	0.1103	0.0583	0.0494	0.0700	0.0841	0.0297	0.0450	0.0337	0.0172	0.0405
1976	0.0930	0.0589	0.0408	0.0848	0.0819	0.0248	0.0366	0.0283	0.0152	0.0401
1977	0.0899	0.0547	0.0369	0.0845	0.0825	0.0247	0.0346	0.0276	0.0144	0.0353
1978	0.0703	0.0528	0.0349	0.0814	0.0826	0.0255	0.0308	0.0278	0.0129	0.0334
1979	0.0736	0.0564	0.0351	0.0823	0.0858	0.0239	0.0289	0.0270	0.0114	0.0290
1980	0.0768	0.0612	0.0396	0.0805	0.0873	0.0239	0.0287	0.0281	0.0107	0.0273
1981	0.0822	0.0696	0.0352	0.0859	0.0893	0.0226	0.0252	0.0289	0.0100	0.0304
1982	0.0817	0.0762	0.0295	0.0968	0.1052	0.0277	0.0329	0.0356	0.0153	0.0445
1983	0.0776	0.0701	0.0226	0.0996	0.1135	0.0314	0.0396	0.0398	0.0172	0.0521
1984	0.0791	0.0568	0.0261	0.1002	0.1167	0.0246	0.0398	0.0358	0.0177	0.0596
1985	0.0757	0.0673	0.0242	0.0983	0.1099	0.0254	0.0388	0.0247	0.0178	0.0614
1986	0.0795	0.0632	0.0278	0.0936	0.1054	0.0275	0.0404	0.0193	0.0226	0.0570
1987	0.0742	0.0588	0.0233	0.0966	0.0949	0.0275	0.0391	0.0172	0.0213	0.0536
1988	0.0603	0.0528	0.0443	0.0671	0.0742	0.0285	0.0284	0.0166	0.0264	0.0430
1989	0.0732	0.0516	0.0649	0.0898	0.0833	0.0326	0.0459	0.0166	0.0216	0.0462
1990	0.0786	0.0690	0.0692	0.0920	0.0926	0.0543	0.0558	0.0161	0.0220	0.0487
1991	0.0789	0.0732	0.0946	0.1044	0.1037	0.0713	0.0616	0.0189	0.0272	0.0626
1992	0.1046	0.0778	0.0945	0.1045	0.1148	0.0864	0.0700	0.0261	0.0297	0.0734
1993	0.0711	0.0724	0.0961	0.0903	0.1134	0.0893	0.0399	0.0287	0.0235	0.0839
1994	0.0877	0.0809	0.1088	0.0910	0.1160	0.0775	0.0686	0.0296	0.0140	0.0954
1995	0.0661	0.0729	0.1080	0.0893	0.1189	0.0876	0.0651	0.0560	0.0145	0.0876
1996	0.0713	0.0706	0.1035	0.0924	0.1188	0.0772	0.0566	0.0541	0.0114	0.0795

Correlation Coefficients, and Additional Estimates by Age, Sex, and Income Class

This appendix contains additional estimation results that were referred to but not included in chapter 6. These include coefficients of correlation between the explanatory variables of the model, correlations between actual and fitted values, and parameter estimates by age, sex, and income class for Models 1 and 2.

Table E1
Correlation Matrix of Explanatory Variables, Three Income Classes, 1974–96

	INCOME	LEISURE	EDUCA-TION	HEALTH	OTHER SPENDING	FEDERAL SPENDING	DISTANCE	QUEBEC	PQ	DSTAY	P2
INCOME	1.0000	-0.6043	0.3550	0.5448	0.3669	-0.4365	-0.1267	-0.1186	0.0158	0.1473	-0.4910
LEISURE	-0.6043	1.0000	-0.0400	-0.2102	-0.3032	0.3346	-0.0257	0.1442	-0.0422	-0.0000	0.9088
EDUCATION	0.3550	-0.0400	1.0000	0.4743	0.5397	-0.2669	0.0062	0.3492	-0.0471	0.0000	-0.0032
HEALTH	0.5448	-0.2102	0.4743	1.0000	0.3916	-0.1191	0.0266	0.0107	-0.1141	0.0000	-0.0829
OTHER SPENDING	0.3669	-0.3032	0.5397	0.3916	1.0000	-0.4683	0.0336	0.0677	-0.0050	-0.0000	-0.2157
FEDERAL SPENDING	-0.4365	0.3346	-0.2669	-0.1191	-0.4683	1.0000	-0.0583	-0.2995	0.0080	-0.0000	0.4168
DISTANCE	-0.1267	-0.0257	0.0062	0.0266	0.0336	-0.0583	1.0000	0.0703	0.0282	-0.9448	-0.0228
QUEBEC	-0.1186	0.1442	0.3492	0.0107	0.0677	-0.2995	0.0703	1.0000	-0.0397	-0.1048	0.0845
PQ	0.0158	-0.0422	-0.0471	-0.1141	-0.0050	0.0080	0.0282	-0.0397	1.0000	-0.0420	-0.0526
DSTAY	0.1473	-0.0000	0.0000	0.0000	-0.0000	-0.0000	-0.9448	-0.1048	-0.0420	1.0000	0.0000
P2	-0.4910	0.9088	-0.0032	-0.0829	-0.2157	0.4168	-0.0228	0.0845	-0.0526	0.0000	1.0000
P3	-0.5610	0.8818	-0.0706	-0.3416	-0.2282	0.3741	-0.0127	-0.1239	-0.0019	-0.0000	0.7810
P4	-0.4908	0.7869	-0.0134	-0.0510	-0.3285	0.0832	-0.0318	0.4277	-0.0647	0.0000	0.5869
P23	-0.5617	0.9459	-0.0437	-0.2427	-0.2358	0.4157	-0.0181	-0.0353	-0.0253	-0.0000	0.9274
FISH	-0.0332	-0.0074	0.0056	0.0915	-0.0067	-0.0007	0.0558	0.0093	-0.0159	-0.0420	-0.0447
FISH2	-0.0226	0.1694	0.0205	0.0897	-0.0343	0.0053	0.0558	-0.0397	-0.0159	-0.0420	0.1481
PQ2	-0.0008	0.0352	0.2538	-0.0593	0.0167	-0.1313	0.0282	0.4010	-0.0159	-0.0420	0.0033
P234	-0.6026	0.9996	-0.0375	-0.1989	-0.2996	0.3391	-0.0255	0.1369	-0.0434	0.0000	0.9097
LP234	-0.5966	0.9575	-0.0782	-0.1478	-0.3660	0.3826	-0.0311	0.1865	-0.0578	0.0000	0.9119
LP2	-0.4300	0.8331	-0.0045	0.0018	-0.2182	0.4058	-0.0251	0.1226	-0.0620	-0.0000	0.9572
LP3	-0.6509	0.8879	-0.2125	-0.4280	-0.3620	0.4787	-0.0289	0.0329	0.0011	-0.0000	0.8419
LP4	-0.5343	0.7977	-0.1047	-0.1010	-0.4381	0.1634	-0.0310	0.3542	-0.0623	-0.0000	0.6131

Table E1 (continued)

	P3	P4	P23	FISH	FISH2	PQ2	P234	LP234	LP2	LP3	LP4
INCOME	-0.5610	-0.4908	-0.5617	-0.0332	-0.0226	-0.0008	-0.6026	-0.5966	-0.4300	-0.6509	-0.5343
LEISURE	0.8818	0.7869	0.9459	-0.0074	0.1694	0.0352	0.9996	0.9575	0.8331	0.8879	0.7977
EDUCATION	-0.0706	-0.0134	-0.0437	0.0056	0.0205	0.2538	-0.0375	-0.0782	-0.0045	-0.2125	-0.1047
HEALTH	-0.3416	-0.0510	-0.2427	0.0915	0.0897	-0.0593	-0.1989	-0.1478	0.0018	-0.4280	-0.1010
OTHER	-0.2282	-0.3285	-0.2358	-0.0067	-0.0343	0.0167	-0.2996	-0.3660	-0.2182	-0.3620	-0.4381
SPENDING											
FEDERAL	0.3741	0.0832	0.4157	-0.0007	0.0053	-0.1313	0.3391	0.3826	0.4058	0.4787	0.1634
SPENDING											
DISTANCE	-0.0127	-0.0318	-0.0181	0.0558	0.0558	0.0282	-0.0255	-0.0311	-0.0251	-0.0289	-0.0310
QUEBEC	-0.1239	0.4277	-0.0353	0.0093	-0.0397	0.4010	0.1369	0.1865	0.1226	0.0329	0.3542
PQ	-0.0019	-0.0647	-0.0253	-0.0159	-0.0159	-0.0159	-0.0434	-0.0578	-0.0620	0.0011	-0.0623
DSTAY	-0.0000	0.0000	-0.0000	-0.0420	-0.0420	-0.0420	0.0000	0.0000	-0.0000	-0.0000	-0.0000
P2	0.7810	0.5869	0.9274	-0.0447	0.1481	0.0033	0.9097	0.9119	0.9572	0.8419	0.6131
P3	1.0000	0.4604	0.9579	-0.0369	0.2217	-0.0322	0.8840	0.7704	0.6586	0.8717	0.4962
P4	0.4604	1.0000	0.5455	0.0724	0.0704	0.1148	0.7847	0.8053	0.5733	0.5620	0.9649
P23	0.9579	0.5455	1.0000	-0.0426	0.2009	-0.0177	0.9476	0.8806	0.8345	0.9091	0.5790
FISH	-0.0369	0.0724	-0.0426	1.0000	-0.0159	-0.0159	-0.0039	0.0077	-0.0271	-0.0472	0.0589
FISH2	0.2217	0.0704	0.2009	-0.0159	1.0000	-0.0159	0.1754	0.1468	0.1225	0.1683	0.0854
PQ2	-0.0322	0.1148	-0.0177	-0.0159	-0.0159	1.0000	0.0307	0.0581	0.0296	0.0355	0.1140
P234	0.8840	0.7847	0.9476	-0.0039	0.1754	0.0307	1.0000	0.9583	0.8357	0.8866	0.7961
LP234	0.7704	0.8053	0.8806	0.0077	0.1468	0.0581	0.9583	1.0000	0.9070	0.8641	0.8527
LP2	0.6586	0.5733	0.8345	-0.0271	0.1225	0.0296	0.8357	0.9070	1.0000	0.7703	0.6173
LP3	0.8717	0.5620	0.9091	-0.0472	0.1683	0.0355	0.8866	0.8641	0.7703	1.0000	0.6098
LP4	0.4962	0.9649	0.5790	0.0589	0.0854	0.1140	0.7961	0.8527	0.6173	0.6098	1.0000

Table E2
Correlations between Actual and Fitted Migration Rates, 1974–96, Model 1

					Destination					
Origin	NFLD	PEI	NS	NB	QUE	ONT	MAN	SASK	ALTA	BC
Low income										
NFLD	0.0003	−0.0011	−0.0290	−0.1929	−0.1336	0.5914	0.5314	0.2703	0.3445	0.2521
PEI	0.1970	0.6000	0.6113	0.2515	0.2912	0.3360	0.4704	0.5408	0.8535	0.5349
NS	−0.0982	−0.1197	0.1011	−0.3124	−0.1912	0.2408	0.4954	0.4283	0.8492	0.6063
NB	0.7746	−0.3576	0.4747	0.6584	0.1652	0.5200	0.6699	0.5857	0.8228	0.5853
QUE	0.4967	0.3377	0.5075	0.1530	0.5197	0.2033	0.6704	0.6425	0.8587	0.4813
ONT	0.3913	0.3681	0.3089	0.2137	0.5226	0.6952	0.6665	0.6392	0.7661	0.7999
MAN	0.1381	−0.3273	−0.5134	−0.3743	−0.1738	0.2492	−0.0440	0.1567	0.8146	0.4633
SASK	0.2521	−0.0274	−0.0999	−0.1367	0.4110	0.6859	0.2999	0.7899	0.5867	0.6007
ALTA	0.3386	−0.1074	−0.0996	−0.1104	0.1732	0.4357	−0.0934	−0.0639	−0.0568	−0.1934
BC	−0.0365	0.0530	0.2875	0.3394	0.4484	0.4669	0.6142	0.5209	0.6199	0.5749
Middle Income										
NFLD	0.2869	−0.1116	0.3750	0.1148	0.1216	0.7303	0.5715	0.2125	0.7051	−0.0409
PEI	0.6326	0.4204	0.3487	−0.3281	0.2135	0.0286	0.3814	0.2752	0.6521	0.6362
NS	0.5952	−0.0942	0.2444	−0.4230	0.0587	−0.0913	0.4825	0.5858	0.7200	0.3883
NB	0.5205	0.2298	0.4834	0.6064	0.2971	0.3230	0.2823	0.5797	0.8070	0.5016
QUE	0.2476	0.4742	0.2988	0.1787	0.6635	0.5239	0.5507	0.7110	0.9002	0.5969
ONT	0.5943	0.1256	0.3066	0.1667	0.3363	0.5657	0.6470	0.6361	0.7223	0.6366
MAN	0.2487	−0.4372	0.1841	−0.2593	−0.1536	0.2107	−0.0185	0.2619	0.7232	0.3033
SASK	0.2859	0.2277	0.3511	0.1973	0.5415	0.6971	0.2667	0.7089	0.8261	0.6262
ALTA	0.5327	0.2896	0.5259	0.3238	0.5902	0.7274	0.0559	0.0179	0.2923	−0.1643
BC	0.1635	−0.1682	0.3249	0.2770	0.5053	0.5305	0.5294	0.5920	0.7450	0.4591

Table E2 (continued)

Origin	Destination									
	NFLD	PEI	NS	NB	QUE	ONT	MAN	SASK	ALTA	BC
High Income										
NFLD	0.2582	-0.0555	0.3745	0.1975	0.1072	0.7161	0.4522	0.0943	0.4962	-0.2443
PEI	0.6574	0.3292	0.2818	-0.4582	0.1457	0.0688	0.2562	0.1828	0.4991	0.5890
NS	0.6018	0.0143	0.1593	-0.4127	-0.0099	-0.0658	0.3759	0.5598	0.5725	0.3908
NB	0.5236	0.3482	0.4897	0.6781	0.5924	0.4823	0.3204	0.5680	0.6777	0.5296
QUE	0.2733	0.5966	0.3571	0.2620	0.7129	0.6829	0.4953	0.7073	0.8641	0.6205
ONT	0.5643	0.1117	0.2521	-0.0020	0.2762	0.4617	0.5038	0.5645	0.5581	0.6631
MAN	0.3381	-0.3148	0.1576	-0.2536	-0.0964	0.3050	-0.0108	0.3238	0.6552	0.3008
SASK	0.2854	0.3148	0.3379	0.2249	0.5273	0.7667	0.2195	0.7245	0.8096	0.6459
ALTA	0.6772	0.4447	0.6305	0.4250	0.6061	0.8284	0.1813	0.0632	0.4267	-0.0543
BC	0.1575	-0.1291	0.3032	0.2020	0.4750	0.5352	0.4934	0.6236	0.6622	0.4245

Note: Values in table are coefficients of correlation between the actual and predicted migration rates for a particular origin-destination pair.

Table E3
Correlations between Actual and Fitted Migration Rates, 1974–96, Model 2

Origin					Destination					
	NFLD	PEI	NS	NB	QUE	ONT	MAN	SASK	ALTA	BC
Low income										
NFLD	-0.1674	0.4774	-0.5209	-0.1686	-0.1228	0.2953	0.7058	0.0373	0.5413	0.2925
PEI	-0.2341	0.2789	0.0647	0.0720	0.1795	0.5304	0.8218	0.3721	0.9163	0.5439
NS	0.1010	0.3055	0.3780	-0.0402	0.3094	0.3897	0.6367	0.4039	0.8617	0.6376
NB	0.6081	-0.0819	0.2716	0.8127	0.3831	0.7154	0.8253	0.7755	0.8945	0.5343
QUE	0.4236	0.4075	0.1359	-0.1933	0.2733	0.1141	0.6810	0.2806	0.7986	0.2982
ONT	0.5189	0.2357	-0.0426	-0.0475	0.4624	0.5686	0.6882	0.4156	0.7464	0.7162
MAN	-0.0395	-0.6269	-0.7648	-0.5328	-0.5169	0.2073	-0.3757	-0.6212	0.7979	0.2761
SASK	0.3110	-0.3608	0.2794	-0.3785	0.0429	0.7994	0.6136	0.4160	0.1514	0.4129
ALTA	0.2488	-0.1523	-0.0897	-0.0941	0.1300	0.4474	-0.0962	-0.5328	-0.1298	-0.3372
BC	-0.0733	0.0949	0.3724	0.3249	0.4531	0.5637	0.6557	0.3788	0.6142	0.7127
Middle Income										
NFLD	0.4930	0.3631	0.3162	0.2905	0.3468	0.5371	0.7329	0.3366	0.7839	0.1954
PEI	0.3923	0.5197	-0.1478	-0.5957	0.4009	0.3200	0.7434	0.3834	0.6636	0.5597
NS	0.5445	0.1772	0.4960	-0.2323	0.4356	0.2261	0.6568	0.5749	0.7624	0.3778
NB	0.3648	0.3946	0.3045	0.8312	0.4966	0.6613	0.5677	0.6617	0.8862	0.5756
QUE	0.0830	0.3995	0.0675	0.0026	0.5708	0.4922	0.5282	0.4905	0.8435	0.4974
ONT	0.4930	-0.1863	-0.1255	-0.1769	0.1110	0.3138	0.6431	0.3538	0.6925	0.4547
MAN	0.1417	-0.7749	-0.1943	-0.5044	-0.5312	0.1924	-0.4822	-0.5709	0.6802	-0.1024
SASK	0.3694	-0.0077	0.3189	-0.2072	0.2944	0.8220	0.6507	0.6620	0.5873	0.5453
ALTA	0.4274	0.1877	0.4886	0.3395	0.5169	0.7483	0.0468	-0.3522	0.2037	-0.3658
BC	0.2436	-0.2500	0.4091	0.1813	0.4372	0.6389	0.6764	0.4913	0.7552	0.6549

Table E3 (continued)

Origin						Destination					
	NFLD	PEI	NS	NB	QUE	ONT	MAN	SASK	ALTA	BC
High Income										
NFLD	0.5165	0.2578	0.3990	0.4530	0.4337	0.5783	0.6651	0.2233	0.6270	-0.0361
PEI	0.4449	0.4747	-0.0810	-0.6113	0.3836	0.3750	0.6159	0.1946	0.4911	0.5196
NS	0.5057	0.1639	0.3075	-0.2715	0.4183	0.1703	0.4940	0.4232	0.5615	0.3682
NB	0.3347	0.4014	0.3557	0.8133	0.7934	0.7112	0.5499	0.6146	0.7378	0.5987
QUE	0.1106	0.5004	0.2282	0.1624	0.6462	0.6444	0.4403	0.5383	0.8189	0.5453
ONT	0.4572	-0.1985	-0.1001	-0.2313	0.1771	0.2098	0.4305	0.1894	0.4400	0.5161
MAN	0.2033	-0.6287	-0.1412	-0.4271	-0.1491	0.3236	-0.4855	-0.5256	0.5482	-0.0341
SASK	0.3753	0.1955	0.2970	-0.0495	0.4498	0.8595	0.6106	0.7683	0.6432	0.6805
ALTA	0.5890	0.4222	0.6353	0.4734	0.5494	0.8603	0.2435	-0.2072	0.3881	-0.1933
BC	0.2368	-0.1468	0.3904	0.1067	0.5536	0.6318	0.6243	0.5549	0.6537	0.5824

Note: Values in table are coefficients of correlation between the actual and predicted migration rates for a particular origin-destination pair.

Table E4
Parameter Estimates for Model 1, by Income Class, Age, and Sex, 1974–96

	Low Income					
Variable	Males 20–24	Females 20–24	Males 25–44	Females 25–44	Males 45–64	Females 45–64
INCOME	2.631	1.721	1.542	1.858	1.893	1.765
LEISURE	1.696	-1.598	1.900	-3.383	1.179	-9.101
HEALTH	-0.335	-0.239	-0.122	-0.561	-0.456	-0.655
EDUCATION	0.595	0.307	0.256	0.402	0.274	-0.031
OTHER SPENDING	-0.125	-0.297	-0.097	-0.471	-0.272	-0.192
FEDERAL SPENDING	0.091	0.101	0.146	0.111	0.027	0.207
DSTAY	1.519	0.985	1.644	1.614	1.868	1.736
DISTANCE	-0.429	-0.517	-0.472	-0.529	-0.602	-0.634
P2	-15.457	-5.906	-30.551	-4.164	-23.691	21.463
P3	-8.145	5.718	-12.569	9.262	-12.207	28.396
P4	-6.263	5.261	-6.250	10.310	4.117	29.364
QUEBEC	-2.359	-2.306	-2.095	-2.290	-2.126	-2.381
PQ	0.389	0.182	0.422	0.253	0.434	0.313
PQ2	0.311	0.137	0.141	0.087	0.017	0.291
FISH	0.103	-0.039	0.015	-0.472	-0.093	-0.148
FISH2	-0.824	-0.743	-0.944	-0.839	-0.724	-0.459
NFLD	0.082	-0.238	0.520	-0.065	0.596	-0.856
PEI	-0.900	-1.188	-0.667	-1.075	-0.463	-1.620
NS	-0.418	-0.586	-0.364	-0.501	-0.220	-0.912
NB	-0.066	-0.414	0.098	-0.279	0.014	-0.821
QUE	1.554	1.486	1.491	1.600	1.589	1.384
ONT	-0.191	-0.160	-0.272	-0.119	-0.080	-0.044
MAN	-0.824	-1.053	-0.962	-0.995	-0.703	-0.925
SASK	-0.927	-1.044	-1.064	-1.038	-0.817	-0.985
ALTA	-0.391	-0.348	-0.616	-0.440	-0.495	-0.484
Log L	-1454088	-1763243	-1137999	-2143256	-194764.2	-366252.2
Log L$_0$	-11460350	-15385430	-12606320	-34263780	-5869767	-12349770
McFadden's R^2	0.9017	0.9100	0.9277	0.9502	0.9729	0.9768
No. of observations	2300	2300	2300	2300	2300	2300

Table E4 (continued)

	Middle Income					
Variable	Males 20–24	Females 20–24	Males 25–44	Females 25–44	Males 45–64	Females 45–64
INCOME	2.873	1.584	2.156	1.579	2.889	1.946
LEISURE	4.205	0.131	6.808	-2.622	5.839	-8.210
HEALTH	-0.409	-0.226	-0.305	-0.357	-0.550	-0.358
EDUCATION	0.295	0.081	0.045	-0.052	0.178	-0.447
OTHER SPENDING	-0.406	-0.477	-0.334	-0.478	-0.404	-0.223
FEDERAL SPENDING	0.304	0.383	0.545	0.404	0.262	0.358
DSTAY	1.627	0.654	2.040	1.721	2.295	1.864
DISTANCE	-0.428	-0.586	-0.473	-0.541	-0.588	-0.651
P2	-20.236	-10.572	-45.224	-8.179	-37.549	17.212
P3	-15.530	-0.640	-27.652	7.406	-25.282	24.941
P4	-13.979	-0.670	-22.306	7.371	-19.170	25.985
QUEBEC	-2.446	-2.271	-2.343	-2.257	-2.580	-2.453
PQ	0.279	0.145	0.391	0.525	0.501	0.671
PQ2	-0.018	0.049	0.031	0.158	-0.029	0.144
FISH	0.298	-0.121	-0.069	-0.395	0.109	-0.409
FISH2	-0.949	-0.912	-1.030	-1.119	-0.591	-0.764
NFLD	0.135	-0.438	0.625	-0.358	0.490	-1.156
PEI	-0.856	-1.601	-0.690	-1.421	-0.553	-1.888
NS	-0.521	-1.092	-0.559	-0.992	-0.321	-1.310
NB	-0.068	-0.747	0.181	-0.645	0.094	-1.134
QUE	1.970	1.531	1.947	1.585	1.937	1.186
ONT	-0.145	-0.274	-0.381	-0.238	-0.265	-0.345
MAN	-0.764	-1.247	-1.118	-1.308	-0.925	-1.320
SASK	-0.597	-1.017	-0.976	-1.247	-0.921	-1.314
ALTA	-0.145	-0.337	-0.505	-0.515	-0.621	-0.792
Log L	-1961228	-1386287	-2693417	-2561848	-467091.1	-504493.2
Log L_0	-17832210	-14641480	-43358290	-48516630	-19771740	-21058070
McFadden's R^2	0.9144	0.9293	0.9511	0.9605	0.9814	0.9822
No. of observations	2300	2300	2300	2300	2300	2300

Table E4 (continued)

| | High Income | | | | | |
Variable	Males 20-24	Females 20-24	Males 25-44	Females 25-44	Males 45-64	Females 45-64
INCOME	2.469	0.631	0.846	1.334	0.558	1.242
LEISURE	4.199	-0.019	3.490	-0.469	-1.929	-7.861
HEALTH	-0.441	-0.038	-0.228	0.002	-0.262	0.127
EDUCATION	0.133	0.066	-0.166	-0.193	-0.532	-0.748
OTHER SPENDING	-0.522	-0.379	-0.280	-0.613	-0.233	-0.372
FEDERAL SPENDING	0.415	0.419	0.589	0.231	0.633	0.337
DSTAY	0.460	0.267	1.197	1.593	1.228	1.290
DISTANCE	-0.607	-0.632	-0.592	-0.566	-0.726	-0.750
P2	-19.398	-10.550	-27.215	-12.659	-8.625	16.564
P3	-16.394	-1.337	-16.946	0.076	0.033	23.105
P4	-14.724	-0.997	-12.307	-0.411	4.844	24.704
QUEBEC	-2.184	-1.801	-2.114	-1.748	-2.109	-1.799
PQ	-0.035	0.095	0.478	0.498	0.615	0.731
PQ2	-0.264	-0.145	0.014	0.164	0.014	0.151
FISH	0.299	-0.198	-0.305	-0.456	-0.168	-0.310
FISH2	-0.701	-1.047	-0.912	-1.146	-0.728	-0.687
NFLD	-0.058	-0.455	-0.165	-0.642	-0.736	-1.721
PEI	-1.693	-2.147	-1.733	-1.585	-2.239	-2.334
NS	-0.971	-1.248	-1.118	-1.007	-1.598	-1.724
NB	-0.501	-0.958	-0.551	-0.820	-1.149	-1.630
QUE	1.686	1.246	1.528	1.310	0.971	0.514
ONT	-0.216	-0.231	-0.165	-0.141	-0.447	-0.523
MAN	-1.094	-1.438	-1.300	-1.384	-1.677	-1.757
SASK	-0.668	-1.139	-1.120	-1.332	-1.553	-1.631
ALTA	-0.197	-0.420	-0.395	-0.512	-0.806	-0.945

Table E4 (continued)

Variable	High Income					
	Males 20–24	Females 20–24	Males 25–44	Females 25–44	Males 45–64	Females 45–64
Log L	-492541.3	-134248.1	-4569235	-1223962	-1205597	-273285
Log L$_0$	-5235716	-1308921	-75612450	-23693470	-45002040	-12061650
McFadden's R²	0.9293	0.9241	0.9555	0.9636	0.9807	0.9842
No. of observations	2300	2300	2300	2300	2300	2300

Note: All coefficients are statistically significant at the 1% level of significance unless otherwise indicated. *Bold* type indicates significance at the 5% level, *bold italic* type indicates significance at the 10% level, and *shaded bold italic* type indicates that the coefficient is not statistically significant at a level of significance less than or equal to 10%. Log L is the value of the log of the likelihood function at the parameter estimates, while Log L$_0$ is the maximum value of the log of the likelihood function for a model with only alternative-specific constants. McFadden's (1974) R² is given by $1 - (Log\ L/Log\ L_0)$.

Table E5
Parameter Estimates for Model 2, by Income Class, Age, and Sex, 1974–96

Variable	Low Income					
	Males 20–24	Females 20–24	Males 25–44	Females 25–44	Males 45–64	Females 45–64
INCOME	1.882	0.429	0.590	0.828	0.703	1.567
LEISURE	0.769	0.798	0.469	0.703	0.384	0.159
HEALTH	-0.052	0.247	0.253	-0.058	0.052	-0.393
EDUCATION	0.670	0.558	0.653	0.714	0.526	0.114
OTHER SPENDING	-0.008	-0.202	-0.386	-0.609	-0.377	-0.266
FEDERAL SPENDING	-0.351	-0.282	-0.796	-0.237	-0.655	0.165
DSTAY	1.496	0.875	1.576	1.528	1.763	1.716
DISTANCE	-0.434	-0.537	-0.485	-0.546	-0.621	-0.638
LP234	-0.870	-0.691	-0.630	-0.575	-0.445	-0.187
QUEBEC	-2.358	-2.303	-2.093	-2.289	-2.127	-2.380
PQ	0.446	0.277	0.437	0.339	0.427	0.3630

Table E5 (continued)

Variable	Low Income					
	Males 20–24	Females 20–24	Males 25–44	Females 25–44	Males 45–64	Females 45–64
PQ2	0.254	0.036	0.123	-0.009	0.017	0.238
FISH	-0.100	-0.080	-0.017	-0.145	-0.172	-0.092
FISH2	-0.637	-0.691	-0.920	-0.742	-0.661	-0.514
NFLD	-0.771	-0.969	-0.456	-0.768	-0.542	-0.979
PEI	-1.105	-1.395	-0.716	1.274	-0.749	-1.616
NS	-0.211	-0.452	0.101	-0.464	0.005	-0.961
NB	-0.405	-0.656	-0.233	-0.540	-0.355	-0.861
QUE	1.327	1.190	1.185	1.322	1.262	1.324
ONT	0.133	0.193	0.178	.103	0.216	-0.007
MAN	-0.598	-0.828	-0.540	-0.758	-0.433	-0.854
SASK	-0.979	-0.951	-0.919	-0.843	-0.726	-0.903
ALTA	-0.533	-0.415	-0.586	-0.407	-0.517	-0.490
Log L	-1453857	-1763931	-1138810	-2143793	-194883.1	-366290.8
Log L_0	-11460350	-15385430	-12606320	-34263780	-5869767	-12349770
McFadden's R^2	0.9017	0.9100	0.9277	0.9502	0.9729	0.9768
No. of observations	2300	2300	2300	2300	2300	2300

Variable	Middle Income					
	Males 20–24	Females 20–24	Males 25–44	Females 25–44	Males 45–64	Females 45–64
INCOME	2.504	0.325	1.049	0.372	1.915	1.602
LEISURE	0.627	0.550	0.508	1.037	0.750	-0.063
HEALTH	-0.254	0.153	-0.041	0.122	-0.142	-0.086
EDUCATION	0.328	0.301	0.426	0.411	0.470	-0.268
OTHER SPENDING	-0.295	-0.412	-0.597	-0.651	-0.500	-0.307
FEDERAL SPENDING	-0.053	0.025	-0.415	0.052	-0.455	0.256

Table E5 (continued)

	Middle Income					
Variable	Males 20–24	Females 20–24	Males 25–44	Females 25–44	Males 45–64	Females 45–64
DSTAY	1.603	0.546	1.965	1.617	2.220	1.832
DISTANCE	-0.433	-0.607	-0.488	-0.561	-0.602	-0.657
LP234	-0.667	-0.588	-0.630	-0.744	-0.521	-0.163
QUEBEC	-2.447	-2.270	-2.343	-2.257	-2.578	-2.451
PQ	0.302	0.220	0.384	0.630	0.483	0.728
PQ2	-0.039	-0.030	0.425	0.048	-0.014	0.081
FISH	0.134	-0.125	-0.133	-0.532	-0.015	-0.348
FISH2	-0.795	-0.889	-0.981	-0.981	-0.484	-0.822
NFLD	-0.558	-1.139	-0.378	-1.181	-0.628	-1.317
PEI	-1.074	-1.860	-0.783	-1.712	-0.774	-1.889
NS	-0.363	-0.989	-0.092	-1.015	-0.031	-1.330
NB	-0.350	-1.020	-0.181	-0.992	-0.258	-1.181
QUE	1.781	1.238	1.598	1.222	1.582	1.099
ONT	0.091	0.047	0.059	-0.028	0.012	-0.279
MAN	-0.618	-1.049	-0.732	-1.076	-0.655	-1.222
SASK	-0.678	-0.931	-0.874	-1.067	-0.853	-1.214
ALTA	-0.275	-0.355	-0.484	-0.493	-0.673	-0.771
Log L	-1961202	-1386969	-2695285	-2562111	467276	-504558.9
Log L$_0$	-17832210	-1308921	-4338290	-48516630	-19771740	-21058070
McFadden's R²	0.9144	0.9293	0.9511	0.9605	0.9814	0.9822
No. of observations	2300	2300	2300	2300	2300	2300

Table E5 (continued)

Variable	High Income					
	Males 20–24	Females 20–24	Males 25–44	Females 25–44	Males 45–64	Females 45–64
INCOME	1.782	−0.752	**0.074**	**0.200**	***0.061***	0.806
LEISURE	−0.251	*0.019*	−0.227	0.506	0.170	−0.513
HEALTH	−0.274	0.413	*0.030*	0.420	0.067	0.369
EDUCATION	0.181	*0.193*	0.101	0.142	−0.274	−0.649
OTHER SPENDING	−0.454	−0.340	−0.472	−0.745	−0.302	−0.446
FEDERAL SPENDING	0.185	*0.037*	*−0.005*	−0.052	0.152	0.126
DSTAY	0.399	0.147	1.147	1.494	1.194	1.248
DISTANCE	−0.618	−0.655	−0.602	−0.585	−0.733	−0.758
LP234	−0.371	−0.451	−0.349	−0.561	−0.394	*−0.009*
QUEBEC	−2.187	−1.798	−2.116	−1.747	−2.109	−1.795
PQ	−0.013	0.173	0.491	0.575	0.613	0.768
PQ2	−0.288	−0.231	*0.005*	0.080	*0.235*	*0.106*
FISH	*0.174*	*−0.189*	−0.309	−0.579	−0.243	−0.222
FISH2	−0.603	−1.095	−0.921	−1.017	−0.662	−0.774
NFLD	***−0.543***	−2.369	−0.825	−1.329	−1.445	−1.778
PEI	−1.956	−1.115	−1.827	−1.849	−2.316	−2.238
NS	−0.967	−1.180	−0.861	−1.044	−1.371	−1.616
NB	−0.746	0.994	−0.794	−1.119	−1.334	−1.583
QUE	1.532	0.125	1.318	1.005	0.754	0.487
ONT	−0.083	−1.216	0.102	0.052	−0.267	−0.403
MAN	−1.070	−1.037	−1.068	−1.197	−1.472	−1.621
SASK	−0.788	−0.383	−1.042	−1.181	−1.489	−1.525
ALTA	−0.292		−0.376	−0.462	−0.879	−0.884
Log L	−492706.5	−134341.6	−4571296	−1224082	−1205742	−273319.5
Log L$_0$	−5235716	−1308921	−75612450	−23693470	−45002040	−12061650
McFadden's R^2	0.9293	0.9240	0.9554	0.9636	0.9807	0.9842
No. of observations	2300	2300	2300	2300	2300	2300

Note: All coefficients are statistically significant at the 1% level of significance unless otherwise indicated. **Bold** type indicates significance at the 5% level, ***bold italic*** type indicates significance at the 10% level, and **shaded bold italic** type indicates that the coefficient is not statistically significant at a level of significance less than or equal to 10%. Log L is the value of the log of the likelihood function at the parameter estimates, while Log L$_0$ is the maximum value of the log of the likelihood function for a model with only alternative-specific constants. McFadden's (1974) R^2 is given by $1 - (\text{Log L}/\text{Log L}_0)$.

Marginal Effect Formulas

In this appendix we provide all of the formulas used for computing marginal effects. For completeness, this list includes those stated in chapter 7. Some of these calculations require a reformulation of after-tax incomes, which is presented at the appropriate point below.

The general formula for the marginal effect on the probability of migration from province i to another province j of a change in some explanatory variable x in province j is

$$\frac{\partial P_{ij}}{\partial X_j} = P_{ij}\left(1 - P_{ij}\right)\frac{\partial EU_{ij}}{\partial X_j}, \tag{F1}$$

while the effect of a change in x in province k on migration from i to j is

$$\frac{\partial P_{ij}}{\partial X_k} = -P_{ij}P_{ik}\frac{\partial EU_{ik}}{\partial X_k}. \tag{F2}$$

The rest of the formulas below are derived by appropriately differentiating expected utility (4.7) and substituting the result into these equations. All the derivatives are based on the assumption that infra-marginal taxes owing and the marginal tax rate will be unaffected by changes in any variables that affect the level of income. To save space, separate derivatives are not given for Quebec, except in the case of provincial taxes. In all other cases, the Quebec counterparts can be obtained simply by replacing τ_{ij} with $(\tau^F_{ij} + \tau^Q_{ij})$ in what follows.

For completeness we give the formulas for marginal effects of a change in a variable x_j on flows from province i to j, along with the effect on migration from i to j of a change in X in province k. We restrict our comments here to the derivative with respect to X_j.

A REFORMULATION OF AFTER-TAX INCOMES

In the case of the explanatory variables that enter into after-tax incomes, the derivation of the marginal effects is complicated by the fact that in most cases a change in before-tax income will also change the individual's income tax liability, even though marginal tax rates remain constant. Thus the derivatives with respect to such variables must incorporate the effect of the change on the total income tax liability of the individual. This task is most easily accomplished by re-writing after-tax incomes in a form that highlights the role of marginal tax rates. We do so using an approach suggested by Phipps (1990), which involves writing after-tax income for each state of the world in terms of τ, the highest marginal tax rate, that is, the rate that applies to the last dollar of income received by the individual. Because only the part of the individual's income that is above some level, say Y^0, is taxed at this rate, this approach involves adding to the budget constraint an adjustment factor, TAX^0, that represents the difference between total taxes owed and the total tax that would be owing if *all* income were taxed at the top marginal rate. Because taxable income in the model varies with origin and destination, as well as the state of the world, so do τ, Y^0, and TAX^0.

The following equations present a reformulation of after-tax income under the stylized tax system described above, for each state of the world, for the nine provinces that between 1966 and 1996 were party to the tax collection agreement with the federal government. In the case of these provinces, the variable Y^0 is determined entirely by the federal rate structure, while τ and TAX^0 reflect the interaction of the federal rate structure and the provincial income tax rates.

More specifically,

$$\tau = \tau^F(1 + \tau^P), \tag{F3}$$

where τ^F is the highest federal marginal tax rate and τ^P is the provincial tax rate, which differs across provinces. Similarly,

$$TAX^0 = BFT(1 + \tau^P),\tag{F4}$$

where *BFT* is Basic Federal Tax.

For state 1, then, after-tax income is given by

$$INC_{ij1} = \begin{cases} (1 - \tau_{ij1})\big[50w_j + B_i - C1_{ij}\big] + TR_i - C2_{ij} - TAX^0_{ij1} \\ \quad + \tau_{ij1}(Y^0_{ij1} + P), \quad t \le 1971 \\ (1 - \tau_{ij1})\big[50w_j + B_i + TR_i - C1_{ij} - C2_{ij}\big] - TAX^0_{ij1} \\ \quad + \tau_{ij1}(Y^0_{ij1} + P), \quad 1972 \le t < 1988 \\ (1 - \tau_{ij1})\big[50w_j + B_i + TR_i - C1_{ij} - C2_{ij}\big] - TAX^0_{ij1} \\ \quad + \tau_{ij1}Y^0_{ij1} + \tau_{1ij1}P, \quad t \ge 1988, \end{cases}\tag{F5}$$

where τ_{1ijs} is the rate of tax credit applying to an individual from province i who moves to province j in state s. For state 2, it is

$$INC_{ij2} = \begin{cases} (1 - \tau_{ij2})\big[w_j MXYR_j + B_i - C1_{ij}\big] + TR_i + UI_{j2} - C2_{ij} \\ \quad - TAX^0_{ij2} + \tau_{ij2}(Y^0_{ij2} + P), \, t \le 1971 \\ (1 - \tau_{ij2})\big[w_j MXYR_j + B_i + TR_i + UI_{j2} - C1_{ij} - C2_{ij}\big] \\ \quad - TAX^0_{ij2} + \tau_{ij2}(Y^0_{ij2} + P), \, 1972 \le t < 1988 \\ (1 - \tau_{ij2})\big[w_j MXYR_j + B_i + TR_i + UI_{j2} - C1_{ij} - C2_{ij}\big] \\ \quad - TAX^0_{ij2} + \tau_{ij2}Y^0_{ij2} + \tau_{1ij2}P, \, t \ge 1988, \end{cases}\tag{F6}$$

where

$$UI_{j2} = \rho w_j^R MXYR_j.\tag{F7}$$

For state 3, after-tax income is

$$INC_{ij3} = \begin{cases} (1 - \tau_{ij3})\big[w_j MXYR_j + B_i - C1_{ij}\big] + TR_i + UI_{j3} + SA_{j3} - C2_{ij} - \\ \quad TAX^0_{ij3} + \tau_{ij3}(Y^0_{ij3} + P), t \le 1971 \\ (1 - \tau_{ij3})\big[w_j MXYR_j + B_i + TR_i + UI_{j3} - C1_{ij} - C2_{ij}\big] + SA_{j3} - \\ \quad TAX^0_{ij3} + \tau_{ij3}(Y^0_{ij3} + P), 1972 \le t < 1988 \\ (1 - \tau_{ij3})\big[w_j MXYR_j + B_i + TR_i + UI_{j3} - C1_{ij} - C2_{ij}\big] + SA_{j3} - \\ \quad TAX^0_{ij3} + \tau_{ij3}Y^0_{ij3} + \tau_{1ij3}P, t \ge 1988, \end{cases}\tag{F8}$$

where

$$UI_{j3} = \rho w_j^R MINWKS_j \tag{F9}$$

and

$$SA_{j3} = \begin{cases} \dfrac{\overline{SA_j}}{52}\left(51 - MIN_j - MINWKS_j\right), & t < 1971 \\[2ex] \dfrac{\overline{SA_j}}{52}\left(50 - MIN_j - MINWKS_j\right), & t \geq 1971. \end{cases} \tag{F10}$$

Finally, before-tax and after-tax incomes for state 4 are assumed to be identical; after-tax income for state 4 is thus

$$INC_{ij4} = SA_{j4} + TR_i - C1_{ij} - C2_{ij}, \tag{F11}$$

where $SA_{j4} = \overline{SA_j}$.

In the case of Quebec, which collects its own personal income tax, one must differentiate between the federal and provincial values of τ, Y^0, and TAX^0. In the equations below, which provide the definitions of after-tax income net of moving costs for Quebec for states 1, 2, and 3, the federal values are indicated by a superscript F, while the provincial values are distinguished by a superscript Q. For state 1, after-tax income net of moving costs is

$$INC_{ij1} = \begin{cases} (1 - \tau_{ij1}^F - \tau_{ij1}^Q)\left[50w_j + B_i - C1_{ij}\right] + TR_i - C2_{ij} - TAX_{ij1}^{0F} - \\ \qquad TAX_{ij1}^{0Q} + \tau_{ij1}^F(Y_{ij1}^{0F} + P^F) + \tau_{ij1}^Q(Y_{ij1}^{0Q} + P^Q), \quad t \leq 1971 \\[2ex] (1 - \tau_{ij1}^F - \tau_{ij1}^Q)\left[50w_j + B_i + TR_i - C1_{ij} - C2_{ij}\right] - TAX_{ij1}^{0F} - \\ \qquad TAX_{ij1}^{0Q} + \tau_{ij1}^F(Y_{ij1}^{0F} + P^F) + \tau_{ij1}^Q(Y_{ij1}^{0Q} + P^Q), \quad 1972 \leq t < 1988 \\[2ex] (1 - \tau_{ij1}^F - \tau_{ij1}^Q)\left[50w_j + B_i + TR_i - C1_{ij} - C2_{ij}\right] - TAX_{ij1}^{0F} - \\ \qquad TAX_{ij1}^{0Q} + \tau_{ij1}^F Y_{ij1}^{0F} + \tau_{1ij1}^F P^F + \tau_{ij1}^Q Y_{ij1}^{0Q} + \tau_{1ij1}^Q P^Q, \quad t \geq 1988. \end{cases} \tag{F12}$$

For states 2 and 3, it is

$$INC_{ijs} = \begin{cases} (1 - \tau_{ijs}^{F} - \tau_{ijs}^{Q})\left[w_j MXYR_j + B_i - C1_{ij} \right] + TR_i + UI_{js} & \text{(F13)} \\ \quad + SA_{js} - C2_{ij} - TAX_{ijs}^{0F} - TAX_{ijs}^{0F} \\ \quad + \tau_{ijs}^{F}(Y_{ijs}^{0F} + P^F) + \tau_{ijs}^{Q}(Y_{ijs}^{0Q} + P^Q),\ t \le 1971 \\[6pt] (1 - \tau_{ijs}^{F} - \tau_{ijs}^{Q})\left[w_j MXYR_j + B_i + TR_i + UI_{js} - C1_{ij} - C2_{ij} \right] \\ \quad + SA_{js} - TAX_{ijs}^{0F} - TAX_{ijs}^{0F} + \tau_{ijs}^{F}(Y_{ijs}^{0F} + P^F) \\ \quad + \tau_{ijs}^{Q}(Y_{ijs}^{0Q} + P^Q),\ 1972 \le t < 1988 \\[6pt] (1 - \tau_{ijs}^{F} - \tau_{ijs}^{Q})\left[w_j MXYR_j + B_i + TR_i + UI_{js} - C1_{ij} - C2_{ij} \right] \\ \quad + SA_{js} - TAX_{ijs}^{0F} - TAX_{ijs}^{0F} + \tau_{ijs}^{F} Y_{ijs}^{0F} \\ \quad + \tau_{1ijs}^{F} P^F + \tau_{ijs}^{Q} Y_{ijs}^{0Q} + \tau_{1ijs}^{Q} P^Q,\ t \ge 1988, \end{cases}$$

where $s = 2$ for state 2 and 3 for state 3; $SA_2 = 0$; and UI_2, UI_3, and SA_3 are defined as in equations (F7), (F9), and (F10) above. Because income taxes are assumed to be zero in state 4, there are no differences between Quebec and the other provinces in the definition of after-tax income net of moving costs in this state of the world.

FORMULAS FOR MARGINAL EFFECTS OF CHANGES IN THE INDICATED VARIABLES

Average weekly wage w, $t \ge 1972$

$$\frac{\partial P_{ij}}{\partial w_j} = P_{ij}(1 - P_{ij})\alpha_1 \left\{ \frac{\pi_{j1}}{INC_{ij1}} 50\left(1 - \tau_{ij1}\right) + \right. \tag{F14}$$

$$\frac{\pi_{j2}}{INC_{ij2}}\left[MXYR_j + \rho MXYR\,WKS_j d_j \right]\left(1 - \tau_{ij2}\right)$$

$$\left. + \frac{\pi_{j3}}{INC_{ij3}}\left[MIN_j + \rho MIN\,WKS_j d_j \right]\left(1 - \tau_{ij3}\right) \right\}$$

$$\frac{\partial P_{ij}}{\partial w_k} = -P_{ij}P_{ik}\alpha_1 \left\{ \frac{\pi_{k1}}{INC_{ik1}} 50(1-\tau_{ik1}) + \right.$$

$$\frac{\pi_{k2}}{INC_{ik2}}[MXYR_k + \rho MXYRWKS_k d_k](1-\tau_{ik2})$$

$$\left. + \frac{\pi_{k3}}{INC_{ik3}}[MIN_k + \rho MINWKS_k d_k](1-\tau_{ik3}) \right\}, \ k \neq j,$$

(F15)

where

$$d_j = \begin{cases} 1 \ if \ w_j < MIE, \\ 0 \ if \ w_j \geq MIE. \end{cases}$$

Changes in the wage result not only in changes in wage income in states 1, 2, and 3 but also in changes in unemployment insurance income in states 2 and 3 if the current wage is less than the weekly maximum insurable earnings. These derivatives are not defined prior to 1972 because the relationship between weekly unemployment insurance payments and weekly wages is discontinuous then.

It is noteworthy that the sign of these derivatives will depend on the sign of the coefficient α_1. A change in the wage in province j will increase in-migration to (and reduce out-migration from) province j from all provinces of origin as long as α_1 is positive.

Finally, it should be noted that these derivatives assume that the foregone wage cost of moving does not change when the wage rate changes. This assumption is not completely consistent with the construction of the data used for estimation. In fact, an increase in the wage in province j would increase the foregone moving cost of all moves from province j. However, the effect is likely to be small and is ignored because the discontinuous nature of the step function used to estimate the foregone wage cost of moving means that it is not differentiable.

Level of Consumption of the Public Good F

There is more than one public good in the model, but for simplicity the superscripts or subscripts that would distinguish one public good from another have been omitted. The marginal effect formulas are

$$\frac{\partial P_{ij}}{\partial F_j} = P_{ij}(1-P_{ij})\left[\frac{\alpha_3}{F_j}\right]$$

(F16)

$$\frac{\partial P_{ij}}{\partial F_k} = -P_{ij}P_{ik}\left[\frac{\alpha_3}{F_k}\right], \; k \neq j, \tag{F17}$$

where α_3 is the coefficient common to all provinces of the fiscal variable F. The sign of the effect of a change in F_j depends entirely on the sign of α_3. As long as this sign is positive, an increase in F_j will increase inflows to and decrease outflows from province j. In general, the sign of the coefficient of a public spending variable determines the sign of the variable's marginal effect.

Social Assistance Income

Like that of the wage derivative, this derivative's sign depends on the sign of α_1. If α_1 is positive, an increase in social assistance spending in province j will increase income in states 3 and 4 and thereby lead to an increase in inflows to and a decrease in outflows from that province. The formulas are

$$\frac{\partial P_{ij}}{\partial \overline{SA}_j} = P_{ij}\left(1-P_{ij}\right)\alpha_1\left[\frac{\pi_{j3}}{INC_{ij3}}\frac{\left(50 - MIN_j - MINWKS_j\right)}{52} + \frac{\pi_{j4}}{INC_{ij4}}\right] \tag{F18}$$

$$\frac{\partial P_{ij}}{\partial \overline{SA}_k} = -P_{ij}P_{ik}\alpha_1\left[\frac{\pi_{k3}}{INC_{ik3}}\frac{\left(50 - MIN_k - MINWKS_k\right)}{52} + \frac{\pi_{k4}}{INC_{ik4}}\right], \; k \neq j. \tag{F19}$$

Minimum Weeks of Work Required to Qualify for Unemployment Insurance Benefits

These derivatives are discussed in the second section of chapter 7, titled "Minimum Weeks Required to Qualify for Unemployment Insurance." The formulas are

$$\frac{\partial P_{ij}}{\partial MIN_j} = P_{ij}\left(1-P_{ij}\right)\left\{\frac{\alpha_1\pi_{j3}}{INC_{ij3}}\left[w_j\left(1-\tau_{ij3}\right)-\frac{\overline{SA}_j}{52}\right] - \frac{\alpha_2\pi_{j3}}{\left(T-MIN_j\right)}\right\} \tag{F20}$$

$$\frac{\partial P_{ij}}{\partial MIN_k} = -P_{ij}P_{ik}\left\{\frac{\alpha_1\pi_{k3}}{INC_{ik3}}\left[w_k\left(1-\tau_{ik3}\right)-\frac{\overline{SA}_k}{52}\right]-\frac{\alpha_2\pi_{k3}}{\left(T-MIN_k\right)}\right\}, \tag{F21}$$
$$k \neq j.$$

Maximum Insurance Benefits Available to a Person with Minimum Qualifying Weeks

These derivatives are also discussed in the main text, in the third section of chapter 7, titled "Maximum Weeks of Unemployment Benefits with Minimum Qualifications." The formulas are

$$\frac{\partial P_{ij}}{\partial MINWKS_j} = \begin{cases} P_{ij}\left(1-P_{ij}\right)\alpha_1\dfrac{\pi_{j3}}{INC_{ij3}}\left[\rho w_j^R - \dfrac{\overline{SA}_j}{52}\right], t \leq 1971 \\[4mm] P_{ij}\left(1-P_{ij}\right)\alpha_1\dfrac{\pi_{j3}}{INC_{ij3}}\left[\rho w_j^R\left(1-\tau_{ij3}\right)-\dfrac{\overline{SA}_j}{52}\right], \\[4mm] t > 1971 \end{cases} \tag{F22}$$

$$\frac{\partial P_{ij}}{\partial MINWKS_k} = \begin{cases} -P_{ij}P_{ik}\alpha_1\dfrac{\pi_{k3}}{INC_{ik3}}\left[\rho w_k^R - \dfrac{\overline{SA}_k}{52}\right], t \leq 1971, \\[3mm] k \neq j \\[4mm] -P_{ij}P_{ik}\alpha_1\dfrac{\pi_{k3}}{INC_{ik3}}\left[\rho w_k^R\left(1-\tau_{ik3}\right)-\dfrac{\overline{SA}_k}{52}\right], \\[4mm] t > 1971, k \neq j \end{cases} \tag{F23}$$

PROVINCIAL TAX RATES

For all the provinces except Quebec, income taxes under the stylized tax system described in chapter 5 can be written as follows:

$$TAX_{ijs} = \begin{cases} FT_{ijs}\left[(1-\alpha)+\tau_j^P\right], & t < 1972 \\[2mm] FT_{ijs}\left(1+\tau_j^P\right), & t \geq 1972 \end{cases} \tag{F24}$$

where FT_{ijs} is income tax payable to the federal government, α is the federal government tax abatement in favour of the provinces, and τ_j^P is the rate of income tax set by province j. The derivative of income tax payable with respect to the provincial tax rate τ_j^P is therefore just FT_{ijs}, and the marginal effects of changes in τ_j^P can be written as

$$\frac{\partial P_{ij}}{\partial \tau_j^P} = P_{ij}\left(1 - P_{ij}\right)\alpha_1\left\{\frac{\pi_{j1}}{INC_{ij1}}FT_{ij1} + \frac{\pi_{j2}}{INC_{ij2}}FT_{ij2} + \frac{\pi_{j3}}{INC_{ij3}}FT_{ij3}\right\} \qquad \text{F25)}$$

$$\frac{\partial P_{ij}}{\partial \tau_k^P} = -P_{ij}P_{ik}\alpha_1\left\{\frac{\pi_{k1}}{INC_{ik1}}FT_{ik1} + \frac{\pi_{k2}}{INC_{ik2}}FT_{ik2} + \frac{\pi_{k3}}{INC_{ik3}}FT_{ik3}\right\}, \qquad \text{(F26)}$$

$$k \neq j.$$

In the case of Quebec ($j=5$), income taxes under the stylized tax system are given by

$$TAX_{i5g} = FT_{i5g}\left(1 - \alpha^Q\right) + QT_{i5g}, \qquad \text{(F27)}$$

where α^Q is the federal abatement in favour of Quebec and QT is Quebec tax payable. A change in the Quebec tax system that would be comparable to a change in the rate τ_j^P set by the other provinces would be an equal percentage change in all Quebec marginal tax rates. One can allow for such a change in the tax system by re-writing the above equation as

$$TAX_{i5g} = FT_{i5g}\left(1 - \alpha^Q\right) + bQT_{i5g}, \qquad \text{(F28)}$$

where the parameter b represents the change in the Quebec rate structure. A value of $b=1$ would imply no change in the rate structure; $b>1$ would imply an across-the board increase in all marginal tax rates. The derivative

$$\frac{\partial TAX_{i5g}}{\partial b} = QT_{i5g} \qquad \text{(F29)}$$

is thus equivalent to $\partial TAX_{ijs} / \partial \tau_j^P$ in the case of the other provinces. For Quebec, then, derivatives of migration rates with respect to tax rates become

$$\frac{\partial P_{i5}}{\partial b} = P_{i5}\left(1 - P_{i5}\right)\alpha_1\left\{\begin{array}{c}\dfrac{\pi_{51}}{INC_{i51}}QT_{i51} + \dfrac{\pi_{52}}{INC_{i52}}QT_{i52} \\[2ex] + \dfrac{\pi_{53}}{INC_{i53}}QT_{i53}\end{array}\right\} \qquad \text{(F30)}$$

$$\frac{\partial P_{i5}}{\partial b} = -P_{ij}P_{i5}\alpha_1\left\{\frac{\pi_{51}}{INC_{i51}}QT_{i51} + \frac{\pi_{52}}{INC_{i52}}QT_{i52} + \frac{\pi_{53}}{INC_{i53}}QT_{i53}\right\}, \qquad \text{(F31)}$$

$$j \neq 5.$$

TABLES OF MARGINAL EFFECTS

Average marginal effects of changes on in-, out-, and net in-migration to each province of changes in variables *in that province* for the period 1978–96 are recorded in summary form in the main text of chapter 7. More detailed results are reported in the technical report on which this book is based, and are available at www.carleton.ca/~winers.

Simulations and Tables

Many important details about the simulations have already been provided in chapter 8. In this appendix we provide additional details regarding the methods we used. Tables containing more detailed simulation results are also provided.

GENERAL METHODOLOGY

As was noted in chapter 8, the simulation results are expressed in terms of numbers of people rather than migration rates. Changes in the number of people moving are determined by multiplying the predicted change in the migration rate in each simulation by the relevant provincial populations. In addition, since the models estimated are best able to predict the average migration behaviour of Canadians over the years, rather than year-to-year changes, the simulations involving the elimination of regional variation in one or more variables are carried out as follows:

1 The probability of migrating from i to j under the simulation is generated for all i and j, for each year from 1978 to 1996. Note that since the models used for the simulations are not dynamic, what happens in one year has no influence on what happens to the predicted migration rates in subsequent years. The "base case" series of predicted migration rates are subtracted from those for the simulation to obtain the predicted change in migration rates due to the simulation.

2 The *actual* populations of the provinces for each year are then used to convert the predicted changes in migration rates into predicted changes in the number of migrants from i to j for all i and j and for each year.

These numbers are summed to obtain the predicted change in the number of in-migrants to and out-migrants from each province for each year.

3 The predicted changes in the in- and out-migration flows for each
province are then averaged over the nineteen years of the 1978 to 1996
period. The average annual predicted change in net in-migration is
computed by taking the difference between the in- and out-migration
numbers.

The change in total in-migration to any province j is given by

$$IN_j = \sum_{\substack{k=1 \\ k \neq j}}^{J} POP_k \cdot \Delta P_{kj}, \qquad (\text{G1})$$

where POP_k is the population of province k, J is the total number of provinces, and ΔP_{kj} is the simulated change in the rate of migration rate from k to
j. The change in total out-migration from province j is given by

$$OUT_j = POP_j \sum_{\substack{k=1 \\ k \neq j}}^{J} \Delta P_{jk}. \qquad (\text{G2})$$

The change in net in-migration to province j is of course the difference
$IN_j - OUT_j$. The populations used in the calculation of the migration flows
are constructed from the sample data by summing actual migration flows
(including the staying option) across all destinations for each province of
origin.

The remainder of this appendix outlines any assumptions underlying
the simulations that have not already been discussed in chapter 8. These
assumptions are especially important in the case of variables that enter into
the composite income or leisure terms of the model. As noted in chapter 8,
it is a special feature of the conditional logit model that if an explanatory
variable enters the model independently of all others, as do the per capita
government spending variables, the level of that variable is irrelevant if it
does not vary across regions. Any variable that does not vary across regions
simply cancels out of the numerator and denominator of equation (4.4).
However, eliminating regional variation in wages, for example, does not
eliminate regional variation in the composite variable INCOME, and thus the
level at which it is set can influence the outcome of the simulation.

As an aid to understanding the simulations, table G1 provides a summary
of which variables in the model are affected by each of the simulations discussed in the chapter, and in the case of the INCOME variable, which states of

Table G1
Variables Affected by Simulations and Numbering of Simulations

| | After-Tax Income | | | | Leisure | Other Variables |
Simulation	State 1	State 2	State 3	State 4		
1 No VER		x	x		x	
2 No EXT		x	x		x	
3 No VER and No EXT		x	x		x	
4 Federal Spending						FEDERAL SPENDING
5 Education Spending						EDUCATION
6 Provincial Income Tax Rates	x	x	x			
7 Social Assistance			x	x		
8 All Policy variables	x	x	x	x	x	FED, ED, HEALTH, OTHER SPENDING
9 Average Weekly Earnings	x	x	x	x		
10 Probabilities		x	x		x	
11 Moving Costs	x	x	x	x		DSTAY, DISTANCE

the world are affected. An "x" in any of the first five columns indicates that the value of the variable changes, while the last column simply lists the variables other than INCOME and LEISURE that are affected. As the table indicates, all but two of the simulations involved changes to the composite INCOME variable. It should also be noted that changes to the LEISURE variable always take the form of changes in the amount of leisure time (i.e., unemployment) in states 2 and 3. None of the simulations altered the amount of leisure time consumed in states 1 and 4.

SIMULATION-SPECIFIC DETAILS

Note that table G1 also assigns a number to each simulation. These numbers are used to refer to the simulations in subsequent tables.

Elimination of the VER

In this simulation, we assume that MIN, the minimum number of weeks of work required to qualify for unemployment insurance benefits, is 13 in all provinces and all years of the simulation, which leads to changes in MIN-WKS, MXYR, MXYRWKS, and weeks of social assistance benefits in state 3 as well. Although MXYR depends primarily on the benefit schedule, it is affected by the change in MIN because MIN is the lower bound for MXYR. For those

Table G2
Estimated Regional Extended Benefits, 1990–94

Range of regional unemployment rate	18 November 1990 to 3 April 1994		3 April 1994 to 31 December 1996	
	Increase in weeks of benefits	Estimated regional extended benefit weeks	Increase in weeks of benefits	Estimated regional extended benefit weeks
under 6.0%	0	0	0	0
6.1% to 7.0%	3	3	2	2
7.1% to 8.0%	3	6	2	4
8.1% to 9.0%	4	10	2	6
9.1% to 10.0%	4	14	2	8
10.1% to 11.0%	4	18	2	10
11.1% to 12.0%	4	22	2	12
12.1% to 13.0%	2	24	2	14
13.1% to 14.0%	2	26	2	16
14.1% to 15.0%	2	28	2	18
15.1% to 16.0%	2	30	2	20
over 16.1%	2	32	2	22

Source: Authors' calculations and schedules of benefits that came into effect on 18 November 1990 and 3 April 1994.

provinces and years for which MXYR was less than 13 weeks, MXYR was raised to 13 weeks and MXYRWKS was adjusted accordingly.

The calculation of MINWKS under this scenario proves somewhat more complicated, since the actual benefit schedules in effect during the 1978 to 1996 period did not always allow for the combination of a high regional unemployment rate and an entrance requirement of 13 weeks of work. Some additional assumptions regarding the benefit schedule therefore have to be made. For the period 1978 to 18 November 1990, it is straightforward to apply the benefit schedule that was actually in effect, which consisted of 1 week of benefits for each qualifying week, plus regional extended benefits that depended on the regional unemployment rate. To derive the value of MINWKS for these years, 13 is added to regional extended benefits as calculated for the purposes of constructing the data required for estimation.

For 18 November 1990 to 3 April 1994, regional extended benefits are derived from the benefits schedule, Schedule 2 of the revised Unemployment Insurance Act, by taking the difference between weeks of benefits at each possible level of the regional unemployment rate and the next, for a given number of qualifying weeks, resulting in the values in the second and third columns of table G2. Regional extended benefits are then calculated for each province, based on the provincial unemployment rate. To obtain total benefits for each province, it is assumed that individuals with 13 weeks of work would be entitled to a minimum of 11 weeks of benefits. This value was derived by first computing the ratio of weeks of benefits to qualifying weeks at 20 qualifying weeks (17/20 = 0.85), and then applying that ratio to the assumed value of 13 weeks for MIN. This ratio is used because 20 is the lowest level of qualifying weeks for which benefit weeks are specified for a regional unemployment rate of 6 percent or less. The schedule does not provide a level of benefits at that regional unemployment rate for 13 quali-fying weeks because the schedule incorporates the VER. Total benefits for each province are computed by adding 11 to the level of regional extended benefits for each province in each year, subject to the constraint that MIN and MINWKS sum to 50. In cases where MIN plus MINWKS exceeded 50, MIN-WKS is set equal to 50 minus MIN.

A similar procedure is used to derive the value of MINWKS between 3 April 1994 and the end of 1996. The revised benefit schedule is somewhat sim-pler; it specifies that every two qualifying weeks, up to 40 weeks, would entitle the claimant to 1 week of benefits. Thirteen weeks of work would therefore entitle an individual to 7 weeks of benefits. Regional extended benefits according to the revised schedule are given in columns four and five of table G2. As before, total benefits are obtained by adding regional extended benefits, computed based on the provincial unemployment rate, to the seven weeks of basic benefits. In this case, the constraint that MIN and MINWKS must not exceed 50 weeks is not binding.

The value of MINWKS for each province and year for this simulation is given in table G3. Weeks of social assistance benefits are computed as the difference between 50 weeks and the sum of MIN and MINWKS, and are given in table G4. Finally, the values are presented in table G5. MXYRWKS can easily be computed by subtracting the values of MXYR in table G5 from 50.

Elimination of Regional Extended Benefits

In this next simulation, regionally extended benefits under unemployment insurance are eliminated by setting θ, the rate at which qualifying weeks are translated into weeks of benefits, equal to 2 weeks of benefits for each week of work in all provinces in all years of the simulation. This change leads to changes in MXYR, MXYRWKS, MINWKS, and weeks of social assistance benefits in state 3. The value of MXYR corresponding to this value of θ is obtained by solving the equation

$$MXYR + 2MXYR = 50;$$

Table G3
MINWKS for Simulation 1, 1978–96

Year	NFLD	PEI	NS	NB	QUE	ONT	MAN	SASK	ALTA	BC
1978	37	37	37	37	37	27	23	17	17	31
1979	37	37	37	37	37	23	19	15	13	29
1980	37	37	37	37	37	25	19	15	13	25
1981	37	37	37	37	37	25	29	17	13	25
1982	37	37	37	37	37	37	31	23	29	37
1983	37	37	37	37	37	37	35	27	37	37
1984	37	37	37	37	37	35	31	29	37	37
1985	37	37	37	37	37	31	31	31	37	37
1986	37	37	37	37	37	25	29	29	37	37
1987	37	37	37	37	37	23	27	27	37	37
1988	37	37	37	37	35	17	29	27	31	37
1989	37	37	37	37	35	19	29	27	27	35
1990	37	37	37	37	37	22	26	24	26	30
1991	37	37	35	37	35	23	23	19	23	27
1992	37	37	37	37	37	31	27	23	27	31
1993	37	37	37	37	37	31	27	19	27	27
1994	31	31	27	25	25	18	18	11	16	18
1995	29	25	21	19	19	13	11	9	11	13
1996	29	25	21	19	19	13	11	9	11	13

Note: For 1990, used 11/12 of the value under the 1977–90 rules, plus 1/12 of the value under the new rules introduced 18 November 1990. For 1994, used one-quarter of the value under the old rules, plus three-quarters of the value under the new rules introduced 3 April 1994.

Table G4
Weeks of Social Assistance Benefits in State 3 for Simulation 1

Year	NFLD	PEI	NS	NB	QUE	ONT	MAN	SASK	ALTA	BC
1978	0	0	0	0	0	10	14	20	20	6
1979	0	0	0	0	0	14	18	22	24	8
1980	0	0	0	0	0	12	18	22	24	12
1981	0	0	0	0	0	12	8	20	24	12
1982	0	0	0	0	0	0	6	14	8	0
1983	0	0	0	0	0	0	2	10	0	0
1984	0	0	0	0	0	2	6	8	0	0
1985	0	0	0	0	0	6	6	6	0	0
1986	0	0	0	0	0	12	8	8	0	0
1987	0	0	0	0	0	14	10	10	0	0
1988	0	0	0	0	2	20	8	10	6	0
1989	0	0	0	0	2	18	8	10	10	2
1990	0	0	1	0	1	15	11	13	11	7
1991	0	0	2	0	2	14	14	18	14	10
1992	0	0	0	0	0	6	10	14	10	6
1993	0	0	0	0	0	6	10	18	10	10
1994	6	6	11	12	12	19	19	26	22	19
1995	8	12	16	18	18	24	26	28	26	24
1996	8	12	16	18	18	24	26	28	26	24

Table G5
Values of *MXYR* for Simulation 1

Year	NFLD	PEI	NS	NB	QUE	ONT	MAN	SASK	ALTA	BC
1978	13	13	13	13	13	18	20	23	23	16
1979	13	13	13	13	13	20	22	24	25	17
1980	13	13	13	13	13	19	22	24	25	19
1981	13	13	13	13	13	19	17	23	25	19
1982	13	13	13	13	13	13	16	20	17	13
1983	13	13	13	13	13	13	14	18	13	13
1984	13	13	13	13	13	14	16	17	13	13
1985	13	13	13	13	13	16	16	16	13	13
1986	13	13	13	13	13	19	17	17	13	13
1987	13	13	13	13	13	20	18	18	13	13
1988	13	13	13	13	14	23	17	18	16	13
1989	13	13	13	13	14	22	17	18	18	14
1990	13	13	14	14	14	20	19	19	19	17
1991	13	13	18	15	18	25	24	25	24	22
1992	13	13	16	15	16	20	22	24	22	20
1993	13	13	14	15	15	18	20	22	20	18
1994	15	15	19	20	20	25	25	29	26	25
1995	16	19	22	23	23	27	28	30	28	27
1996	16	19	22	23	23	27	28	30	28	27

the solution is 17 weeks. However, this value has to be subjected to the constraint that *MXYR* be at least as great as *MIN* in all provinces and years, which results in some regional variation remaining in *MXYR*. The values of *MXYR* for all provinces and years for this simulation are presented in table G6. *MXYRWKS* is simply 50-*MXYR*.

The values of *MINWKS* under this simulation display considerably more variation than do those of *MXYR* and *MXYRWKS* because *MIN* is unaffected by this simulation. However, the appropriate value of *MINWKS* was easy to compute, since it is just 2*MIN* in this case. The values of *MINWKS* for this simulation are given in table G7, while those for weeks of social assistance benefits in state 3, calculated residually as before, are given in table G8.

Elimination of All Regional Variation in the Employment Insurance System

This simulation is a combination of the previous two. Under this simulation, the various UI variables take on the values specified in the section of chapter 8 that deals with this case, in all provinces and all years.

Table G6
Values of MXYR for Simulation 2

Year	NFLD	PEI	NS	NB	QUE	ONT	MAN	SASK	ALTA	BC
1978	17	17	17	17	17	17	17	17	17	17
1979	17	17	17	17	17	17	17	17	17	17
1980	17	17	17	17	17	17	17	17	17	17
1981	17	17	17	17	17	17	17	17	17	17
1982	17	17	17	17	17	17	17	17	17	17
1983	17	17	17	17	17	17	17	17	17	17
1984	17	17	17	17	17	17	17	17	17	17
1985	17	17	17	17	17	17	17	17	17	17
1986	17	17	17	17	17	17	17	17	17	17
1987	17	17	17	17	17	17	17	17	17	17
1988	17	17	17	17	17	17	17	17	17	17
1989	17	17	17	17	17	17	17	17	17	17
1990	17	17	17	17	17	17	17	17	17	17
1991	17	17	17	17	17	17	17	18	17	17
1992	17	17	17	17	17	17	17	17	17	17
1993	17	17	17	17	17	17	17	18	17	17
1994	17	17	17	17	17	17	17	19	17	17
1995	17	17	17	17	17	17	18	19	18	17
1996	17	17	17	17	17	17	18	19	18	17

Table G7
Values of MINWKS for Simulation 2

Year	NFLD	PEI	NS	NB	QUE	ONT	MAN	SASK	ALTA	BC
1978	20	20	20	20	20	24	26	28	28	22
1979	20	20	20	20	20	26	28	28	28	24
1980	20	20	20	20	20	26	28	28	28	26
1981	20	20	20	20	20	26	28	28	28	26
1982	20	20	20	20	20	20	22	26	24	20
1983	20	20	20	20	20	20	20	24	20	20
1984	20	20	20	20	20	20	22	24	20	20
1985	20	20	20	20	20	22	22	22	20	20
1986	20	20	20	20	20	26	24	24	20	20
1987	20	20	20	20	20	26	24	24	20	20
1988	20	20	20	20	20	28	24	24	22	20
1989	20	20	20	20	20	28	24	24	24	20
1990	27	27	28	27	28	29	28	29	28	28
1991	20	20	28	26	28	32	33	32	33	32
1992	20	20	24	26	26	30	32	33	32	30.
1993	20	20	22	26	24	30	32	32	32	32
1994	22	22	24	26	26	32	32	31	33	32
1995	24	24	26	28	28	33	32	31	32	33
1996	24	24	26	28	28	33	32	31	32	33

Table G8
Number of Weeks on Social Assistance in State 3, Simulation 2

Year	NFLD	PEI	NS	NB	QUE	ONT	MAN	SASK	ALTA	BC
1978	20	20	20	20	20	14	11	8	8	17
1979	20	20	20	20	20	11	8	8	8	14
1980	20	20	20	20	20	11	8	8	8	11
1981	20	20	20	20	20	11	8	8	8	11
1982	20	20	20	20	20	20	17	11	14	20
1983	20	20	20	20	20	20	20	14	20	20
1984	20	20	20	20	20	20	17	14	20	20
1985	20	20	20	20	20	17	17	17	20	20
1986	20	20	20	20	20	11	14	14	20	20
1987	20	20	20	20	20	11	14	14	20	20
1988	20	20	20	20	20	8	14	14	17	20
1989	20	20	20	20	20	8	14	14	14	20
1990	10	10	9	9	9	7	7	7	7	8
1991	20	20	8	11	8	2	0	0	0	2
1992	20	20	14	11	11	5	2	0	2	5
1993	20	20	17	11	14	5	2	0	2	2
1994	17	17	14	11	11	2	2	0	0	2
1995	14	14	11	8	8	0	0	0	0	0
1996	14	14	11	8	8	0	0	0	0	0

No Regional Variation in Real per Capita Federal Spending

This simulation is carried out by setting the variable equal to zero in all provinces in all years.

No Regional Variation in Real per Capita Spending on Education

This simulation is also carried out by setting the variable equal to zero in all provinces in all years.

No Regional Variation in Provincial Income Tax Rates

The income tax rates used for the simulation are shown in table G9. All other details are provided in the third section of chapter 8.

No Regional Variation in Social Assistance Benefits

The level of social assistance benefits used for the simulation are given in table G9. All other details are provided in the section of chapter 8 titled "Regional Variation in Social Assistance Payments."

Table G9
Values of Variables for Simulations 6, 7, and 9[1]

Year	Provincial Income Tax Rates, Simulation 6	Annual Nominal Social Assistance Benefits, Simulation 7	Average Weekly Earnings, Simulation 9	WUI, Simulation 9
1978	0.4998	4709.50	242.91	160.01
1979	0.4972	5485.30	263.85	158.31
1980	0.4974	6094.30	290.52	174.00
1981	0.4999	6845.50	325.21	189.00
1982	0.5100	7573.50	357.71	210.00
1983	0.5152	8086.90	382.78	229.67
1984	0.5241	8554.80	398.66	239.20
1985	0.5228	8920.10	412.75	247.65
1986	0.5245	9303.70	425.16	255.10
1987	0.5350	9767.40	441.23	264.74
1988	0.5394	10211.80	460.67	276.40
1989	0.5406	10661.60	484.23	290.54
1990	0.5461	11201.40	506.24	303.74
1991	0.5472	11912.90	529.48	317.69
1992	0.5533	12439.40	547.98	328.79
1993	0.5644	12470.70	557.94	322.21
1994	0.5667	12507.80	568.27	318.23
1995	0.5667	11996.20	573.75	315.56
1996	0.5639	11453.10	586.06	322.33

[1] See table G1 for definitions of simulation numbers.

Regional Variation in All Policy Variables Eliminated

This simulation is a combination of simulations 3, 4, 5, 6, and 7 with the elimination of regional variation in real per capita spending on health and other functions by the provincial governments. The latter two variables are set to zero in all provinces and years – any constant level would do, since a variable that does not change across destinations drops out of the equation for predicted probabilities – while the values of the other variables are set in the manner described above or in the relevant section of chapter 8.

No Regional Variation in Average Weekly Earnings

The simulation values of both w_j and WUI_j are given in table G9. For further details, see the section of chapter 8 dealing with regional variation in wages.

Table G10
Probabilities of States of the World for Simulation 10

Year	State 1	State 2	State 3	State 4
1978	0.8878	0.0481	0.0197	0.0444
1979	0.8989	0.0445	0.0127	0.0439
1980	0.9013	0.0469	0.0077	0.0441
1981	0.9014	0.0470	0.0073	0.0442
1982	0.8587	0.0763	0.0119	0.0531
1983	0.8488	0.0772	0.0162	0.0579
1984	0.8557	0.0705	0.0166	0.0572
1985	0.8640	0.0651	0.0157	0.0552
1986	0.8698	0.0618	0.0139	0.0544
1987	0.8796	0.0579	0.0118	0.0507
1988	0.8897	0.0558	0.0108	0.0437
1989	0.8850	0.0551	0.0101	0.0498
1990	0.8695	0.0605	0.0084	0.0616
1991	0.8442	0.0694	0.0121	0.0744
1992	0.8346	0.0674	0.0124	0.0855
1993	0.8411	0.0615	0.0124	0.0850
1994	0.8549	0.0514	0.0100	0.0836
1995	0.8626	0.0432	0.0069	0.0873
1996	0.8706	0.0418	0.0060	0.0816

No Regional Variation in the Probabilities of the States of the World

The simulation values of the probabilities are given in table G10. All additional information is given in the section of chapter 8 dealing with the probabilites of the four states.

The Elimination of Moving Costs

All relevant details are provided in the section of chapter 8 dealing with moving costs.

The Effects of Extraordinary Events in Quebec and Newfoundland

To simulate the effects of the events associated with the dummy variables OCT, OCT2, PQ, PQ2, FISH, and FISH2, we predict migration rates when the values of these dummy variables are set to zero. In these simulations, each pair of dummy variables is set to zero by itself, without changing the original values of the other two pairs. The associated changes in migration flows are then computed for each year, and summed over the relevant years.

DETAILED SIMULATION RESULTS

The remainder of this appendix consists of detailed tables of simulation results.

Table G11
Elimination of Variable Entrance Requirement, Average Annual Change in Inflows and Outflows, 1978–96

	NFLD	PEI	NS	NB	QUE	ONT	MAN	SASK	ALTA	BC
						Model 1[1]				
Low Income										
In-migration	-51	-24	-1	-32	0	92	22	22	27	3
Out-migration	82	27	8	46	6	-65	-20	-18	-13	6
Net In-migration	-133	-50	-9	-79	-6	157	42	40	40	-3
Middle Income										
In-migration	-183	-95	-13	-126	-7	288	65	68	73	-7
Out-migration	221	96	17	139	21	-246	-73	-68	-61	18
Net In-migration	-404	-191	-30	-265	-28	534	138	136	134	-25
High Income										
In-migration	-86	-43	-17	-70	-14	161	30	33	29	-26
Out-migration	93	37	12	68	23	-140	-37	-37	-39	16
Net In-migration	-179	-80	-29	-139	-37	301	67	70	68	-42
All Income Classes[2]										
In-migration	-320	-162	-30	-229	-21	541	117	123	130	-29
Out-migration	396	160	37	254	50	-451	-130	-123	-113	40
Net In-migration	-716	-322	-67	-483	-71	992	247	246	242	-70
						Model 2[1]				
Low Income										
In-migration	-7	-3	0	-4	0	12	3	3	4	1
Out-migration	11	4	1	6	1	-9	-3	-2	-2	1
Net In-migration	-17	-7	-1	-11	-1	21	6	5	5	0
Middle Income										
In-migration	-13	-7	-1	-9	-1	21	5	5	5	0
Out-migration	15	7	1	10	2	-18	-5	-5	-4	1
Net In-migration	-29	-14	-2	-19	-3	39	10	9	10	-1

Table G11 (continued)

	NFLD	PEI	NS	NB	QUE	ONT	MAN	SASK	ALTA	BC
						Model 2¹				
High Income										
In-migration	4	2	1	3	0	−6	−1	−1	−1	2
Out-migration	−3	−1	0	−2	−1	6	2	2	2	−1
Net In-migration	7	3	1	5	1	−12	−3	−3	−3	2
All Income Classes²										
In-migration	−16	−8	0	−11	−1	27	6	6	8	2
Out-migration	23	9	2	14	3	−21	−6	−6	−4	1
Net In-migration	−39	−17	−2	−25	−3	48	13	12	12	1

¹ Based on parameter estimates in table 6.2. See also figures 8.1a and 8.1b.
² Totals may differ from sum across income classes due to rounding error.

Table G12
Elimination of Regional Extended Benefit, Average Annual Change in Inflows and Outflows, 1978–96

	NFLD	PEI	NS	NB	QUE	ONT	MAN	SASK	ALTA	BC
						Model 1¹				
Low Income										
In-migration	−76	−22	−31	−79	−38	217	48	68	62	−6
Out-migration	126	29	52	106	73	−142	−42	−59	−21	23
Net In-migration	−202	−51	−83	−185	−111	360	90	127	83	−29
Middle Income										
In-migration	−253	−118	−139	−268	−152	694	146	222	175	−59
Out-migration	323	130	159	297	258	−544	−147	−203	−94	72
Net In-migration	−575	−248	−297	−565	−409	1238	293	425	269	−131
High Income										
In-migration	−119	−54	−88	−143	−120	396	69	114	70	−79

Table G12 (continued)

	NFLD	PEI	NS	NB	QUE	ONT	MAN	SASK	ALTA	BC
					Model 1[1]					
Out-migration	132	50	81	137	180	-335	-75	-114	-61	52
Net In-migration	-251	-103	-169	-280	-300	731	144	228	131	-131
All Income Classes[2]										
In-migration	-448	-194	-257	-490	-310	1308	262	404	307	-145
Out-migration	580	208	292	540	511	-1022	-264	-377	-176	146
Net In-migration	-1028	-402	-549	-1030	-820	2329	527	781	483	-291
					Model 2[1]					
Low Income										
In-migration	-13	0	-4	-16	-6	32	7	10	9	-1
Out-migration	19	1	6	21	11	-22	-7	-10	-4	3
Net In-migration	-32	0	-10	-37	-18	54	14	20	13	-4
Middle Income										
In-migration	-25	0	-9	-36	-15	57	12	18	14	-6
Out-migration	28	1	10	36	23	-49	-13	-19	-10	5
Net In-migration	-53	-1	-20	-71	-37	106	25	37	24	-11
High Income										
In-migration	3	5	4	0	3	-11	-2	-3	-2	3
Out-migration	-3	-4	-3	-1	-5	10	2	3	2	-2
Net In-migration	6	9	7	1	8	-22	-5	-6	-4	5
All Income Classes[2]										
In-migration	-35	5	-9	-52	-18	77	17	25	22	-4
Out-migration	44	-3	13	56	30	-61	-17	-25	-12	6
Net In-migration	-79	8	-22	-107	-47	139	34	51	34	-10

[1] Based on parameter estimates in table 6.2. See also figures 8.2a and 8.2b.
[2] Totals may differ from sum across income classes due to rounding error.

Table GI3
No Regional Variation in UI, Average Annual Change in Migration Flows by Income Class, 1978–96

	Model 1[1]			Model 2[1]			Model 1[2]		
	In-migration	Out-migration	Net In-migration	In-migration	Out-migration	Net In-migration	In-migration	Out-migration	Net In-migration
Low Income									
NFLD	-101	170	-271	-15	24	-39	-27	52	-78
PEI	-42	50	-92	-4	5	-9	-13	16	-29
NS	-31	56	-86	-4	8	-12	-8	17	-25
NB	-82	115	-196	-15	19	-34	-21	33	-53
QUE	-34	72	-106	-6	11	-17	-9	22	-31
ONT	252	-163	415	36	-24	60	76	-45	120
MAN	56	-49	105	8	-7	15	17	-13	30
SASK	80	-70	151	12	-11	23	24	-19	43
ALTA	74	-26	101	10	-4	15	21	-7	29
BC	1	22	-20	-0	3	-3	1	6	-6
Middle Income									
NFLD	-341	454	-795	-30	34	-64	-39	53	-92
PEI	-183	200	-383	-9	10	-19	-21	24	-45
NS	-137	167	-303	-11	12	-23	-16	19	-35
NB	-294	338	-632	-32	33	-65	-34	40	-74
QUE	-142	256	-399	-14	22	-36	-17	32	-49
ONT	813	-623	1436	63	-54	117	97	-73	171
MAN	173	-172	344	13	-15	28	20	-20	40
SASK	264	-242	506	21	-22	43	32	-28	59
ALTA	212	-118	329	16	-11	27	24	-14	38
BC	-37	67	-104	-4	4	-9	-5	8	-13

Table G13 (continued)

	Model 1[1]			Model 2[1]			Model 1[2]		
	In-migration	Out-migration	Net In-migration	In-migration	Out-migration	Net In-migration	In-migration	Out-migration	Net In-migration
High Income									
NFLD	-147	186	-333	6	-6	12	-23	28	-52
PEI	-28	76	-104	5	-4	9	-12	12	-24
NS	-31	89	-120	4	-3	7	-13	13	-26
NB	-83	173	-256	3	-3	6	-23	24	-48
QUE	-101	188	-289	3	-5	8	-18	29	-47
ONT	477	-67	544	-14	13	-27	71	-57	128
MAN	151	-48	198	-3	3	-6	12	-13	25
SASK	199	-95	294	-4	4	-8	20	-20	40
ALTA	202	-9	211	-3	3	-5	12	-11	24
BC	12	158	-146	3	-1	5	-11	8	-19
All Income Classes[3]									
NFLD	-589	810	-1399	-39	52	-91	-89	133	-222
PEI	-253	326	-579	-8	11	-19	-47	52	-99
NS	-198	311	-509	-11	17	-28	-37	49	-86
NB	-458	626	-1083	-43	49	-93	-78	97	-175
QUE	-278	516	-794	-16	29	-44	-44	83	-127
ONT	1542	-854	2395	85	-66	151	244	-175	419
MAN	380	-268	647	18	-19	37	49	-46	95
SASK	543	-408	951	29	-29	57	76	-66	142
ALTA	488	-153	641	24	-13	37	58	-32	90
BC	-24	247	-270	-1	6	-7	-16	22	-38

[1] Based on parameter estimates from table 6.2. See also figures 8.3a and 8.3b.
[2] Based on parameter estimates in table 6.6. See also figure 8.3c.
[3] Totals may differ from sum across income classes owing to rounding error.

Table G14
No Regional Variation in UI, Average Annual Change in Migration Flows by Age, Sex, and Income Class, Model 1, 1978–96[1,2]

	20–24 Years Old			25–44 Years Old			45–64 Years Old		
	In-migration	Out-migration	Net In-migration	In-migration	Out-migration	Net In-migration	In-migration	Out-migration	Net In-migration
Low Income Men									
NFLD	-14	29	-43	-10	14	-24	0	1	-1
PEI	-4	5	-9	-4	4	-8	0	0	0
NS	-5	12	-17	-3	5	-8	0	0	0
NB	-16	25	-40	-7	9	-16	0	0	-1
QUE	-6	15	-22	-3	7	-10	0	-1	0
ONT	44	-24	68	21	-13	34	1	0	2
MAN	10	-8	17	5	-5	10	0	0	0
SASK	16	-14	29	8	-7	15	0	0	1
ALTA	16	-3	19	6	-2	8	0	0	0
BC	1	4	-3	0	2	-2	0	0	0
Low Income Women									
NFLD	36	-58	94	65	-78	143	15	-17	33
PEI	21	-21	42	32	-30	61	10	-8	18
NS	12	-18	30	19	-22	41	5	-5	10
NB	25	-34	59	42	-44	86	10	-9	19
QUE	12	-22	34	19	-30	49	5	-8	13
ONT	-86	61	-147	-122	98	-220	-28	29	-58
MAN	-19	17	-35	-25	27	-52	-6	7	-13
SASK	-26	24	-50	-34	34	-69	-7	9	-16
ALTA	-28	11	-38	-31	22	-53	-5	5	-11
BC	4	-9	12	5	-8	13	4	-1	5

Table G14 (continued)

	20–24 Years Old			25–44 Years Old			45–64 Years Old		
	In-migration	Out-migration	Net In-migration	In-migration	Out-migration	Net In-migration	In-migration	Out-migration	Net In-migration
Middle Income Men									
NFLD	-70	87	-157	-96	127	-223	-9	12	-20
PEI	-27	29	-56	-47	58	-105	-4	5	-9
NS	-33	40	-73	-32	43	-75	-2	3	-5
NB	-75	86	-161	-76	88	-163	-7	7	-14
QUE	-34	51	-85	-29	53	-81	-3	5	-8
ONT	150	-127	277	202	-147	349	17	-15	33
MAN	38	-36	75	47	-45	92	4	-4	8
SASK	69	-64	133	71	-64	135	6	-6	12
ALTA	54	-21	74	52	-27	79	4	-3	6
BC	-11	17	-28	3	12	-9	-1	1	-2
Middle Income Women									
NFLD	4	-4	8	48	-49	97	15	-13	28
PEI	3	-3	6	32	-28	59	12	-9	21
NS	2	-2	4	20	-18	38	8	-5	13
NB	3	-3	5	33	-29	62	12	-9	21
QUE	2	-3	5	21	-32	53	7	-12	19
ONT	-9	8	-18	-101	90	-192	-30	36	-67
MAN	-2	2	-5	-18	23	-41	-5	8	-14
SASK	-3	3	-6	-25	28	-53	-7	10	-17
ALTA	-3	2	-4	-22	22	-44	-5	9	-13
BC	2	-2	4	12	-7	19	9	-1	11

Table G14 (continued)

	20–24 Years Old			25–44 Years Old			45–64 Years Old		
	In-migration	Out-migration	Net In-migration	In-migration	Out-migration	Net In-migration	In-migration	Out-migration	Net In-migration
High Income Men									
NFLD	-16	12	-29	-69	71	-140	8	-8	16
PEI	-4	3	-7	-31	29	-60	5	-4	9
NS	-10	8	-18	-38	37	-75	5	-3	8
NB	-18	16	-34	-69	66	-135	7	-6	13
QUE	-14	14	-27	-46	63	-109	5	-10	15
ONT	33	-34	67	176	-151	327	-20	21	-42
MAN	7	-8	15	34	-35	69	-3	5	-8
SASK	21	-18	39	56	-55	111	-5	6	-11
ALTA	9	-7	15	33	-26	59	-3	4	-7
BC	-11	9	-21	-25	21	-47	5	-1	7
High Income Women									
NFLD	0	0	0	5	-7	12	5	-6	11
PEI	0	0	0	4	-3	7	5	-4	9
NS	0	0	0	3	-3	6	4	-2	6
NB	0	0	0	3	-3	7	5	-4	8
QUE	0	0	0	4	-6	10	5	-10	14
ONT	0	0	0	-15	13	-28	-17	18	-35
MAN	0	0	0	-2	3	-5	-3	4	-6
SASK	0	0	0	-3	4	-7	-3	5	-8
ALTA	0	0	0	-3	3	-6	-2	5	-7
BC	0	0	0	3	-1	4	7	-1	8

Table G14 (continued)

	All Low Income			All Middle Income			All High Income		
	In-migration	Out-migration	Net In-migration	In-migration	Out-migration	Net In-migration	In-migration	Out-migration	Net In-migration
NFLD	93	-109	202	-108	159	-267	-67	63	-130
PEI	55	-49	104	-32	52	-84	-21	21	-42
NS	28	-28	56	-37	61	-97	-37	37	-74
NB	53	-54	107	-110	140	-251	-72	69	-141
QUE	26	-37	63	-36	61	-97	-46	51	-97
ONT	-171	150	-321	228	-155	383	157	-132	289
MAN	-34	38	-72	64	-52	116	33	-32	66
SASK	-43	46	-89	110	-93	203	65	-58	123
ALTA	-42	33	-75	80	-18	98	34	-20	55
BC	13	-12	25	15	20	-5	-21	27	-48

[1] Parameter estimates from table E4. See also figures 8.4a to 8.4f.

[2] See table G15 for corresponding base case average annual migration flows.

Table G15
Base Case Predicted Average Annual Migration Flows by Age, Sex, and Income Class, Model 1, 1978–96[1]

	20–24 Years Old			25–44 Years Old			45–64 Years Old		
	In-migration	Out-migration	Net In-migration	In-migration	Out-migration	Net In-migration	In-migration	Out-migration	Net In-migration
Low Income Men									
NFLD	450	934	-483	382	554	-172	50	67	-17
PEI	372	457	-85	316	326	-9	53	51	2
NS	882	1227	-344	649	786	-138	95	91	4
NB	842	1119	-277	645	741	-96	90	92	-2
QUE	773	1276	-503	659	1012	-352	91	126	-36
ONT	2586	2334	252	1878	1643	235	229	226	3
MAN	927	1153	-226	747	954	-207	109	133	-24
SASK	795	1043	-249	717	860	-143	116	127	-12
ALTA	1956	848	1108	1174	901	273	145	130	14
BC	1558	751	807	1253	642	611	152	86	66
Low Income Women									
NFLD	588	1009	-421	760	1006	-246	97	128	-31
PEI	523	629	-106	631	654	-23	105	103	2
NS	1178	1404	-226	1371	1491	-120	204	204	0
NB	1139	1385	-246	1410	1477	-67	207	204	3
QUE	1014	1477	-463	1186	1666	-480	163	260	-97
ONT	3040	2751	289	3336	2913	423	458	458	0
MAN	1061	1350	-289	1229	1518	-289	187	232	-45
SASK	1006	1258	-253	1228	1438	-210	183	220	-37
ALTA	2083	1220	863	1888	1704	184	251	233	18
BC	1819	967	853	2015	1188	827	318	131	187

Table G15 (continued)

	20–24 Years Old			25–44 Years Old			45–64 Years Old		
	In-migration	Out-migration	Net In-migration	In-migration	Out-migration	Net In-migration	In-migration	Out-migration	Net In-migration
Middle Income Men									
NFLD	651	777	–126	931	1091	–160	123	150	–27
PEI	480	528	–48	811	851	–40	132	127	4
NS	1155	1163	–8	1661	1705	–44	254	235	20
NB	1127	1180	–53	1682	1739	–57	254	237	17
QUE	1057	1305	–249	1435	1990	–555	170	293	–123
ONT	2721	3022	–301	3697	3589	108	485	508	–23
MAN	1106	1386	–280	1405	1771	–366	204	247	–43
SASK	1080	1361	–281	1379	1662	–283	211	245	–34
ALTA	2123	1436	688	2162	1983	179	264	278	–14
BC	1775	1117	658	2453	1236	1218	358	136	222
Middle Income Women									
NFLD	367	408	–41	677	768	–91	96	100	–4
PEI	305	324	–19	694	683	11	124	110	14
NS	742	741	2	1466	1460	6	258	215	43
NB	709	712	–3	1453	1355	98	251	217	33
QUE	788	1147	–358	1437	2106	–669	180	401	–221
ONT	2111	2099	13	3883	3793	91	595	685	–89
MAN	786	1048	–262	1387	1828	–441	245	325	–80
SASK	811	933	–122	1352	1615	–263	241	296	–55
ALTA	1387	1240	148	2126	2262	–136	315	409	–94
BC	1406	763	644	2708	1314	1394	598	145	453

Table G15 (continued)

	20–24 Years Old			25–44 Years Old			45–64 Years Old		
	In-migration	Out-migration	Net In-migration	In-migration	Out-migration	Net In-migration	In-migration	Out-migration	Net In-migration
High Income Men									
NFLD	141	102	40	1203	1191	12	231	242	–11
PEI	68	60	7	915	891	24	246	215	31
NS	242	218	25	2513	2430	83	623	505	118
NB	229	199	30	2370	2282	88	571	491	80
QUE	300	286	14	2893	3657	–764	549	1150	–602
ONT	706	757	–51	6989	6886	103	1525	1689	–164
MAN	282	341	–59	2484	2937	–453	554	691	–137
SASK	356	376	–20	2492	2844	–352	546	661	–116
ALTA	535	644	–109	3956	4395	–439	744	980	–237
BC	522	399	123	4512	2813	1699	1421	383	1038
High Income Women									
NFLD	36	51	–15	252	333	–81	35	47	–12
PEI	21	19	2	259	240	18	57	48	10
NS	76	59	18	678	589	89	136	97	39
NB	62	65	–3	604	557	47	121	98	23
QUE	108	115	–7	962	1225	–263	138	316	–179
ONT	249	220	29	2082	2115	–32	366	428	–63
MAN	87	109	–22	665	836	–171	124	168	–44
SASK	96	116	–20	639	784	–145	126	161	–35
ALTA	153	192	–38	1055	1326	–271	170	269	–99
BC	163	105	58	1501	691	810	432	72	361

[1] Parameter estimates from table E4. These base case predicted flows correspond to table G14 and figures 8.4a to 8.4f.

Table G16
Equal Income Tax Rates, Average Annual Change in Inflows and Outflows, 1978–96

	NFLD	PEI	NS	NB	QUE	ONT	MAN	SASK	ALTA	BC
					Model 1[1]					
Low Income										
In-migration	58	-10	5	40	469	-402	-16	-41	-308	-104
Out-migration	-102	1	-30	-68	-641	289	-10	29	185	39
Net In-migration	160	-11	35	108	1110	-691	-5	-70	-494	-143
Middle Income										
In-migration	98	-11	24	85	857	-600	-9	-49	-433	-138
Out-migration	-114	5	-32	-92	-1019	567	-4	57	380	74
Net In-migration	212	-16	55	176	1876	-1167	-6	-105	-814	-212
High Income										
In-migration	42	-4	10	36	523	-373	4	-15	-207	-59
Out-migration	-42	3	-10	-35	-615	360	-5	20	239	40
Net In-migration	83	-7	20	71	1138	-733	9	-36	-446	-99
All Income Classes[2]										
In-migration	198	-25	39	161	1850	-1374	-21	-105	-949	-302
Out-migration	-258	9	-71	-194	-2274	1216	-19	106	805	153
Net In-migration	456	-34	111	355	4124	-2591	-2	-211	-1753	-455
					Model 2[1]					
Low Income										
In-migration	23	-4	2	16	187	-172	-7	-19	-133	-45
Out-migration	-44	0	-14	-29	-276	115	-5	9	75	15
Net In-migration	68	-4	15	45	463	-286	-3	-28	-208	-61
Middle Income										
In-migration	48	-6	10	41	410	-314	-6	-29	-229	-74
Out-migration	-60	2	-19	-47	-537	273	-3	23	186	34
Net In-migration	109	-8	29	88	948	-586	-4	-52	-415	-109

Table G16 (continued)

	NFLD	PEI	NS	NB	QUE	ONT	MAN	SASK	ALTA	BC
						Model 2[1]				
High Income										
In-migration	11	-1	2	10	138	-107	1	-5	-59	-18
Out-migration	-12	1	-3	-10	-177	95	-2	4	64	10
Net In-migration	23	-2	6	19	315	-203	2	-10	-123	-28
All Income Classes[2]										
In-migration	83	-11	14	66	735	-593	-13	-54	-421	-137
Out-migration	-117	3	-36	-86	-991	482	-9	37	325	60
Net In-migration	200	-14	50	152	1726	-1075	-4	-90	-746	-197

[1] Based on parameter estimates in table 6.2. See also figures 8.5a and 8.5b.
[2] Totals may differ from sum across income classes owing to rounding error.

Table G17
Equal Social Assistance Benefits, Average Annual Change in Inflows and Outflows, 1978–96

	NFLD	PEI	NS	NB	QUE	ONT	MAN	SASK	ALTA	BC
						Model 1[1]				
Low Income										
In-migration	-7	-6	-20	-10	-16	-53	-8	-4	-2	-16
Out-migration	-8	0	-2	-64	-51	-12	6	-9	-8	5
Net In-migration	1	-6	-19	54	35	-41	-14	5	7	-22
Middle Income										
In-migration	-13	-11	-35	-22	-35	-79	-10	-2	8	-29
Out-migration	-9	0	-3	-90	-79	-30	11	-15	-20	9
Net In-migration	-4	-11	-32	68	44	-49	-21	14	28	-38
High Income										
In-migration	-6	-4	-18	-12	-28	-48	-4	1	11	-18
Out-migration	-3	0	-1	-38	-50	-22	5	-8	-16	6
Net In-migration	-2	-5	-17	27	22	-26	-9	8	26	-24

Table G17 (continued)

	NFLD	PEI	NS	NB	QUE	ONT	MAN	SASK	ALTA	BC
All Income Classes[2]										
In-migration	-26	-21	-73	-44	-79	-181	-22	-5	17	-63
Out-migration	-20	1	-6	-193	-180	-65	21	-32	-44	20
Net In-migration	-5	-22	-68	149	101	-116	-44	27	61	-84
					Model 2[1]					
Low Income										
In-migration	-3	-2	-9	-4	-7	-22	-3	-1	0	-7
Out-migration	-3	0	-1	-27	-21	-5	2	-3	-4	2
Net In-migration	0	-3	-8	23	15	-17	-6	2	3	-9
Middle Income										
In-migration	-7	-5	-18	-11	-18	-41	-5	0	5	-15
Out-migration	-5	0	-1	-46	-41	-15	5	-7	-10	5
Net In-migration	-2	-6	-17	35	23	-26	-10	6	15	-19
High Income										
In-migration	-2	-1	-5	-3	-8	-13	-1	0	3	-5
Out-migration	-1	0	0	-11	-14	-6	1	-2	-4	2
Net In-migration	-1	-1	-5	8	6	-7	-2	2	7	-7
All Income Classes										
In-migration	-12	-9	-32	-18	-32	-76	-10	-2	8	-27
Out-migration	-9	1	-2	-84	-77	-26	9	-12	-18	9
Net In-migration	-3	-10	-30	66	44	-50	-18	11	26	-35

[1] Based on parameter estimates in table 6.2. See also figures 8.6a and 8.6b.
[2] Totals may differ from sum across income classes due to rounding error.

Table G18
Equal Spending on Education, Average Annual Change in Inflows and Outflows, 1978–96

	NFLD	PEI	NS	NB	QUE	ONT	MAN	SASK	ALTA	BC
Model 1[1]										
Low Income										
In-migration	-27	22	129	191	-158	-230	140	80	-390	304
Out-migration	46	-21	-134	-196	250	232	-155	-91	307	-177
Net In-migration	-73	43	263	387	-408	-461	295	170	-697	482
Middle Income										
In-migration	1	-1	-3	-4	3	5	-3	-2	7	-7
Out-migration	-1	0	3	4	-6	-6	3	2	-8	4
Net In-migration	1	-1	-6	-8	9	10	-6	-4	16	-11
High Income										
In-migration	5	-10	-61	-79	69	69	-65	-45	137	-183
Out-migration	-11	5	47	63	-121	-122	62	36	-207	85
Net In-migration	15	-15	-108	-142	190	191	-127	-81	345	-268
All Income Classes[2]										
In-migration	-22	11	65	108	-86	-157	72	33	-245	114
Out-migration	34	-16	-84	-130	124	103	-89	-53	91	-89
Net In-migration	-56	27	149	237	-210	-260	161	86	-337	202
Model 2[1]										
Low Income										
In-migration	-49	37	228	332	-260	-367	245	143	-637	545
Out-migration	76	-34	-220	-327	445	418	-256	-148	551	-288
Net In-migration	-125	71	448	659	-705	-785	501	291	-1189	833
Middle Income										
In-migration	-26	27	160	220	-157	-198	156	101	-337	378
Out-migration	37	-14	-123	-180	285	310	-157	-85	420	-170
Net In-migration	-62	41	283	400	-442	-508	312	186	-758	547

Table G18 (continued)

	NFLD	PEI	NS	NB	QUE	ONT	MAN	SASK	ALTA	BC
High Income										
In-migration	-2	3	21	27	-22	-21	22	16	-44	63
Out-migration	3	-1	-15	-20	42	43	-20	-11	71	-27
Net In-migration	-5	5	36	47	-64	-64	42	27	-115	90
All Income Classes[2]										
In-migration	-76	67	409	579	-439	-586	423	259	-1019	985
Out-migration	116	-50	-357	-527	772	771	-433	-245	1042	-486
Net In-migration	-192	118	767	1106	-1211	-1357	856	504	-2061	1471

[1] Based on parameter estimates in table 6.2. See also figures 8.7a and 8.7b.

[2] Totals may differ from sum across income classes owing to rounding error.

Table G19
Equal Federal Spending, Average Annual Change in Inflows and Outflows, 1978–96

	NFLD	PEI	NS	NB	QUE	ONT	MAN	SASK	ALTA	BC
					Model 1[1]					
Low Income										
In-migration	78	-177	-748	-112	394	48	-161	311	608	487
Out-migration	-41	214	1057	202	-440	158	282	-244	-289	-172
Net In-migration	119	-391	-1805	-314	834	-111	-443	554	897	660
Middle Income										
In-migration	195	-477	-1884	-302	1152	99	-429	827	1508	1350
Out-migration	-76	633	2804	515	-1135	480	800	-626	-894	-462
Net In-migration	271	-1110	-4688	-818	2287	-381	-1229	1453	2402	1812
High Income										
In-migration	103	-302	-1524	-269	1081	-226	-437	615	1086	1047
Out-migration	-42	359	2109	365	-1094	577	691	-499	-886	-406
Net In-migration	145	-661	-3633	-634	2176	-803	-1128	1114	1972	1453

Table G19 (continued)

	NFLD	PEI	NS	NB	QUE	ONT	MAN	SASK	ALTA	BC
All Income Classes[2]										
In-migration	376	-956	-4156	-683	2627	-79	-1027	1753	3202	2884
Out-migration	-159	1206	5970	1083	-2669	1215	1773	-1368	-2068	-1040
Net In-migration	536	-2162	-10126	-1766	5296	-1294	-2800	3122	5270	3924
					Model 2[1]					
Low Income										
In-migration	-91	431	1918	312	-595	141	375	-485	-951	-752
Out-migration	160	-317	-1498	-243	1043	-52	-425	554	668	413
Net In-migration	-252	748	3416	554	-1637	193	800	-1039	-1619	-1165
Middle Income										
In-migration	-49	272	1131	204	-392	116	232	-294	-535	-467
Out-migration	70	-210	-885	-140	627	-35	-276	329	481	257
Net In-migration	-119	482	2016	343	-1019	151	508	-623	-1016	-724
High Income										
In-migration	-2	10	52	10	-24	13	14	-14	-25	-24
Out-migration	2	-8	-44	-7	35	-9	-16	15	27	13
Net In-migration	-4	18	96	17	-59	21	29	-30	-52	-37
All Income Classes[2]										
In-migration	-142	713	3100	525	-1011	270	620	-794	-1511	-1243
Out-migration	233	-536	-2428	-389	1704	-96	-718	898	1176	683
Net In-migration	-374	1248	5528	914	-2715	365	1338	-1692	-2687	-1925

[1] Based on parameter estimates in table 6.2. See also figures 8.8a and 8.8b.

[2] Totals may differ from sum across income classes owing to rounding error.

Table G20 (continued)

	NFLD	PEI	NS	NB	QUE	ONT	MAN	SASK	ALTA	BC
High Income										
In-migration	24	134	-290	-86	562	-1662	-256	430	1738	-567
Out-migration	-32	-104	273	86	-651	1815	341	-386	-1678	362
Net In-migration	56	238	-563	-172	1213	-3477	-598	816	3416	-930
All Income Classes[2]										
In-migration	-167	1170	2300	669	240	-4748	236	653	2076	-1838
Out-migration	227	-868	-1808	-552	55	5250	-173	-620	-2035	1116
Net In-migration	-393	2038	4108	1221	185	-9998	408	1273	4111	-2954

[1] Based on parameter estimates in table 6.2. See also figures 8.9a and 8.9b.

[2] Totals may differ from sum across income classes due to rounding error.

Table G21
No Regional Variation in Average Weekly Earnings, Average Annual Change in Inflows and Outflows, 1978-96

	NFLD	PEI	NS	NB	QUE	ONT	MAN	SASK	ALTA	BC
					Model 1[1]					
Low Income										
In-migration	96	532	629	509	52	-872	530	581	-390	-580
Out-migration	62	-318	-361	-231	264	1350	-301	-394	472	545
Net In-migration	33	850	991	740	-212	-2222	831	975	-862	-1125
Middle Income										
In-migration	188	996	1170	966	163	-1261	930	1057	-460	-862
Out-migration	104	-504	-480	-305	489	2709	-469	-614	1007	951
Net In-migration	84	1500	1650	1272	-326	-3970	1399	1671	-1467	-1813
High Income										
In-migration	95	367	586	460	162	-574	501	576	-167	-417
Out-migration	24	-184	-242	-150	219	1407	-261	-324	585	516

Table G20
No Regional Variation in Policy, Average Annual Change in Inflows and Outflows, 1978–96

	NFLD	PEI	NS	NB	QUE	ONT	MAN	SASK	ALTA	BC
					Model 1¹					
Low Income										
In-migration	-151	-350	-781	-242	717	-492	22	471	1311	952
Out-migration	358	449	1191	379	-802	877	168	-296	-570	-298
Net In-migration	-509	-799	-1972	-621	1519	-1369	-146	767	1881	1250
Middle Income										
In-migration	-233	-747	-2151	-841	2221	-211	-337	1307	3798	1353
Out-migration	554	1149	3651	1328	-1933	1489	954	-812	-2029	-191
Net In-migration	-787	-1896	-5802	-2169	4154	-1700	-1291	2119	5827	1545
High Income										
In-migration	-106	-412	-1787	-671	1972	-891	-542	923	3319	622
Out-migration	233	554	2818	930	-1769	1726	1016	-635	-2434	-11
Net In-migration	-339	-966	-4605	-1600	3741	-2617	-1559	1559	5753	633
All Income Classes²										
In-migration	-490	-1509	-4719	-1754	4910	-1594	-858	2701	8428	2927
Out-migration	1145	2152	7659	2637	-4504	4092	2138	-1744	-5033	-500
Net In-migration	-1635	-3661	-12378	-4391	9414	-5686	-2996	4445	13462	3427
					Model 2¹					
Low Income										
In-migration	-119	595	1852	558	-489	-1263	426	-63	-555	-575
Out-migration	191	-424	-1458	-475	870	1362	-461	45	400	319
Net In-migration	-310	1019	3310	1033	-1359	-2625	887	-108	-955	-893
Middle Income										
In-migration	-72	441	738	197	167	-1823	66	286	892	-696
Out-migration	67	-340	-623	-162	-164	2074	-53	-279	-757	435
Net In-migration	-139	781	1362	360	330	-3897	119	566	1649	-1131

Table G21 (continued)

	NFLD	PEI	NS	NB	QUE	ONT	MAN	SASK	ALTA	BC
Net In-migration	71	551	828	610	-57	-1980	762	899	-752	-932
All Income Classes²										
In-migration	379	1895	2385	1935	377	-2706	1961	2214	-1017	-1859
Out-migration	190	-1007	-1083	-687	972	5466	-1032	-1332	2064	2011
Net In-migration	189	2901	3468	2622	-595	-8173	2992	3546	-3081	-3870

Model 2¹

	NFLD	PEI	NS	NB	QUE	ONT	MAN	SASK	ALTA	BC
Low Income										
In-migration	39	206	249	201	18	-366	208	235	-171	-250
Out-migration	22	-138	-158	-100	102	535	-130	-164	186	214
Net In-migration	17	344	407	301	-83	-901	338	399	-357	-464
Middle Income										
In-migration	93	461	556	460	74	-641	437	515	-247	-447
Out-migration	46	-267	-257	-162	229	1299	-247	-308	479	450
Net In-migration	48	728	813	622	-155	-1940	684	823	-726	-897
High Income										
In-migration	26	94	153	120	42	-162	130	153	-49	-119
Out-migration	6	-54	-71	-44	56	371	-75	-90	152	135
Net In-migration	20	147	223	164	-15	-533	205	243	-201	-254
All Income Classes²										
In-migration	158	761	958	781	134	-1170	775	903	-467	-817
Out-migration	73	-458	-486	-306	387	2204	-453	-562	817	799
Net In-migration	85	1220	1443	1087	-253	-3374	1227	1465	-1284	-1616

1 Based on parameter estimates in table 6.2. See also figures 8.10a and 8.10b.

2 Totals may differ from sum across income classes owing to rounding error.

Table G22
No Regional Variation in Probabilities, Average Annual Change in Migration Flows, 1978–96

	Model 1[1]			Model 2[1]			Model 1 (UI benefits unchanged)[2]		
	In-migration	Out-migration	Net In-migration	In-migration	Out-migration	Net In-migration	In-migration	Out-migration	Net In-migration
Low Income									
NFLD	8550	-2686	11237	1302	-1230	2532	8907	-2705	11612
PEI	2648	-881	3529	673	-467	1140	2783	-896	3679
NS	2431	-570	3001	647	-561	1209	2582	-585	3168
NB	6583	-2416	8999	1768	-1394	3162	6855	-2438	9292
QUE	2501	-1207	3708	1402	-1483	2885	2650	-1238	3888
ONT	-5296	12709	-18005	-2481	2802	-5283	-5367	13314	-18681
MAN	-788	2506	-3294	-207	311	-518	-803	2648	-3452
SASK	-1200	2992	-4192	-770	1066	-1836	-1252	3215	-4466
ALTA	-2358	3433	-5791	-2558	2282	-4840	-2375	3577	-5952
BC	1031	223	808	1035	-514	1549	1143	232	911
Middle Income									
NFLD	12592	-2455	15046	1439	-982	2420	13980	-2490	16471
PEI	4283	-1101	5384	882	-526	1408	4845	-1146	5990
NS	4007	-412	4419	1030	-627	1658	4601	-438	5039
NB	10499	-2727	13226	2255	-1427	3682	11605	-2774	14380
QUE	4070	-1389	5459	1906	-1846	3751	4656	-1465	6121
ONT	-6116	20194	-26310	-2608	3661	-6269	-6292	22671	-28963
MAN	-740	3666	-4406	-82	362	-444	-773	4186	-4960
SASK	-1323	4242	-5565	-839	1325	-2163	-1480	5030	-6510
ALTA	-2569	6190	-8759	-2891	3536	-6427	-2604	6844	-9448
BC	2076	571	1506	1737	-648	2385	2513	633	1880

Table G22 (continued)

	Model 1[1]			Model 2[1]			Model 1 (UI benefits unchanged)[2]		
	In-migration	Out-migration	Net In-migration	In-migration	Out-migration	Net In-migration	In-migration	Out-migration	Net In-migration
High Income									
NFLD	6483	-1393	7876	1194	-680	1874	6984	-1411	8395
PEI	2191	-610	2801	566	-301	868	2393	-629	3022
NS	2415	-335	2751	662	-302	964	2693	-362	3055
NB	6035	-1746	7781	1740	-980	2721	6497	-1777	8274
QUE	3308	-1527	4836	1771	-1635	3406	3673	-1611	5284
ONT	-4496	12327	-16822	-2205	3221	-5426	-4630	13473	-18103
MAN	-387	1776	-2162	-72	328	-401	-406	1974	-2379
SASK	-821	2270	-3091	-547	908	-1455	-919	2608	-3527
ALTA	-1583	4270	-5853	-1719	2740	-4459	-1603	4586	-6188
BC	1957	74	1884	1426	-482	1908	2242	74	2167
All Income Classes[3]									
NFLD	27625	-6534	34159	3935	-2891	6826	29871	-6607	36478
PEI	9121	-2593	11714	2121	-1294	3415	10021	-2671	12692
NS	8853	-1318	10171	2339	-1491	3830	9877	-1385	11262
NB	23117	-6889	30006	5764	-3801	9564	24957	-6989	31946
QUE	9880	-4123	14003	5078	-4964	10042	10979	-4314	15292
ONT	-15908	45229	-61137	-7294	9684	-16978	-16289	49458	-65747
MAN	-1915	7948	-9863	-362	1001	-1363	-1982	8809	-10791
SASK	-3344	9504	-12848	-2155	3298	-5454	-3650	10852	-14503
ALTA	-6510	13893	-20403	-7168	8558	-15726	-6582	15007	-21588
BC	5065	867	4198	4198	-1644	5842	5898	939	4959

[1] Based on parameter estimates from table 6.2. See also figures 8.11a and 8.11b.
[2] Based on parameter estimates in table 6.2.
[3] Totals may differ from sum across income classes due to rounding error.

Table G23
No Moving Costs, Average Annual Change in Migration Flows, 1978–96

	Model 1[1]			Model 2[1]		
	In-migration	Out-migration	Net In-migration	In-migration	Out-migration	Net In-migration
Low Income						
NFLD	105406	67180	38226	106092	67141	38951
PEI	58155	12436	45719	58013	12437	45575
NS	143575	84108	59467	143806	84069	59737
NB	135488	71953	63535	134717	71935	62783
QUE	92762	392524	-299762	92784	393237	-300453
ONT	315390	604774	-289384	312650	605457	-292806
MAN	158991	97208	61783	157985	97236	60749
SASK	151020	81455	69565	151593	81485	70108
ALTA	285983	173641	112342	288710	173369	115342
BC	326285	187776	138510	327922	187906	140016
Middle Income						
NFLD	184419	87019	97399	190061	87559	102502
PEI	113844	22061	91782	103795	22138	81657
NS	274790	131189	143601	257425	131941	125484
NB	255967	112428	143539	242043	112891	129152
QUE	171111	707760	-536649	163244	745518	-582274
ONT	543943	1105826	-561882	548955	1106139	-557185
MAN	269073	158938	110136	283007	158360	124647
SASK	259493	133441	126053	271233	133207	138026
ALTA	455840	324037	131803	512290	318267	194022
BC	591531	337313	254218	583609	339641	243968

Table G23 (continued)

	Model 1[1]			Model 2[1]		
	In-migration	Out-migration	Net In-migration	In-migration	Out-migration	Net In-migration
Low Income						
PEI	91335	10871	80464	90784	10867	79916
NS	288045	108696	179349	286747	108687	178060
NB	246114	79880	166235	244818	79861	164957
QUE	219726	688198	-468471	219700	689628	-469929
ONT	613499	1338858	-725359	609446	1340624	-731178
MAN	284367	142946	141421	283373	142972	140401
SASK	275560	125224	150336	278145	125242	152903
ALTA	478176	386715	91461	482682	386210	96472
BC	710850	441870	268980	713016	442421	270595
All Income Classes[2]						
NFLD	461075	209865	251210	469616	210361	259255
PEI	263334	45369	217965	252591	45443	207148
NS	706410	323993	382417	687977	324697	363280
NB	637568	264260	373308	621578	264686	356892
QUE	483599	1788481	-1304882	475728	1828384	-1352656
ONT	1472832	3049457	-1576625	1471050	3052220	-1581169
MAN	712431	399091	313339	724365	398568	325797
SASK	686074	340120	345954	700971	339934	361037
ALTA	1219999	884393	335605	1283682	877846	405836
BC	1628666	966958	661708	1624547	969968	654579

[1] Based on parameter estimates from table 6.2. See also figures 8.12a and 8.12b.
[2] Totals may differ from sum across income classes due to rounding error.

Notes

CHAPTER ONE

1 This is so despite the regional economic convergence that has occurred since 1945, which is still far from complete. On the nature of regional convergence in Canada, see for example Coulombe and Tremblay (2001).

2 A useful review of Canadian trends and developments in migration in the 1976 to 1986 period is found in Beaujot (1991). This is updated to include the 1986–96 period in the second edition (Beaujot and Kerr 2004).

3 As pointed out by Beaujot and Kerr (2004), Gilbert et al. (2001) find that these internal migration flows are especially important relative to international migration for growth and the decline of non-metropolitan areas. International migrants are disproportionately attracted to large urban areas.

4 We will ignore the CC line in figure 1.1 for the moment.

5 Sharpe, Arsenault, and Ershov have made a rough calculation of the gain in output due to interprovincial migration in Canada in the 1987–2006 period, assuming such an equilibrium occurs every period. If all migrants produce at the average productivity level (measured by output per worker) in the province of origin and destination at any point in time, they calculate that real output gains due to interprovincial migration were equal to $6,227 million (in 1997 dollars), or an average of 1.27 percent of total real output growth over the period (2007, 32).

6 CC can also be regarded as representing the difference between total compensation in region S and that in region D, a difference assumed to be positive because of the receipt of fiscal benefits in S that are greater than those received by a person residing in region D. Only the differential between the two regions in net public sector benefits matters.

7 Another diagram that explicitly shows net fiscal benefits in both regions, rather than just a line reflecting the policy differential, is found in Wilson (2003, 387).

8 In fact, people have been leaving the poorer provinces like Newfoundland to go to central Canada for decades, at least prior to the quite recent development of offshore oil. But this net outflow, in Courchene's view, is (or was) not large enough.

9 For a recent contribution to this literature, which emphasizes the importance of interregional mobility, see Boadway and Tremblay (2010).

10 In addition, one may note that it has been argued that the equalization system helps to support the proper functioning of the federal system of government itself, by insuring that the poorer provinces can continually challenge the federal government (see Breton 1996).

11 See Usher (1995) concerning the resulting complexities and for a negative assessment of the extent to which the Canadian equalization system may be successful in accomplishing this task.

12 Moreover, the economic benefit – measured by the area 123 in figure 1.1 – must be greater than the full cost of taxation required to finance the equalization payments. A truly complete assessment of the efficiency of grants must also allow for the inevitable moral hazard created by all subsidy programs, in this case the incentive for provinces to strategize against the equalization program formulas, which lead to greater payments (to some extent) if a province reduces its tax effort. On the latter issue, see, for example, Smart (1998) and Dahlby (2008, chapter 9) and the references cited therein.

13 Both Watson (1986) and Wilson (2003) have made benefit-cost calculations concerning the potential for efficiency gains from implementation of the Canadian equalization system. Watson uses the Winer-Gauthier (1982a) estimates of the migration effects of setting equalization in 1977 to its 1971 level, while Wilson combines the Winer-Gauthier estimates with the Mills, Percy, and Wilson (1983) estimates of a long-run adjustment parameter. The model used by Watson extrapolates from the effect on year-to-year changes in migration, while Wilson makes an estimate of the long-run effects using a stock adjustment model of migration, in which the flow of migrants every year is assumed to be a fixed proportion of the stock of potential migrants in each province in each year. Not surprisingly, Wilson's estimates of the benefit-cost ratio due to equalization, after allowing for the efficiency cost of taxation to finance the grants, is about 1.6, which is higher than the 0.02 figure arrived at by Watson. The difference in the estimates depends heavily on the stock-adjustment coefficient used to compute the long-run migration flow. We have more to say about predicting migration flows in the following chapters. But it can be noted here that interregional migration flows are highly variable, and we think that estimating a long-run model, which depends on lifetime migration patterns, is a difficult enterprise. Nonetheless, the general point Wilson makes seems to us valid: a substantial long-run effect may arise even if year-to-year changes in migration patterns as a result of government policy are modest.

14 Wellisch (2000, chapters 6 and 7) provides a detailed technical analysis of the argument, along with associated references to the literature.

15 Moreover, if scale or other factors require that one government can efficiently provide public services with a larger public sector, governments will voluntarily cooperate to transfer resources between them so that the kind of inefficient migration we discussed earlier is prevented. Otherwise, welfare for the representative citizen, both at home and in other places, will be lower than it could be.

16 The Salmon (1987a,b) mechanism of yard stick intergovernmental competition (see also Besley and Case 1995) – the tendency of citizens to look at what is going on in other jurisdictions and to hold their own representatives accountable for inferior public sector performance – may reduce the importance of migration costs in this second context.

17 See Kreuger and Mueller (2010) for a recent study of the relationship between job search and unemployment insurance in the United States and for references to the literature on job search.

18 Grady and Macmillan (2007) provide further background concerning the issue of regulatory barriers in Canada and the Agreement on Internal Trade. See also the discussion in Harris and Schmidt (2005) concerning labour market integration in the NAFTA region.

19 It is worth pointing out here that the task of a central government that wishes to protect and enhance the common labour (and any other) market in a federal country is not an easy one. A difficult problem it must face is that federal policies that offset the adverse economic consequences of provincial policies also limit the degree of autonomy effectively exercised by those governments. The adverse consequences of fiscal differentials that result from provincial government policies can be offset by federal transfers of various kinds that, when appropriately computed, even out net fiscal benefits across the country. From the point of view of a provincial government, however, this policy amounts to the negation of its right and responsibility to differentiate itself within the federal system. In a similar manner, federal actions of one sort or another that offset or reduce restrictive labour market regulations infringe on the ability of lower levels of government to exercise authority over internal (e.g., provincial) economies. The objections in the Québec government's Commission on Fiscal Imbalance (2002) – the Seguin Report – to almost all federal economic involvement in the province of Québec can be understood in this context. Thus there are both benefits and costs to central government action to deal with provincial policies that presently distort the allocation of labour. The benefits of appropriate federal policies stem from the gain in average earned income that results from a more efficient national allocation of labour, as well as from a corresponding reduction in regional disparities. The cost of policies that limit or offset autonomous provincial regulation of labour markets are more difficult to assess even in qualitative terms. At some point, the virtues of competitive federalism pointed to by Breton and Scott (1982) and Breton (1996) will be attenuated. The question of how best to balance these benefits and costs remains unanswered in economic theory.

CHAPTER TWO

1 We set aside here the role of labour market regulations, since measures of such regulations that can be used in our statistical analysis do not exist.

2 Details regarding data sources and construction of these variables are provided in the first section of appendix A.

3 Although provincial differences in average incomes may influence our income tax measure, the rate structure of the federal personal income tax does not differentiate between individuals based on their province of residence.

4 In all of these calculations we use unweighted means and/or standard deviations. While measures weighted by population or labour force shares might provide a more accurate picture of provincial differences in overall welfare, from the point of view of the individual migrant who is concerned only about herself, the unweighted values provide a more accurate picture of the incentives to migrate.

5 There is a structural break in the first three variables in 1996, due to a change in Statistics Canada's definition of the government sector. Both the Financial Management System and Provincial Economic Accounts data were revised by Statistics Canada as part of a general revision of the national accounts in 1997, and the new data were pushed back to 1992. The new data differ from the old in some cases. The old data series are available until 1995. We are indebted to Dan Finnerty for assistance in constructing data for 1996 on the old basis.

6 See chapter 5 and appendix C for more details.

CHAPTER THREE

1 Representative examples of that work can be found in papers cited by Cebula (1979, 1980), Goss and Paul (1990), Charney (1993), Dowding, John, and Biggs (1994), Antolin and Bover (1997), Blank (1998), Tervo (2000), Rhode and Strumpf (2002), Bailey (2005), Boerner and Uebelmesser (2007), Banzhaf and Walsh (2008) and Sasser (2010), among many, many others.

2 Winer and Gauthier also estimate linear models similar to Courchene's in the first part of their study in an attempt to reproduce Courchene's results. Although these results are included in table 3.1, only their conditional logit results are discussed here.

3 In early applications, little distinction was made between the terms "conditional logit model" and "multinomial logit model." Today the term "multinomial logit model" is used to refer to a model in which the explanatory variables are characteristics of individuals, not the alternatives under consideration as in the conditional logit formulation, and the parameters $\beta_1, ..., \beta_K$ vary across alternatives. Hybrid models are also possible. For further details regarding the two models see Greene (2000).

4 The error term in (3.4) is interpreted as an approximation error. See Day (1989) for further details.

5 As noted earlier, it is impossible in linear models to include the attributes of all potential destinations. Foot and Milne (1984) get around this problem by defining "all other provinces" versions of each explanatory variable that are distance-weighted aggregates of the values for nine provinces.

6 Day includes the provincial unemployment rate as a separate explanatory variable in her estimating equations and finds that a higher unemployment rate in province i, holding all else equal, will significantly reduce in-migration to province i.

7 Their measure of expected before-tax income is the ratio of the average employ-ment income of migrants from i to j divided by the average employment income of stayers in province i, lagged one period, multiplied by the average employment income of stayers in province j in the current year.

8 Transfer payments are less highly correlated with income than are income tax pay-ments, and they thus pose less of a problem from an econometric point of view.

9 Liaw and Ledent do not provide a precise definition of their government transfers variable, but the associated discussion suggests that they used transfers to persons rather than intergovernmental transfers.

10 Of course, a high correlation between unemployment rates and unemployment insurance variables when the two are entered separately would also be problematic from an econometric point of view.

11 A time series is said to be stationary if its mean and variance are constant and if the correlations between observations at different points in time depend only on how far apart the two observations are. Regression of nonstationary variables on each other will yield unreliable results unless appropriate estimation and modelling techniques are used.

12 Although on page 175 of their paper Basher and Fachin describe their federal transfers variable as including intergovernmental transfers such as equalization as well as transfers to persons, their list of data sources on page 174 says otherwise. In a personal communication with us Syed Basher has confirmed that the correct definition of the variable is the one on page 174.

13 The Basher and Fachin study did not include age as an explanatory factor, so it can-not consider the hypothesis that the aging of the population over the sample period is also partly responsible for the downward trend in interprovincial migration rates.

14 Note that they do not model migration rates or probabilities like most other authors. Their dependent variable is the log of the number of migrants from prov-ince i to province j in year t.

15 Some regional convergence also appears to characterize the United States and Japanese experience (Barro and Sala-i-Martin 1992).

16 Vanderkamp (1988) and Rosenbluth (1996) actually estimate all the equations of their model simultaneously.

17 It may be interesting to note that compared to the tax data used by Winer and Gauthier, and in this book, the SLID appears to have thinner tails (the lowest- and highest-income individuals are under-represented). This is likely because, unlike tax forms, the survey on which the SLID is based is voluntary.

18 This problem has come to be known in the econometric literature as the Moulton effect. It can be traced to a combination of groupwise heteroskedasticity and cor-relations between the model error terms of individuals within the same group, a problem that is referred to as "clustering." See Angrist and Pischke (2009, chapter 8) for a relatively accessible discussion of this issue.

19 Note that Shaw's fiscal variables are defined on a provincial basis. Dion and Coulombe (2008) provide a more recent study of inter-CMA migration but do not include any fiscal variables in their model.

20 Recall that the probability of migrating lies between zero and one.

21 Finnie also estimates a model that includes a social assistance dummy variable, but owing to data limitations this model could be estimated only for the period 1992–95. In this model receipt of unemployment insurance benefits significantly increases the mobility of only four age-sex groups. Receipt of social assistance benefits also significantly increases the mobility of four age-sex groups.

22 "Moderate" attachment to the labour market in Audas and McDonald corresponds to our state 2 (strongly attached), while their "weak" attachment state corresponds to our state 3 (weakly attached). "Strong" attachment in Audas and McDonald corresponds to our state 1 (employed all year).

23 On the labour market attachment of frequent unemployment insurance claimants, see also Schwartz et al. (2001).

24 Audas and McDonald use industry dummies as their instruments but do not offer any defense for this choice. These instruments are likely to be weak at best, though we do not have obvious alternatives to suggest.

25 While Ostrovsky, Hou, and Picot (2008) do consider destination choice, they limit the choice of options to not moving, moving to Alberta, and moving to another province.

26 Annual rates of net in-migration to the ten provinces ranged in absolute value from 0.01 percent to 2.04 percent during the 1971–2009 period. During the same period, rates of in-migration ranged from 0.26 percent to 4.99 percent, and rates of out-migration ranged from 0.33 percent to 4.21 percent. (Migration rates were calculated using data from CANSIM Tables 510001 and 510018, retrieved on 26 October 2010.)

27 Note that this change also makes it possible for part-time workers to more easily add together experience from different part-time jobs.

CHAPTER FOUR

1 In fact, in certain years of high unemployment in the provinces of Newfoundland, Prince Edward Island, and New Brunswick, the number of people receiving unemployment insurance benefits exceeds the number of people counted as unemployed by the Labour Force Survey by substantial amounts. Our treatment of unemployment insurance is intended to be robust with respect to this measurement issue.

2 The discussion that follows is in terms of weeks, not hours, of work because our sample period ends prior to the 1996 reform that redefined qualifying employment in terms of hours.

3 Since April 1993, individuals who quit without "just cause," are fired, or refuse to accept suitable employment have been ineligible for benefits. Prior to April 1993, such individuals were eligible for benefits but were subjected to a penalty in the form of a reduction in their weeks of benefits.

4 There is a two-week waiting period for unemployment insurance, and those fully employed do not receive social assistance.

5 In particular locations it may be possible for some individuals to receive limited forms of social assistance while employed. (This is so under the the federal working income tax (WITB) program which began in 2007, which is outside of our sample period). We simplify a complicated situation by assuming that social assistance and work are mutually exclusive. Relaxing this assumption is a difficult task in practice that requires data concerning the work-related income of social assistance recipients. We do not think that variation across provinces in the conditions concerning work and receipt of social assistance is likely to be a significant determinant of the interprovincial migration decisions of tax filers, though one can never be sure without actually doing the required empirical work. In any event, we must leave this extension of the model for the future.

6 In addition to allowing for the existence of a two-week waiting period for receipt of unemployment insurance, the value 50 also allows us to work with a logarithmic utility function in which leisure time in state 1 enters as the term $\log(T - X)$, where $T = 52$ and X is weeks of work in state 1.

7 The log-linear functional form that we choose for the direct utility function would be undefined in state 1 if this state did not include any leisure time.

8 A model in which migration and labour supply decisions and the aggregate state of the labour market in each location are all simultaneously determined would be desirable. Such models have, to our knowledge, not yet been estimated because of their complexity and associated data requirements (but see Rosenbluth 1996).

9 The migration data are defined so that international migrants and those tax filers moving to or from northern territories are excluded. See chapter 5 and appendix B.

10 It may be of some interest to note the difference between (4.7) and the corresponding indirect utility function when the direct utility function is assumed to be of the linear expenditure (LES) type. In the LES case, the nominal value of the subsistence expenditure bundle is subtracted from each of the INC (income) terms within the first set of square brackets; the subsistence leisure bundle is subtracted from each of the leisure terms in round brackets within the second set of square brackets; and the subsistence bundles for the real fiscal variables and the amenities A are subtracted from (each component of) F and A respectively. The presence of these unknown subsistence bundles would substantially complicate the problem of empirical implementation of the model, and this complication is avoided by proceeding as we have.

11 In one specific application of the model in chapter 8, we will explicitly allow for calculation by prospective migrants of the present value of future earnings in each location. This does not alter the nature of our results reported there, and this estimation is referred to in the footnotes in that chapter.

CHAPTER FIVE

1 Beginning with the 1991 Census, respondents have also been asked where they lived one year previously.

2 Immigrants will "reappear" in the data in the year after they have arrived in Canada if they file a personal income tax form.

3 See appendix B for further details regarding the tuition fee amounts used.

4 The condition that we use to eliminate students will not eliminate all students, since many transfer the tuition deduction to a parent.

5 In 1995, for example, median total income for all tax filers in our sample of people aged 20–64 is about $24,142 or about 62.5 percent of the median "family and unattached individuals" income of $37,130 reported in Statistics Canada publication S.C. 13–207. The lower median in the tax data in part reflects the fact that since families do not file joint tax returns in Canada, the income of each spouse is reported on separate tax forms. As a result, the upper income of our lowest income group in 1995 is somewhat lower than the level of 0.5 times median family income that is sometimes used to distinguish between those who are poor and those who are not. The 0.625 ratio does not apply for all years in our sample, in part because the definition of total income for tax purposes changes over time. However, median total income in the tax files is consistently lower than median family income.

6 There are, for example, very few high-income, younger women moving from Prince Edward Island to Saskatchewan in any year.

7 Since the migration data are based on individual tax files, strict confidentiality conditions apply even to the release of grouped data. These conditions require that cells containing less than a specified number of individuals must be written to zero before the data can be released to the public. Additional cells that do not actually violate the confidentiality conditions might also be written to zero if they could be used to make inferences about the true contents of other empty cells when combined with row and column totals.

8 To be completely accurate, we never actually saw these tapes, let alone individual tax files. All processing of our computer programs was remote and only aggregated statistical results were available to us.

9 Thus a scaled flow is set to zero whenever the scaled value of an origin-destination flow is less than one.

10 Further details regarding the construction of the migration data are provided in appendix B.

11 Interprovincial migration estimates by age, sex, province of origin, and province of destination for the period 1977–96 were purchased from the Demography Division of Statistics Canada.

12 This phenomenon appears to be less evident in the highest-income group, in our data set. Although this income group does experience a decrease in the number of out-migrants in 1982, the subsequent increase in 1983 is extremely small.

13 We are unable to explain the large spikes in in- and out-migration rates for British Columbia in the mid- to late 1980s. In the case of out-migration, the spike is no doubt related to the jump in total outflows from British Columbia observed in figure 5.10.

14 We would like to thank Tim Sargent and Marcel Bédard for their advice about the data in this section.

15 For a more complete summary of the many changes to Canada's unemployment system over this period, see Dingledine et al. (1995) or Lin (1998).

16 Note that the provincial tax rate may be greater or less than the federal rate of abatement.

17 For the years 1966–71, the income thresholds for Quebec are the same as the federal ones, but the Quebec marginal rates differ. After 1971, both the marginal rates and the income thresholds differ.

18 Once again we look at the value of INCOME for stayers only. Recall that if moving costs were included, the effect would be to reduce the value of INCOME in the potential migrant's province of destination.

19 See appendix A for details regarding data sources.

20 Recall that the standard deviation of the natural log of each per capita government spending variable is almost identical to the coefficient of variation of the variable computed before taking logs. The latter is plotted in chapter 2.

CHAPTER SIX

1 Since the probabilities by definition lie between 0 and 1, the coefficient of variation of the transformed series is greater than that of the untransformed series, which may give the logarithmic series a greater influence on the estimates.

2 The values of the likelihood ratio test statistics for the three income classes respectively are 22,074, 32,836, and 13,044 for Model 1, and 16,076, 8,956, and 6,390 for Model 2.

3 It is important to note that DSTAY is *not* an indicator of the staying choice. For each individual (or more accurately in our case, for each group, where groups are defined by year, province of origin, and personal characteristics), DSTAY is one for the staying option and zero for other options regardless of the choice that the individual actually makes. Were data available on the determinants of the fixed costs of moving, it would be possible to model them in a more sophisticated manner.

4 Note that we consider the staying option to be a destination as well. Thus the variable NFLD takes on the value 1 for flows from Newfoundland to Newfoundland (the staying option), and the value 0 for flows from Newfoundland to all other provinces. The other eight provincial dummies are constructed in the same fashion.

5 This result follows from the first-order conditions for maximizing the log-likelihood function after alternative-specific constants have been added to the model. We also note here that since variation across provinces in the quality or character of the health, education, and other components of public sectors may exist and may not be revealed by fiscal aggregates, we also tried interacting each public spending variable with an alternative-specific constant. These additional interactive, alternative-specific variables did not improve the results concerning the

role of public spending or the results as a whole, and they are omitted from the following discussion.

6 The TI files do indicate the language in which tax forms were completed. However, defining groups on the basis of language as well as income class, age, and sex would have resulted in even more empty cells in the mobility matrix for each year.

7 This includes responses to Bill 101 (1977), which placed restrictions on the ability of parents to choose the language of instruction of their children in public schools.

8 These results conflict with those of Day (1992), who included per capita government spending on health, education, social services, and all other goods in a conditional logit model of aggregate interprovincial migration in Canada from 1961 to 1981. She found that per capita government spending on both health and education had a positive effect on in-migration, while the effect of spending on social services was negative. The effect of other spending was not statistically significant in most cases. One should note that the sample considered here, 1974–1996, involves quite a different pattern of public expenditure than in the spending heydays of the 1960s and 1970s. In particular, there were large swings in public spending in the 1980s and 1990s. Moreover, it is possible that aggregate spending on social services may act to some extent as a proxy for employment prospects in Day's work (since only a single aggregate unemployment rate was included), while here social assistance to individuals is explicitly modelled and included in the variable *INCOME*.

9 See appendix E for a complete correlation matrix.

10 All the potential specifications of the probabilities we tested suffered from similar collinearity problems. Results for alternative specifications including *P234* (the sum of *P2*, *P3*, and *P4*) and *LP2*, *LP3*, and *LP4*, estimated using the 1974–96 data for three income classes, can be found in Day and Winer (2001). In these alternative specifications, the coefficient of *INCOME* is always positive.

11 As table E1 of appendix E indicates, *DSTAY* and *DISTANCE* are also highly correlated, but primarily with each other. For this reason we will vary them together in the simulations in chapter 8 that are designed to investigate the quantitative importance of moving costs.

12 The correlation coefficients for each origin-destination pair for the two models can be found in table E2 of appendix E.

13 Although it has become increasingly common for women to postpone child bearing till after age 35, during the majority of years included in the sample such behaviour would have been less common.

14 For the interested reader, additional models are discussed in Day and Winer (2001).

CHAPTER SEVEN

1 Detailed tables showing the average marginal effect on in-, out-, and net in-migration to every province of a change in the value of a specific variable in province *j*

are provided in the technical report on which the book is based. See appendix G in Day and Winer (2001).

2 Changing the policy parameter may influence migration in the opposite direction to a change in wages. In this case, the entry in tables 7.3 and 7.4 will have a negative sign in front of it.

3 We recall that social assistance payments in the calculations are for a single parent with two children, which is the only series available on a consistent basis for all province and years in the sample.

4 The calculation of the corresponding tax rate for Quebec is discussed in the section "After-Tax Incomes Net of Moving Costs" of chapter 5 and in appendix F.

CHAPTER EIGHT

1 More detailed results can be found in table G12

2 In Winer and Gauthier (1982a), "low income" means having an income of $10,000 or less, in 1977 constant dollars. Since we found the median total income of tax filers to be $11,024 in 1977, Winer and Gauthier's low-income (or PNTP) class would include some individuals included in our middle-income group.

3 More detailed results corresponding to figures 8.3a, 8.3b, and 8.3c can be found in table G13 of appendix G.

4 More detailed results can be found in table G14. The corresponding base case in migration flows by age, sex, and income class can be found in table G15.

5 More detailed results can be found in table G16.

6 See also appendix G, table G17

7 Detailed results are in table G18.

8 For detailed results, see table G19.

9 More detailed results can be found in table G20.

10 Detailed results are in table G21.

11 More detailed results can be found in table G22.

12 These results are, however, reported in the last three columns of table G22.

13 More detailed results can be found in table G23.

14 Note that the sum over provinces of gross inflows must equal the sum over provinces of gross outflows, so looking at in-migration instead would yield exactly the same results.

15 This figure is based on the ex ante (i.e., before migration) number of Quebec tax filers in our sample at the beginning of 1976.

16 We also computed the preceding simulations using the intertemporal model introduced at the end of chapter 4, using both the 10 percent sample and the 100 percent sample. We use that model here, and not for the policy simulations discussed earlier, because of the difficulty in those simulations of constructing counterfactual incomes, which the extraordinary event simulations do not require. For both events in Quebec and for both samples, the numbers produced using the intertemporal

model are about the same as those reported in table 8.4. We have therefore left the precise results out of the table to make it more compact. These results can be found in table 16a of our technical report (Day and Winer 2001).

17 We are grateful to Michael Hatfield of Human Resources Development Canada for suggesting this explanation.

CHAPTER NINE

1 The connection is of course that the lower-income class is likely to contain a high proportion of individuals who are not strongly attached to the labour force (and vice versa), though direct evidence on the matter is missing from our data.

2 Wilson (2003) has proposed a model of this sort.

3 We mean one in which there is some well-defined connection between an individual's migration decision today and those that he or she makes in the following years of their life.

APPENDIX B

1 While 100 percent tapes for the years 1970–73 exist, record layouts for these years can no longer be found, despite intensive efforts to locate them.

2 There are several ways of assigning location using tax files. In addition to the province of residence code, one could use the province to which a filer's taxes are assigned (tax province), or the postal code. The latter is not always available, and may be unreliable when a commercial tax preparation firm is involved. The tax province code is not directly based on the question answered by the tax payer in every case (although use of this code and of residence province appear to yield almost the same migration flows). Province of residence is the most desirable basis upon which to assign location because it is the result of an answer by the tax filer to an easily understood question.

3 On the 1996 tax return, the tax filer reports his or her province of residence on 31 December 1996. On the 1995 return, province of residence on 31 December 1995 is reported. If the two addresses are different, the tax filer has changed his or her province of residence sometime between 1 January 1996 and the end of the same year.

APPENDIX C

1 We would like to thank Tim Sargent and Marcel Bédard for their advice and help in assembling these data.

2 Seasonal benefits can be ignored in the calculation of MXYR for the period prior to the 1971 revisions, since an individual who qualified for seasonal benefits but not regular benefits would be unlikely to be entitled to enough weeks of benefits to satisfy the definition of MXYR.

Bibliography

Afxentiou, P.C., and A. Serletis. 1998. "Convergence across Canadian Provinces." *Canadian Journal of Regional Science* 21: 11–26.

American Automobile Association. 1992. *AAA Road Atlas.*

Angrist, Joshua D., and Jörn-Steffen Pischke. 2009. *Mostly Harmless Econometrics: An Empiricist's Companion.* Princeton: Princeton University Press.

Antolin, Pablo, and Olympia Bover. 1997. "Regional Migration in Spain: The Effect of Personal Characteristics and of Unemployment, Wage and House Price Differentials Using Pooled Cross-sections." *Oxford Bulletin of Economics and Statistics* 59 (2): 215–35.

Audas, Rick, and James Ted McDonald. 2003. "Employment Insurance and Geographic Mobility: Evidence from the SLID." Ottawa: SRDC Working Paper Series 03-03, April.

Bailey, M.A. 2005. "Welfare and the Multifaceted Decision to Move." *Amercian Political Science Review* 99 (1): 125–35.

Bakhshi, Samira, Mohammad Shakeri, M. Rose Olfert, Mark D. Partridge, and Simon Weseen. 2009. "Do Local Residents Value Federal Transfers? Evidence from Interprovincial Migration in Canada." *Public Finance Review* 37(3): 235–68.

Banzhaf, H. Spencer, and Randall P. Walsh. 2008. "Do People Vote with Their Feet? An Empirical Test of Tiebout's Mechanism." *American Economic Review* 98(3): 843–63.

Barro, Robert J., and Xavier Sala-i-Martin. 1992. "Regional Growth and Migration: A Japan-United States Comparison." *Journal of the Japanese and International Economies* 6: 312–46.

Basher, Syed A., and Stefano Fachin. 2008. "The Long-Term Decline of Internal Migration in Canada: The Case of Ontario." *Letters in Spatial and Resource Sciences* 1 (2): 171–81.

Beaujot, Roderic. 1991. *Population Change in Canada: The Challenges of Policy Adaptation.* Toronto: McClelland and Stewart.

Beaujot, Roderic, and Don Kerr. 2004. *Population Change in Canada*. 2d ed. Don Mills, ON: Oxford University Press.

Bélanger, Alain. 2002. *Report on the Demographic Situation in Canada 2001*. Ottawa: Statistics Canada, Catalogue no. 91–209.

Benarroch, Michael, and Hugh Grant. 2004. "The Interprovincial Migration of Canadian Physicians: Does Income Matter?" *Applied Economics* 36 (20): 2335–45.

Besley, Timothy, and Anne Case. 1995. "Does Electoral Accountability Affect Economic Policy Choices? Evidence from Gubernatorial Term Limits." *Quarterly Journal of Economics* 110(3): 769–98.

Blanchflower, David G., and Andrew J. Oswald. 1994. *The Wage Curve*. Cambridge, MA: MIT Press.

Blank, Rebecca M. 1988. "The Effect of Welfare and Wage Levels on the Location Decisions of Female-Headed Households." *Journal of Urban Economics* 24 (2): 186–211.

Boadway, Robin, and Frank Flatters. 1982a. *Equalization in a Federal State: An Economic Analysis*. Ottawa: Supply and Services Canada for the Economic Council of Canada.

– 1982b. "Efficiency and Equalization Payments in a Federal System of Government: A Synthesis and Extension of Recent Results." *Canadian Journal of Economics* 15(4): 613–33.

Boadway, Robin, and A.G. Green. 1981. "The Economic Implications of Migration to Newfoundland." Discussion Paper 189. Ottawa: Economic Council of Canada.

Boadway, Robin, and Jean-Francois Tremblay. 2010. "Mobility and Fiscal Imbalance." *National Tax Journal* 63 (4, part 2): 1023–54.

Boerner, Kira, and Silke Uebelmesser. 2007. "Migration and the Welfare State: The Economic Power of the Non-Voter?" *International Tax and Public Finance* 14 (1): 93–111.

Bolduc, Denis, Bernard Fortin, and Marc-André Fournier. 1996. "The Effect of Incentive Policies on the Practice Location of Doctors: A Multinomial Probit Analysis." *Journal of Labor Economics* 14 (4): 703–32.

Breton, Albert. 1996. *Competitive Governments: An Economic Theory of Politics and Public Finance*. New York: Cambridge University Press.

Breton, Albert, and Angela Fraschini. 2007. "Competitive Governments, Globalization, and Equalization Grants." *Public Finance Review* 35 (4): 463–79.

Breton, Albert, and Anthony Scott. 1982. *The Economic Constitution of Federal States*. Toronto: University of Toronto Press.

Cahill, Ian. 1993. "The Effect of Unemployment Insurance on the Geographic Mobility of Labour in Canada." Ottawa: Program and Policy Analysis, Employment and Immigration Canada.

Canadian Tax Foundation. 1966–95. *The National Finances*. Toronto: Canadian Tax Foundation.

– 1996–97. *The Finances of the Nation.* Toronto: Canadian Tax Foundation.

*Canadian Unemployment Insurance Legislation and Relevant Employment Legisla-
tion.* 1977. 6th ed. Don Mills, ON: CCH Canadian Limited.

Cebula, Richard J. 1979. "A Survey of the Literature on the Migration Impact of
State and Local Government Policies." *Public Finance* 34 (1): 69–84.

– 1980. "Voting with One's Feet: A Critique of the Evidence." *Regional Science
and Urban Economics* 10 (1): 91–107.

Charney, Alberta H. 1993. "Migration and the Public Sector: A Survey." *Regional
Studies* 27 (4): 313–26.

Christofides, Louis, and Chris McKenna. 1995. "Employment Patterns and
Unemployment Insurance." UI Evaluation Brief #7, May. Ottawa: Human
Resources Development Canada.

Cochrane, John H. 1991. "A Simple Test of Consumption Insurance." *Journal of
Political Economy* 99(5): 957–76.

Collins, Kirk A. 2008. "The 'Taxing' Issue of Interprovincial and Cross-Border
Migration." *Canadian Public Policy* 34(4). 481–99.

Commission on Fiscal Imbalance. 2002. *A New Division of Canada's Financial
Resources.* Québec. (The Seguin Report).

Corak, Miles. 1996. "Unemployment Insurance and Canada-US Unemployment
Rates." *Policy Options* July–August.

Coulombe, Serge. 2006. "Internal Migration, Asymmetric Shocks, and Interprovincial Economic Adjustments in Canada." *International Regional Science Review*
29 (2): 199–223.

Coulombe, Serge, and Kathleen M. Day. 1999. "Economic Growth and Regional
Income Disparities in Canada and the Northern United States." *Canadian Public
Policy* 25 (2): 155–78.

Coulombe, Serge, and Frank Lee. 1995. "Regional Productivity Convergence in
Canada." *Canadian Journal of Regional Science* 18 (1): 39–56.

Coulombe, Serge, and Jean-François Tremblay. 2001. "Human Capital and
Regional Convergence in Canada." *Journal of Economic Studies* 28 (3), 154–80.

Courchene, Thomas J. 1970. "Interprovincial Migration and Economic Adjustment." *Canadian Journal of Economics* 3 (4): 550–76.

– 1978. "The Transfer System and Regional Disparities: A Critique of the Status
Quo." In *Canadian Federation at the Crossroads: The Search for a Federal-
Provincial Balance,* ed. Michael Walker. Vancouver: The Fraser Institute, 145–86.

– 2006. "Energy Prices, Equalization and Canadian Federalism: Comparing Canada's Energy Price Shocks." *Queen's Law Journal* 31 (2): 644–96.

Cousineau, Jean-Michel, and François Vaillancourt. 2001. "Regional Disparities,
Mobility and Labour Markets in Canada." In *Adapting Public Policy to a
Labour Market in Transition,* eds. W. Craig Riddell and France St.-Hilaire.
Montreal: Institute for Research on Public Policy, 143–74.

Dahlby, Bev. 2008. *The Marginal Cost of Public Funds: Theory and Applications.*
Boston: MIT Press.

Daveri, Francesco, and Riccardo Faini. 1996. "Where do Migrants Go? Risk-Aversion, Mobility Costs and the Locational Choice of Migrants." Discussion Paper 1540. London: Center for Economic Policy Research.

Day, Kathleen M. 1989. "Government Policies, Unemployment Rates, and Inter-provincial Migration in Canada." Unpublished PHD diss., University of British Columbia.

– 1992. "Interprovincial Migration and Local Public Goods." *Canadian Journal of Economics* 25 (1): 123–44.

Day, Kathleen M., and Stanley L. Winer. 1994. "Internal Migration and Public Policy: An Introduction to the Issues and a Review of Empirical Research on Canada." In *Issues in the Taxation of Individuals,* ed. Allan Maslove. Toronto: University of Toronto Press, 3–61.

– 2001. "Interregional Migration and Public Policy in Canada: An Empirical Study." Working Paper W-01-3E, Ottawa: Applied Research Branch, Human Resources Development Canada, July, 294 pages. Available at www.carleton.ca/~winers.

– 2006. "Policy-Induced Migration in Canada: An Empirical Investigation of the Canadian Case." *International Tax and Public Finance* 13: 535–64.

Dean, James M. 1982. "Tax-Induced Migration in Canada, 1972–79." *Western Economic Review* 1 (2): 17–31.

DeJuan, J., and M. Tomljanovich. 2005. "Income Convergence across Canadian Provinces in the 20th Century: Almost but Not Quite There." *Annals of Regional Science* 39:567–92.

Dingledine, Gary. 1981. *A Chronology of Response: The Evolution of Unemployment Insurance from 1940 to 1980.* Prepared for Employment and Immigration Canada. Ottawa: Minister of Supply and Services Canada.

Dingledine, Gary, John Hunter, and Chris McKillop. 1995. *The History of Unemployment Insurance.* Ottawa: Human Resources Development Canada. Available at http://www.hrdc-drhc.gc.ca/insur/histui/hrdc.html.

Dion, Patrice, and Simon Coulombe. 2008. "Portrait of the Mobility of Canadians in 2006: Trajectories and Characteristics of Migrants." In *Report on the Demographic Situation in Canada 2005 and 2006.* Statistics Canada Catalogue no. 91-209X. Ottawa: Minister of Industry.

Dowding, Keith, Peter John, and Stephen Biggs. 1994. "Tiebout: A Survey of the Empirical Literature." *Urban Studies* 31 (4/5): 767–97.

Emery, J.C. Herbert. 1999. "Some Regions Are More Equal than Others: Evidence on the Sources of Regional Income Differentials from the Canadian Labour Market before 1930." Unpublished, Department of Economics, University of Calgary, October. In Papers in Political Economy, Political Economy Research Group, University of Western Ontario, 92–5, 2000.

Ferris, J. Stephen, and Stanley L. Winer. 2007. "Just How Much Bigger Is Government in Canada: A Comparison of the Size and Structure of the Public Sectors in Canada and the United States." *Canadian Public Policy* 33 (2): 173–206.

Finnie, Ross. 1998a. "The Patterns of Inter-provincial Migration in Canada, 1982–95: Evidence from Longitudinal Tax-Based Data." School of Policy Studies, Queen's University, and Bureau of Labour Market Analysis Division, Statistics Canada, October.

– 1998b. "Interprovincial Mobility in Canada: The Effects of Interprovincial Mobility on Individuals' Earnings. Panel Model Estimates." Working Paper No. W-98-5E.c, Applied Research Branch, Strategic Policy, Human Resources Development Canada, November.

– 2004. "Who Moves? A Logit Model Analysis of Inter-Provincial Migration in Canada." *Applied Economics* 36 (16): 1759–79.

Foot, David K. 1984. "The Demographic Future of Fiscal Federalism in Canada." *Canadian Public Policy* 10(4): 406–14.

Foot, David K., and William J. Milne. 1984. "Net Migration in an Extended Multiregional Gravity Model." *Journal of Regional Science* 24 (1): 119–33.

Gilbert, Stéphane, Alain Bélanger, and Jacques Ledent. 2001. "Immigration, migration interne et croissance urbaine au Canada pour la période de 1976 à 1996."
Paper presented at the Association des Démographes du Québec, Sherbrooke, May.

Gillespie, W. Irwin. 1991. *Tax, Borrow and Spend: Financing Federal Spending in Canada 1967–1990*. Ottawa: Carleton University Press.

Glaeser, Edward L., and Andrei Shleifer. 2005. "The Curley Effect: The Economics of Shaping the Electorate." *Journal of Law, Economics and Organization* 21 (1): 1–20.

Gordon, Roger. 1983. "An Optimal Taxation Approach to Fiscal Federalism." *Quarterly Journal of Economics* 98: 567–86.

Goss, Ernie, and Chris Paul. 1990. "The Impact of UI Benefits on the Probability of Migration of the Unemployed." *Journal of Regional Science* 30 (3): 349–58.

Grady, Patrick, and Kathleen Macmillan. 2007. "Interprovincial Barriers to Labour Mobility in Canada: Policy, Knowledge Gaps and Research Issues." Industry Canada Working Paper 2007-10, Ottawa. Also available as MPRA Paper 2988, May 2008 at http://mpra.ub.uni-muenchen.de/2988/.

Graham, John. 1964. "Fiscal Adjustment in a Federal Country." In J. Graham, A. Johnson, and J. Andrews, *Inter-Government Fiscal Relationships*, Canadian Tax Paper No. 40. Toronto: Canadian Tax Foundation, 3–34.

Grant, E. Kenneth, and John Vanderkamp. 1976. *Economic Causes and Effects of Migration: Canada 1965–71*. Ottawa: Economic Council of Canada.

Green, David A., and Kathryn Harrison. 2006. "Races to the Bottom versus Races to the Middle: Minimum Wage Setting in Canada." In *Racing to the Bottom? Provincial Interdependence in the Canadian Federation*, ed. K. Harrison. Vancouver: UBC Press, 193–228.

Greene, William H. 1998. *Limdep Version 7.0 User's Manual*. Revised ed.. Plainville, NY: Econometric Software Inc.

– 2000. *Econometric Analysis*. 4th ed. Upper Saddle River, NJ: Prentice Hall.

Greenwood, Michael J. 1996. "Frontier Issues in the Determinants and Consequences of International Migration." *International Regional Science Review* 19
(1/2): 179–84.

Gunderson, Morley. 1994. "Barriers to Interprovincial Labour Mobility." In *Interprovincial Trade Wars: Why the Blockade Must End*, ed. Filip Palda. Vancouver:
Fraser Institute, 131–54.

Grunfeld, Yehuda, and Zvi Griliches. 1960. "Is Aggregation Necessarily Bad?"
Review of Economics and Statistics 42 (1): 143–55.

Harris, John R., and Michael P. Todaro. 1970. "Migration, Unemployment and
Development: A Two-Sector Analysis." *American Economic Review* 60 (1):
126–42.

Harris, Richard G., and Nicolas Schmitt. 2005. "Labour Mobility and a North
American Common Market: Implications for Canada." In S.T. Easton, R.G
Harris, and N. Schmitt, eds,. *Brains on the Move: Essay on Human Capital
Mobility in a Globalizing World and Implications for the Canadian Economy*.
Policy Study 42. Toronto: C.D. Howe Institute, 133–74.

Harrison, Kathryn, ed. 2006. *Racing to the Bottom? Provincial Interdependence in
the Canadian Federation*. Vancouver: UBC Press.

Health and Welfare Canada. 1989. *Social Security Statistics, Canada and Provinces,
1963–64 to 1987–88*. Ottawa: Supply and Services Canada.

Heckman, James. 1979. "Sample Selection Bias as a Specification Error." *Econometrica* 47: 153–61.

Helliwell, John. 1994. "Convergence and Migration among Provinces." 29 Special
Issue: S324–30.

Hettich, Walter, and Stanley L. Winer. 1986. "Vertical Imbalance in the Fiscal
Systems of Federal States." *Canadian Journal of Economics* 19 (4): 745–65.

Hou, Feng, and Roderic Beaujot. 1995. "A Study of Interregional Migration
between Ontario and Atlantic Canada: 1981–1991." *Canadian Journal of
Regional Science* 18 (2): 147–60.

Islam, Mohammed N. 1989. "Tiebout Hypothesis and Migration-Impact of Local
Fiscal Policies." *Public Finance* 44 (3): 406–18.

Kapsalis, Constantine. 2008. "Measuring Occupational Migration Using Employment Insurance Data." Paper prepared for HRSDC, Ottawa.

Krueger, Alan B., and Mueller, Andreas. 2010. "Job Search and Unemployment
Insurance: New Evidence from Time Use Data." *Journal of Public Economics*, 94
(3–4): 298–307.

LaForest, Gérard V. 1981. *The Allocation of Taxing Power under the Canadian
Constitution*. Canadian Tax Paper No. 65. 2d ed. Toronto: Canadian Tax
Foundation.

Lazar, Fred. 1992. "Labour Market Policies and the Jurisdictional Distribution of
Powers." In D. Brown, F. Lazar, and D. Schwanen, eds., *Free to Move: Strength-
ening the Canadian Economic Union*. C.D. Howe Institute, 99–146.

Létourneau, Raynald. 1992. "Un indice de prix régional de biens et services comparables au Canada et son application aux disparités de revenu." Working paper no. 92-2, Department of Finance, Ottawa, Canada.

Liaw, Kao-Lee, and Cornelius P.A. Bartels. 1982. "Estimation and Interpretation of a Nonlinear Migration Model." *Geographical Analysis* 14 (3): 229–45.

Liaw, Kao-Lee, and Jacques Ledent. 1987. "Nested Logit Model and Maximum Quasi-Likelihood Method." *Regional Science and Urban Economics* 17 (1): 67–88.

– 1988. "Joint Effects of Ecological and Personal Factors on Elderly Interprovincial Migration in Canada." *Canadian Journal of Regional Science* 11 (1): 77–100.

Lin, Zhengxi. 1995. *Interprovincial Labour Mobility in Canada: The Role of Unemployment Insurance and Social Assistance.* Ottawa: Human Resources Development Canada.

– 1998. "Employment Insurance in Canada: Recent Trends and Policy Changes." *Canadian Tax Journal* 46 (1): 58–76.

Mace, Barbara J. 1991. "Full Insurance in the Presence of Aggregate Uncertainty." *Journal of Political Economy* 99 (5): 928–56.

MacNevin, Alex S. 1984. "Fiscal Integration and Subcentral Public Sector Inducements to Canadian Interprovincial Migration." Unpublished PHD diss., McMaster University.

Maddala. G.S. 1983. *Limited Dependent and Qualitative Variables in Econometrics.* Cambridge, UK: Cambridge University Press.

Mansell, Robert, and Ronald Schlenker. 1995. "The Provincial Distribution of Federal Fiscal Balances." *Canadian Business Economics* 3 (2): 3–22.

Martinez-Vasquez, J., and B. Searle, eds. 2007. *Fiscal Equalization: Challenges in the Design of Intergovernmental Transfers.* New York: Springer.

Massey, D.S., J. Arango, G. Hugo, A. Kouaouchi, A. Pellegrino, and J. E. Taylor. 1993. "Theories of International Migration: A Review and Appraisal." *Population and Development Review* 19(3): 431–66.

McFadden, Daniel. 1974a. "Conditional Logit Analysis of Qualitative Choice Behaviour." In *Frontiers in Econometrics,* ed. P. Zarembka. New York: Academic Press.

– 1974b. "The Measurement of Urban Travel Demand." *Journal of Public Economics* 3 (4): 303–28.

McFarlane, David S., Gregory S. Pun, and Antonio D. Loparco. 1992. *The Annotated Unemployment Insurance Act 1993.* Toronto: Carswell.

McLeman, Robert, and Barry Smith. 2006. "Changement climatique, migrations et sécurité." *Les Cahiers de la sécurité* 63 (4): 95–120.

Mendelsohn, Matthew, and Jon Medow. 2010. "Help Wanted: How Well Did the EI Program Respond during Recent Recessions?" Mowat Note, Mowat Centre for Policy Innovation, School of Public Policy and Goverenance, University of

Toronto, September 8, 2010 (http://www.mowatcentre.ca/research-topic-mowat.php?mowatResearchID=22).

Mills, K.E., M.B. Percy, and L. Sam Wilson. 1983. "The Influence of Fiscal Incentives on Interregional Migration: Canada 1961–78." Canadian Journal of Regional Science 6(2): 207–9.

Myers, Gordon. 1990. "Optimality, Free mobility, and the Regional Authority in a Federation." Journal of Public Economics, 43 (1): 107–21.

National Council of Welfare. 1997a. Welfare Incomes 1995. Ottawa: Minister of Supply and Services Canada.

– 1997b. Welfare Incomes 1996. Ottawa: Minister of Public Works and Government Services Canada.

Newbold, K. Bruce. 1996. "Income, Self-Selection, and Return and Onward Interprovincial Migration in Canada." Environment and Planning A 28 (6): 1019-1–34.

Newbold, K. Bruce, and Stefania Cicchino. 2007. "Inter-regional Return and Onwards Migration in Canada: Evidence Based on a Micro-regional Analysis." Canadian Journal of Regional Science 30 (2): 211–30.

Newbold, K. Bruce, and Kao-Lee Liaw. 1994. "Return and Onward Interprovincial Migration through Economic Boom and Bust in Canada, from 1976–81 to 1981–86." Geographical Analysis 26 (3): 228–45.

Osberg, Lars, Daniel Gordon, and Zhengxi Lin. 1994. "Inter-regional Migration and Inter-industry Labour Mobility in Canada: A Simultaneous Approach." Canadian Journal of Economics 27 (1): 58–80.

Ostrovsky, Yuri, Feng Hou, and Garnett Picot. 2008. "Internal Migration of Immigrants: Do Immigrants Respond to Regional Labour Demand Shocks?" Analytical Studies Branch Research Paper No. 318, Catalogue no. 11F0019M. Ottawa: Statistics Canada, December.

Oswald, Andrew. 1996. "A Conjecture on the Explanation for High Unemployment in the Industrialized Nations: Part I." Warwick Economic Research Papers, No. 475. University of Warwick, December.

Padovano, Fabio. 2007. The Politics and Economics of Regional Transfers: Decentralization, Interregional Redistribution and Income Convergence. Cheltenham, UK: Edward Elgar.

Phipps, Shelley. 1990. "Quantity-Constrained Household Responses to UI Reform." 100 (399): 124–40.

Pissarides, Christopher, and Jonathan Wadsworth. 1989. "Unemployment and the Inter-regional Mobility of Labour." Economic Journal 99 (397): 739–55.

Polachek, Solomon W., and Francis Horvath. 1977. "A Life Cycle Approach to Migration: Analysis of the Perspicacious Peregrinator." In Research in Labour Economics, vol. 1, ed. R.G. Ehrenberg. Greenwich Conn: JAI Press, 103–50.

Pommerehne, Werner, Gebhard Kirchgässner, and Lars Feld. 1996. "Tax Harmonization and Tax Competition at State-Local Levels: Lessons from Switzerland." In Developments in Local Government Finance: Theory and Policy, eds. G. Pola and G. France. Cheltenham, UK: Edward Elgar, 292–330.

Pudney, Stephen. 1989. *Modelling Individual Choice: The Econometrics of Corners, Kinks and Holes*. Oxford, UK: Basil Blackwell.

Revenue Canada. 1968–96. *Taxation Statistics*. Ottawa.

Rhode, Paul W., and Koleman Strumpf. 2002. "Assessing the Importance of Tiebout Sorting: Local Heterogeneity from 1850–1990." *American Economic Review* 93 (5): 1648–77.

Robinson, Chris, and Nigel Tomes. 1982. "Self-Selection and Inter-provincial Migration in Canada." *Canadian Journal of Economics*, 15 (3): 474–502.

Rosenbluth, Gideon. 1996. "Interprovincial Migration and the Efficacy of Provincial Job Creation Policies." *Canadian Business Economics* 4 (2): 22–34.

Rudner, Karen L. 1995. *The 1996 Annotated Unemployment Insurance Act*. Toronto: Carswell.

Salmon, Pierre. 1987a. "The Logic of Pressure Groups and the Structure of the Public Sector." In Albert Breton, Gianluigi Galeotti, Pierre Salmon, and Ronald Wintrobe, eds., *Villa Colombella Papers on Federalism, European Journal of Political Economy*, 3 (1&2): 55–86.

– 1987b. "Decentralization as an Incentive Scheme." *Oxford Review of Economic Policy*. 3 (2): 24–43.

Sargent, Timothy C. 1995. "An Index of Unemployment Insurance Disincentives." Working Paper No. 95-10, Department of Finance, Ottawa, Canada.

Sasser, Alicia, C. 2010. "Voting with Their Feet: Relative Economic Conditions and State Migration Patterns." *Regional Science and Urban Economics* (40): 122–35.

Schwartz, Saul, Wendy Bancroft, David Gyarmati, and Claudia Nicholson. 2001. "The Frequent Use of Unemployment Insurance in Canada: The Earnings Supplement Project." Ottawa: Social Research and Demonstration Corporation.

Schweitzer, Thomas T. 1982. "Migration and a Small Long-Term Econometric Model of Alberta." Discussion Paper No. 221, Economic Council of Canada, Ottawa, Canada.

Scott, Anthony, and Greg Bloss. 1988. "Interprovincial Competition." In *Taxation and Fiscal Federalism: Essays in Honour of Russell Mathews,* eds. Geoffrey Brennan, Bhajan S. Grewal, and Peter Groenwegen. Sydney: Australian National University Press, 180–201.

Sharpe, Andrew, Jean-Francois Arsenault, and Daniel Ershov. 2007. "The Impact of Interprovincial Migration on Aggregate Output and Labour Productivity in Canada, 1987–2006." *International Productivity Monitor* 15: 25–40.

Shaw, R. Paul. 1985. *Intermetropolitan Migration in Canada: Changing Determinants over Three Decades*. Ottawa: Statistics Canada.

– 1986. "Fiscal versus Traditional Market Variables in Canadian Migration." *Journal of Political Economy* 94 (3): 648–66.

Shroder, Mark. 1995. "Games the States Don't Play: Welfare Benefits and the Theory of Fiscal Federalism." *Review of Economics and Statistics* 77 (1): 183–91.

Sjaastad, Larry A. 1962. "The Costs and Returns of Human Migration." *Journal of Political Economy* 70 (5): 80–93.

Smart, Michael. 1998. "Taxation and Deadweight Loss in a System of Intergovernmental Transfers." *Canadian Journal of Economics* 31 (1): 189–206.

St-Amour, Martine, Jacques Ledent, and Jean-François Lachance. 2008. "La redistribution spatiale des immigrants selon leur localisation initiale à ou hors Montréal : Une analyse longitudinale par cohorte." Paper presented at the 2008 Conference of the COOL Research Data Centre, "Comings and Goings: Migration, Policy and Society," October 17–18, 2008, Ottawa, Ontario.

Stark, Oded. 1991. *The Migration of Labour*. Oxford: Basil Blackwell.

– 1996b. "Frontier Issues in International Migration." *International Regional Science Review* 19 (1/2): 147–77.

Statistics Canada. 1966–72a. *Annual Report on Benefit Periods Established and Terminated under the Unemployment Insurance Act*. Catalogue no. 73-201. Ottawa.

– 1966–72. *Statistical Report on the Operation of the Unemployment Insurance Act*. Catalogue no. 73-001. Ottawa.

Statistics Canada. 1979–82. *Air Carrier Financial Statements*. Catalogue 51-206. Ottawa.

– 1983. *Employment, Earnings and Hours*. Catalogue no. 72-002. Ottawa.

– 1983–97. *Canadian Civil Aviation*. Catalogue 51-206. Ottawa.

– 1987–98. *Rail in Canada*. Catalogue no. 52-216. Ottawa.

– 1995. *Unemployment Insurance Statistics 1995*. Catalogue no. 73-202S. Ottawa: Ministry of Industry, June.

– 1997. *Report on the Demographic Situation in Canada 1996*. Catalogue no. 91-209 XPE, March.

Statutes of Canada, various volumes. S.C. 1959, c. 36; S.C. 1967–68, c. 33; S.C. 1976–77, c. 54; S.C. 1978–79, c. 7; S.C. 1990, c. 40; S.C. 1993, c. 13; S.C. 1994, c. 18; S.C. 1996, c. 23.

Tervo, Hannu. 2000. "Migration and Labour Market Adjustment: Empirical Evidence from Finland 1985–1990." *International Review of Applied Economics* 14 (3): 343–60.

Tiebout, Charles M. 1956. "A Pure Theory of Local Expenditures." *Journal of Political Economy* 64 (5): 416–24.

Townsend, Robert. 1994. "Risk and Insurance in Village India." *Econometrica* 62 (3): 539–91.

Usher, Dan. 1995. *The Uneasy Case for Equalization Payments*. Vancouver: The Fraser Institute.

Vachon, Marc, and François Vaillancourt. 1999. "Interprovincial Mobility in Canada, 1961–1996: Importance and Distribution." In *How Canadians Connect: Canada – the State of the Federation, 1998/99*, eds. H. Lazar and T. McIntosh. Montreal and Kingston: McGill-Queens' University Press, 101–22.

Vanderkamp, John. 1988. "Regional Disparities: A Model with Some Econometric Results for Canada." In *Regional Economic Development: Essays in Honour of François Perroux*, eds. B. Higgins and D.J. Savoie. Boston: Unwin Hyman, 269–96.

Watson, William G. 1986. "An Estimate of the Welfare Gain from Fiscal Equalization." *Canadian Journal of Economics* 19 (2): 298–308.

Wellisch, Deitmar. 2000. *Theory of Public Finance in a Federal State*. Cambridge, UK: Cambridge University Press.

Wilson, L. Sam. 2003. "Equalization, Efficiency and Migration: Watson Revisited." *Canadian Public Policy* 29 (4): 289–308.

Wilson, L.S., M.B. Percy, and K.H. Norrie. 1980. " Oil Prices, Interregional Adjustment, Fiscal Transfers and the Canadian Economic Union." University of Alberta, Unpublished.

Winer, Stanley L. 1986. "Challenging Issues in the Study of Fiscally-Induced Migration." *Canadian Journal of Regional Science* 9 (3): 381–7.

Winer, Stanley L., and Denis Gauthier. 1982a. *Internal Migration and Fiscal Structure: An Econometric Study of the Determinants of Interprovincial Migration in Canada*. Ottawa: Economic Council of Canada.

– 1982b. "Internal Migration Data: A Supplement to Internal Migration and Fiscal Structure." Technical Paper, Ottawa: Economic Council of Canada.

Zabalza, Antoni, Christopher Pissarides, and Margaret Barton. 1980. "Social Security and the Choice between Full-time Work, Part-time Work and Retirement." *Journal of Public Economics* 14 (2): 245–76.

Index